Which way?

What way?

Your way Lord.

By Carol S. Lovely

Which Way? What Way? Your way Lord.

Copyright c 2002

Scripture quotations are taken from the new open bible, King James Version, unless stated otherwise.

PRINTED BY

BOOKMASTERS INC.

MANSFIELD, OHIO

ACKNOWLEDGMENTS

The fact of being told daily that I should have never been born, along with mental and physical abuse by my father and sexual abuse by others, led me down a path of hopelessness, drugs, and anti-depressants. I was born the eleventh child in a poverty-stricken family of thirteen children to an alcoholic father and a Christian mother. We lived in roach, waterbug-infested, half-double house's in an old section on the west side of Dayton, Ohio just so my father could be near the neighborhood bars.

I looked for answers as hopeless situations continually harassed my life. Rape, spousal abuse, children hooked on drugs, a son placed in a foreign prison, and being told I could never see my grandchild again left me not only broken financially, but broken in spirit. My story, <u>Which</u> way? <u>What way</u>? <u>Your way Lord</u> is the type of book for which I looked in Christian book stores to help me as I struggled to, "walk on water" and sought miracles that offered hope. No one seemed to help and my constant cry to God was, "Lord, teach me to pray!"

When I discovered a caring friend, Sandy, I found someone who would believe with me. We began to pray together and learned to practice the principle of agreement as touching anything, IT SHALL BE DONE. Together we formed a business-a cleaning service. We never had so much fun in our entire lives as we began to clean "for Him" and pray on our job. When we prayed about the medication I took, the Lord spoke to me, "Trust Me and I will bring you out." Then miraculously I was free of the drugs the doctors had said I would be on for the rest of my life. The yoke-destroying power of God began to work in the lives of two normal, every-day housewives.

Soon my life was filled with "hope that maketh not ashamed." God gave me dreams and visions and I found like Joseph of the old Testament, when God reveals it to you, it will surely come to pass. Supernatural encounters with angels brought me further courage that God loved me and was with me. The knowledge

3

imparted showed me how to pray and internalize the scripture. Knowing and using the word of God brought me from a fearful, negative, defeated person to a compassionate woman of prayer.

Out of respect for others, whether or not they have asked for mine or God's forgiveness- confirmed in my heart to change most of the names excluding my own name and Sandy's, some family, and friends. It is not my intention or desire to hurt, expose, or get even with anyone who's lives could be hurt from the past mistakes which now rests under the blood of Jesus. I am telling my story for one purpose, to glorify God in all the wonderful things He has done for Sandy and me. He told me to write this book, I obeyed. It's also my deepest desire to help someone else. My testimony of searching, researching, and the results have inspired my story. I pray in the name of Jesus that this book will help others to know God the Father as their own true and most wonderful Papa. He has been so patient, kind and loving to me, like no other ever has.

"Thank You so much, Lord for never giving up on me, and helping me not to give up on myself. Thank You, dear Lord for suppling the finances to publish this book myself. I love You!"

"Thank you my dear precious husband, Roy Lovely for believing in me, and helping me to be able to finish running the race God has set before me. I love you." Thanks to my sons, daughter-in -laws, and grandchildren whom I love with all my heart too. Thanks to all my sisters, and brothers, who I love and cherish. "Thank you for all your prayers for me and this book." A great big thank you to all of my friends, who are also mentioned inside the pages of this book. "God bless all of your hearts! You have been so faithful to pray for me, and the publishing of this book. Thank you all for encouraging me and praying for me." Last but not least, "I thank you Sandy for being such a faithful friend always. Thank you for your prayers and encouragement. Thanks for never losing sight of the vision we shared for this book. Thank you more then anything else for always agreeing with me in prayer, night or day. God bless you! Of course through it all we have witnessed God do the miraculous otherwise this book could not have been written."

Most of all, I dedicate this book to my loving heavenly Father who taught me. I am made in His image. I can do all things through Christ Jesus who strengthens me. His strength is made perfect in my weakness. "I am so thankful to You, Papa God. You taught me how to be a writer, and an author. I've seen a glorious light! You dispelled the dark shadows from my past. You gave me beauty for ashes. Your joy, dear Lord Jesus, is my strength. Thank You, dear Papa for the blood of my sweet Lord Jesus that covers me, my family, and every page in this book, in the name of Jesus. Thank You, dear Lord Jesus for healing my broken heart and restoring my shattered dreams. Thank You for giving me hope to go on, knowing You'll never leave me nor forsake me, dear Lord Jesus. Thank You sweet precious Holy Spirit for leading and guiding me into all truth. The knowledge of Your truth has set me free, again, and again! I love You dear Papa, wonderful Lord Jesus, and sweet precious Holy Spirit!" A special thank you to my friend, Nancy Trimbach, who critiqued this book one last time.

I also dedicate this book, in loving memory of my precious Christian mother, Lydia Fraley. I'm so thankful she introduced all of us to Jesus. All throughout her life she showed us by her own example, God's unconditional love. Moreover, I dedicate this book to all of my brothers and sisters who were not called to write a book, but lived through the hard times before me, or with me. I especially dedicate this book to my sister Peggy who in childhood was my body guard, and has been my lifelong close friend. We were given to each other as gifts from God. I have no doubt, our lives would have been completely different without each other to hold onto through all the tough times. I also dedicate this book to any woman, man or child who needs inner healing. "Please don't ever give up. There is hope, because God loves you! There isn't a sin that God will not forgive. There isn't a broken heart He can't mend. He'll help you to forgive those who have hurt you, and He will heal you through His Son, Jesus. The Lord will turn your fear into faith, and you'll fearlessly be able to say with confidence, 'The Lord is my Shepherd and I shall not want." (Psalm 23:1)

Foreword

By Wanda J Herman

Carol's story is an inspiring and encouraging story of one woman's struggle to believe for a better life against all odds. Carol is an individual who had no formal training, no one to encourage her, but has been led step- by- step into fulfilling an important role for God-to be an example of believing God for the unbelievable. He is still working in her life.

Carol's personal encounters with angles, dreams and visions are real. She had to trust in an all powerful, supernatural Heavenly Father when her earthly family failed to provide her emotional, physical, and spiritual needs.

Hers is a story with which many women (and many men) can identify. Carol grew up in an environment that is all too commonplace for many of America's children. Through this book parents can become aware of thoughtless behavior and careless, cruel, critical words that affect the lives of their children. Christians can learn to be a little less judgmental of those who are crying out for help and not "shoot they're wounded."

I became acquainted with Carol because of her friendship with my sister-in-law. Hearing her story has helped me become more compassionate in my counseling with women subjected to sexual, physical, and emotional abuse. Seeing her emerge from her self-imposed cocoon into a spiritual "butterfly" typified by her new married name- she changed from Carol S. Fraley, to Carol S. Lovely.

Rev. Wanda J. Herman, Assembles of God
Writer, "Miracle of Murlin Heights"
Ghost Writer: "Sego" and "God's got your number"

Table of Contents

Chapter One

When I was a child

I was born on a farm in Portsmouth Ohio. Most of my formative years were a series of nightmares. During the years we lived on the farm, my childhood innocence was stolen. A man who worked on the farm, took me up into the loft of our barn and molested me. He threatened me with a pitchfork, and told me he'd make me jump into the hay wagon below, if I didn't do what he wanted. He also threatened to kill me if I told on him. I never even told my mother. I'm not sure how old I was when the molesting started, or how many times it happened. I was seven years old when we left the farm, and the molesting stopped. I had terrible feelings of guilt, fear, and shame. I was afraid of any kind of farm animal, and dogs, or cats. I had a terrible fear of men and large bodies of water too.

Daddy got into very violent moods. He threatened to kill us many times. He hit us with his cruel large hands and pulled our hair, or else, he'd whip us with his belt! We dodged things he threw at us! He also kicked my brothers with his shoes on, and sometimes they bled. Daddy used terrible foul language and he cursed us daily. Mommy prayed and asked God, to take the fear of daddy out of her heart. She told us about a strange thing that happened the last time daddy threatened her with a gun. He laid the cold smooth steel of a double barreled shotgun behind her ear, and cocked both barrels while her back was turned washing dishes! He said, he'd kill her if she made one wrong move! She knew it was the Lord, when a powerful anointing came over her. She turned around, looked daddy square in the eye, pointed her finger at him and boldly said,

"IN THE NAME OF GOD, YOU WON'T HURT ME, BECAUSE GOD WON'T **LET YOU!**" Instantly, he fell backwards. His eyes rolled back in his head, and his body lay lifeless on the cold linoleum floor. She told us, the Lord asked her the same question three times firmly, while daddy was laying on the floor unconscious, "LYDIA, DO YOU WANT THIS MAN?"

After God asked her that same question the third time, she finally answered, "Yes Lord. Please don't let him die in his sins and go to hell?" Sure enough, the Lord answered her prayer. My younger sister Peggy and I, felt guilty because we were so disappointed that daddy lived. God forgave us, because we repented. We just wanted all the fighting, yelling, hitting and cursing to stop. We desperately needed to be a happy, normal family and live in peace and quiet. Mommy cried and told us, if she divorced him, he'd die, in the street, a drunk. At least he worked and kept a roof over our heads.

I am the eleventh child of our parents thirteen children. I'm the seventh daughter, and Peggy is the eighth. Our younger brother, David died. We also had four older brothers. Daddy treated all of us the same. He was mean to everyone. Our heritage is a mixture of Cherokee, Shawnee, Black Foot Indian, German, Irish and Dutch. We were very poor, living in roach and water bug infested old half doubles on the west side of Dayton. Sometimes we lived in upstairs apartments. We moved as much as five times in one year, but we always stayed close to the bars. There were never any nice curtains on our windows, just shredded dirty plastic ones. We had roll-a-way beds with feather tic mattresses'. We'd try to clean as best we could, with what we had, which wasn't much. Daddy always thought someone was trying to kill him. He was constantly on edge, so he carried a knife inside his right boot. He was very superstitious. He never sat in front of an open window or door. It was also un heard of for him to keep any promise he made to us. He'd throw his head back laughing hysterically if we cried.

I remember when we moved into our first, and only brand new

2

red brick half double, in a nice clean low income housing complex, without inside bugs. Park side homes in Dayton was our new home. I'd never seen brightly lit lamp posts and lots of green grassy fields to run and play in before. I felt so safe there. I used to sit outside in the summertime after dark singing gospel songs to the top of my lungs! We even had a nice shopping center with a theater. It was hard for me and Peggy to believe there weren't any winos laying near our streets, offering us gum or candy. We had a nice large yard, with lots of green grass, instead of a tiny yard with patches of brown or yellow grass surrounded by mostly dirt. We even had our very own big park within the complex. It was filled with brand new swings, monkey bars, and slides to play on. Mommy bought my sister Peggy a bike from the Salvation Army store. My sister learned to ride her bike really well. People from the Salvation Army church gave us a pair of skates. My sister and I shared them, until our wonderful brother Gene made a racing cart out of a piece of old flat wood, and used the wheels off our skates.

I couldn't believe Peggy actually dared to hope again, wishing Santa might bring her a present. We'd always thought something was wrong with us. Santa never came to our house or brought us presents, not even once. No matter where we lived, every year the other kids on our block showed off their new dolls and toys on Christmas day. Sometimes Peggy got so mad, a big fight broke out with the other kids! I didn't get mad at anybody. I just held it all inside. I finally realized Santa wasn't real. It didn't bother me anymore, but it still did Peggy. Before we went to bed on Christmas Eve, we never got tired of hearing mommy read us the story from the bible about baby Jesus, born in a manger. We'd sit on the floor beside her creaky rocking chair listening to her read. We strung pop corn for the little tree, our brother Gene bought us.

I felt so sorry for Peggy as she lay there in bed beside me crying. She wanted the new doll, she saw in the store window in town. I yawned, and with heavy eye lids, I whispered, "Listen, Peggy, and you can hear mommy's old foot peddled sewing machine humming

3

downstairs. I wonder what pretty clothes she'll make for our doll's this year?" My younger sister bellowed, "I told you, I don't want that same old doll this year! I'm getting a new one from Santa this time, remember?" I went to sleep, hoping and praying Peggy wouldn't be too, disappointed again. I was so thankful that was the last year she cried for a new doll. The love in mommy's tired eyes Christmas morning did something inside Peggy's heart. Nothing had changed. They were still our same old dolls, cleaned up, wearing pretty new matching bonnets, socks and dresses made from clothing we'd long since outgrown. The new bonnets on our dolls always covered up the fact that half their hair was missing.

A few of our older brothers and sisters who still lived close to us, sometimes bought us a small present. We understood that they had their own children to buy for. And besides, they were almost as poor as we were. Our oldest brother Jim, sometimes brought us bags of candy, nuts, potato chips and fruit. Waiting for us under the tree on Christmas morning was a brown paper bag with our names on it. Mommy was the most wonderful cook in the world! I remember special times on Sundays, sometimes, when she'd fix crispy fried chicken, delicious whipped potatoes with gravy, corn on the cob, green beans, and flaky brown biscuits. Before we left the farm, she'd make us a blackberry cobbler with flaky brown crust. We'd pour fresh cold milk over it. We also had pinto beans, fried potatoes, and cornbread many times, for several days in a row. No matter what the meal was, it always tasted good when mommy made it. We bowed our heads and thanked God for it too.

During the winter months, at our new house we had so much fun. We ran and played in the fluffy clean white snow for hours. We made snow angels' and ate great big ice cycles. I can still picture mommy standing on the front porch, calling to us. Her apron strings flapped in the wind, while whips of her salt and pepper grey hair blew softly across her face. She'd make us snow, milk with white sugar, and vanilla. She also put different colors of food coloring in it to make it pretty. In the spring and summer we loved to play in the big grassy green fields. We had lemon aid

4

stands, picnics and peaceful long walks in the park. We also jumped in big piles of leaves in the autumn, and we never got tired of looking at all the different beautiful colors of leaves on the trees. Daddy still came home drunk, cursing and yelling at us, but somehow we found comfort living in the nice neighborhood. Un expectedly, one day an awful darkness came and disrupted everything. Peggy was only seven and I was ten. It started in early spring when daddy decided to take us, and a couple of our friends to get ice cream. Peggy blinked her big blue eyes, and starred up at me, frowning, "Carol, can you believe daddy wants to, not only take us to get ice cream, but our friends too?" I shrugged my shoulders, and returned her puzzled gaze. Of course, I was thinking the exact same thing. We were confused, but nevertheless, we obeyed daddy and asked our two friends if they wanted to go along with us to get ice cream. We didn't argue with daddy or mommy, not ever. Our mother never raised her voice at us. She just called our name if she wanted our attention, and we quickly obeyed her. Or else, she'd whip us with a skinny small switch from a tree, which most of the time we had to go pick out ourselves. Daddy, grabbed us by our hair, and whipped us good, so we always obeyed them both without talking back or asking why.

After we got our ice cream, daddy asked if we'd like him to take us on a nice long drive? Not thinking, we all said, "Yes!" It was still pretty cold out. It started raining really hard with sudden bright flashes of lightning, and loud crashes of thunder! Suddenly he stopped the car, and made me and Peggy get out! He told us to keep walking until we reached the levy wall where it was slippery, wet, muddy and dangerous! He stayed in the car with the girls, and ordered my sister and me to keep walking on up around, behind the levy wall! We were told not to look back, or come back, until he called for us! Horrified, sobbing, and steeped in fear we huddled together in the cold drenching rains behind the levy wall. She and I tried not to think about what daddy was doing to those girls back there in the car. We were soaking wet and covered with mud when daddy finally called for us out of the storm. Mommy was furious

5

with him when we got home. She asked us all some very rapid questions. Daddy had already instructed us to lie. I believe we told her, we helped him fix a flat tire. I felt so guilty inside. I wanted with all my heart to tell her the truth, but we were threatened severely before hand by daddy. He said, he'd kill us if we told what happened. A couple of months later it happened again. It was really warm outside and daddy made my sister and me stay in the car while he took the two girls for a long walk up to the levy. We were told to stay inside the hot car with the windows rolled up and lay down on the floorboard until they came back. The heat in that old two toned green car was terrible, but the fear of daddy was much worse. Once again, daddy threatened to kill every one of us if we told anyone. Thank God, daddy's nightmarish sickness ended, when mommy finally realized something was terribly wrong and called the police. We had to leave that happy place where we lived. We moved back into the inner City, ashamed and humiliated. Once again, Peggy and I clung together and cried bitter tears.

Sometimes daddy stood over us, and squeezed our collarbone with his big hand! He'd pressure us to tell a lie on mommy. He wanted to know if she'd had a strange man in the house, and if she was in bed with him that day. I felt so sorry for mommy with most of her teeth rotted, and broken off. She'd had so many of us kids, her calcium was depleted. She suffered horribly, but we couldn't afford a dentist. She had two old dresses to her name that were fastened together with latch pins, because half the buttons were missing. I felt like screaming at daddy! "WILL YOU PLEASE LOOK AT HER!" We couldn't understand how he could even ask us such a question? Everyone loved and respected mommy, not only as a Christian but as a good neighbor and a wonderful lady. We got so tired of him cross examining us. Every single night daddy came home drunk, angry and cursing about everything, before, during and after dinner! Finally, he'd stagger off into the living room to watch T V. We were always so grateful when he'd fall asleep on the couch, even if it was in a drunken stupor.

I squinted in school at my books, and the blackboard. I had trouble hearing the Teacher too. The school board was able to help us financially. They got the glasses I needed. One day, mommy's friend from the Salvation Army Church told her about an Oral Roberts healing crusade in our town. She called it, 'A big tent meeting!' The nice lady came and picked us up and took us there. Peggy and I kept our arms around mommy as we inched our way to the front stage where Mr. Roberts was praying for people. We saw all kinds of miraculous healing! Jesus visited Oral Roberts tent meeting that day in an awesome way! Our faith grew stronger as we witnessed Jesus healing so many people right before our very eyes! When it came my turn, mommy explained to Oral Roberts about the school sending me to the doctor and why. He smiled, and took off my glasses. He handed them to mommy, and told her I wouldn't need them anymore! When he put his hands over my eyes, and asked Jesus to heal me, I saw two big fire balls swirling around, and I felt heat in both my eyes! He also put his hands over my ears, and asked Jesus to heal my ears. I heard them pop really loud! Suddenly, I could hear clearly too. I started crying, "Thank You Jesus for healing my eyes and ears!" Tears were pouring from mommy's eyes too, as she thanked the Lord Jesus for healing me.

When Oral Roberts asked if someone in the audience could please step out in the aisle, a slim dark haired man stepped out. Mr. Roberts asked if I could tell him the color of the man's clothing? Even though he was a good distance away, I described his yellow shirt, brown tie with matching brown pants and jacket exactly as it was. I even gave a perfect description of the tiny yellow sea horse woven into the center of his brown tie. I could hear and see perfectly, "Thank You, Jesus!" Before we left the tent meeting someone on Mr. Roberts staff asked mommy to fill out a card if we'd like them to help us find a church closer to us?

Mommy signed the card, and we were contacted by Reverend Percy Herman. The church bus started picking up mommy, our older brother Gene, Peggy and myself to attend the church of God in Dayton, every Sunday. Even though the church bus came, we missed church some Sundays. Mommy made us hide if she wasn't feeling well. Brother Herman introduced us to his daughter Brenda, and we became good friends. It felt like we'd known each other all our lives. Brenda's hair and eyes were dark like mine. Her birthday's six months before mine, and we were born in the same year. One day, she realized we sang well together, so she coaxed me into singing with her on stage. I was so afraid. My knees were knocking together. Brave Peggy dressed like an angel in a play. She sang a beautiful song all by herself. We started having prayer meetings in Brenda's basement, and ours. I kept listening to Brenda pray in another language, and when I finally asked her about it, I received the baptism of the Holy Spirit at the tender age of twelve! God filled me with His love, joy and peace that day.

Sometimes at night, suddenly, daddy came bursting into our room, and woke us up out of a sound sleep. He'd grab us by our hair, shake us, and yell awful curse words at us. He'd get right up in our face, and yell! His breath was thick with stale alcohol and tobacco, "You blank, blank, lazy girls', wake up! Hurry, get up, quick, and get dressed! Help your mammy pack, we're moving! Somebody's trying to kill me!" Poor mommy looked so tired and disgusted, but she never quarreled with daddy about anything. She was our example of Jesus unconditional love. We never knew if we were moving because he drank the rent money, or if someone from the bar he frequently attended was really trying to kill him. We had no doubt someone might try to kill him. He was really mean.

I'll never forget what happened one day in my sixth grade class at recess. My Teacher, Mrs. Kramer told the others to run along outside and play, but she asked me to stay behind. I thought I'd done something wrong, so I was afraid. She smiled really nicely at me, and said with compassion in her voice, "Carol, I've learned a lot about you from reading your school attendance records. I know something about your background, and your family life at home

8

too. I also know your daddy is an alcoholic." She handed me a dictionary. She told me. She thought I was a very smart little girl. She asked if I'd be willing to make her a very important promise. Mrs. Kramer wanted me to study the words in the dictionary, and learn their meanings. She said, if I'd learn the words and use them often in my vocabulary, my reading and writing skills would improve dramatically. She hugged me, and told me, the dictionary would help me throughout my whole life. I thanked her shyly, and I agreed to do what she requested. I gladly kept that promise.

I was walking to school one morning when I noticed this rather handsome dark haired man standing on the curb starring at me. I had just turned thirteen. I desperately needed to wear a bra, but I was wearing tee shirts and slips. I looked much older then thirteen. As I walked closer to him, he just kept starring at me. I got a really funny feeling as I walked passed him. I was wishing Peggy hadn't stayed home sick that day. Suddenly, he jumps me from behind, reaches around and grabbs me with his strong right hand and arm! He held my right breast firmly in a twisted painful grip. Before I could scream, he clasped his left hand over my mouth. My mind was racing as he dragged me into the ally! I tried to get free, but the pain in my upper body was horrible. He held me firm, and just kept dragging me. Finally, I was able to get my front teeth into one of his fingers, and I bit him until he bled. He let me loose! He cursed me and hit me hard across the face!

I took off running. I never stopped screaming until I reached home. My brother Gene took off after him as soon as I calmed down enough to tell him what was wrong with me. Mommy called the police and told them what street I was on when the strange young man attacked me. I was badly bruised, and shook up. Right after that I started having nightmares and trouble sleeping and eating. I kept getting sick in school a lot and having to be brought home. The school board decided to put me in an all girls' school.

I had to walk over a big, scary, long bridge before daylight and catch a bus to get to the new school every morning. I was so scared! Peggy got up early and walked me across town to the bus stop. She was so brave, it was incredible. She refused to fear anything or anyone, including older, larger, and tougher girls or boys. She wasn't even afraid of stray dogs, cats, or drunk's. Peggy's love for me, and her fighting spirit far out weighed her fear. Even though she was three years younger then me, she always fought my battles. I was shy and afraid, the exact apposite of her. We cried at the bus stop, because for the first time in our lives we were being separated from each other. The new school was about a half an hour away, by bus. My first day there I met a few decent girls, but the others were some of the nastiest, meanest girls I'd ever met in my entire life.

Those mean girls had been abused, and they had been unwanted all their lives. They were from fostering homes, and believe me they had learned how to abuse others, especially fearful girls like me. They lived in a foster home right across the street from the school we attended. They hated me from the first day we met, because I was afraid of them and they knew it. They found out I was a Christian girl, and that made things even worse. They hit me, pushed me around, and made fun of me. They called me names, and I just took it. They used the four letter awful 'F' word in stereo, as much or more than daddy. I failed miserably as a Christian witness to them. The other three new friends that I'd made, treated me decent. They taught me how to dance, too. After a few hard weeks of being ridiculed, I finally said yes to my first cigarette. We were crossing a busy street after getting off the bus. I kept on smoking, just so I could be cool, and look bad, mean, and tough, like all the others. My nerves were so bad I'd developed terrible stomach problems. Most of the time these mean, hateful girls took my lunch money that I babysat for in the evenings, and my bus tokens. I was forced to walk home on the west side of Dayton with the winos, and hungry stray, ugly dogs in all kinds of weather.

One particularly terrible day, I was walking home from school in the pouring rain. I was terrified of the loud crackling of thunder, and scary lightning! All of a sudden this real tough looking girl came out of an ally, and started walking beside me. She started having a conversation with me, as if she'd known me all her life. I was soaking wet, and all I could think of was, how cold, hungry, and tired I felt. Even though she was a stranger, it was comforting to have someone to talk to. She asked if she could come home with me and stay the night, and I didn't even know her name yet. I was too afraid of her to tell her no. I was even more afraid of the rest of the long walk home in the storm alone, so I said, "Sure!"

Mommy said, she could stay without much of an argument. We lived in an upstairs apartment at that time. Peggy and I slept in the living room on an old fold out couch, and the new girl named Terry slept between us. Late that night the girl tried to touch us in places that weren't very nice. Peggy threatened to beat her up, and she left sometime that night. After almost a year of being beat up at school, going without lunch, and walking home, I cried and told mommy the truth. I told her the mean girls took my lunch money and bus tokens, and they pushed me around, cursed me, and called me bad names. Mommy decided, not to send me back to that school, or any other school. We walked up the street to the corner pay phone the next day, in case there were any nosy listeners on our party line at home, I guess. Before mommy picked up the phone, she looked up to heaven and asked God to forgive her for what she was about to do. Mommy whipped us quicker for lying then anything else. She called the school, and told them she was sending me out west to California to live with my older sister Helen, until I graduated. Mommy said, those mean girls would never get another chance to hurt me again. I was so grateful and relieved.

I don't know how we kept it a secret, but I never went back to any school. However, I did become an avid reader and I kept my promise to Mrs. Kramer. I studied and used the dictionary. Daddy never suspected anything, nor did the authorities ever check up on us, thank God. I continued to babysit for different people with Peggy in the evenings just like nothing had changed. I was fourteen when that happened, and I remained in hiding during the cold dark winter months. I was so thankful for the summertime. If anyone saw me, they'd think I was visiting. When I turned seventeen I met Joe. After just three short months of dating Joe, he purposed, and I said yes. Everyone was happy for us except mommy. She cried and begged me not to marry Joe, because he was an unbeliever. I never tried to hurt or disobey her in my life, but that time my mind was made up. When she finally realized she couldn't talk me out of it, she hugged and kissed me, and gave me her blessing.

My wedding day was nearly a disaster when daddy started cursing and yelling at me. He accused me of doing all kinds of terrible things. In a drunken rage, he threw me out on the porch, and called me a no-good whore! The door slammed behind me so hard, it made my teeth rattle! Black mascara mixed with hot tears streamed down my face as I stood there on the front porch, shivering in my wedding gown. I was so hurt and angry, I wanted to run back in the house and scream, "That's a lie, daddy! I am still a virgin!" Mommy and Peggy tried to comfort me, but I was so humiliated and shaken by the time Joe arrived to pick us up, I just wanted to get, what was supposed to be, the happiest day of my life, over with. Even though it was a warm lovely day in April, I was freezing. My brother-in-law Don was kind enough to walk me down the aisle. I thank God for my loving sister Sally and Don.

I remember when I was about eight and a half months pregnant with my first son David. I'd spent the day with my mother again, and visited with my sister Peggy after she came home from school while Joe was at work. I was huge and miserable, so Joe didn't want me staying home by myself, especially since my time was so close to have the baby. I kept looking at my watch, pacing the floor, and watching for Joe at the front door of mommy's house. He was never late. Joe knew what time daddy came home from work, and he always picked me up before he arrived. Mommy nervously watched the clock on the wall too. I loved and missed her and Peggy so much. Joe dropped me off there early in the morning on his way to work, after daddy left, and I always left long before daddy came home. It worked out really well, usually. I anxiously stood there with my things, but I knew it was too late when I heard daddy's angry curse words as he slammed the back kitchen door! I thought, "Oh dear Lord, please have mercy on me!" He was drunk as always. He staggered into the living room, and collapsed on the couch. He started in asking me some really nasty questions about my pregnancy, only in a twisted, ugly manner. He used the four letter dreaded 'F' word that I hated, instead of saying the word, sex. I kept thinking, "Where is my husband?" For the very first time in my entire life I talked back to my dad. I was scared, but I answered him in a low, humble voice. "Why, daddy. You and mommy had thirteen of us kids when you were young and in love. There isn't anything dirty about having children."

Before I knew what was happening, he was right up in my face screaming slurred curse words at me, his knife pressed against my stomach! I was afraid to breathe, knowing he could hurt or even kill me, and my baby! My brave little sister Peggy who was only four feet eleven inches tall, jumped in between us! Somehow, she grabbed his strong hand that held the knife, and forced the knife to her own chest, yelling, "GO AHEAD YOU BLANK, BLANK, OF A BLANK, KILL ME, WHY DON'T YOU? I'M NOT AFRAID OF YOU!" Just then, I heard Joe come barreling through the door with a crow bar raised to hit daddy, "WHAT IN THE BLANK, IS GOING ON HERE? LOOK OLD MAN, WHY DON'T YOU PICK ON SOMEBODY YOUR OWN SIZE, INSTEAD OF THESE WOMEN?" It was a miracle none of us were hurt, thank God. I'd never heard Peggy curse like that before. It startled daddy enough to hold him off me until Joe could get there to help us.

Shortly after my first son David was about a year old, I started seeing a stomach specialist. He took several x-rays, put me on a strict diet, and tried different medications to help me. Sometime later, he brought Joe into his office and said, "Joe, your wife, Carol, is going to need a lot of help to remain calm and quiet. Treat her gentle and be kind to her. She needs your love and care right now. Well, I'm sure you'll take good care of your wife. She needs

13

you to be as patient and soft spoken with her as you can right now. Please make sure she continues to take this medication I've prescribed for her." I tried to do what the doctor said. I stayed on the strict diet and hoped to live in peace and quiet, but a few weeks after the doctor had that serious talk with Joe, I caught him in the arms of a friend of mine, Lisa! Several weeks later, I remember it was actually easier to forgive Lisa then it was Joe. She was just a young girl of sixteen and single. He was married, older, and should have known better. However, Joe never stopped begging me to come back home with him until I finally gave in. I said yes to Joe much sooner then I wanted to, because it was even more horrible living back home in the same house with daddy.

With the passing of time through the years, I thought staying busy, and raising our two beautiful sons, David and now Joey would stop the empty ache in my heart. After all, we had a nice home, furniture, a car, and even pretty curtains on the windows, so why wasn't I happy? Joe worked nights and went to school to learn blue printing for his work in tool and die casting. I felt lonely and afraid. He was also gone much of the time, fishing and hunting, while I stayed home with the boys. He enjoyed having parties with drinking and playing cards. I hated parties and drinking, and except for our children, we didn't have a whole lot in common. If it hadn't been for Peggy, I don't know what I would have done. I loved her children and she loved mine. We took them shopping with us, out to parks, and the movies. We did just about everything together. Her husband Harry was a truck driver, and he was gone a lot too.

Joe and I rarely went to church, except on Easter, sometimes. I lost contact with my friend Brenda. I sure missed singing on stage with her. Instead I sang with Joe, his dad, and brother. We sang secular country songs about drinking and men leaving their wives, and etc. All though it had been many years since I'd left home, the scars inside me were not healing from my past. I still had serious stomach problems, and I carefully stayed on a strict diet. I took stomach pills, nerve pills, and we had very large doctor bills.

Horrible flash backs of the rape in my childhood began to surface, and torment my mind, day and night! I could only remember scattered parts of my childhood. But because it was too painful, I'd blocked out whoever it was that raped me, many years ago. My doctor suggested a hypnotist could perhaps help me remember, but things only got worse. Also, my therapist strongly recommended shock treatments each time I tried suicide. There seamed to be no hope for my recovery. I couldn't even die successfully. I plunged deeper into depression, and further suicide attempts were made.

I was taking about twenty-eight pills a day. My psychologists had me on so much medication, I took a pill to calm me down or to go to sleep. I took pills for pain, and I took pills to help me cope with life. It was even getting more, and more difficult for the doctors to keep me sedated while giving me the shock treatments. During one of the shock treatments, they forgot to put the heavy plastic mouthpiece inside my mouth to cushion the blow of my teeth hitting together. It was horrible! I woke up right in the middle of the shock treatment, and I was in excruciating pain! Electricity charged through my body at a tremendous jolt, without the mouthpiece, and knocked nearly all of my perfectly good teeth loose. I was so scared! I wouldn't let them put me to sleep again. They had to pull all my top teeth and half my bottom, by numbing my mouth, and giving me nerve gas. The pain was almost unbearable. My swollen, black and blue, face, neck, and eyes looked like someone had beat me up really bad. In the middle of everything else, Joe walked into my hospital room looking really sad one day, and announced my dad had just died.

I couldn't even cry without terrible pain. My mouth was full of gauze, and my jaws were swollen and sore. I was furious, thinking, "How dare him die on me. I didn't even get to ask him why he hated me all these years." I couldn't believe the odd mixed feelings I had that day, trying to figure out how I could love, and hate daddy at the same time. I felt guilty because I was still angry with him, and he was dead. The sudden news of daddy's death made my already depressed state of mind even more confused. Even though

15

my heart had somewhat softened toward daddy over the years, watching him love, and care about my sons, I was still having trouble forgetting what he'd done to me, or why? To my knowledge he never gave me money, or hugged me, or touched me affectionately, and yet he always gave my children money, and affection. In the middle of the suffering, God graciously intervened and gave me beautiful false teeth for an extremely low price.

For seven years, I was in and out of hospitals. I lost track of who God was. I tried finding Him again in 'mind cosmology' books, the horoscope, and palm reading. I'd drifted so far away from God, I began to think praying didn't even help. I certainly couldn't comprehend the bible, especially since I was taking all those pills. I was thankful Joe, at least had compassion in his heart for our sons. He stayed with us through all that darkness that seemed to have no end. I still loved him even though he was mean to me. Joe abused me verbally, by calling me names, like stupid and looser. He put me down in front of others, and encouraged our sons to degrade me, and talk back to me, too. I tried to shrug it off.

Voices still rang almost constantly in my ears, telling me to kill myself. Day, and night the voices whispered, "No one wants, or needs you around here. Why are you causing all this sadness in their lives? Why don't you just do everyone a big favor, and kill yourself? Let your husband find a nice wife for himself, and a good mother for your children. Why should you stick around in everybody's way?" Joe hated my tears, and wanted nothing to do with my painful memories, so he stayed away from home as much as possible. I could hardly stand the responsibility of me, let alone the boys, without his help. Our finances were putting a terrible strain on our shaky marriage. Joe had his problems within himself, and so did I. Here we were carrying all this extra baggage from our past, and neither of us was getting the inner healing we needed. It was like being caught in an awful trap, with no way out. At that time I had no idea it was demon oppression, nor did I know how to break free from its control over our lives. I didn't know how to use the name of Jesus, or plead the blood of Jesus over us, either.

I'd never been baptized, because of my fear of water. However, I became even more afraid of going to hell, than I was of being baptized in water. I somehow managed to find my friend, Brenda Mays, and tell her I wanted to be baptized. Joe took me to meet Brenda at the First Pentecostal Church of Murlin Heights in Dayton Ohio. Brother Snoddgrass himself baptized me. He was Brenda's sister-in-law, Wanda Herman's daddy. When I came up out of the water, everyone, including Joe, said I looked like an angel. They said my appearance was a bright, shiny, golden color. There was a prophecy given over my life that night. They wrote it down on paper and gave it to me. It scared me so bad I cried, and begged God to forgive me when I tore it up, and threw it in the waste basket. No matter how hard I tried to forget though, I remembered a small part of the prophecy, "You will stand in the gap, and repair the breech." (I didn't know that simply meant a prayer warrior.) I was completely healed that very night of all stomach problems, "Thank You Jesus!" I was able to eat anything I wanted after that.

Although I still wasn't walking closely with God the way I should have been, He was merciful to me again, and helped me out of another horrible pit. I was introduced to a young therapist, Jack Blackburn. He started taking me off the drugs, a little at a time. He encouraged me to take long walks, and eat lots of fresh fruits and vegetables. He was so kind, gentle, and patient with me. With a lot of hard work, and many prayers I came off most of the pills, except for ten a day. My family doctor insisted I take those last ten pills a day for the rest of my life, but I felt like a butterfly breaking out of its cocoon. I no longer felt like a worm. After all those years of darkness, I saw a ray of hope, a light at the end of the long tunnel. I walked five miles a day, lost twenty five pounds, and felt like I was worth something to someone, including myself. I thank God for His great love, and tender mercies. I also thank God, for my sweet mother, and my sisters and brothers, who kept on praying for me, and didn't give up on God or me.

On the sixth day of December 1983, about three thirty in the afternoon, I came back to God and made a vow, I'd never turn away from Him again. I'd picked up my youngest son Joey at a Christian school in Springfield, and we were on our way back home. It was a cold, grey day. Here and there, spots of unmelted dirty snow dotted the edges of the roads, yards, and fields. Seat belts were not mandatory at that time, so we weren't wearing any. We were talking and joking as we drove along, when all of a sudden Joey stretched out his arm across me, (acting as a seat belt), "LOOK OUT MOM! THEY'RE NOT GOING TO STOP AT THE STOP SIGN!" I caught a glimpse of the car just as it pulled out in front of us! Both our cars were speeding along at about fifty-five miles per hour, and neither of us could stop! I heard myself scream, "GOD SAVE US ALL!"

I slammed on my brakes, just seconds before we hit head on! The other driver's small car spun around on impact. I pulled as hard as I could on the steering wheel and pushed on my brakes with all my strength to stop the car! By the time I finally stopped the car, I couldn't see anything through the shattered windshield except a green liquid spewing out from under the hood. Joey's head had hit the rear view mirror, and was bleeding badly. In my dazed state of mind, I heard him yelling, "Come on, mom, hurry! We've got to get you out of this car!" I really panicked when I finally understood what he was trying to tell me. We were parked at the bottom of a steep hill, on the wrong side of the road. School busses, cars and trucks traveled down that hill at a pretty fast speed. They wouldn't be able to see us in time to stop.

We struggled, but we couldn't get my door open on the driver's side. I was wedged in tight under the steering wheel which had caved in from the crash. To my right, a leather cup and cassette holder was built in between the two lower front seats, making it impossible for me to move. The car that hit us, was still spinning out of control. It kept on hitting us repeatedly on Joey's side of the car where the gas tank was. Joey refused to quit, until he somehow pulled me out from under the steering wheel, up over the built-in cup and cassette holder, and out to safety. During that whole

18

process his head spurted out blood every time his heart beat! God, and Joey saved my life that day, and I am thankful to them both. No one was killed, "Thank God!" He saved us all. "Thank You Jesus!" Joey had a concussion, and I had several broken and fractured ribs, and my knee caps were loosened, but I wasn't afraid.

Joe was really angry that I'd wrecked our new car, until he found out it was the other driver's fault, and her insurance was paying for everything. Not even Joe's anger or his insults toward me could take away my joy, because I had fallen in love with Jesus again. Jesus was my first love, and I'd come back to Him, forever. Even though I was black and blue, in pain, and very sore, I had peace and hope in my heart again. Two weeks after the accident, Joe went on a deer hunting trip at our cabin for a week, and took David and Joey with him. I'd been ordered by the doctor, not to climb stairs or lift anything heavy for at least six weeks. Our only source of heat was a wood burning stove downstairs in our basement which had to be loaded night and day with the firewood that we kept outside. The basement door was old and heavy. It had a stubborn black, rot iron latch. I had to push my weight against the door to open the latch and close it. The door was exceptionally hard to push closed against the snow drifts! "I am strong in Christ Jesus."

I'd never had a vacation in our twenty-one years of marriage. Joe always said, we couldn't afford it. However, neither money nor circumstances ever stopped him from going on his fishing and hunting trips spring, summer, fall and winter. If we had any extra money, it was spent on important things like, any and all kinds of ball cards, guns, knives, golfing, and fishing acquitment, or hunting gear. Joe always said, those things were important investments in our future. "God have mercy on us!" I was so thankful I'd found Jesus again. He gave me hope. Only God can change a hopeless situation and turn it around for good. I found great comfort reading God's word. I was getting to know Jesus, who taught me about my heavenly Father's love for me. I wanted Joe to know God's love. I wanted so much for Joe to go to heaven one day too.

My sister Peggy, who was not just my sister, but my lifelong best friend, cried and told me, she and her family were moving out west to Arizona. She and I had no choice, but to finally accept the move. We cried many, many tears, wrote long letters, and as often as we could afford it, we called each other long distance. Words cannot express how much I missed Peggy, and her family. God, through His mercy and His word, soothed the terrible sadness in my heart. I begged Jesus to fill the empty void, and He did while I read His word and learned about Him. I promised myself, I was going to read every word in the bible, and believe it was written just for me. I dug into God's word so much the pages started falling out. I was happy to go and buy a new bible. I was so thankful Jesus had not left me. I began to pray in tongues again, as if I'd never stopped. The Lord's love and mercy swept over me in waves of sheer joy. I started praising, and worshiping the Lord in spirit and in truth.

(John 42:23-24) "But the hour is coming, and now is, when the true worshipers will worship the Father in spirit and truth; for the Father is seeking such to worship Him. "God is Spirit, and those who worship Him must worship in spirit and truth." I wanted everything God had freely given me, through the blood Jesus sacrificed for me on the cross. I was making up for all the years I'd missed. (1 Corinthians 14:15) "What is it then? I will pray with the Spirit, and I will pray with my understanding also: I will sing with the Spirit and I will sing with the understanding also."

One day while I was reading through the scriptures, I realized what God was trying to say to me through the prophesy given me. (Isaiah 58:12) (Ezekiel 22:30) I will, through prayer, stand in the gap and repair the breech for others. I repented for running from His call on my life. I wanted to obey God's word, so He gave me the grace to forgive my dad and everyone who had ever hurt me, including Joe. Through forgiveness Jesus healed me from the inside out. I wanted to learn how to pray for others who were depressed and broken like I'd been, even though I felt I was just a new babe in Christ myself. I wanted to become like Jesus, and do what He did. Jesus said in, Luke 4:18-19, "The Spirit of the Lord is upon Me, Because He has anointed Me to preach the gospel to the poor. He has sent Me to heal the brokenhearted, To preach deliverance to the captives And recovery of sight to the blind, To set at liberty those who are oppressed, To preach the acceptable year of the Lord."

Joe and I didn't go to church anywhere, and I was thankful for Christian Television, but I needed someone to fellowship with. Little did I know that God already had a plan. I'd met Sandy at the bowling alley several different times, but we never really had a chance to talk much or get to know each other. She was Joe's best friend, Ron's wife. One night at the bowling alley, Sandy asked if I'd like to come to her house for lunch the next day. I accepted. She was a recent, rededicated Christian herself. We laughed and talked the entire afternoon. It was as if we'd known each other all our lives. We had so much in common. She told me her people were from Kentucky, too, and there were traces of Indian in her bloodline. Sandy's two beautiful daughters, Betsy and Jenny were just a couple of years younger then my two sons. We even liked the same southern style cooking. Sandy's light brown hair, green eyes, and lighter complexion, were apposite my dark brown hair, hazel eyes and olive looking skin, but we felt like sisters. Even our high moral standards were similar, but more then anything else, our love for Jesus, prayer, and the word of God were identical.

We started calling each other every morning, to pray together. Sandy was as tired of idle gossip as I was, and that was before we discovered it's a sin. We studied God's word and received it as if God wrote it just for us. Our friendship grew. (Matthew 5:6) "Blessed are they that do hunger and thirst after righteousness for they shall be filled." Sandy and Ron didn't just say they hated abortion, they took in young pregnant unwed girls, and let them stay with them, long after they had their baby's. They helped them, until they were able to get back on their own two feet. Betsy and Jenny unselfishly gave up their bedrooms for the pregnant teens. Also, a couple of times Sandy and Ron took in young boys that had no where else to go. They fed them, did their laundry, and most of all, they gave them love. I couldn't count the times I witnessed Ron and Sandy help their neighbors and strangers, pay their electric, phone, rent and grocery bills.

Sandy, Ron and their daughters were a living example of the love of Jesus in, Matthew 25:35-40 'For I was hungry and you gave Me food; I was thirsty and you gave Me drink; I was a stranger and you took Me in; 'I was naked and you clothed Me; I was sick and you visited Me; I was in prison and you came to Me.' "Then the righteous will answer Him, saying, 'Lord, when did we see You hungry and feed You, or thirsty and give You drink? When did we see You a stranger and take You in, or naked and clothe You? 'Or when did we see You sick, or in prison and come to You?' "And the King will answer and say to them, 'Assuredly, I say to you, inasmuch as you did it to one of the least of these My brethren, you did it to Me.' I felt privileged that God had picked me to be Sandy's friend. Together, we found God's word has the power to save us, heal us, and set us free from everything that binds us, past present, and future. We were excited about reading God's word, especially when we learned, we have a blood bought covenant with Almighty God which cannot be broken.

I had cleaned houses for other people to make extra money, and Sandy liked the idea of us working together. We kept talking about starting our own cleaning business, and after seeking the Lord awhile, we decided to do it. We called it C & S Cleaning Company and put our add in the local newspaper. It wasn't long before we had a few regular customers. I'll never forget Wendy. She had two pretty blond, blue eyed little girls, and a really busy husband who was never home. She had a lovely home filled with new furniture. She also drove a nice car, and she had pretty clothes. Wendy told us, she had been suffering from depression, and she'd been taking anti-depressants for a long time. She gave us a house key, and we started cleaning for her every week. Sandy knew I had an extra amount of compassion for Wendy, because of what I'd suffered with depression too. Although I had told the Lord, I wanted to see people set free from depression, I never dreamed He'd hold me to that promise so soon.

One afternoon, I was cleaning Wendy's main big bathroom. Sandy was cleaning the kitchen. Wendy had stayed home that day, she wasn't feeling well. She was laying in her king size bed, resting, while I was scrubbing the tub, when suddenly the Lord spoke to me about her. He told me, she'd planned to kill herself at midnight, that night. He wanted me to go pray for her. He told me, to lay hands on her in His name, and He'd set her free. I was petrified! I wanted to obey Him, but I just couldn't do it! He spoke to me again, "Carol, Wendy has planned to kill herself at midnight tonight. I want you to go lay hands on her and set her free, in My name." I shook my head, and frantically went on scrubbing the tub! I argued, "But Lord, I don't even hardly know this woman! How can I know this is You telling me to do this, for sure?" On and on, the argument went between me and the Lord, until I was worn out! I said, "Lord, I just can't do this, I'm too afraid! I know Lord! Go, and ask Sandy to do it, she's right there in the kitchen?" He wouldn't change His mind. He wanted me to do it. I continued to argue with Him and perspire, when suddenly a force I couldn't explain, picked me up under my arms, supernaturally brought me to my feet, and stood me outside Wendy's bedroom doorway.

I was glad she was turned toward the wall, and her back was facing me when I stuttered, "A, a, Wen, Wendy?" She looked back over her shoulder, "Yes, Carol, what is it?" I broke out in a cold sweat, and gulped out, "Oh, oh, nothing Wendy! Really it's nothing, go back to sleep, please!" I swung around, and ran into the kitchen where Sandy was cleaning the refrigerator. Breathing heavily, I stood there and explained everything to her quickly, hoping she might help me, "Oh Sandy, You've just got to help me, please?" She looked at me rather puzzled, shrugged her shoulders and said, "No, Carol. God spoke to you, and told you to do this, not me. If you really feel this is the Lord speaking to you, then you'd better go do it right now. I'll just wait here." I swallowed hard, and smiled at her through my clenched chattering teeth. I said, "And what do I say to Wendy, if this is not the Lord?" I knew she was right. If I doubted it was the Lord, and I was scared, then how could I expect her to obey His voice, when she didn't hear it.

God's Spirit pulled me like a magnet back to Wendy's bedroom doorway again, only this time a boldness came over me as I blurted out everything! Before I could finish speaking, Wendy jumped straight up in the middle of her bed and started jumping up and down, screaming to the top of her lungs, "OH, GOD, THANK YOU FOR HEARING, AND ANSWERING MY DESPERATE CRIES FOR HELP! YOU HEARD ME LORD! YOU REALLY, REALLY HEARD ME, AND YOU SENT SOMEONE TO DELIVER ME, JUST AS I PRAYED, DEAR LORD!" Sandy came rushing into the room to see what was going on. After Wendy calmed down a little, and got off the bed, we laid hands on her, in Jesus name, and Jesus set her free! "Hallelujah!" I was set free too, from the fear of wondering if I truly heard God's voice.

(John 10:27) "My sheep hear My voice, and I know them, and they follow Me." Wendy needed our services less, and less after that glorious day. Her life was never the same. After Wendy's husband saw the transformation in her, he got saved. He started taking their whole family to a really strong word church. Only the Lord knows how many people's lives they have touched, by the power of the dear precious sweet Holy Spirit. Sandy and I fell more and more in love with Jesus every day! We never hesitated to pour our prayers out to God in Jesus name, and He never failed to amaze us when He answered our childlike prayers for ourselves or others.

A lady named Joyce called about our cleaning add. We saw she was an attractive dark haired, small framed women when she answered her doorbell. A closer look at her inside the house showed dark circles under her large sad brown eyes. She told us. She'd been sick for a long time. We told her, we were Christian women who loved to pray. Joyce told us, she was a non- practicing Catholic. She believed in Jesus. We told her about, Isaiah 53:4-5,

"Surely He hath born our griefs, and carried our sorrows; yet we did esteem Him stricken, smitten of God, and afflicted. But He was wounded for our transgressions, He was bruised for our iniquities, the chastisement of our peace was upon Him, and with His strips we are healed." Joyce welcomed our prayers, and our cleaning experience, so we prayed for her, and we cleaned for her weekly.

I'll never forget the time Sandy and I cleaned an apartment for Joyce near a large, busy town. Her renters had moved out and left the place in really bad shape. It was nearly dark by the time we'd finished cleaning. Joyce surprised us when she said. She couldn't pay us until the following Thursday. Not wanting to embarrass her or ourselves, we smiled and said, "Oh sure, that's fine." We gathered our cleaning supplies and left, knowing the gas tank was close to empty, and we had no money. As we walked out to the car, I heard, "Oh, where is your great faith now, ladies?" The minute we got in the car we started praying in the Spirit LOUD, and we quoted God's word as LOUD as we could too, "It is written, 'MY GOD SHALL SUPPLY ALL, CAROL AND SANDY'S NEED ACCORDING TO HIS RICHES IN GLORY, BY CHRIST JESUS!" (Philippians 4:19) As if things weren't bad enough already, we discovered we were lost in that huge, big, busy City! We must have sounded like machine guns to the enemy, quoting scriptures, praying in tongues, and praising God as loud, hard, and as fast as we could, because suddenly our sorrow turned into outrageous joy!

Sandy started laughing so hard she could hardly keep the car on the road. She was so funny! I started slapping my leg, and laughing uncontrollably too. It felt like we were intoxicated with joy. I hollered, "Hey Sandy, I think the Holy Spirit has anointed us with His joy, don't you?" She kept laughing, and pointed toward the back seat. Finally she caught her breath, and squealed, "Carol look, there in back seat! Can't you see that BIG, HUGE, bright glowing white angel riding in the car with us?" We roared with laughter as tears rolled down our cheeks. I looked over at the gas gage which was steadily rising and yelled, "Sandy, will you look at your gas gauge! God is filling your tank up, supernaturally?" She yelled at the same time, pointing at the road sign in front of us, "Hey Carol, look, there's our exit! We're not lost anymore! Oh, praise God!" (Psalm 34:4-7) "I sought the Lord, and He heard me, And delivered me from all my fears. They looked unto Him, and were radiant, and their faces were not ashamed. This poor man cried out, and the Lord heard him, And saved him out of all his troubles. The angel of the Lord encamps all around those who fear Him, And delivers them." (Psalm 126:2) Then our mouth was filled with laughter, and our tongue with singing. Then they said among the nations, "The Lord has done great things for them."

I couldn't help remembering when Joe didn't like the way I laughed. He ridiculed me, until I changed my naturel, God given laugh. It was difficult, but I did it so he wouldn't be ashamed of me. I wanted Joe to love and except me the way I was. He never could. I'd sit and cry, praying I could get Joe to stop treating me that way in front of our sons and others. When I tried to say grace at the table, Joe made fun of me in front of Joey and David, until I was in tears. It hurt and angered my family to see and hear the way Joe put me down and called me names right in front of them.

I had no self esteem, until I came back to Jesus and let Him do surgery on my broken heart, my broken past, and my broken dreams. Every time I'd go to God in tears, whether it was from a past hurt, or a problem right then, I'd see myself as a little girl on my Papa's lap. Sometimes I'd see myself leaning my head on my heavenly Father's chest, and other times He'd bounce me on His knee. Each time I went to Him, I wondered why I was seeing a vision of myself on His lap as a little child, and not the age I was? I finally realized, not only was I a new babe in Christ, but the child inside of me had been crushed, bruised and wounded throughout my childhood years, and much of my adult life.

I knew I had to let go, and let God heal the broken child inside of me, before I could have faith in my heavenly Father's love. It was a serious challenge, but I kept looking at Jesus, because He said in,

26

John 14:9 Jesus said to him, "Have I been with you so long, and yet you have not known Me, Philip? He who has seen Me has seen the Father; so how can you say, 'Show us the Father'?" I didn't know how to receive a fathers love, except by trusting Jesus to reveal Him to me. As I constantly studied the four gospels, I saw my Papa while looking at Jesus. I saw the colors of the rainbow around my heavenly Papa's face when I'd see myself sitting on His lap or standing in front of His Great thrown. I was falling in love with my wonderful heavenly Father and getting to know Him as my own personal Papa, God. Jesus was teaching me, one step at a time, how to receive a Father's love. "By faith, I believe, I receive Your love, Papa God. Please, keep helping me to receive Your love Papa, in the name of Jesus."

Chapter Two

If two on earth agree

When our oldest son David married his young wife Carrie, they came to live with us in our small house. After we knew for sure Carrie was pregnant, we were all very happy. We were even happier when our little granddaughter Rebecca was born. She had curly red hair, and big blue eyes, and I fell in love with her immediately. She was a small wonderful gift from God, and I thanked Him for her. She was nearly five months old when David decided to join the military. Six weeks later he came home from boot camp with the shocking news. He was being stationed in London, England, four years. He and Carrie weren't very happy about moving so far away from her family, or ours, either. Our little granddaughter, Rebecca had brought us so much joy and laughter since the day she was born. I couldn't bare the thought of her leaving us too. I was so stunned by the sudden news, I held Rebecca close in my arms and I cried out to God from my broken heart, "Oh Lord, surely there's been a mistake."

Sandy's eyes welled up with tears of compassion when I cried and told her the news about David, Carrie and the baby leaving. I said, "Sandy, my heart is breaking, and I don't even know how, or what I should pray. We've never been separated from our sons before. Little Rebecca has lived with us since she was born. How can we stand not seeing her cheery, small face every day?" Sandy had never been separated from her daughters before either, so she knew it was not going to be easy for me to say good-by to all of them. None of us were pleased with the situation, but there seemed to be nothing we could do, accept to try and make the best of it. I felt so lost, hurt, and empty, I couldn't seem to do anything, but cry. I just kept praying, "Oh dear Lord, please help us! This decision made for David, Carrie and the baby to move three thousand miles away from us, isn't Your will, is it Lord?" I had to trust God. He was in control. Before we knew it, it was time for us to take them to the airport. We were all crying. Carrie's mom, dad and sisters were all wiping the tears from their eyes too. Just knowing the plane, David, Carrie and the baby boarded was going to carry them three thousand miles away from us, it was more than I could bear. I bawled like a baby calf lost from its mother, all the way home from the air port. I just couldn't seem to pull myself together. Joe's silent anger made the long drive home even more unbearable. I was miserable. I knew Joe was hurting deeply too.

I thought. "Joe and I should be comforting each other. We should be looking forward to our future together, with or without our children living close to us." But instead, Joe and I hardly ever talked without an argument. He wanted to argue about anything, and everything. Joe was even more angry and dissatisfied with me since I'd come back to the Lord. It felt like the valley we were in was so deep. I simply didn't know what to do? Even though I prayed constantly, it felt like I was not getting any peace when it came to Joe or our marriage.

My youngest son, Joey, hated sad farewells, so he'd refused to go to the air port with us. Instead, he went off somewhere by himself. The two of them had always done things together. The house was so empty and quiet. It felt strange not to hear Rebecca jabbering baby talk with her mother and daddy. Suddenly, Joe yelled as he slammed the kitchen door, "I'm going to play some blank, blank golf. I'll see ya later!" I ran out on the porch just as he was pulling out of the driveway, and said, "Joe, please wait! Will you be coming home in time for dinner tonight?" I knew our neighbors heard Joe's angry voice shouting back at me, "Just go ahead and eat without me again! I don't know what the, blank time I'll be home!" Everything in me wanted to take control of my life, and my marriage. My whole world, as I knew it was falling apart, and I couldn't seem to do anything to stop it. Once again, I was frustrated, hurt and angry. The tears flowed freely from my eyes as I walked back into the house. Seeing my precious little granddaughter's empty playpen, made me cry much harder. I found David's shirt laying on my bedroom floor. He must have taken it off in a hurry, and in the middle of the last minute rush, left it there. His shirt reminded me of how much I missed him. I picked his crumpled shirt up off the floor, clutched it to my heart, and fell on the bed sobbing uncontrollably!

Suddenly, right in the middle of all my overwhelming sadness and sorrow, I heard a still small voice say, "Daughter, if you want Me to help you, than get up and read Psalm 40." Instead of obeying God's voice, I fell back on the bed and kept on moaning and wailing about all my troubles. The Lord repeated His words, but I continued to cry aloud and tell Him how bad I was hurting. The third time the Lord spoke to me, however, it was so loud and so firm, I felt His suggestion start at the top of my head, and continue all the way down to my feet, "DAUGHTER, IF YOU REALLY WANT ME TO HELP YOU, THAN GET UP AND READ PSALM 40." Reluctantly, I got up and went into the living room. I hurriedly scooped my bible up from the coffee table, and read Psalm 40:1-3 "I waited patiently for the Lord; And He inclined to me, And heard my cry. He also brought me up out of a horrible pit, Out of the miry clay, And set my feet upon a rock, And established my steps. He has put a new song in my mouth-- Praise to our God; Many will see it and fear, And will trust in the Lord." I thanked the Lord, for gently rebuking me.

I felt like I was trying to climb a steep mountain, and the Lord threw me a rope, and gave me a hope to hold onto, especially when I read, Psalm 40: 11- 14 "Do not withhold Your tender mercies from me, O Lord; Let Your lovingkindness and Your truth continually preserve me. For innumerable evils have surrounded me; my iniquities have overtaken me, so that I am not able to look up; They are more then the hairs of my head; Therefore, my heart fails within me. Be pleased O Lord, to deliver me; O Lord make haste to help me! Let them be ashamed and brought to mutual confusion who seek to destroy my life; Let them be driven backward and brought to dishonor who wish me evil."

I read Psalm 40 to Sandy over the phone the next morning. His word, which was written thousands of years ago is alive, and full of power. The fact that God's word identified with my situation in 1984, amazed me. I was so happy, God intervened and gave me hope again, after I finally obeyed His voice. As I searched the scriptures and memorized them, they were like warm soothing oil pouring over me. (2 Corinthians' 12:10) "When I am weak, then am I strong in Christ Jesus." (Deuteronomy 31:6) "Be strong and of good courage, do not fear nor be afraid of them; for the Lord your God, He is the One who goes with you. He will not leave you nor forsake you." My arms actually ached to hold my little granddaughter, Rebecca. I'd held her in my arms every day for the first six months of her life. I felt God's love comforting me.

I was learning to trust God to take care of David, Carrie, and Rebecca, who were three thousand miles away from us. It wasn't easy, but I knew I had to learn to trust Him to heal my marriage to Joe, too. I surprised Joey when I suggested completely redoing the bedroom he and David had shared growing up. A small love-seat which let out into a bed replaced the bunk beds, and made his room more like a den. We hung bamboo blinds, and I made new white curtains to brighten his room, too. It gave me something to do to take my mind off other things, and it made Joey happy.

Sandy and I were desperate to learn how to pray effectively for ourselves and our families. We cried out to God constantly, "Lord, teach us how to pray?" We were like baby birds, with our mouths open wide, crying out for God's wisdom, knowledge, and truth. I needed to learn to pray and trust God, because my marriage was in deep trouble. When I prayed, God gave me more grace to love Joe unconditionally, even though he was treating me like I was a total stranger. Our cleaning company was growing every day. I liked being busy. It helped, having my own money to spend, even though Joe made excellent wages where he worked. The dear precious Holy Spirit helped me remember scriptures that comforted me. (Galatians 6:9) And let us not grow weary while doing good, for in due season we shall reap if we do not lose heart.

The first time Sandy and I met our friend Jean. We were browsing through her lovely gift shop. A tall, thin, attractive woman with short, reddish blond hair and large trusting, blue grey eyes, spoke to us in a soft gentle voice, "Hi, welcome to the country gift shop. How may I help you, ladies?" We knew almost immediately, we were going to be good friends with Jean. She told us she, too, was a Christian. After we'd talked awhile, she asked us if we'd like to start having a prayer group, right there in her big comfortable, old farmhouse. We all agreed we should have our prayer group on Mondays, the beginning of every week. Our early Monday morning prayer group was exactly what we all needed. We had so much fun talking, and getting to know each other, over coffee and pastry, before prayer. All of us contributed delicacies.

One beautiful, sunny afternoon while Sandy and I were helping Jean with her yard sale, she introduced us to a couple of her friends, Dixie, and Barb. They just happened to stop by her yard sale. I smiled when Jean asked Dixie and Barb if they would like to join the prayer group. Instantly, they said, "Yes, we'd love to come!" We all laughed, because we knew it wasn't an accident, that these two women who loved to pray visited Jean's yard sale. Jean's next door neighbor, Barb, was about five feet, five inches tall. The pretty blond, blue eyed, slender Barb, could hardly wait to join us in our Monday morning prayer group. Dixie's small five foot frame, had nothing to do with her 'giant slayer' spirit. Her fiery red hair, with her freckled, fair complexion, caused her big blue eyes to be even more expressive when she talked about her great love for Jesus. We loved to talk about our dear, Lord, Jesus!

Jean's cousin Betty, a sweet robust lady with salt and pepper grey hair and blue eyes, joined our Monday morning prayer group too. Every week, the six of us looked so forward to our prayer group. Because ours was a prayer of agreement, God answered them quickly. He was also revealing exciting, and awesome things to us, through the dear precious Holy Spirit. One day the six of us were standing in a circle, praying. Barb requested prayer for her husband, Joe's knee. He'd had surgery on his knee cap, but it didn't help him. He was still in terrible pain. As we continued to pray, I saw a vision of Barb's husband, Joe, sitting at his desk in his office. He was leaning back in his chair, relaxing with his feet propped up on his desk. His legs were crossed, and his hands were behind his head. I can't remember now which knee cap it was, but suddenly a ball of fire started swirling in a circle on Joe's knee. The ball of fire swirled for a few seconds, and then disappeared. Joe jumped up, and walked around happy, and smiling. "Praise God!" Barb told us at our next prayer meeting, Joe was instantly, completely healed at the exact, precise moment God showed me the vision. She said. "Joe praises the Lord for his healing!" Later, glory to God, Joe also received the baptism of the Holy Spirit. "God, You're so good!" We were all so thankful Jesus healed Joe.

As long as I live, I'll never forget when I had the most incredible, open-eyed vision I've ever seen! It was during our regular Monday morning prayer group. We were all sitting at Jean's big kitchen table having coffee, and enjoying our time of fellowship before prayer. I was listening to Jean talk one minute, then suddenly, I had a vision. I was with Jesus, in the garden of Gethsemane the night of His arrest. I could barely hear or see Jean and the other ladies any longer. Instead, I saw my beautiful sweet Jesus standing in the garden. I heard the voices of angry men, and I saw them holding fiery blazing torches, coming to take our wonderful Lord, Jesus away. The Lord's face was so innocent and precious as the cruel, angry men tried to take hold of Him.

I had absolutely no control over what was happening to me, and I was afraid. One instant I felt the Lord's deep overwhelming sorrow, and the next instant I was standing at a distance, helplessly watching Him suffer. It was a strange feeling, being part of two worlds. In the vision, I wanted to run to Jesus and comfort Him, but I couldn't move in any direction. I also wanted to answer Jean, and Sandy, and my other friends who kept asking me, "What's wrong Carol? Are you all right?" I couldn't do anything except moan in my spirit and weep as I watched Jesus suffer. His wonderful face had looked like pure gold, in the reflection of the burning torches. The vision changed and shifted quickly from time to time. Thank God, none of us will ever have to bear the horrible, indescribable suffering our Savior was enduring spiritually, physically, or mentally, because He went through it all for our salvation, peace and healing. He'd quickly shift the vision again, and I'd see myself standing at a distance watching Him. John 3:14-16 "And as Moses lifted up the serpent in the wilderness, even so must the Son of Man be lifted up, " that whoever believes in Him should not perish but have eternal life. "For God so loved the world that He gave His only begotten Son, that whoever believes in Him should not perish but have everlasting life."

I couldn't answer any of my friend's questions, accept with deep sounds of moaning, and uncontrollable weeping. I had to strain very hard to hear their muffled voices asking me, "Carol, please answer us! Are you all right?" Finally, they picked me up under my arms and drug me into Jean's family room, where we usually prayed. They all stopped shaking me, and asking me questions, when they realized, I couldn't answer. Instead, they sat me down really easy on the floor. Then they all gathered around me, and prayed in the tongues. I was filled with compassion for Jesus, as the cruel, angry men violently beat His precious back, until it was bloody and bruised. Isaiah 53:5 "But He was wounded for our transgressions, He was bruised for our iniquities; the chastisement for our peace was upon Him, And by His stripes we are healed."

For an instant I watched as He walked under the burden of the cross. Those horrible nails were pounded in His precious hands and feet. I watched Him in the vision. He endured suffering for us and He was blameless, as they raised Him on the cross. The love in His heart for His people, for us, and for the whole world, was beyond my human ability to describe it. My friends were all crying too. They realized something holy was happening, and not just to me, but to all of us in the prayer group. "Dear precious, Jesus."

When the vision finally ended, I was completely drained emotionally, and physically. I shared my unbelievable experience with my friends, "In the vision, every step Jesus took toward the cross, He took me with Him." I was so thankful Jesus refreshed and healed me immediately from the pain of watching and feeling

Him suffer. My friends tried to comprehend, but it was almost impossible to explain the dramatic experience I'd had with Jesus. The vision God allowed me to participate in that day was so deeply felt. (Hebrews 9:22) "And according to the law almost all things are purged with blood, and without shedding of blood there is no remission." The book of Ephesians says. His love is incomparable love. Matthew 16:24 Then Jesus said to His disciples, "If anyone desires to come after Me, let him deny himself, and take up the cross, and follow Me."

On our way back to my house, I told Sandy, "I don't think I should go back to the prayer group again for a while. I need to quietly seek God for some answers, and find out why He gave me the vision. I couldn't bear to ever go through that experience again, and I pray the Lord never requires it of me." She said. She didn't want to return to the prayer group for a while again either. She was afraid, too. She and I usually laughed a lot together, because we had the joy of the Lord, but that day we were serious. Thank God, we knew Jesus was no longer suffering on the cross, but is seated at His Father's right hand. When we got back to my house we decided we'd just sit quietly, and pray in the spirit. While we were praying, and waiting on God to tell us what to do next, all of a sudden, Sandy jumped up, and said, "Carol, I know what we'll do! We will call the 700 hundred club, and see what they say about it. I'm sure someone there can answer our question."

Sandy listened on the extension in the bedroom, while I talked with the prayer counselor on the living room phone. As I told her my story, I was a little fearful of her reaction. I almost hung up the phone several times. The enemy was trying to spook me into believing, the vision God gave me, was too strange. However, I pressed on, until I finished my story. The prayer counselor on the other end of the line startled me when she boldly said, "Well, praise God, sister! You are privileged like Habakkuk! Read his story, and see how he was able to still see the vision the Lord gave him clearly, right in the middle of all the adversity!" She prayed for me, and encouraged me to read Habakkuk.

Later that day, I read the book of Habakkuk, but I didn't

understand how it related to my vision of the Lord. I still felt I needed more reassurance concerning the vision God gave me. I knew God understood my questioning heart, because He said in, Psalm 138:8 "The Lord will perfect that which concerns me." One of my very favorite scriptures in the bible is, Numbers 23:19 "God is not a man that He should lie, nor the Son of man that He should repent." God kept His promise, and gave me the final confirmation I needed in my heart. He sent my friend Dixie over to my house with a book that answered all my questions, once and for all, about the open-eyed vision of Jesus and the cross. "Thank You, Jesus."

Dixie laughed and told me, God didn't tell her why she had to bring me this certain book, but He did tell her to come right over and bring it to me, immediately. She said, she felt she urgently needed to hand the book to me personally. She said, she didn't know what the book was about, she hadn't even read it yet. The book belonged to her husband, Ronnie. She asked her husband, Ronnie, if she could let me borrow his book because God told her, "Dixie, take this book to Carol, and do it quickly." She said Ronnie gladly gave his permission. Dixie told me, the Lord wouldn't let her rest until she obeyed Him, and brought me the book. I thank God for Dixie's obedience. "Following the fire." The book was written, by Gerald Derstine, as told by Joan Derstine. What happened to me in the vision of Jesus going to the cross? Also, happened to this one man in their prayer group, and it was right before they all suffered persecutions. It happened to me in our prayer group almost identically. As I read through the pages of this wonderful book, it opened my eyes. "Hallelujah!" Sandy, and I were no longer afraid to return to our prayer group. God is so faithful to keep His word. "Praise God, for the blood of Jesus!"

We started getting odd phone calls at all hours, day and night. I'd say, "Hello?", But the other person wouldn't answer. I always sensed the other person was really trying to intimidate me. I suspected it was another woman in my husband's life. If Joe answered the phone, the mystery person talked to him. He'd quickly take the phone off into our bedroom, and shut the door. If

I asked who it was, Joe always said, it was just an old friend who wanted to talk to him privately, or else, it was just one of his hunting buddies, and sometimes he said, it was an important business associate. However, after each of his long, and very private phone conversations, he'd leave for long periods of time without telling me where he was going. I constantly prayed in tongues to strengthen myself. I also kept asking God to expose the other woman, who Joe kept denying existed. I was getting very uneasy, so I stayed close to Jesus. I kept on trusting in the Lord to bring us through, what seemed like an awful nightmare.

I knew Joe was an unbeliever. I also knew what the bible said about the subject, but I still loved Joe, and I just couldn't let him go. (1 Corinthians' 7:13) "And the woman who has a husband who does not believe, if he is willing to live with her, let her not divorce him." I wanted to fight for my marriage to Joe, but sometimes it was taking every bit of strength I had left in me to hold on and wait, until Jesus calmed the storm. One night Joe finally returned home after going to the store three hours earlier for bread and milk. I was so furious! I tried to calm down, but I couldn't. Once again he'd left right after another one of his mysterious, and very private phone conversations. Joe's strange disappearances had gone on long enough. I couldn't be silent anymore, not this time. I thought of Jesus in the vision of the cross.

Tears were streaming down my cheeks when I cornered him in the kitchen, yelling, "I want the truth Joe, and I don't care how much it hurts me! I can't take your lies anymore, do you hear me Joe? The secret phone calls, and the sneaking around has got to stop, now Joe! I believe I've been a good wife to you for twenty-three years! Haven't I earned enough respect from you, to at least hear you tell me the truth Joe?" He leaned his back against the kitchen sink, put his face in his hands, and started to weep like a baby. His reaction startled me. I'd never seen him cry like that before. I had a feeling this truth was going to hurt, and hurt really badly. I tried to brace myself for what I knew was coming so I sat down at the kitchen table. I whispered, "God have mercy on us." I thought about the time I caught Joe in Lisa's arms. I whispered under my breath, "Oh dear Lord, why can't Joe ever just love me? Please help me dear Lord Jesus, I don't want to go through this again, it's just too painful!" I already knew in my heart what Joe was going to say when he finally broke through the silence, "Carol, I don't love you anymore, I'm sorry. I haven't loved you for a long time. I want a blank, blank divorce, and don't fight me! I am in love with someone else." I'd suspected and feared what Joe was going to say, but when he spoke those cruel, angry words out of his mouth, I still wasn't at all prepared to hear them.

What little hope I had left for mine and Joe's marriage to be restored, drained out of me. Instead I felt hopelessness, fear and panic! I sat there in disbelief, I was so stunned. I heard myself whisper, "Dear, precious, Lord Jesus, please give us peace in the midst of this storm?" Immediately, I felt something like a warm blanket wrap around me, and I felt peace. I tried to speak quietly and rationally to Joe, but he told me he was moving out. He said he was leaving, and he'd be back later to get the rest of his things. I really couldn't see how Joe's death or this divorce could be any different, the emptiness and the feelings of loss was so similar.

I couldn't believe I was watching the only man I'd ever loved, walk out the door. I cried, "Oh dear God, please help me?" I felt like Jesus' merciful arms were around me, comforting me. I held onto Him tightly as I made my way to the phone in the living room. I knew Sandy was home with her family, so I called my friend Jean. She ministered to me, for nearly two hours, after listening quietly to my story. Jean encouraged me, and prayed comforting prayers over me too. I felt stronger, and I had a ray of hope hearing Jean read God's word, in Psalm 34:18 "He is close to the broken hearted." I knew, no matter how I felt inside, God was very near to me, because He said so in His word. After Jean finished praying for me, I went to bed and slept peacefully.

As soon as I opened my eyes the next morning, the demons started talking to me before I could get out of bed, "Joe wants a younger woman, not you! You are so old and ugly. You'll never get him back this time!" I sensed a dark, thick cloud of hopelessness and despair hovering over me. The grotesque darkness tried to smother the very life out of me with horrible thoughts of suicide and depression. A demonic spirit of fear gripped hold of me, and tried it's level best to overpower me, too. I threw back the covers, and leaped out of bed, screaming, "JESUS, PLEASE HELP ME! OH PLEASE HURRY, LORD, JESUS! HELP ME! I plead the blood of Jesus, in the name of Jesus, over my mind, and I thank You Lord for Your holy angels, and Your ministering spirits that watch over me, and keep me safe. And I rebuke this torment off my mind in the name of Jesus!" I started praying in tongues, as loud, hard, and as fast as I could.

Even though it was a bitter cold day, Joey had gone outside to run. He was in training. He wanted to win the Golden Gloves Boxing Championship that year. He ran early every morning for at least a couple of hours. I was afraid, and I felt so alone. Suddenly, someone was pounding on my back door! I knew it wasn't Joey, knocking. He didn't have a key, so he always left the back door unlocked on the mornings he ran. I was on my knees at the foot of my bed, crying, when I looked up and saw my friend Jean standing there. Her eyes filled with tears when she said, "Hi Sweetie. I was so worried about you, I just had to stop by and check up on you. You're door was unlocked, so I came on in. I hope that's ok?" She fell to her knees beside me, and scooped me up in her arms. I felt like a helpless child with Jean holding me while I cried. The Lord sent Jean by to keep His word. Isaiah 66: 13 "As one whom his mother comforts, so I will comfort you . . . "

About a half hour after Jean left, I heard someone else knocking on my back door. All of a sudden, I came to my senses! I glanced at the clock, and said, "Oh dear Lord! It must be Sandy picking me up for work, and I'm not ready!" I was still sitting on the floor in my bedroom. My hair wasn't even washed or combed, and I had on no make up. Sandy took one look at me when I opened the door, and said, "I knew something was wrong, because God kept bringing you before my face last night. What's wrong Carol?"Even though she knew I'd suspected another woman in Joe's life, she was still shocked when I told her what had happened. We cried and talked for over an hour, and nearly forgot about our jobs.

Thank God. We had the keys to most of our customer's houses. I was really thankful for the hard work, it kept me busy, and gave me extra spending money. I also liked the feeling of being physically stronger, but tired enough to sleep at night. It kept me from constantly thinking about everything.

Later that day after work Sandy dropped me off at my house. Before I got out of the car, she said quietly, "Carol, why don't you just come on home, and stay the night with the girl's and I? You know Ron work's nights. We could stay up late and talk." I thanked her for asking me, and I said, "Sandy, I think I'd better stay home tonight, just in case Joe comes back to get his clothes. Remember, he said he was coming back to get the rest of his things? I want to fix him and Joey a nice dinner. Don't worry about me, my friend, I'll be fine." Reluctantly, she said, "Well all right Carol, if you're sure that's what you want to do. If you change your mind, or if you need me, don't hesitate to call, no matter what time it is, ok? Otherwise, I'll be here to pick you up for work about eight o clock tomorrow morning." I agreed, and I waved bye as I ran up the front steps to my house.

As soon as I put the key in the lock and turned the door knob, I felt a strange urgency to go straight back to my bedroom, and look in the closet. I was so hurt and shocked when I opened the closet door! All of Joe's clothes were gone. While I was at work, he came back and got the rest of his things. Joe's old, faded blue wedding suit was the only piece of his clothing he left behind. My yellowed wedding gown hung there beside it, as if to laugh at me in a mocking manner. Hurt, anger, and dozens of memories flooded over my mind. I reached up and grabbed the sleeves of our wedding clothes and screamed out in agony, "Oh Father, You said in Your word; Joe and I are no longer two, but one flesh! Therefore, what You have joined together, Oh God; Please don't let any man, or another woman put our marriage asunder!" (Matthew 19:6)

I fell to my knees, sobbing, and crawled to the foot of my bed, praying in the spirit in order to by pass my tormented mind. I raised my weary arms in praise, and reach up with everything I had left in me, to take hold of the hem of Jesus' garment. Without even realizing what I was doing, I walked into the bathroom and cut off most of my long hair. I'd always seen myself in the mirror of my husband's eyes. I thought, "If Joe is no longer attracted to me, I must be so ugly." The enemy kept harassing me. He said he was going to kill me. He taunted me, and told me I was too weak to fight back. The dear precious Holy Spirit quickly reminded me, His word says in, 2 Corinthians 12:10 "...For when I am weak, then I am strong in Christ Jesus." I also read, 2 Corinthians 29:9."My grace is sufficient for you, for My strength is made perfect in weakness." God did surgery on me that day. Through the power of His word, He supernaturally ripped the fear from my heart. I grew stronger each day, by hearing myself read, speak, and pray God's word. Jesus never left me. I felt His presence so close, gently whispering hope into my spirit, and healing me physically from the top of my head to the soles of my feet, daily.

Even though I knew Joe was selfish, and his words against me were cruel and abusive, I still loved him. I didn't want to lose him, no matter how crazy it seemed to my family or anybody else. I needed to know wisdom, so I studied God's word concerning divorce to see how He felt about it. (Malachi 2:16) "God hates divorce." (2 Corinthians 6:14-15) "Do not be unequally yoked together with unbelievers. For what fellowship has righteousness with lawlessness? And what communion has light with darkness? And what accord has Christ with Belial? Or what part has a believer with an unbeliever?"Joe and I used to sing an old country song with his family, called, "The shoe goes on the other foot tonight." Somehow, I knew I wasn't just remembering that old song, because we used to sing it, but it was the Lord, He was bringing it to my mind. "The joy of the Lord is my strength."

I soon realized what the Lord was up to, when Joe called and told me he couldn't afford to move in anywhere, accept with his mother, and dad. Joe sounded so sad, and miserable, I had to put my hand over my mouth to keep from laughing out loud. He said he hated living with his parents, because they constantly told him how wrong he was for leaving his sweet, wonderful wife, (me.) I called Sandy the minute Joe and I hung up the phone. I couldn't wait to tell her the good news! I think she was almost as happy as I was. But she and I knew the battle was just heating up. However, we also understood, the battle belongs to the Lord, and by faith, I'd already claimed that His promised victory was mine. Joe started calling me every day. He said, I was the only one who treated him decent. He also said, "Carol, no one in my family speaks to me, without giving me a dirty look. You are the only one who talks nice to me." I had a good feeling, God was breaking up Joe's relationship with the other woman, because he was calling me. Every time Joe called, I said in my heart, "Oh thank You, dear, sweet, Jesus for healing my husband Joe, and our marriage!" "Glory to Your wonderful name, precious Lord, Jesus!"

I was so very grateful the Lord lead me to read the book, "Love Life.", By Dr. Ed Wheat. The Lord put that book in my hands to give me the ammunition I needed to fight the good fight of faith for my marriage. The storm that raged through our home and tried to tear mine and Joe's marriage apart caused such confusion. I felt stranded; and without a battle plan, a strategic clear set course to follow, how could I possibly reach my goal, out smart the enemy, and find my way out of the storm? God knew I desperately needed the vital information this wonderful book provided. It was like a remarkable flashlight, piercing through the horrible darkness, shedding God's great light onto my pathway. I felt secure and confident when I read through the pages of the book. I knew God was guiding me safely through the storm. No matter how mean, angry, or down right nasty Joe treated me, I kept on forgiving him with the agape love and mercy in my heart through God's grace.

God kept giving me more grace to love Joe, even when it got really rough. Sometimes I had to leave the room, rather then stand there and listen to Joe's cruel, abusive words. Each time the Lord helped me calm down. His peace and love flooded my heart, and I forgave Joe and went on loving him, anyway. Sandy and I prayed in agreement against, any, and all women who Joe might be attracted too, or tempted to have an affair with. We asked God, too either remove the other woman from Joe's life, by turning them against each other, or get them saved. It was totally awesome how quick God answered our prayers. Sheila, Joe's young, pretty, tall and slender, blond, blue eyed secretary started calling me from work, on her lunch break several times a week. She said she just called to talk, but she wound up telling me all her troubles. I asked Sandy, "My friend, can you believe Joe's secretary, Sheila, is calling me from work to tell me, HER TROUBLES? I don't know how God did it, but He sure answered this prayer, exceedingly, abundantly, above ALL that we could ask, or even possibly think. Wow!" Sandy laughed, and said, "Oh Carol, God is so good, He can do anything." We praised the Lord, "Thank You, dear Jesus!"

Every day, without let up, the enemy argued his case against me, asking, if I was such a good Christian woman, and such a faithful wife, why was Joe being unfaithful to me? He asked why I kept paying my tithes too? I got so irritated, I just started praising God as loud as I could for giving me more seed to sow into His Kingdom! I thanked Him for the work so I could give. I pled the blood of Jesus, in the name of Jesus over my marriage vows. We also dwell in the secret place of the Most High God, who's power no foe can withstand. (Psalm 91) "Dear sweet Jesus, O how I love You, and thank You for teaching me how to trust You more!"

I knelt at the foot of my bed, and cried out to God, "Please Papa, I'm not asking You to change Joe, I'm asking You to change me, in the name of Jesus!" As I lifted my face toward heaven, praying in tongues, I saw a clear vision of myself standing at a crossroad. I was wearing an old yellowed torn dress, and I was all bent over with heaviness. I looked real sad. Tears gushed from my eyes, both in the natural, and in the vision I saw of myself in. I heard the Lord speak to me clearly. He said, "Daughter, that is a spirit of self pity you are wearing. That thing is dangerous. I want you to take that thing off, leave it at the side of the road, And I want you to NEVER pick it up again." I watched myself in the vision as I took off the old yellowed torn dress. I stood there holding it between the index finger and thumb of my right hand. When I dropped it at the side of the road, I felt a new freedom take place on the inside of me. I prayed, "Oh God, in the name of Jesus, please help me to never pick up that old yellowed, ragged, worn out, garment of self pity again? Give me the strength to exchange it for a garment of praise today, Lord. Thank You, Lord Jesus, for rescuing me."

I listened carefully as the Lord gave me several clear instructions that day. He told me, each day of my life, I have a choice. I knew He'd help me to put on the spirit of praise, in exchange for the garment of heaviness. He told me to put my gospel tapes in my stereo, turn the knob up on one setting, LOUD, and leave it there. Every morning, as soon as my eyes popped open, He said, I needed to go into the living room, turn on the stereo, and play my gospel tapes, LOUD! He told me, I needed to do this every morning, before coffee, bathroom, prayer, breakfast, or before doing anything else. I knew demons hated the blood of Jesus, and God's praise music. They were screaming and running as fast as they could, and getting as far away from my house as possible. "Thank You, Jesus!" As I listened, danced, praised God, and sang with the beautiful praise and worship songs, I found myself falling more, and more in love with Jesus. I loved to dance with Jesus. I'd bow and say, "Well good morning, dear Lord Jesus! May I have this dance?" I saw us dancing on a sandy beach next to a beautiful blue body of water. Lovely green palm trees stood waving in gentle breezes along the shore. The sky was always an awesome perfect blue as my wonderful Savior and I joyfully danced to the music.

I kept my praise music turned up on LOUD, while I ate my breakfast, showered, did my hair, put on my make up, and dressed for work too. By the time I turned off the music, I was so pumped up with faith. I said my prayers and read my bible, believing God was going to perform supernatural miracles for me that very day. The Lord instructed me to do exactly the same thing in the evening before bed. Afterwards, I'd shower again, fall into bed, and sleep peacefully. I found scriptures to confirm everything God showed me in the vision, and the clear instructions He gave me. Isaiah 61:3 "To console those who mourn in Zion; To give them beauty for ashes; The oil of joy for mourning; The garment of praise for the spirit of heaviness; That they might be called trees of righteousness; The planting of the Lord, that they might be glorified. (Psalm 22:3) "God inhabits the praises of His people." I literally danced my blues away. I felt a significant change, physically, and spiritually. The dancing made me too tired to worry. But most of all, I wanted the Lord to be able to move freely, and accomplish His will for my life. Dancing also relieved stress, and helped tone up my muscles. I'm sure cleaning houses helped too. "Thank You, sweet Jesus for teaching me to trust You more."

My good friend and neighbor, Elaine, brought my dinner several times while Joe was living with his parents. She knew I wasn't eating correctly, so she'd show up at my door with steeping, hot plates of delicious food. Sometimes she'd have crispy fried chicken, mashed potatoes with gravy, green beans that were fresh picked from her garden, along with corn on the cob, already buttered and salted, sliced red ripe tomatoes, salted, and a big slice of fresh hot buttered cornbread. And she never brought me a meal without a home made desert which she usually made from scratch. Elaine always sat and talked to me while I ate every last bite. I couldn't help but love this woman who cared about me, prayed for me, and fed me so well. The Lord made sure I had no reason to be envious of Joe, whose mother was also an excellent cook. Joey was seldom home. Most of his time was spent down at the gym working out. He was on a high protein diet. He ate his breakfast omelet with so much garlic on it I had to open a window, or door, and I definitely left the room. I like garlic, but not for breakfast.

The Lord instructed me not to discuss the status of my marriage with anyone else but Him or my strong, Christian friends. He told me, if I asked for anything He'd supply it, and He did, according to His riches in glory by Christ Jesus. He told me not to worry about losing weight. I felt Joe would love me more if I were skinnier. Between cleaning houses, and dancing both morning and evening, I quickly lost twenty pounds. Psalm 113:3 says, "From the rising of the sun to the place where it sets; The name of the Lord shall be praised." Sandy looked at me and said, "Carol, you've lost so much weight, we need to go shopping, and buy you some new clothes." We had fun shopping for my new wardrobe. Joe couldn't help but notice how peaceful I was. He also noticed I never once had to ask him for a dime. God, my provider supplied us with plenty of work. Sandy and I tithed ten percent off of every penny we made from our cleaning company, and the Lord caused our business to prosper. I bought everything I needed, including groceries, new clothes, and even new furniture. I paid every bill on time too, and I did it without Joe's financial support.

(Neh. 8:19) "The joy of the Lord is my strength." I never told Joe how broken my heart was. I didn't tell any of my family members about my marriage troubles, because the Lord told me not to. When they called long distance, I'd laugh and talk, and act as if everything was fine, and by faith it really was. I didn't tell David and Carrie either. I asked Joey not to tell any of his friends about his dad moving out. I felt the Lord cautioning me not to speak anything negative about our marriage. Sandy was the only one who knew how difficult it was for me to even go shopping in our local grocery store. When Joe came over for dinner, he'd make spiteful remarks about the women cashiers flirting with him. At first, I felt almost paranoid. I'd look at all the different pretty female cashiers, and wonder which one Joe was having an affair with?

Early one afternoon, Sandy and I stopped by her house to rest and have lunch, before going back to work. We were cleaning two, and sometimes three, large houses a day. After lunch, Sandy insisted I lean back and relax in her husband, Ron's, big, soft recliner, while she collapsed on the couch. I was so exhausted, I quickly agreed. I laid there praying softly in the spirit as I tried to push tormenting thoughts of Joe, and the divorce, that I refused to give him, from my mind. My eyelids were heavy, but I wasn't asleep. Suddenly, I saw a vision of a small young girl hopelessly crying. She seemed to be lost at night by herself out on the dark, stormy sea. Her frail, trembling body shook with terror as she stood all alone in an old, rotted wooden boat. The wind and heavy rains tossed the old boat violently, back and forth! The young girl's left hand clutched an old ragged rope that hung down from a rusty pole still standing in the center of the old boat. She was

47

hanging on for dear life, as huge angry waves violently hit her again and again! The strong winds and waves nearly capsized the old wooden boat! The poor child's clothes and hair were soaking wet from the drenching blasts of the cold wind and rain.

I felt strangely afraid for the shivering, terrified little girl, and I was overwhelmed with compassion for her. She looked so horrified and helplessly lost, out in the middle of the violent storm. She had no one to help her, no one to save her. The loud, terrifying crashes of thunder, and bright flashes of dangerous lightning, relentlessly streaked across the dark, angry sky. Suddenly, I felt the cold, hard blasts of wind and heavy rains stinging my face, and my body. I shook so hard. I identified way too much with the little girl's fear, dread, and panic, so I asked the Lord from my heart if the little girl was me, from my childhood? His answer was a definite, "Yes." When the Lord opened my eyes, I recognized the fearful, little girl in the old boat was from my distant past. She stood there freezing. She was being tossed by the storm, wind, and waves. The frail, little girl was the broken, abused memory of the child inside of me that wasn't yet healed.

I, myself, who was the hurting little girl standing ridged in the old boat, scarcely hanging onto the old ragged rope, looked up and saw Jesus coming straight toward me. For whatever reason, Jesus didn't calm the storm, but instead, He kept gliding across the mighty, raging waters, with His beautiful face against the elements. He did not stop until He stood directly in front of me, the shivering fearful child in the old boat. I never took my eyes off His. I just stood there in the old boat staring up into His beautiful, blue eyes. His lovely eyes that were the color of the ocean, and sky on a clear perfect day. He gazed into my eyes with such compassion and love. I was overwhelmed. I felt like I was the only person on earth who mattered to Jesus right then. His wonderful blue eyes danced with love's pure energy. Powerful healing love and acceptance flowed from Him. We communicated without speaking a word audibly. As I looked deep into His eyes, I knew He was searching my very soul. He knew my past, present and future. The storm continued to rage, but I kept my eyes on Jesus.

Without taking my eyes off His, out of the corner of my eye, I saw He was slowly raising His right hand and arm. He stopped when His precious hand was within easy reach of mine. I knew in my heart, exactly what He wanted me to do. However, I was too afraid to completely abandon myself to Him. I knew He wanted me to let go of the rope, (the past), I was holding on tightly with my left hand. I didn't even try to reach out to Him with my free hand. In my heart, I wanted to trust Him. I wanted to let go of the rope, and let Him heal me of every hurt, fear, broken promise and rejection of my past, but I couldn't let go. He just stood there with His precious nail scarred hand stretched out in front of me, waiting patiently. From deep down inside my heart, I kept screaming, "CAROL, JUST LET GO OF THE ROPE, AND TAKE HIS HAND!" But my mind, my will and my emotions kept resisting Him, "HOW CAN YOU TRULY ABANDON YOURSELF TO COMPLETELY TRUST HIM? WILL HE HURT YOU LIKE EVERYONE ELSE HAS?" I said in my heart, stubbornly. "No He won't, not ever! He said, He will never leave me or forsake me."

With everything I had in me, and all the strength I could muster, with only the faith the size of a tiny mustard seed, I let go of the rope and reach for His powerful strong hand! In that one swift instant, when I touched the tip of His finger, instantly, I was resting secure in His wonderful strong, loving arms. Immediately, the storm ceased, the seas calmed, and blue peaceful skies and sunshine surrounded us. I was so peaceful, calm and happy. I just wanted to stay there in His wonderful sheltering arms forever. I was crying and praising the Lord so loud, I woke Sandy up from her nap. I was so excited. When I told her about the vision, she was so happy for me, especially when I told her how very beautiful the Lord's blue eyes were. I felt so free. I was changed on the inside. The Lord changed me and made me different that day. (2 Chronicles 20:15) "For the battle is not yours, but God's." My faith in God was stronger since I'd had my encounter with Jesus. (2 Corinthians 5:17) "Therefore if any man be in Christ, he is a new creature, old things are passed away and behold all things have become new." (Isaiah 40:31) "My strength is renewed like the eagles." Praise God! I kept saying, "Jesus, You are so wonderful. Thank You for healing the child inside of me. I love You Jesus!"

Sandy and I kept on paying our tithes and offerings out of our earnings from C & S, cleaning Company, and God kept blessing us. We even expanded it into C & S cleaning & painting Company. We hired my son Joey, and Sandy's daughters, Betsy and Jenny, and some of our nieces and nephews, to help us, too. Joe noticed, I kept growing happier in the Lord. He grew more miserable and discontent living with his parents, and trying to be a playboy. I couldn't help but feel sorry for him. I was hurting, but at least, I had joy and peace in the Lord. God was so attentive to my needs during the time Joe was away. He gave me another wonderful surprise. Carrie and the baby came back to the States to visit with her parents for a couple of months, hallelujah! I hadn't told David or Carrie about Joe moving out. I was walking by faith, seeing things as though they were not, so I was expecting him to move back home any day. Carrie never once suspected Joe wasn't living at home, and I never told her anything different.

Nearly every day for two months Carrie left Rebecca with me, at my request. She was busy having fun visiting and going shopping with her family and friends. Sandy knew how much it meant to me, to be able to spend time with my little granddaughter. She was delighted to adjust our work schedule around my time with Rebecca. Sometimes when Sandy and I needed to clean several houses, Betsy babysat Rebecca. I had so much fun getting to know my little curly, red-haired baby girl again. She was the absolute apple of my eye. When she'd look up at me with those big blue eyes and smile, I couldn't stop hugging her, or kissing her sweet little face. My broken heart was so soothed by her hugs and kisses. We ate sticky candy, cookies, and ice cream, but we ate lots of good healthy food too. That little one year old bundle of joy even caused her grandpa, Joe, to go out and buy a video camera. Joe came over every evening to have dinner, and take movies of Rebecca. God had a full proof plan to bring Joe and I together at every given opportunity. Joe didn't dare curse around his granddaughter, at least not very often, so I had some relief for awhile, and I'd always say, "Thank You so very much, my wonderful, Papa God, for making my home peaceful, and thank You for bringing Rebecca to visit us too, sweet Lord."

We danced, and we laughed with our precious little granddaughter. I crawled around on the floor with her, bounced her on my knees, and played peek-a-boo until we were exhausted. She grew so attached to me, I couldn't leave the room without her crying for me, so Joe really had no other choice but to take movies of Rebecca and me playing together. On the evenings Carrie came to pick Rebecca up, Joe was there, and in the mornings when she dropped her off, she knew Joe was at work anyway, so she never suspected anything. Sometimes Carrie stayed there, and visited with me for a couple of hours. She did the same thing in the evenings, but I never indicated to her that anything was wrong. Joe seemed happy with my decision, not to tell David or Carrie, too. We did every, goofy thing imaginable, just to make our little Rebecca laugh. We loved her so much. She had become a bridge.

Joe had been living with his parents for about a month before Carrie came and brought Rebecca. That first month I wouldn't have wanted my little granddaughter there, because I was such a mess before Jesus got a hold of me. Joe was even worse. The first two weeks were awful when Joe came home just for his manly needs to be met. I'd have to grit my teeth when he made love to me. He was so cruel, especially when he'd sit and brag about all his other extra marital affairs. At one time, I was even afraid of him giving me a disease, until the Lord reassured me that wouldn't happen to me. I was reminded, I'm protected under the shed blood of Jesus. Joe also came over quit often for dinner. Afterwards, he'd sit in his favorite easy chair and watch television, until he fell asleep. When I'd finally wake him up, he'd say, "It's too late for me to go back to mom and dad's house. They're probably already in bed asleep. I might as well just stay the night here." I'd simply smile and say, "Whatever you say, sweetheart." I was happy when he wanted to stay the night, but I missed praising the Lord, and dancing before I went to bed. So many times I wanted to throw in the towel, and quit trying. Each time, though, the Lord filled me up again with His agape love that never quits, or gives up on anyone.

I constantly read, and reread 1 Corinthians 13. The Lord taught me how to love Joe unconditionally. His steadfast, longsuffering, compassionate mercy always amazed me. The Lord, never gives up on us, and He doesn't want us to give up on anyone else either. A few days after Carrie and our little Rebecca went back to England, I was walking through the house, when all of a sudden, Joe stopped me in the hallway. He put his hands on my shoulders and starred deep into my eyes. Without saying a word, he took me in his arms, and kissed me passionately. When we finally came up for a breath of air, he hugged me and whispered in my ear, "Carol, honey, I'm falling in love with you all over again. Would it be all right with you, if I move back in with you and Joey today?" I hugged his neck really hard, and squealed out, "Yes Joe! OH ABSOLUTELY, YES! YES! YES, JOE! PLEASE COME ON HOME!" He asked me that question exactly three months after the day he'd told me he didn't love me anymore, and moved out. However, after the first three weeks since he'd moved out, he came home almost every single night, for one reason or another.

The Lord taught me many things during the time I waited for Joe to return home. I studied God's word and obeyed it, no matter how difficult it was for me to do. With the Lord's help, I didn't allow myself to become bitter toward Joe, I forgave him quickly. I suffered really badly. I thought sometimes, I didn't even want Joe to come back home, but nevertheless, I laid down my own will, and did it God's way. I received great rewards from doing it God's way, too. Joe bought me a beautiful sapphire and diamond gold ring. My favorite. He also bought me, an expensive gold necklace. My new necklace had a wonderful gold cluster, an anchor, a cross, and a solid gold heart, too. The beautiful necklace reminded me of the scripture in 1 Corinthians 13:13 "And now abide faith, hope, love, these three; but the greatest of these is love." The Lord taught me so much about faith through that experience. (Matthew 11:12) "The violent take it by force." I wanted Joe to see Jesus in me. I had a bull dog faith to believe for my marriage, too. Someday, I

want to hear Jesus say, "Well done, My good and faithful servant."
More than anything else, the Lord taught me more about His love.
He taught me how to love Joe with His agape love, instead of my
own. "Dear precious Lord Jesus, I'm learning more about You!"

The Lord put the icing on the cake when Joe asked me to go to
our cabin with him for a week. We went on our very first real
vacation together. We went fishing, and he did some wild turkey
hunting while we were there too. Joe was so grouchy, and down
right hateful to me. I felt so unwanted sometimes, but when I'd
think of what the Lord had done for us, I'd just start laughing at
the enemy! The Lord had done some great things for us, in spite of
Joe's attitude. The most wonderful thing happened before Joe
moved back home. Our youngest son Joey won the Golden Gloves
Boxing Championship, not once, but twice! Parts of both Joey's
winning fights were shown on television, and on two different
popular news channels. His pictures were in all the local news
papers. On two of our local, and most popular news channels, well
known sports casters interviewed him on prime time television.
Joey thanked everyone for praying for him on live television
during one of the interviews. Joey was awesome to watch. His
boxing was very professional. His long months of training, and
hard work, really paid off. We were all so proud of him. Joey
agreed, we are all God's champions. I told Joey, he's a winner,
whether he was in the ring, or out of the ring in my eyes.

A brand new friend name Ivy joined our Monday morning prayer
group. When I first met Ivy, I sensed she had a troubled heart. Her
long jet black hair, and piercing dark eyes made her small frame
more distinguished looking. She loved Jesus with her whole heart,
and she was baptized in the precious Holy Spirit. She was a new
believer, but she was already keenly sharp in the things of God.
Jean had moved from her big comfortable farmhouse, so we were
meeting regularly at my house for prayer. Early one Monday
morning, Sandy, Ivy, Dixie, and Jean and I were kneeling around
my king size bed. We were all holding hands while we prayed in
the spirit. Sandy was on Ivy's right side, and I was on her left. All

of sudden, Ivy started shaking us violently! She prayed in tongues really loud, too! Someone else began to boldly interpret, "Quit you like men, Carol and Sandy! Stand upon your feet! Gird up the loins of your minds! Keep your armor on and in place at all times, and above all keep your shield of faith up! DO NOT SLEEP, spiritually, BUT STAY AWAKE AND PRAY!" Ivy had not been aware of how hard she was gripping Sandy's and my hands. She wasn't even aware of how hard she was shaking us.

A terrible fear rose up on the inside of me, and I said, "This can't be right, can it? I mean, I, I just came out of a terrible battle! Surely now, the Lord wants me to just sit back and relax for a while, doesn't He? After all, the Lord does say in His word. We are to try every spirit, to see if it is from God." I looked at everyone, especially at Ivy, and sighed. I said, "Who am I kidding? I don't have to try the spirits to see if this is from God. I know it's from God! The reason I know this, is because I've known for quite some time, something was wrong with David, Carrie and little Rebecca. For several weeks now, every time I've tried to pray for them, I've felt such a heaviness. I haven't been able to kneel, stand, or sit when I pray for them either. I feel such a heavy burden to pray for them, constantly. All I can do is to lay prostrate on the floor before God, and cry out to Him in their behalf."

Sandy, looked at me and shrugged her shoulders. She said, "Carol, to my knowledge, not too much is wrong in my own life, yet. But I do not know what is coming tomorrow. We will do all that the Lord has instructed us to do." Sandy had been concerned about David, and his family too. I'd been confiding in her for several weeks about it. I'd told her, how terrible the burden on my heart was to pray for them. I'd lain prostrate on the floor, praying for David and his family, week after week, with little or no relief in sight, from the heavy burden of prayer. Although I'd wanted to deny the fact that something was terribly wrong in David, Carrie and Rebecca's lives, I couldn't. I'd hoped I'd stop having these unfamiliar grave forebodings, but I didn't. I apologized to Ivy and to the rest of my friends. I especially apologized to the Lord, for trying to deny something I knew He was warning me about. Night and day I prayed for David and his family, fervently. Even when I'd try to dust the furniture, I knew something was wrong, wrong, wrong. Naturally, I'd pick up one of David, Carrie or Rebecca's pictures to dust underneath it, but instead of continuing on with my cleaning, I was compelled to fall to my face and pray for them.

Each time I spoke to David on the phone, I asked him, "Son, is everything all right with the three of you?" David's answer was always the same, "Sure mom. Everything's great here with us. Why do you keep asking me that question?" I couldn't answer, truthfully, because I didn't understand it myself. I didn't want to cause him to worry, so I'd just say, "Oh, David, you know me. I'm just being a concerned mother, that's all." Carrie's mother, Janet and I had become closer since our children and grandchild had gone to England. She'd been coming to our prayer group on Mondays too. I remember one particular day, everyone else had gone home after our prayer meeting, except Sandy and Janet. The two of them were sitting on the couch in the living room talking, while I was finishing up some of my laundry. I was on my way up the basement steps with a basket of laundry, to sit and fold clothes while I visited with my friends, when suddenly, I heard the Lord speak to me, really LOUD! He said, "CAROL, READ JOB 12, 29, AND THE END OF JOB!" I whirled around so fast, I nearly dropped my laundry basket, and fell back down the basement stairs! God's command was so loud and so bold. I felt it start at the top of my head and vibrate all the way down to my feet.

I hurried and ran up stairs! I interrupted Janet and Sandy's conversation, "Hey! Did you two hear what the Lord just said to me? He said it so loud, I thought perhaps you might have heard Him, too?" Sandy and Janet looked a little perplexed when they answered, "Hear what, Carol?" As soon as I finished telling them what the Lord said, Sandy grabbed my bible from off the coffee table. She quickly found the book of Job, and read chapters 12, 29, and the last three chapters of Job, out loud. We always knew what the Lord meant when He wanted us to read the whole chapter. He'd say, the name of the book, and the chapter. Otherwise, He specified chapter and verse. I'd had an uneasy feeling, since the day the Lord told me, (personally) to read those particular chapters of Job. Although, for some strange reason, I felt it involved Janet, too. A couple of weeks later, Janet stopped calling me, and she stopped coming to the prayer group, too. We were all concerned. I tried calling her for several weeks, but she wouldn't answer her phone. Finally, one day she answered, and I talked to her briefly. She said she just didn't have time to come to the prayer meetings any more, she was busy. She seemed very nervous. That was our last phone conversation. I knew something was wrong, but what?

David called and told us some really excellent news! He said. The three of them were coming home for Christmas! I was so happy, I could hardly stand it! Once again, David reassured me that everything was fine with him and his little family. Sandy was thrilled when I shared the good news with her. Joe, helped me paint the whole house, from top to bottom. Joey helped us paint the basement. We wanted to be prepared for their homecoming. The time passed quickly and before we knew it, it was time to pick them up at the airport. I sensed something was wrong as soon as we arrived. When I greeted my old friend, Janet, she acted sort of strange and distant. I was hurt when Carrie treated Joe and I like we were total strangers. I couldn't quite figure out what was happening, when she avoided us too. Suddenly, I looked up and saw David. I thought, "Lord, why, is my son, David wearing sun glasses, inside the airport terminal, at night?" Everyone seemed on edge, including our little Rebecca. Someone broke the ice, and suggested we should all go and get something to eat. Later, in the restaurant, I noticed David was still wearing his sunglasses. Carrie sat with her parents, across the table, opposite us. The entire time we were at the restaurant, Carrie continued to pass dirty looks to David. It was obvious. Something was wrong. I had a feeling, this strange scenario had everything to do with the fact that I laid on my face the past year, in fervent prayer for the three of them.

After a slight argument between David and Carrie in the parking lot outside the restaurant, Carrie and the baby got in the car and left with her parents. David climbed into the back seat of our car. He talked all the way home, without even once mentioning

Carrie's name. The sunglasses were no longer a mystery. When we arrived back home, I saw David's red swollen eyes. The next morning, after Joe left for work, David told me everything. He said his marriage to Carrie had been very rocky for quite some time. I told David, "Son. I know how it feels to be in love with someone who says they aren't in love with you anymore." He didn't believe me, until I told him what had happened recently with his dad and I. I said, "David, the Lord will help your's and Carrie's marriage too. If you'll only pray, and believe God can do it, He will help you. If the Lord can salvage your mother and dad's marriage, as bad as it was, then He can save your marriage too, son."

A few days later, Janet called, distraught, and yelling, "Carol! Please help me? The devil is in my house and he's in my daughter too!" After she calmed down a little, she told me David found a love letter Carrie had written to a man name Jim. She'd only just met the man a few weeks earlier while she was working at the officer's club in England. According to the letter; Carrie and Rebecca were supposed to fly to Texas to meet this man, Jim. Apparently she was waiting until David left for 'T.D.Y.' duty in California, as soon as Christmas was over. The words of the Lord kept ringing in my ears, "Carol, read Job, 12, 29, and the end of Job." Ivy's interpretation, "Quit you like men, Carol and Sandy. Stand upon your feet. Do not sleep, spiritually. Stay awake and pray. Keep your shield of faith up." As soon as I hung up the phone, I fell to my knees, then onto my face in prayer. I asked the dear precious Holy Spirit to help me pray for David, Carrie and our granddaughter, Rebecca. I prayed, "Dear God, help me to always remember what You said in your word? The battle is Your's, Lord, and the victory is mine!"

Right in the middle of all the confusion, a special blessing came when I finally obeyed God, and went to see Carrie. It was less then two weeks before Christmas, but instead of snow, we had unseasonably warm weather, and thick, heavy fog that night. I didn't want to go over to Janet's house to see Carrie, because I knew she didn't want to see me. I didn't want to drive in that terrible heavy fog, after dark, either. I kept arguing with the Lord about it, until He convinced me to go. I didn't even know why, I was going over there to see Carrie, or what I was going to say to her when I got there. The Lord did not tell me why He wanted me to go see Carrie. He just kept urging me to go on over there and talk to her. Rebecca was spending the evening at our house. We were all having a great time, enjoying her company. It was hard for me to want to leave my comfort zone, and do what the Lord was telling me to do, especially when He didn't even give me a hint as to why He was sending me out in the fog. I told David, and Joe where I was going, and why. I prayed, "God have mercy on me?"

I left Rebecca there with her daddy, grandpa, and Uncle Joey. I barely pressed my foot on the gas peddle. As I crept along in the awful, thick fog. I kept thinking, "Carrie has made it very clear to me, she doesn't want me around. Her dad and mom will be home. How can I possibly talk to her about whatever it is I'm supposed to talk to her about?" I kept praying in tongues, and asking God to help me, all the way there! I breathed a sigh of relief as I slowly rounded the corner to Janet's house where Carrie was staying, just in time to see Carrie's dad's car pulling out of their driveway. When Carrie answered the door, I shrugged my shoulders and said, "Carrie, I have no idea why I'm hear, except to tell you I love you. I pray you'll allow me to remain your friend no matter what happens between you and David?" She looked really sad, but she asked me to come in. I said in my heart, "Thank, You God. But what am I supposed to do now, Lord?" Carrie told me her mother was in bed asleep, and her dad was gone for the entire evening. I relaxed a little after she gave me that information. Suddenly, by the leading of the dear precious Holy Spirit, the direction of our conversation changed drastically.

Carrie broke down and started to cry. She told me she'd been depressed and suicidal for a long time. She told me she often visualized herself in a coffin. She said she could see her family and friends standing around her coffin, crying and mourning her death. I knew Carrie had gone to church all her life, but I asked her, "Carrie, have you ever said the sinner's prayer?" She looked up at me from the couch where she was sitting. She told me her Pastor had never given an altar call. When I asked her if she wanted to say the sinner's prayer, after me, and ask God for forgiveness, she eagerly answered me in tears, "Yes, Carol! Please help me say the sinner's prayer?" I knelt on the floor in front of her, and took hold of her hands. I was so happy. I led her in the prayer of salvation! She asked the Lord to forgive her and come into her heart, and He did. (Romans 10: 9-10) "That if you confess with your mouth the Lord Jesus and believe in your heart that God has raised him from the dead, you will be saved. For with the heart one believes to righteousness, and with the mouth confession is made to salvation." I cried, "Oh, thank You Jesus!"

With Carrie's permission, I laid hands on her and rebuked the spirits of suicide and depression off her life, in Jesus name. I saw seven gold rings lift up off her body and disappear, like smoke. We hugged each other, and laughed. She said she felt lighter. We celebrated her name being written down in the Lamb's book of life. "Hallelujah!" I praised the Lord all the way home. I could have cared less about the foggy streets. "Thank You my dear, sweet Jesus, for saving Carrie's soul!" By the time I reached home, Carrie had already called David. They decided to try and work things out in their marriage. I was so happy for them. I could hardly stand it. David and Carrie started reading their bibles, and memorizing the scriptures together. They talked about the Lord with enthusiasm. We had a wonderful Christmas. David said he wasn't even worried about Carrie remaining in the States until his T. D. Y. duty was over. Carrie and the baby were going to fly back to England and meet David at their home. So why worry?

I confessed to Sandy that I still had the same awful, and uneasy feeling to pray for them. I said, "Sandy, why am I still having these strange feelings when I obeyed God. I went to see Carrie that night, and led her to the Lord. So, why am I still falling prostrate before Him, in prayer for them? This burden of prayer is so intense, it hasn't let up, even though they are happy. Why can't I feel peace about David and his family in my heart, yet, Sandy?" She just smiled, shook her head, and said, "I wish I knew all the answers to your questions, Carol, but unfortunately, I don't understand it either. Only God knows why you're still feeling this terrible burden to pray for them. Maybe it's because they still need special prayer for their marriage."

At sometime around three o clock in the morning, on New Years Eve, 1986, I had a dream that deeply troubled me. I knew in my heart it was a direct warning dream sent from God, Himself. In the dream, I was shopping in a large department store with Carrie and Rebecca. I was standing there leisurely searching through some clothes on a rack when suddenly, a horrible fear swept over me! A terrible, demonic panic gripped me! In the dream I knew something was very wrong. I sensed a serious danger lurking all around us! My eyes darted quickly back and forth, as I frantically searched through the store isles, looking for Rebecca. When I looked up and saw Carrie standing at the end of the clothes rack with her empty shopping cart, it was as if she were transparent like glass. I could see straight through her. I yelled, "Carrie! Where is little Rebecca?" Carrie had a horrified look of surprised terror on her face as she answered me with frightened, jerking sounds, "I, I don't know? She was right here just a minute ago!"

Immediately, something evil began to jerk, bump, and move violently through the clothes on the rack, right in front of me! The evil jerking vibrations, began at one end of the clothes on the rack, and kept on moving through them wildly! Whatever it was, it moved swiftly, bumping, and jerking something, or someone inside the clothes on the rack, until it reached the other end of the rack! In the same constant, violent manner, it came all the way back the other way, moving through the clothes on the rack, until it stopped again. Instinctively, I knew it was my little granddaughter, Rebecca, who was violently being dragged through the clothes against her will! I knew she was the one struggling to get free from whoever, or whatever evil thing it was that made her go with them, involuntarily! The fight was so intense and violent, everything around us, including the floor underneath us, vibrated like a small earth quake! This weird, crazy thing wrestling with my granddaughter inside the clothes on the rack couldn't be human? Everything was happening so fast, I felt helpless. Suddenly, everything stopped, as quickly as it started, and it became deadly silent, and still. In the next swift second, though, at mock speed, a demonic looking woman, popped up out of the clothes on the rack, and stood there boldly starring me in the face!

I felt extreme panic! A horrible attack from a spirit of fear tried to grip hold of me. It tried to overwhelm me! The extremely hateful, ugly woman looking demon, had straw- like blond hair, sticking out in every possible direction. That thing snarled its mean upper lip at me, clenched its jaws stubbornly in a look of defiance, and then growled at me like a crazed, angry animal! The awful women looking demon resembled Carrie in a strange, horrid sort of way. Hate oozed out of the pores in it's grotesquely cruel twisted face! It continued to try and intimidate me with an ungodly glare from its inhuman bulging, bloodshot eyes. The ugly demon had purple and red streaks running through its bulging, red, blood shot eyes, and purple veins ran down through its scarred face, reminding me of a road map to hell. The terrible women looking demon had on a dirtied white jacket, blue jeans, and a faded blue jean shirt. Hate, disgust, and murder blazed from its bulging blood shot eyes, and the veins in its neck and face stood out! Even in the dream, I knew how to use the name of Jesus against it. I grabbed my black leather purse from off my shoulder, and started swinging it in a circle above my head, toward the women looking demon. I screamed, "YOU LET GO OF MY GRANDDAUGHTER, REBECCA, NOW IN THE NAME OF JESUS! I SAID, YOU WILL LET GO OF HER NOW, IN THE NAME OF JESUS!"

That old, ugly demon kept ducking, and I kept swinging my purse at it, and screaming, until I woke Joe up! Joe shook me really hard, and yelled, "Carol, blank, it! Wake up! Do you know what the, blank, time it is? It's three o-clock in the morning! Who in the blank, are you screaming at? Wake up!" I apologized the minute Joe was able to get me awake. As soon as he calmed down. I told him about the dream. He just shrugged it off. He said, "Well Carol, it's probably because we ate sour kraut and pork ribs before midnight, at mom's, remember? Go back to sleep." Long after Joe went back to bed, I sat in our darkened living room stunned and didn't move. I just couldn't stop thinking about the dream. I kept reliving it, over, and over again. I asked God, "Papa, Carrie is all right, now that she's given her heart to You, isn't she? Lord, what are You trying to tell me through this dream?" He didn't answer me. Instead He gave me a burning desire to pray. Once again, I laid on my face on the floor. I prayed the rest of the night. I didn't stop praying until the alarm clock went off to wake Joe up for work. I felt refreshed. I got up and fixed Joey and his dad breakfast, and got them off to work, without feeling sleepy at all. I had plenty of energy left, to do whatever I needed to do.

Later that morning when Sandy stopped by to pick me up for work, I told her about the dream. She interpreted my dream. "Carol, I see you like David, in the bible. He whirled his slingshot above his head, just like you did with your purse! God is telling you, to be like David! Kill the giant and take off his head, once and for all, in the name of Jesus!" Although, I knew the dream involved spiritual warfare, I was confused as to why I needed to do it? I said, "Yes, but Sandy, what am I fighting for? Carrie asked Jesus to forgive her of her sins. She, and David, and Rebecca are a happy family now, I think.?So why did I have this dream?" The Lord answered that hard question the very next morning when David called from California, frantically asking me, "Mom, have you seen Carrie or Rebecca?" I hesitated, "No son, I haven't. Why?" David's voice was shaky, "Mom, I know Carrie's gone to meet with that guy, Jim, in Texas, just like she told him in the letter. Remember the letter I found before Christmas? She hasn't changed, mom. She only made us think she'd changed, so we wouldn't suspect her. Carrie has not only endangered herself, but my little girl too! Mom, I'm worried about my daughter. I pray she's all right! Carrie just met this guy. She hardly knows him."

I tried to calm David down, but he was so angry and upset, he wouldn't listen to me. He told me he had talked to Carrie's mother and sisters. David said her mother and sisters were all really nervous when they evaded his questions. I was so concerned about

David, and especially Rebecca. I immediately called Joe at work. Finally, Joe answered the phone. He was quite rattled by the news. David was three thousand miles away. In his state of mind, we didn't know what he was capable of doing. Carrie and our little granddaughter were thousands of miles away from us too. At Joe's suggestion, I called the Red Cross. They were so kind to us, and they helped David, which helped us greatly. Within one hour, after I'd called the Red Cross, David's commanding officer called me from California. He reassured us that everything was under control, at least where David was concerned. David's commanding officer told me, he'd talked with David's Sergeant. His Sergeant, in turn contacted some of David's buddies, who were being supportive to David. I kept praising the Lord, silently, from my heart, until I hung up the phone. (2 Corinthians 10:4-6) "For the weapons of our warfare are not carnal but mighty in God for the pulling down of strongholds, casting down arguments and every high thing that exults itself against the knowledge of God, bringing every thought into captivity to the obedience of Christ, and being ready to punish all disobedience when your obedience is fulfilled."

I couldn't stop thinking about Rebecca, Carrie and the dream. Carrie had allowed the cares and riches of this world to tear God's word out of her heart. (Mark 5:18-19) David had always bought Carrie pretty clothes and everything he could afford to buy her. But she wanted more expensive things, things he couldn't possibly give her. I lay prostrate on the floor on my face, praying for David, Carrie and Rebecca, once again. I desperately cried out to God, "Oh, dear Lord! This is why You gave me that unusual dream about Carrie and our sweet little Rebecca, isn't it? God, please don't let Carrie drag my precious little granddaughter wherever she wants to against her will, in the name of Jesus!" The enemy didn't waste any time. He tried to scare me, by showing me vivid color pictures of David hanging himself from a rope. He tried to show me pictures of Carrie's lover, Jim, who was violently hitting Rebecca, because she didn't know him, she was crying and afraid. So he hit her, and knocked her clear across the room! Her small body, slammed against the wall! I plead the blood of Jesus over us.

As I ran to the phone to call Sandy, I screamed as loud as I could, I bound the enemy off my mind and life, in the name of Jesus! I started pleading the blood of Jesus in the name of Jesus, over myself and my family, and thanking the Lord, for His great warring angels and ministering spirits that stand watch over us and keep us safe. I yelled out against those awful pictures in my mind, "CASTING DOWN, EVERY, EVIL, IMAGINATION THAT TRIES TO SET ITSELF UP AGAINST THE POWER OF CHRIST, AND BRINGING INTO SUBMISSION, EVERY THOUGHT, UNTO THE OBEDIENCE OF CHRIST!" (2 Corinthians 10:5) I leaned against the kitchen wall, and I cried out to God, "Lord, please help me to dial Sandy's number!" Sandy's words were so comforting. She said, "Carol, I'm coming right on over. Just hold onto Jesus. Everything is going to be alright, my friend. God will take care of David, and Rebecca, you'll see. Ron and I will stay with you and Joe, until they find Rebecca, and bring her back home again safely. We will not allow you to go through this darkness alone." I kept saying, "Sweet Jesus, please help us!"

While I waited for Sandy and Ron to get there, I called Jean, Dixie, and Ivy. I called my sister Peggy right away, too. I knew they would be praying for all of us. I knew Peggy would call my other sisters and brothers who lived near her, out West, to ask them to pray for us. I rebuked the spirit of fear, in the name of Jesus off me. I prayed almost constantly in tongues, and I drew strength from His word. He is my God. He cannot lie. (Psalm 118:6) "The Lord is on my side. I will not fear. What can man do to me?" Carrie and Rebecca were missing for what seemed like the longest three days and nights of our entire lives. The only time any of us slept, was out of sheer exhaustion. Sandy and I spent most of our time shut up in my bedroom praying together at the foot of my bed. Finally, we knew the Lord had heard our desperate cries for help, when David called and told us. The military had apprehended Carrie and our little Rebecca, and they were on their way back home. Sandy and I praised God, "Hallelujah to the Lamb!" We were all so happy, even Joe and Ron were teary eyed. The military allowed David three days leave. Somehow, David hoped he and Carrie could try and salvage what was left of their marriage in that short amount of time. "God have mercy on him."

Carrie's lover Jim, the man in Texas was stripped of his rank, because he was still a married man. David tried to talk to Carrie during his three-day leave, but she refused all his calls. So he went back to England, broken- hearted and alone. However, those three days were not completely lost. David received the baptism of the dear precious Holy Spirit. I gave David all my books and tapes on how to save your marriage, alone. I wanted him to take them back to England with him. I kept hearing the precious Holy Spirit whisper, "Let not your heart be troubled, neither let it be afraid." I answered Him, "Oh, dear Lord, I believe. Help Thou my unbelief?" The house was finally quiet. I laid on the floor on my face again. The burden of prayer was so heavy. I had to lay flat on the floor on my face. I cried out to God, "Dear Lord, what happened to Carrie? I obeyed You. I went to her house that foggy night, and I led her to You, Lord. I know she meant it when she said the sinners prayer. I laid hands on her, in Your name, and You set her free from those evil tormenting spirits. So, what went wrong, Lord?" I cried for a long time, then I reached up on the coffee table and grabbed my bible.

When I let the bible, fall, open on its own, God answered me from His word, in, Luke 11:24-26 Jesus said, "When an unclean spirit goes out of a man, he goes through dry places, seeking rest; and finding none, he says, 'I will return to my house from which I came,' and when he comes, he finds it swept clean and put in order. "Then he goes and takes with him seven more spirits more wicked then himself, and they enter and dwell there; and the last state of that man is worse then the first." I wept in bitter tears, and then I cried out to God again, "Oh, dear, Lord, what have I done wrong, I only tried to obey You! Now, what am I supposed to do?" When I heard His one and only stern, strong answer, I didn't want to obey Him, "But I say to you who hear: Love your enemies, do good to those who hate you, bless those who curse you, and pray for those who spitefully use you." (Luke 6:27-28) The Lord knew my heart was full of anger toward Carrie. For the love of material things that money could buy her, she placed herself and especially our little, innocent Rebecca in the direct path of danger. He knew what I was thinking too. I just wanted to pray for David, Rebecca, and the rest of our family, but I didn't want to pray for Carrie. I repented and obeyed God. I had to keep on praying for Carrie and believe she would come back to her first love, our sweet Lord, Jesus. (1 Timothy 6:10-12) "For the love of money is a root of all kinds of evil, for which some have strayed from the faith in their greediness, and pierced themselves through with many sorrows. But you, O man of God, flee these things and pursue righteousness, godliness, faith, love, patience, gentleness. Fight the good fight of faith, lay hold of eternal life." "Dear Jesus, help me pray for her."

While I was praying in tongues one day, I saw a vision of Jesus standing with His back to me. He was reaching His loving arms out to a cute, playful little lamb who kept its distance from Him while joyfully playing games, running and leaping. Our precious Lord Jesus never gave up on the little lamb, but stood there with His arms outstretched, patiently waiting for it to come to Him. Every now and then the cute little lamb would stop leaping and running and jumping playfully, and look longingly up into the Lord's precious face. However, each time the little lamb would again, suddenly take off running and skipping, and playfully leaping. Finally, the little lamb leaped into the Lord's arms and snuggled its head under Jesus' neck. The little lamb looked so peaceful and happy, I said, "Aw, dear Lord, who was that?" Immediately, He answered, that it was Carrie, Rebecca's mother. (Matthew 18:11-14) "For the Son of man has come to save that which was lost. "What do you think? If a man has a hundred sheep, and one of them goes astray, does he not leave the ninety-nine and go to the mountains to seek the one that is straying? And if he should find it, assuredly, I say to you, he rejoices more over that sheep than over the ninety-nine that did not go astray. Even so it is not the will of your Father who is in heaven that one of these little ones should perish." No matter how I felt about Carrie's actions, the Lord wanted me to pray for her. He was patiently waiting for her to come back to Him. He loves us unconditionally.

Chapter Three

He that has ears to hear

The Lord made me a promise, back in 1984. I was fixing breakfast one morning for Joe and myself at our cabin, and I was listening to my Christian gospel tapes playing in the kitchen. Joe sat in the living room having coffee, visiting with a couple of his hunting buddies. In my heart, I was thinking, "Oh Lord, what kind of a witness am I for You, while I'm still taking these pills? The doctor says I can never get off these last ten pills a day, but Your word says, I am healed!" I had a cigarette in my hand, and I put it in the ash tray. It made me even more ashamed, and inside my heart, I cried out, "Oh dear Lord, Jesus! How can I possibly see such miracles, and still smoke these dumb things?" He answered me with such love and tenderness. He called me 'daughter' and told me to keep my eyes on Him, and to trust Him and not be afraid. He said He would help me, "I will help you go off the pills one day at a time, and then the cigarettes will leave your life forever." His words were so gentle and kind. I felt an overwhelming acceptance from Him, and I received His unconditional love. I whispered, "Just as I am, without one plea, but that His blood was shed for me." I'd sang that wonderful old hymn, over and over since I was a child. I felt like I was His child.

I could hardly wait to tell Sandy. When we got home, I called her and said, "Sandy, you aren't going to believe what happened to me at the cabin? The Lord promised He'd help me get off the pills one day at a time! He also said the cigarettes are going out of my life forever!" Sandy was excited for me, and so were all my friends and family! However, after a couple of years passed and nothing had changed, I think everyone except Sandy and Peggy thought I hadn't really heard from God, but I knew I had. God planted that tiny seed in my heart in 1984, but it didn't start to manifest until 1987, three years later. He chose to manifest His promise at what I thought was the most unlikely time in my life. Here I was, in all the turmoil with David, Carrie and little Rebecca. God spoke to me as I was walking through my living room. He said, "Carol, it's time for you to stop taking your first set of pills now." I was happy, and scared all at the same time. I knew it was God's timing, because I felt a change taking place inside of me. The Lord gave me both the will, and the strong desire, to obey Him. I said, "O Lord, thank You, I love You so."

I knew what the Lord meant, when He said it was time for me to stop taking my first set of pills. Normally, I took one pain pill four times a day, one nerve pill four times a day, and twice a day I took an extra strong pill for arthritis. The arthritis pills cost a lot of money, because they actually had real flecks of gold in them. With God's help, that day, I adjusted myself to taking three sets a day of the pain pills and nerve pills. I no longer took two of the stronger arthritis pills, but only one per day. I was just as addicted to those prescription drugs, and the cigarettes as any drug addict or alcoholic. I had a new hope in my heart. The pills were leaving and I knew it wouldn't be long until the cigarettes were out of my life forever, too. I wondered why the Lord chose to help me off the pills first, instead of the cigarettes? Everyone, including other Christians, can smell the cigarettes, and also condemn me, but they would never condemn someone for taking prescription drugs. I figured God had His reasons. Soon, I realized it was much easier for me to read, comprehend, and memorize scriptures, just by cutting back on the prescription drugs I was taking. The enemy tried to tell me I was making a big mistake, but God gave me strength, day by day. "I love You so much wonderful Jesus!"

Some days were harder than others, but God gave me His word to stand on when the going got tough. (Romans 8:1) "There is therefore now no condemnation to them that are in Christ Jesus, who walk not after the flesh but after the Spirit." I love this Scripture. (Philippians 4:13) "I can do all things through Christ who strengthens me." (Psalm 138:8) "The Lord will perfect that which concerns me; Your mercy, O Lord, endures forever; Do not forsake the work of Your hands." One day at a time, over a period of several months I quit taking three sets of my pills a day, and I did it only by the grace of God. I was getting ready to take my shower one evening when I heard the Lord say, "Carol, it's time to stop taking your last set of pills now." The enemy fought me the hardest, all that night, and when I woke up the next morning, it was horrible! The pressure to give in was so great I could hardly stand it! The demons of doubt and unbelief had me almost convinced it was not God telling me to quit taking my pills! Not now! They brought up some really strong accusations against me. For instance. The words my family doctor said to me a couple of months earlier. I'd told him, "God is taking me off my pills. So I'll probably only need this one last prescription from you."

His face and neck got red, when he yelled, "Carol, no! You've been on this medication for many years, and I'm afraid you'll have to stay on it for the rest of your life! I've been your family doctor for several years now, and I strongly suggest you go back to taking all your pills, four times a day, the way they were prescribed for you; And I suggest you start right now; today!" I answered him, with bold, righteous anger, "God has been taking me off the pills for several months now, and I'm doing just fine. I'm only on half the dosage I was taking before, and look? Jesus has healed me of the arthritis, so I don't need the pain pills. I've stopped shaking too. This will be the last time I come back to your office and get my prescriptions refilled." I'd no sooner filled that last prescription, when God told me to quit taking the third set of pills, which left me taking only one set a day. The last several weeks really hadn't been so hard that I couldn't stand the pressure. That is, until God said, "Carol, it's time to quit taking your last set of pills, and go off them completely." "Sweet Jesus!"

I felt so much pressure coming at me from every direction that strange day! It seamed like those demons were talking to me in stereo, "Why, Carol. It wasn't God who told you to quit taking your pills! Not, while all this other horrible, awful stuff is going on in your life with your children, and your precious little granddaughter, who you love so much! Hurry up! Take your pills! Remember, even your doctor, who is a licenced physician told you to take them! Go ahead and do it! Why, you poor thing, you. Maybe you can quit some other time, after things settle down a little?" On and on, this raging battle went, from the time God had spoken to me the night before. Within the exact moment my eyes opened that morning, the terrible temptation to start taking my pills again, was unreal! It continued throughout the long morning hours, and picked up enormous speed as the day wore on! Finally, the enemy of my soul had me convinced. It wasn't God telling me to go off the pills. I was weak and shaky inside, and I felt so overwhelmed by the pressure, I couldn't think rationally any longer! I ran to the kitchen cabinet, and had my medicine in my hand, ready to take it, when Sandy knocked on my door.

With tears gushing from my eyes, I flung the door open and blurted out everything, "Oh Sandy, I, I can't go off my medication right now! I just can't do it! I don't believe it was God who spoke to me last night!" Sandy looked at me, sort of stunned. She said, "What was it God said to you last night, Carol?" I told her. He said, "Carol, it's time for you to quit taking your last set of pills, and go off of them completely, now." Sandy looked almost angry when I said, "This can't be God, Sandy. Not now! David's heart is broken, and he's so alone and far from home. Just look at what's happening with my little granddaughter, Rebecca, and her mother? Only God knows what will happen next. I can't handle any more of this stress, without taking my pill's, Sandy! This can't be God telling me to quit taking them at a time like this! I've decided to go back on them, four times a day, and as soon as I get a glass of water I'll take them."

I will never forget the look on Sandy's face. The boldness, and the power of God came over her. She grabbed my shoulders and shook me hard, when she said, "CAROL, NO! DON'T DO IT! YOU, PUT THOSE PILLS DOWN RIGHT NOW, DO YOU HEAR ME? HAS GOD GIVEN US A SPIRIT OF FEAR? NO, HE HASN'T! IT SAYS IN, 1 Timothy 1:7, "GOD HAS NOT GIVEN US A SPIRIT OF FEAR; BUT OF POWER; AND OF LOVE;

AND OF A SOUND MIND!" She shook my shoulders really hard again, and said, "Carol, the devil has been lying to you today! Don't you dare listen to him? God's word says, he is a liar, and he is the father of lies, too! Listen to me, Carol! God would not have brought you this far. He wouldn't have helped you get off all your other pills, one day at a time, and then stop at the last minute. The Lord finishes what He starts, and you know it! This is nothing but an attack of the enemy. I rebuke the devil off you, Carol, in the name of Jesus, right now! His plan was defeated two thousand years ago, at Calvary, by the precious blood of Jesus! Carol, my friend, you can do all things through Christ who strengthens you! Now act like you know the word!" (Philippians 4:13)

I stood there starring at Sandy in disbelief! In all the years I'd known her, she'd never raised her voice at me. However, when Sandy spoke God's word, His truth pierced right through the darkness, and destroyed that yoke of bondage and fear off me! Suddenly, I burst into hilarious laughter, and so did she! We couldn't contain our joy! I pointed at her and said, "Sandy, I know you, remember? I've never heard you raise your voice at anyone, including me. Well, that is accept, of course when you're in a battle, yelling! I have to admit, at first my feelings were hurt, but after the shock of your bold, righteous anger wore off, I realized it was God Himself who sent you here. He sent you here, at that precise moment to rescue me from making a BIG mistake! You could not have acted that way on your own. Thank God, and thank you for obeying God and walking in His anointing."

We celebrated by throwing all of my pills in the garbage can. If I'd had any doubt before, as to whether it was God who sent Sandy to do what she did for me that day, that doubt was destroyed forever. I knew I'd never be tempted to take that medication again. We sang praise and worship songs to the Lord, "We praise You blessed, Father, Son, and Holy Ghost! Hallelujah, to the Lamb of God!" "Oh, Victory in Jesus, my Savior, forever!"

Later that evening, after dinner, Sandy called. She asked if I'd like to go with her to pick up her youngest daughter, Jenny from a high school football game. Joe didn't mind, so I went. It was so foggy and dark out. We could barely see the road in front of us. As we crept along, we came to a stop sign. I immediately, recognized where we were. We were sitting at the bottom of the hill, (on the correct side of the road), where Joey and I had wrecked back in December of 1983. Just as I started to say something about it, Sandy squealed, "Carol, God, just told me, you're going to write a book about our lives, and the miracles He's done for us! You are to call it, Which Way? What Way? Your Way Lord."

I was so excited! I clapped my hands and hollered, "Sandy, while God was speaking to you about the title of the book, I was seeing a vision of the front cover of the book, at the same time! It's a dark powder blue, and it has Which Way?, at the top. What Way?, in the middle, and Your Way Lord; at the bottom. All of the letters were in large bold black print!" I continued, "Sandy, I saw the cover of the book plain like that, but I also saw the same cover, only in a different form. The second time I saw the cover of the book, I saw a picture of you standing sideways at the top left-hand corner on the front cover of the book, beside the big black bold letters, Which Way? I'm standing sideways, looking in the apposite direction on the right side of the letters in the middle of the cover, What Way? I am wearing a red bandanna, and a solid red matching sweat shirt, and you're wearing blue. Both of us are wearing blue jeans and old tennis shoes. Our hair is all frizzled, and we are carrying mops, brooms, and cleaning supplies. However, at the bottom of the cover we are all cleaned up, wearing dresses. Our hair is combed neat and shiny, our heads are bowed, and our hands are folded in reverent prayer. We are kneeling underneath, Your Way Lord."

We were so ecstatic! We acted like two young school girls, laughing hysterically, and praising God, "Thank You, Lord Jesus, we love You!" We had such joy and fun, we laughed all the rest of the way there and back home again, after we picked up Jenny. I was so thankful. Jesus sent Sandy to visit me that day. Jesus not only delivered me from the pill's I'd been taking for many years, but He also healed me. God blessed our obedience and gave me a book to write about the miracles He keeps on preforming in our lives. I kept crying, "Thank You, Jesus, for being so good to me." What had started out to be a hard day, God turned into one of the happiest and most wonderful days of my life.

The next morning, I called Carrie and asked if she'd like to come over. She instinctively declined. I told her how much we missed seeing her and especially our little Rebecca, but she still gave me a defiant "No!" I'd known and loved Carrie for years, and yet, she was very cold toward me. She acted like a complete stranger, someone I'd never known or loved. I offered to watch Rebecca for her, if she wanted to go out, but nothing I said worked. So I hung up in tears! I had that same awful feeling inside my heart and I was so heavy burdened with prayer. I fell prostrate on the floor before the Lord again. I prayed, "Oh, dear Lord, please help Carrie? Lord, open her eyes, and show her how much we love our little Rebecca! We have a right to see her, too, don't we Lord?" It had never once crossed my mind that Carrie wouldn't allow us to see our granddaughter, who we loved with all our hearts. With David gone, Carrie called all the shots, as to when, and if, we could see our little curly red headed pumpkin.

The persecution grew worse. When I'd call and beg Carrie to let us see the baby, she'd tell me Rebecca had plans to go to one of her cousins birthday parties. Or else she had to be with one of her sisters, Rebecca's aunts, not to mention all the of other excuses she gave me. It was very hard for me to constantly swallow what little pride I had left, and keep begging Carrie to let us see Rebecca. Although, my granddaughter was worth anything I had to go through, just to see her beautiful little face. I never gave up trying, periodically, until finally, if Carrie was in a good mood that day, she'd give in, and let us see her. Sometimes it took six weeks of my begging Carrie to let us see her. At other times, it took a little longer, before Carrie decided if we could see Rebecca. I soon realized Carrie was being highly influenced by the enemy, to try and punish us by withholding Rebecca. So, I prayed for her even more. Each time I saw Carrie, she took on more and more of the demonic looking woman's images whom I'd seen pop up out of the clothes on the rack in the dream I'd had New Years Eve. Her appearance was so unlike Carrie. She was sloppy and dirty looking. Carrie had always been clean and neat. Rebecca was so precious to me, I did whatever I had to, to see her.

At that time we didn't have three hundred dollars to pay a lawyer, and take Carrie to Court. Carrie had left us no other choice. We didn't want to hurt her. All we wanted were our grandparent's rights to see Rebecca enforced by the law. I was tired of begging. I couldn't afford a pity party, and I knew I had to forgive Carrie from my heart on a daily basis. It was a must. I couldn't let anything stand in the way of the miracles I so desperately needed. So, the best place for me, was laying on my face in prayer, before the Lord. Each, and every day, I had to get rid of the bitterness I felt in my heart toward Carrie. I prayed for God to help me love her unconditionally, like Jesus loves all of us. I stayed in the word, praised God, and prayed almost constantly to keep my faith strong. Every day someone else in our family, or our friends, called or stopped by to ask about David, Carrie, and Rebecca. By the time I'd finish answering all their questions, and hearing their sighs, worries, and concerns, my faith would be a little shaky again. I not only listened to their well meaning concerned questions, but I heard my own trembling voice get louder and more afraid when I answered them.

Before I knew it, I was saying negative things myself. (Romans 10:17) "Faith comes by hearing, and hearing by the word of God." Day after day, I heard about all of the things Carrie was doing, including riding on a motorcycle with another man. People asked, "Why is Carrie seeing another man? Isn't she still married to David?" David called us collect every day, too. He never failed to ask us, "Mom, have you and dad seen my little girl? Do you know if she's all right?" As always, as soon as I hung up the phone, I'd lay on my face in the floor again, crying out to God to help us! The Lord showed me why it is so important to stay in His word. Whether it was Joe's family, mine, or even my strong Christian friends constantly calling to ask how David and his family were doing, or if they were telling me the information they thought I needed to know about Carrie or Rebecca, I was being strongly affected by it. No matter if it was good, bad or indifferent. I prayed, "Lord help me to obey Your word, and do it Your way?"

Maybe we were wrong, but Joe and I agreed not to tell David about the other man Carrie was seeing, or any of the other bad news, either. His heart was already broken. He was three thousand miles away from us, and all alone. Why add to his pain? After all, what could he possibly do about it, but worry and be more depressed? We made our decision, and agreed it was the right thing to do. We wanted to wait until we saw David, face to face. At least we could be there to comfort him, then.

We were accepting David's collect calls from England almost daily, because he needed us so desperately! Although Joe kept cursing me every time we received another large unaffordable phone bill, I just couldn't tell David not to call us. One day, after I was finished talking to David, I said, "Son, your father has something he wants to say to you about calling us." I handed the phone to Joe, and I whispered in his ear, "You tell David not to call us any more, Joe. I just can't do it." I heard Joe laugh and say, "Oh, no, now son, listen? You call us anytime. No, I wasn't going to say anything about you not calling us. I don't know what your mother meant when she said that." Joe just looked at me and shrugged his shoulders after he hung up the phone. I was surprised when he said, "Your right Carol, I couldn't tell him not to call us. Not when he needs us the most. We'll get the money to pay those phone bills, somehow. God help us." Thank God, Joe finally agreed with me. He didn't want to discourage David from calling. It was our only link to help encourage David, to help him make it through one of the toughest times of his young life. His divorce.

Early one Saturday morning, before daylight, I heard the phone ringing way off in the distance. I forced my heavy eye lids open, and I glanced at the clock on the night stand. I thought, "Lord, it's five thirty in the morning! Who in the world could be calling us at this hour?" I hardly recognized David's voice, when he said,

"Mom, I'm sorry I woke you and dad up this early, but I'm afraid I've got some really bad news to tell you!" I heard muffled sounds of him crying, and I sat straight up in the bed. I thought maybe I was dreaming. Still half asleep, I said, "What is it, son? Please tell me? What's wrong David, are you hurt?" He was still crying so hard, I could barely understand him, "Mom, I'm in really bad trouble, and I mean it's bad! I thought it was just a silly game, because nothing made any sense, or mattered to me anymore! Mom, I was caught stealing and I am facing a possible prison sentence!" I lay there in the darkness, engulfed in fear and grief. A river of tears washed over my face as I listened to my first born son, three thousand miles away, tell me he could possibly go to prison. He was so terrified of going to prison, where he said, he'd heard that men rape other men. He said he was lifting weights.

I kept praying in the spirit underneath my breath as I listened to his unbelievable story. His voice was so raspy. He said, "Mom, I'm so ashamed. How could I have done this? I've let you and dad down, my wife and my daughter, and my Country and my God. I've failed everyone I love and care about. I don't want to live anymore! I'm so sorry. Mom, can you and dad ever forgive me?" My heart was breaking as I searched for the right words to say to comfort him. Finally, I whispered, "Son, Jesus loves you, and your dad and I love you so dearly. Of course, we forgive you. Son listen to me? I praise God you got caught, and I praise God, you've repented from your heart to the Lord, and us. I also praise God that you weren't seriously hurt, or even killed! Jesus is right there with you, and He will never leave you or forsake you. You need to know and understand, I'm telling you what I know is the truth, David. God will help us, and we will help each other get through this nightmare. We will get through this together, with His help, one day at a time." I told him to read, Hebrews 13:5, so he could understand, this was a spiritual battle. I told him, now that he'd repented, God would help him out of his trouble. (Ephesians 6:12) "For we wrestle not against flesh and blood, but against principalities, against powers, against the rulers of the darkness of this world, against spiritual wickedness in high places."

I wanted so much to put my arms around my son and comfort him, but all I could do was quickly remind him of all the good things he had done. He was always a good example in school, and he was well liked by all his teachers, principals, and classmates. He made mostly A's and B's all through his school years, and most everyone liked David's easy going personality. He had lots of good friends who liked and respected him. David had never once received a speeding ticket, and he'd never been in any bad trouble with the law, either. Joe had been listening to our conversation long enough to drink a couple of cups of coffee while he waited for his turn to talk to David. I handed him the phone. I could see the fear and concern for David in Joe's eyes as he tried to comfort him, "Son, anyone can make a mistake. It's what you do from this point on that counts." I ran and locked myself in the bathroom, fell to my knees, sobbing, and prayed in the spirit for David! My heart was so broken. I couldn't possibly even think of how, or what, to pray effectively for my son. I relied totally on the dear precious Holy Spirit to help me pray for him.

Sandy came over to comfort me as soon as she heard the terrible news. She knew we'd been under great pressure almost constantly. The extra expenses of the large monthly seven and eight hundred dollar phone bills had been a steady problem for us, but all our other bills were getting unbearably harder to pay and farther behind too. We juggled them back and forth until I got my faith in line with the knowledge of God's word, (Philippians 4:19) "And my God WILL SUPPLY ALL, Carol & Joe's need according to His riches in glory by Christ Jesus." Every time I came into agreement with Sandy, the money came, without fail. Praise God!

Even though, I was walking by faith and not by sight, determined to see things as though they were not, and praising and thanking God for hearing and answering my prayers to let us see our little granddaughter, I was still shocked when Carrie called and asked if I'd watch her for three days! It had been several months since we'd seen Rebecca, and I was so overwhelmed with joy when she wrapped her little arms around my neck and gave me a big hug! However, about an hour later when I tried to lay Rebecca down on the couch to change her diaper, utter terror struck me! I was horrified when she violently grabbed hold of me and the sides of the couch! She was screaming, "Please don't hurt me grandma? Please don't hurt me!" I quickly scooped her up in my arms and tried to quiet her down, and comfort her, "It's all right, baby girl. Sh. Hush now sweetheart, grandma won't hurt you, I promise." As her loud screams pierced my ears and heart, I cried out to God, "Oh dear Lord, what has happened to my precious little granddaughter? What's causing her to act this way? Who has hurt this little, innocent child, and made her act so afraid like this, Lord?" I was so relieved when I saw Sandy at the door.

I knew it was God who told Sandy to stop by my house that day. I was so thankful she was there with me. She helped me, as I tried to calm Rebecca down. Sandy was as furious as I was when she witnessed my own little granddaughter's violent, terrified reaction as I tried to change her diaper! Rebecca's small private area looked raw and extremely red, and I found a tiny piece of red plastic inside her, too. I had to keep holding her close and rocking her, in between tries to change her. It broke my heart each time she cried, "No grandma! Please don't hurt me!" It felt so strange for me to have to reassure my own grandchild I wouldn't hurt her. It took me nearly twenty minutes to finally be able to put a clean diaper on her. I had to constantly stop, and talk gently to her. I was worn out! Rebecca finally fell asleep in my arms, out of sheer exhaustion. Sandy and I wasted no time. We prayed for Rebecca's protection, and cried out to God! We asked Him to teach us how to pray more effectively for Rebecca, and her dad and mom.

Tears of compassion ran down our faces, as we sat there praying in the spirit for little Rebecca while she slept. I felt a mixture of deep sadness, a broken spirit, and righteous anger, when I said between clenched teeth, "Sandy, when Carrie comes to pick Rebecca up, I'm going to ask her, why she is allowing this to go on? If she really loves her child, surely she will want to make whoever it is, stop whatever it is their doing to the baby, that makes her so afraid?" Sandy's cheeks were burning red with anger too. She said, "Carol, God will bring your little granddaughter out of this trouble, because He promised to deliver our children, and grandchildren." I thought of, Daniel 3:25 I said, "Sandy, God delivered the three Hebrews from the burning, fiery furnace, and He will deliver us, too! In the Mighty name of Jesus, He will deliver us!" Sandy agreed, "Amen, Carol. God will deliver all of us, His children, out of trouble." I held onto God's word, His promises, for dear life! I felt like a salmon swimming up a stream, against the current. "God, I know You'll help my grandchild."

Even though Joe saw what happened when I tried to lay Rebecca down to change her diaper, he still told me not to say anything to Carrie, or the police! He was afraid she'd withhold Rebecca from us even more. He wanted me to wait until we could afford a lawyer and get 'grandparents' rights to see her, and then contact the police. I panicked, "Joe, please let me call the police, or at least Children's Services? We have to tell someone! We cannot allow this abuse to continue! Can't you see? Rebecca needs our help, now, Joe!" I watched Rebecca as she played innocently with her toys in the living room, while Joe and I stood there in the kitchen talking quietly so she couldn't hear what we were saying. I usually listened to Joe's authority, but I couldn't just leave Rebecca in that condition until goodness knows how long it might take to get a lawyer, and then wait who knows how much longer to get a Court date. I knew I had to do something quickly, with or without Joe's approval. The three days passed by much too quickly. I was so afraid to let Rebecca go back to that abuse. When Carrie stopped by to pick up Rebecca, I thought, "Surely Joe is wrong, this time? Carrie loves Rebecca. I know she'll want the person who's hurting Rebecca to stop it. After all, she is her mother." "When I am weak, than am I strong in Christ Jesus."

So, I took a chance and asked Carrie if she knew the reason why Rebecca cried so hard when I tried to change her diaper? Wow, did Carrie ever get mad at me! She told me. Rebecca was none of my business! She then, grabbed the baby up in her arms, while she was reaching her little arms out to me! Carrie left in a whirlwind, she slammed the door behind her! My nerves were shattered. I cupped my hands over my ears to try and drown out the memory of little Rebecca's cries! I fell prostrate on my face on the floor, and I begged God to help me pray for her, "Lord, I forgive Carrie again! Please protect my little granddaughter? Cover her with the precious blood of Jesus, in the name of Jesus. Keep Your angels standing watch over her to keep her safe, please, Lord!"

When Joe came home from work, I confessed I'd talked to Carrie about Rebecca. He got really mad at me, too! When it came to Rebecca's safety, I felt like a mother bear watching over her cub, "Look Joe, I don't care if you are mad at me, or if you hit me, or curse me out! At least Carrie knows I'm asking questions about Rebecca. She knows I'm upset about Rebecca's abnormal behavior! She should be, too! I have every right to ask questions about my own granddaughter, and I want some answers! I will not stop until Rebecca gets the help and protection she needs. No one helped me when I was little and in trouble! I've got to do the right thing and get that baby some help. So, don't even try and stop me Joe!" I suspected Carrie's boyfriend was hurting Rebecca.

I called the police and told them everything that happened, and Joe didn't say a word. I told the police I had saved the small piece of red plastic for them in a sealed plastic bag. I also had to give them a written report of how I found the small piece of red plastic. I never dreamed I would have to call the police for my own little granddaughter. I labored over that police report. I also laid my head over my typewriter and cried several times before I was able to finish it. It was one of the hardest things I have ever done. When I called Children's Services, they said the investigation would be very difficult to do without my son's permission. After I explained the situation to them, about David awaiting trial, they were more sympathetic and understanding. They agreed, David couldn't do anything, but get more frustrated, depressed and heart broken, if he knew. They also understood why we didn't want to tell David the ugly truth, until we were with him.

Little did we know that right after the authorities investigated, Carrie had already gone back to England and told David I was trying to break up their marriage by calling the police and

Children's Services on her. She said I was accusing her of being a bad wife and mother! David, blinded by his love for her, and not knowing anything about what was going on, stopped the investigation. Ten days later, after the charges were dropped, she left him even more devastated, confused, hurt and broken hearted than before. When David called asking questions about Rebecca, I told him as little as possible. I did not want to crush or damage his fragile state of mind. By the grace and mercy of God, David finally stopped asking questions as to why I had called the police.

After a couple of months had gone by, I couldn't stand it anymore. I had to see for myself how Rebecca was doing. I asked Sandy to go with me to try and reason with Carrie and Janet, but they wouldn't answer their door. We could hear Rebecca talking, so I kept knocking. Finally, Janet opened the door in a rage of anger! She yelled, "What do you want? Haven't you caused us enough trouble already?" While I was standing there humbly trying to reason with Janet, Rebecca kept crying for me. She tried several times to come past Janet's legs and out the door to get to me, but Janet kept shoving her backwards! I cried, "But Janet, I was just trying to help little Rebecca. Don't you understand? I wasn't accusing Carrie of being a bad mother. I was afraid for the baby. Surely, you've seen Rebecca cry when her diaper is being changed? Please Janet, remember we are Christians, and remember the . . . " She yelled, "NO! LEAVE US ALONE!" She slammed the door, as hard as she could, in our face! I stood there weeping uncontrollably! My heart was so broken.

When Sandy put her arm around me to walk me to the car, she said, "Carol, always remember, the devil is a liar! God promised you the blessings that are in the end of the book of Job. The blessings are coming to you. You are going to get everything back double, because God promised it, in His word. In the meantime, the Lord, WILL help you to get three hundred dolors to pay a lawyer! You WILL take Carrie to Court, and then you WILL see Rebecca, according to the law." I kept thinking of, Galatians 6:7 "Do not be deceived, God will not be mocked . . . " As we pulled out of the driveway, Rebecca's small face was pressed up against the window glass, crying. She couldn't understand why her grandmothers were arguing. Within seconds after Sandy dropped me off at my house, I lay prostrate on the floor again. I wept and prayed in the spirit. When I reached up and pulled my bible down from off the coffee table, I cried, "Please Papa, help me to understand all this?" Once again, God faithfully answered me from His word in, 2 Corinthians 4:8-9 "We are hard pressed on every side, yet not crushed; we are perplexed, but not in despair; persecuted, but not forsaken; struck down, but not destroyed."

That same day, the Lord also led me to read, 1 Peter 4:12-13 "Beloved, do not think it strange concerning the fiery trial which is to try you, as though some strange thing happened to you; but rejoice to the extent that you partake in Christ's sufferings that when His Glory is revealed, you may also be glad with exceeding joy." When the Lord gave me, Matthew 10:37 I thought, "Now, He's going to tell me, He will harshly judge Janet and Carrie for being so mean to me." But instead, He made ME judge MYSELF. I said, "Oh, dear, Lord, please help me not to put mother, father, Rebecca, Joe, David, Joey, Janet, or Carrie in front of You? If I do, I know I'm not worthy to serve You, Lord?" I was suffering utter torment in my mind and heart, until the Lord helped me repent of that anger and self righteousness, and focus my eyes on Him, where they belonged. I could almost see Him sitting up there on His thrown smiling down at me. He also reminded me, Many others have already gone His way before me, and they came out victorious. (1 Corinthians 10:13) "There hath no temptation taken you but such as is common to man; but God is faithful, who will not suffer you to be tempted above that which you are able; but will with the temptation also make a way of escape that you are able to bear it." "Thank You, Lord for making a way of escape."

If God hadn't given me Sandy to stand in faith with me daily, I don't know what I would have done. My sister, Sally, and her family, had moved out West. Mommy and daddy lived there, too. My sisters, Janie and Helen, moved out West long before anyone else did. My sister Phillis also moved out West. All of my sisters and brothers are very special to me. I love each and every one of them so much, but they live far away. I see them when they come to visit me on vacation. My sister Louise is the only sister who lives within driving distance, but I hardly ever saw her either. My brothers, Gene, and my oldest brother Jim, might as well have lived on Mars. We mostly visited Joe's family. I hadn't seen my brother Marilyn in nearly thirty years. The only brother I saw, rarely, was my precious brother, Ben. Joe said we didn't have the money. We never went to see them in Arizona. So, God graciously gave me my friend Sandy. She is my sister in Christ.

Sandy knew our situation. Our large phone bills were climbing outrageously high. Every single month she stood with me, believing in faith for our bills to be paid. Thank God! Somehow the money came to pay them. We were calling our Congressman regularly, asking for his help for David. We were also making frequent calls to David's Parole Board Officer in Washington, D.C., and David's Commanding Officer in England. On top of all that, we were continually accepting collect calls from David, too. Sandy and I prayed in agreement, reminding God of His promises, "Many are the afflictions of the righteous, but the Lord delivers us from them all." (Psalm 34:19) "Thank You, dear Papa God for our deliverance according to Your word!"

I received another alarming phone call from David. He'd broken his leg sliding into home base while playing ball for the military! David told me he was wearing a cast clear up to his thigh. He lived in an upstairs apartment, in the barracks on the base. He couldn't go up and down the stairs or take care of himself. I was shaken so badly by the news, all I could do was pray for him from my heart, "Lord, David's three thousand miles away from us. He's without the support of his wife and daughter, and he has no other family member there to help him. Some of his friends have turned their backs on him since he got in trouble. Now, he's sick, in pain and alone, facing a Court Martial, and a possible prison term. What am I going to do, Lord?" We had no extra money for a trip to England. I said, "Come into agreement with me son?" We asked the Lord, "Dear, Father, in the name of Your Son Jesus, we ask You to either, help David's dad and I to get the money to go to England or else, please send someone else to help him? We also ask You to please answer this prayer quickly? Thank You, Lord, for answering our prayer, in the wonderful name of Jesus."

The very next day Joey walked in the house, and started pacing the floor. He was talking really fast! He said, "Mom, I can't stop thinking about my brother being way over there in a strange country, all alone, without his family. He doesn't have his wife and child to comfort him. He's going through all of this horrible stuff, alone! Mom, I've made up my mind, I'm going over there. Don't try and talk me out of it, I'm going! I've already bought my plane ticket with the money I've saved. I told my boss, 'I don't know how long I'll be gone.' Since this is an emergency, he said I can go. I leave in the morning!" I fell back in my chair laughing hysterically! When Joey heard me start praising and thanking the wonderful loving God that I serve for His goodness and mercy, he smiled at me and said, "What's going on, mom?" I laughed and told him, "Son, you are the answer to our prayer." Joey told me. He made his decision when I told him that David broke his leg, the day before. (Isaiah 45:2) "I will go before you to make the crooked places straight." "Thank You, and praise You dear God."

Several hours after Joey left for England, I was cleaning his room and praying in the spirit when the Lord spoke to me clearly, "Go too now, and pray for thy son." As God was speaking to me, I saw myself in the spirit, sitting on the couch in my living room with my feet propped up on the coffee table, relaxing while I prayed. As I was walking toward the living room, I knew it was Joey, the Holy Spirit was praying for, through me. I continued to pray in tongues for Joey. I no sooner relaxed and put my feet up, when I saw a clear vision of him sitting in the air plane talking to a young, tall Air Force man, seated beside him. In the vision, I was sitting in a cross legged position on the floor directly in front of them. I was looking up at them. They were completely unaware of my being there. Joey sat in the seat beside the window. The young, handsome, African American Air Force man seated beside Joey nervously started to undo his dark blue tie. He folded it neatly and placed it in his coat pocket. He then unbuttoned the top two buttons on his light blue shirt. The plane stared rocking violently back and forth. I realized there was a terrible storm outside!

I could not hear Joey and the young Air Force man's conversation, but I could both see and feel their uneasiness and fear as they crossed their legs, and shifted back and forth, from one position to the other. I watched as Joey went back and forth crossing his legs to the right and then back to the left again, while he leaned on apposite elbows. Suddenly, the Lord picked me up by the hair of my head, whisked me outside, and stood me on top of the extremely fast moving plane! Amazingly, I was not afraid. I boldly stood there with my feet spread apart, feeling like a high ranking military officer! I was fearless, inside God's supernatural armor. God's armor covered me from head to foot. I knew that nothing evil could penetrate that armor. In the vision, I had no fear of the storm, the height, falling, or the speed of the plane. Absolutely nothing made me afraid. I could feel God's power surging through me. I was One with Him, Jesus, and the dear Holy Spirit. The storm was raging in all it's fury around me! Great flashes of lightning, lite up the entire sky, like fire works! Furious winds whipped all around me, but I knew nothing could harm me, or make me afraid. My legs were covered in God's supernatural armor just like the rest of my body and I felt strong and powerful!

The Lord spoke to me above the noise of the storm. He said, "Speak to the storm, Carol; Tell it, 'Peace, be still,' in My name." With a feeling of indescribable power, and a force of God's supernatural strength flowing through me, I stretched my right hand and arm out in the direction of the storm. I saw myself do this, in the vision, but I also did it in the natural. I boldly said, "PEACE, BE STILL, IN THE NAME OF JESUS!" Instantly, the storm ceased. It was like watching a video movie, on fast forward. The dark angry clouds swirled into nothing, and disappeared like vanishing smoke. I turned and looked in every direction. As far as my eyes could see, there were calm, peaceful skies, and sunshine. Also, the instant the skies cleared, I saw a huge, shiny silver object move swiftly away from the right side of the plane. It disappeared somewhere into the heavens. The dear precious Holy Spirit kept helping me pray for Joey. In the vision, I was quickly brought back inside the plane. I was seated again on the floor in front of Joey and the young Air Force man. I was exactly where I was before. As I looked up at Joey, he was smiling, and relaxed. He seamed really happy now that the storm was over. The young Air Force man, smiled. He reached out his right hand to shake Joey's hand first. Joey was grinning from ear to ear as he shook the young man's hand. Thanks to Jesus, the atmosphere in that plane was charged with peace instead of chaos, and joy, instead of fear.

The two of them were laughing and joking. I felt the Holy Spirit release me from that prayer. So, I got up and went back to my cleaning. Later that day, I told Sandy, "When I stood on top of that plane, out against the elements, I felt like I was wearing God's heavy, protective, supernatural armor. I felt like David, in the bible, when he ran toward Goliath the giant, killed him and took off his head!" (1 Samuel 1:23-58) Weeks later when I talked to Joey, I told him about the vision, and he yelled with excitement, "Mom, the plane I was in had flown off course, because of the terrible storm! The air traffic that day was so heavy the pilot could not fly above it! Didn't you watch the news that night?" I told him our television set had not been working. We were waiting until we could afford to get it fixed. Joey said, "Oh, Mom, listen to me? The man on the news said another plane had flown off course because of the storm, also! The other plane nearly crashed into us! They said if the storm hadn't stopped at the exact moment it did, both planes would have collided in mid air, and exploded, leaving no survivors! Thank God. He saved my life, and many others too! Thank you for praying for me mom, I love you so much."

I couldn't get over the fact that, of course, the shiny metal object I saw in the vision was another plane. The other plane being lost in the storm too, could have caused such a horrible disaster! I'd had such peace after I prayed for Joey that day, I knew the Lord took care of whatever it was that was wrong, so I didn't worry about it, not even once. I thought, "Oh dear, Lord, no wonder You allowed our television to go on the blink." All of a sudden, it dawned on me, how serious it could have been for my son. God, in His mercy, kept that thing hidden from me until Joey was back home and safe. Everything I told Joey I saw in the vision was precise and exact, right down to the minutest detail, including the young tall, Air Force gentleman. Joey agreed. He loosened and removed his tie, and unbuttoned the top two buttons on his shirt, just like it was in the vision. God left no room for doubt in our hearts or minds. Joey agreed, He is our wonderful heavenly Father, God who loves us. Wow! We were so thankful for His divine intervention. "Oh my sweet Lord Jesus, how I love You."

When Sandy came over, I told her everything. She and I were so amazed at the goodness of God. We were both so happy we know Jesus, and we will never be without the comfort of the dear Holy Spirit. "Thank God!" We agreed, we will never turn back from following Jesus. We love our sweet Jesus, and we know He will never leave us nor forsake us. "Thank You for loving us Papa, Jesus, and dear precious Holy Spirit!" Now that I understood why I'd had the vision of Joey's plane, it overwhelmed me when I thought of God's tender mercy to us. "Thank You sweet Jesus!"

One, really hot August afternoon, Joe and I were sitting in the living room, visiting with Diane, Joey's girlfriend, when Carrie happened to stop by with the baby. We were so excited to see our little red headed, blue eyed pumpkin! We hadn't seen her in several months, and we'd missed her terribly. Carrie refused our hugs, but Rebecca ran toward me, and I scooped her up in my arms! I couldn't help but notice, Carrie was wearing old clothes, and her hair was dry and bleached so harshly it looked like straw. Red and purple streaks ran through her eyes and down across her once beautiful face, just like the evil woman in the dream. Since the day I'd first met Carrie, she took pride in how she looked. She was always clean and neatly dressed. Her hair and makeup usually looked nice, too. Carrie acted jumpy and really nervous. Joe, myself, and Diane were there that day to witness the ridiculous horror that was about to take place! Joe had bought Rebecca her own little fishing tackle box, a fishing pole, and her own rubber worms, without hooks. They were some of her most favorite things she played with, when she was allowed to come over. She loved to pretend she was catching great, big fish like her grandpa, Joe and I. We couldn't believe what happened when Joe attempted to show her some of the shinny new colorful rubber worms he'd added to her tackle box. "God have mercy on us."

I was sitting on the love seat with Rebecca on my lap. Carrie was sitting directly across from me in Joe's recliner. Joe was seated on the floor to my left, and Diane was on the couch to my right. Joe opened Rebecca's bright, yellow tackle box, and he held out his hand to show her it was full of the new colorful rubber worms. He said, "See what grandpa bought you. So, now you can catch bigger fish, just like me and grandma!" All of us, excluding Carrie, were in shock over Rebecca's abnormal behavior! She grabbed me tightly around the neck, and started climbing up the front of me, crying and screaming, "PLEASE GRANDMA, MAKE GRANDPA PUT THEM AWAY! I DON'T LIKE THEM GRANDMA, THEY'RE SCARING ME!" She kept crying and screaming the same words, over and over, nearly chocking me! Joe quickly tried to put the worms back in her tackle box!

We were all so confused and stunned when Carrie fell back in her chair, laughing wildly, until Joe started to close the lid on the tackle box! Suddenly, Carrie stopped laughing, and shot up out of the chair! She forced Joe's hand away from the tackle box, flung the lid open, and grabbed a handful of the rubber worms! We all stared at Carrie in amazement, bewildered at her weird behavior. Again, she roared with a loud outburst of wild, crazy laughter! I was still trying to calm Rebecca down. I held her close and rocked her. It was so strange to see and hear Carrie get oddly quiet again. It was spooky! She just sat there in the chair, for a couple of long minutes, quietly, while she laid the handful of rubber worms in the chair beside her. Suddenly, she jumped up again, and ran over and forcibly grabbed Rebecca out of my arms! I couldn't believe it! I was frantic, watching her! She sat back down in Joe's chair with Rebecca on her lap. She kept talking, abnormally sweet to her, "Aw now honey, calm down. Mommy won't let anyone hurt her little baby girl." Carrie was usually a good mother.

I couldn't believe my eyes and ears when Carrie started roaring with wild crazy laughter again! She dumped a whole handful of the rubber worms in Rebecca's red curly hair, and started rubbing them, and swirling them around in circles, until they were all painfully tangled up, in her hair! The baby was screaming to the top of her lungs, as she tried to get away from her mother! Carrie kept laughing, wildly. She kept making fun of Rebecca as she continued to tangle those awful rubber worms into her hair! We were all begging Carrie to stop hurting Rebecca and making her cry! Everything was happening so fast, and yet I felt as if I were moving in slow motion. In my heart, I kept begging God to make the nightmare end! I wanted to shake some sense into Carrie, and make her stop acting like a crazy person; but I couldn't do anything except beg her to stop scaring, and hurting her own baby! I felt as helpless as Joe and Diane. Within seconds, Carrie stopped laughing, and became serene and calm again. She tried to quiet Rebecca down and talked sweetly to her while she pulled small clumps of her beautiful red curly hair out, along with the rubber worms. This weird behavior was not like Carrie!

I knew she was hurting Rebecca on purpose, but why? I thought I was going to hit her, listening to my little grand-baby scream and cry! I ran and got the scissors, and tried to cut some of the worms out of Rebecca's hair. I worked as gently as I could while Carrie glared at me. Her eyes darted fire, as if she were daring me to make one wrong move! God help me? I knew if I did make a wrong move, I may never see Rebecca again. Only God knew how long it was going to take us to get our grandparents rights to see Rebecca. Finally, we removed all of the rubber worms from Rebecca's tender, sore little head. I thought, maybe I could rock the baby and calm her down, but Carrie jerked her from my arms! She was laughing wildly again! As soon as Carrie sat down, she became eerie calm, again, and with her hands on Rebecca's small shoulders, she said, "Oh, mommy's so sorry for scaring her baby. Come here, and give mommy a kiss?" We sat there in disbelief, watching Rebecca's little body still tremble. Short, jerking sobs, caused her little chest to heave back and forth. Rebecca timidly stepped closer and gave her mother a kiss. Suddenly, Carrie jerked Rebecca's shoulders forward, and slammed the baby's lips tightly up against her own! Carrie forced one of the rubber worms from her own mouth, which she had apparently hidden previously, into Rebecca's unsuspecting small mouth! We couldn't believe she used her tongue to push the rubber worm from her mouth into Rebecca's mouth! Rebecca started gagging, and, after she spit out the worm and caught her breath, she cried so loud it sent chills all over us! She was turning blue around her little mouth! Before I could reach her, she ran behind her mother's chair, to get away from her! By the time I got to her, she was still screaming and sliding down the wall! The little granddaughter we loved so much, nearly passed out from fear! When I bent over to pick up Rebecca, Carrie grabbed her up in her arms, and ran out the door, laughing viciously! "What's happening to Carrie, dear Lord?"

Again, I had to put my hands over my ears to try and drown out the awful memory of Rebecca's loud cries! I ran to the phone to call the police, but just as I started to dial the number, Joe clicked the receiver down. He said, "Carol, stop and think for a minute. What are you going to say to the police?" He had a hollow look of deep sadness in his eyes, too. I realized he was right. How could I describe the insane madness that went on that horrible afternoon? After all, Rebecca's daddy was in England, facing a possible prison sentence. Our hands were tied. I reluctantly hung up the phone and went to my room. I fell to my knees and onto my face, as I cried out to God, "Papa, please help me to learn how to effectively pray for my little granddaughter! Please, help me, to know how to pray for her mother, too, Lord!"

While Joey was still visiting his brother, David in England, the Lord gave me a beautiful dream. In this dream, I was casually walking through a lovely garden with Jesus. It was so peaceful there. It's hard to describe it. It was the most beautiful, restful place I've ever seen, and unlike anywhere on earth. Everything was perfect in color. The sky was a deep, awesome blue. Even the grass and trees were a lush resilient green. The flowers were the most brilliant beautiful colors I've ever seen in my entire life! The weather, and the temperature were absolutely so perfect, they couldn't possibly get any better. While Jesus and I walked together through the peaceful garden, there was a soft breeze gently blowing. As we walked along, I asked Him, "Lord, there is something I don't understand, about Your word?" He stopped walking and stood still. I alone, had His undivided attention. When He looked at me, His beautiful blue eyes searched deep into my soul with such love and compassion. I knew it was His desire to answer my question. It was His delight and joy to help me.

I stood there leafing through my bible, until I turned and looked up into His glorious blue eyes again. I said, "Lord, will You please show me something in Your word, just for David? He's the one in so much trouble! I desperately need something from Your word for us to hold onto. I need something specifically for him. Please help us, dear Lord?" His beautiful blue eyes seamed to dance with pure energy, light, and joy, as He gently took my bible. He turned the pages, until He stopped, and pointed with His index finger at the top right-hand corner of the page. On the second line down and third word over, there was the word, 'wood.' I started jumping up and down, and thanking Him since David's middle name was Elwood! Family and friends, nicknamed him, Woody! I woke Joe up, screaming hallelujah to Jesus, "Oh, dear Lord Jesus, I thank You so much! I praise You, Lord, for giving me Your promise to hold onto for David! Hallelujah!" Joe, woke me up! He shook me, and yelled, "Carol, what in the world is wrong with you, screaming, and laughing like that? Are you crazy? You better be blank, thankful it's time for me to get up and go to work, or I'd really be mad at you!" I humbly asked him for his forgiveness, than I squealed with excitement, "Oh Joe, I've just been walking in the most beautiful garden with Jesus! He showed me something in His word, specifically for David, to help him!"

I leaped out of bed, and ran into the living room to get my bible! However, on the way there, suddenly the terrible realization dawned on me! I forgot to look at the scripture and verse reference. Where is it located in the bible? I cried, "Oh no!" Joe was headed for the bathroom when he stopped and asked me, "What's wrong, Carol?" After I told him, he made a joke out of it. With a big smirk on his face, he said sarcastically, "Well, missy. Why don't you just let your bible fall open? You, and your mother are always saying, that's how God speaks to you. So, why not put it to the test this time?" I stared at him, standing there in his wrinkled, blue pajamas, his dark curly hair sticking out in every direction. I said, "Oh Joe, of course that's it! That's exactly what I'll do! I praise God, for giving you wisdom! Wow! I'm amazed. The Lord spoke through you! Oh, thank you, honey! Thank you so much, Joe!" I hugged my large print, King James' bible, and I prayed, "Father, please let Your word fall open to the exact place where Jesus showed me to read the word 'wood', in the dream, in Jesus name? Papa, You said in Your word, You do not want us to be ignorant. So, I thank You for showing me exactly where it is Lord, amen." I could hardly wait to seek and find the answer!

I took a deep breath, and then I let the bible fall open. I looked at the top right-hand corner, but the word 'wood' wasn't there. I read through Isaiah 59:19-21. God's word washed over me, especially the last verse, "As for Me," says the Lord, "this is My covenant with them: My Spirit who is upon you, and My words which I have put in your mouth, will not depart from your mouth, nor from the mouth of your descendants, nor from the mouth of your descendants, descendants," says the Lord, "from this time and forevermore." I kept on reading in, Isaiah 60:1. "Arise shine for your light has come! And the glory of the Lord is risen upon you. For behold, the darkness will cover the earth, And deep darkness the people; But the Lord will arise over you, And His glory will be seen upon you." Each time God gives me scriptures like this from His word, I know He understands everything troubling my heart. I thought, "He established His word for me, today, thousands of years ago." I got so excited, I praised God!

(Isaiah 60:4) " . . . Your sons shall come from afar, and your daughters shall be nursed at your side." I thought, "Wow, God! You are so awesome! David and Joey shall come from afar, and Rebecca shall be nursed at my side, hallelujah!" Finally, I came to verse 17, "Instead of bronze I will bring you gold, Instead of iron I will bring you silver, Instead of 'WOOD,' bronze, and instead of stones, iron. I will also make your officers peace, And your magistrate's righteousness." I started hollering for Joe, "Come here and see this, Joe? I found it! I found the word, WOOD!"

When Joe came running into the living room, he looked sort of pale. He just stood there staring blankly at the bible, as I read it to him. He couldn't believe the advice he jokingly gave me, actually worked. I said, "Look at this Joe? God even knows how many officers David has, including all those over him in the military. He will certainly have them, if he goes to prison, not to mention his parole board officer, in Washington, D.C. Isn't it exciting Joe? God gave us His word. He will make all David's officer's, peaceful toward him. God is so good, isn't He Joe?"He mumbled something under his breath, as he left for work. When Joe slammed the kitchen door behind him, the thought crossed my mind, "If God can speak through a donkey, He can certainly speak through a stubborn, mule headed man like Joe."

When I told Sandy about it later, she laughed, too. God forgave us for laughing at Joe. We needed a good laugh. I said, "Sandy, God is bringing us out of trouble, according to His word! And not even unbelief in Joe will stop it." We agreed, God was in control! Sandy knew I was spending a lot of my time on my face before the Lord in prayer for my family. She understood. I'd had no other choice. God was steadily closing the doors to our cleaning company. We recognized it was His timing. Suddenly, we'd had a dramatic drop in our work. It was strange, how even our elderly customers were going to live with either relatives, or moving into convalescent homes. Our regular, steady, military couple was being transferred to another country. Sandy and I knew it was God, not our work. We had only a couple of customers left. My new freedom gave me more time to spend in the word and prayer.

By the time Rebecca was three years old, Joe and I started hearing reports of seeing her at her grandma Janet's house, alone with only the dog to babysit her. We were furious! We knew the person personally who told us this information, and she was very trustworthy. We also knew her life style. Sandy and I knew her walk with God was pure, too. When I finally got to spend a few hours with Rebecca while Carrie went shopping one day, I asked her about it. She started crying! She told me. She was really scared when they left her there alone with the dog. She said her mommy and her grandma Janet told her she's not allowed to tell anyone they leave her there at the house by herself with the dog. My little, three-year-old granddaughter told me they had forbidden her to call me, or anyone else, either, while she was there alone with the dog. I held her on my lap, and I looked deep into her pretty, big, blue eyes. I said, "I promise you baby girl, that I won't tell on you. I will not get you in trouble if you'll call me when you are there alone. Please call me when your alone and afraid?" I wanted the police to catch Carrie and make her stop it.

Sure enough, a couple of days later Rebecca called me crying! She was there alone in the big empty house with the dog again. She was crying because she was so afraid! Joey had my car that day so I couldn't go over there and comfort her. I sat there wishing I could call the police. Instead, Janet came home unexpectedly, and started yelling and screaming at little Rebecca for being on the phone. I heard Janet yell, "Who are you talking to, Rebecca?" Rebecca answered, "My grandma Carol. I'm sorry, grandma Janet! Please don't be made at me? I was so scared, I, I!" Janet yelled, "You give me that phone, little lady!" Janet slammed the phone down! I was so angry. I sat there weeping, praying for my little granddaughter. I'd promised her I wouldn't get her in trouble, but I did. We'd also heard facts from reliable family members who told us they found her asleep and locked in the back seat of a car at night by herself, while Carrie was inside, tanning! Again, the police were notified too late. When they got there, Carrie's car was gone. The police told us if they caught Carrie leaving Rebecca alone at her young age, it would be an automatic jail sentence. Carrie would also lose custody of her. I broke down again in tears! All I seamed to do was cry and pray for God to protect our little Rebecca. I realized God was dealing with Carrie, and Janet's selfish will. I was so frustrated. I asked Sandy, "I can't understand how two responsible adults like Carrie and Janet, could leave a three year old child alone with a dog, or in the back seat of a car unattended, can you? I mean what kind of nonsense is that? How can they just go off and leave Rebecca, who is just a baby, alone with a dog? She could get into anything! Oh, and what's the dog gonna, do? I know. He'll bark and tell her, "No, no Rebecca!" Sandy, please pray that I can let go of this, and lay Rebecca at Jesus' feet! God help me to trust Him and leave her there at His feet. I forgive them, God please forgive me." Sandy answered, "Carol the Lord knows your heart, and He understands, this is not easy. He will help you, my friend. God will help you."

Early one morning, Sandy and I were sitting in my living room praying in the spirit, when I began to see a vision of David. He was standing with his back to me, looking up toward heaven. He stood there with his feet spread apart, and his arms a little way out from his sides, holding his bible in his left hand. He was wearing his casual clothes, and high top tennis shoes. A bright, vibrant light was shinning down on him from heaven. It moved with intense energy as it flowed from the top of his head, and down to his feet. Suddenly, a huge black spiked ball came hurling down toward him, aimed at the left side of his head! I heard myself scream, "IN THE NAME OF JESUS, I COMMAND THAT EVIL THING TO GO BACK WHERE IT CAME FROM, NOW!" Immediately, the black spiked ball stopped dead in its tracks, just inches from David's head! As suddenly as it came down, it hurled itself backwards until it was completely gone out of sight. Praise God! Only seconds after I'd finished telling Sandy about the vision, David called. Before I could tell him about the vision I'd just had concerning him, he told me why I'd had it. He said. The military authorities grabbed him up out of his bed, and took him in for interrogation earlier that morning! My heart broke, when he told me how scared he was. They put him in a dark metal room with heavy metal doors. Inside what's called a holding tank. I was grateful to God, when David told me. While he was in the metal tank, the Lord spoke to him about his future. The Lord showed David a vision. In the vision David saw himself standing upon a stage. He was preaching to a large crowd of people. David said they were all happy and praising God! I was overwhelmed with joy when David said he wanted God's will for his life to be done! David saved the hardest and most startling news, for last. He said, the military authorities told him he was facing the grave possibility of serving ninety-one years behind bars! "Sweet Jesus!"

We talked about how harsh that sentence was, compared to what he'd done wrong. I pushed back the tears and said, "David, I believe you told us the truth. I can assure you, son, you haven't done anything bad enough to warrant that kind of a sentence!" David told me again exactly what he had done wrong. We both agreed, he should serve his time for what he did, but not ninety one years! Sandy gently squeezed my arm before she left. She whispered, "Call me, later." I felt David's terrorizing fear and panic when he said, "Mom, I may never see my little girl again! Or, I may never see you, and dad, or my brother either. I may never see any of my family or friends again!" I said boldly, "David, God has given us His promises, and we will hold onto them, in faith believing, His word. He will give your officers peace, and bring you back to us, from afar! He brought Joey home safely, and look what the enemy tried to do to him. In the name of Jesus, we will always triumph over our enemies in God's strength. We are covered in the protective blood of Jesus! Son, please don't give up? Remember the vision God just now gave me about you? His bright light from heaven was shinning down upon you. I believe He was telling us not to worry, but instead trust that He will watch over you and Rebecca. He will bring this nightmare to a holy end, once and for all, in the name of Jesus!" My mind had so many questions, but I stayed calm and strong for David until our conversation ended. "Jesus, please help us, dear Lord!"

I walked on into the kitchen. It was one of my favorite places to pray. I always left the top of my window blinds open on the kitchen door so I could look outside toward the heavens and talk to the Lord. The enemy was firing all kinds of questions at me that day! My tears were falling like a steady rain as I looked out through the window blinds toward heaven and cried out to God, "Lord, I will lift up my hands and praise You, even in this situation!" I dropped to my knees, and onto my face on the cold kitchen floor, praying fervently in the spirit. I was trying to drown out the enemy's loud accusations! He kept saying, "You are never going to win this battle! You are never going to see your little granddaughter, or your oldest son again! You are probably going to lose this house, too! You have no hope of David coming back home to you now! You are going to be receiving collect phone calls from England for the rest of your life! You are not going to make it!" I say, "Let God be true and every man or devil a liar."

All during this crazy, one-sided conversation from the enemy, I kept hearing a still small peaceful voice, whispering, "Sunday. Sunday." Finally, I lifted my face up from the floor. I said, "Lord is this You, saying, Sunday? If so, then please tell me why You are saying Sunday?" He answered softly, "Daughter; Remember the vision I gave you of the cross." He reminded me of how terrible and dark everything looked on that Friday night for Him. The angry mob spat on Him, pulled out handfuls of His precious beard. They bludgeoned His back, for our healing, and they hung Him on the cross. He told me, He went there for me and David, and although the situation may look like a dark, fearful Friday night, Sunday is on the way! Because He lives, victory Sunday is on the way for everyone one of us. He said that same resurrection power that raised Him up from the dead, lives inside of us, too! Jesus said if we will always remember this, no situation we are going through will ever look so dark or scary again. Faith exploded inside my spirit! I cried out loud, "Yes Lord, I remember when You took me to the cross in the vision that day!" I will always remember, He lives inside of me, and He is the resurrection and the life! He is The Way, The Truth and The Life! I quoted, I John 4:4 "Greater is He that is in me, then he that is in the world!"

I sat up on my knees, and smiled, while I retrieved another tissue from the box. I wiped the tears from my eyes, and blew my nose, and then I started singing praise and worship songs about the blood of Jesus, and victory in Jesus! I stood to my feet with the Lord's strength and hope flowing through me. I quoted Psalm 42:5 "Why are you cast down, O my soul? And why are you disquieted within me? Hope in God, for I shall yet praise Him for the help of His countenance." At that time, my circumstances hadn't changed around me, yet, but I'd changed on the inside. I knew, beyond a shadow of a doubt, God would help us. I'll always have the victory, because of the blood of Jesus! I knew Jesus loved me! Every time I watched God stretch our bill money, I said out loud, "Thank You sweet wonderful Jesus." I kept thanking and praising the Lord for encouraging me that day. Romans 8:9, 11 "But if the Spirit of Him that raised up Jesus from the dead dwell in you, He that raised up Christ from the dead shall quicken your mortal bodies by His Spirit that dwelleth in you."

When David called discouraged, I told him what happened to me the day Jesus broke through enemy lines and gave me hope about victory Sunday. I felt such compassion for David. He was awaiting trial not knowing when he'd go to prison, or how long he'd be there. After we talked a while he firmly agreed that victory Sunday was on the way, because God loved us enough to allow His precious Son Jesus to go to the cross for us. So, now we can have hope in any situation. David was not ignorant of God's word either, we knew the truth. (2 Corinthians 12:10) "When I am weak then am I strong in Christ Jesus." (Zechariah 4:6) "Not by power, nor by might but by My Spirit says the Lord." I quoted those scriptures over and over, until I got them down in my heart.

I held on for dear life to my promised victory Sunday, on the day I got one of the most horrible phone calls I've ever received in my life! When I picked up the phone. I said, "Hello?" A stranger asked if I was David's mother? He barely gave me time to answer, "Yes, I am." He quickly introduced himself as David's appointed lawyer. This man who I'd never met before was so rude. Once again, before I could say another word, he blurted out in an extremely loud, harsh, dictating voice, "Your son is about to be sentenced to at least ninety-one years in prison! Madam, I feel it is my duty, as your son's lawyer to tell you the truth! I will not hold anything back from you!" David's so called, appointed lawyer, proceeded to rudely, almost scream in my ear! He had the audacity to tell me that he was representing my son! He gave me absolutely no hope when he told me in a cruel, unfeeling and stern voice! "Surely, you cannot expect me to win this case for David?" He said he thought it was his duty to inform me that David would probably spend the rest of his life behind bars!

I was so angry! I could hardly get a word in, but I shouted, right over the top of his loud irritating voice, "Now you listen to me Captain, whatever you said your name was? I'll have YOU to understand something, sir! The military doesn't own my son David. God does! My son, David, dedicated his life to the Lord. So, his heavenly Father will take care of him! God will be his lawyer! If you are trying to pin something on him that he's not guilty of, God will prove him innocent! God will fight for him, and He will uncover the hidden truth!" The rude Captain kept trying to interrupt me, but I continued to yell louder. I yelled right over the top of his negative words against David, "Jesus promised me, sir. Everything covered must be uncovered, and everything hidden must be revealed. (Matthew 10:26.) God is a righteous Judge, and He will judge David fairly, whether you like it or not, sir! I know God will not let me down, and whether you believe me or not, doesn't matter! Oh, and one more thing, sir; If one single hair on my son David's head is harmed, either by himself, or your military, I'm holding you personally responsible! If you are his lawyer, than why don't you act like it? Stop trying to prove him guilty, before he's even had a trial! If God be for us, then who can be against us? Nobody! Not even you, sir! Goodbye!" (Romans 8:31) (John 7:24) I prayed in tongues until I calmed down again.

The next morning I sat in my living room, drinking coffee and enjoying my quiet time with the Lord as usual. I looked so forward to my time with the Lord, after Joey and his dad left for work. I asked the Lord, "Oh dear Lord, if I ever needed to tithe, it's now! We need miracles, but Joe is the head of this house and he won't go to church or tithe. So, what am I to do, Lord?" He answered me with three words, "Forgive your debtors." I argued, "But Lord, no one owes us anything? We owe them!" Instantly, He reminded me of the car we had sold to Joe's brother, who'd never paid us our seven hundred dollars. Instead, he sold it to their sister, and when she couldn't pay us, she in turn sold it to her son-in-law, Joe's Nephew. He'd been driving our car for a couple of years and he hadn't paid us anything, either. In the meantime we were still paying for the insurance on the car, all those years. I looked up and I said, "Hey, Lord that is a great idea! That car has caused us nothing but trouble. Joe's had hard feelings toward all those in his family who haven't paid us anything, for years!" The Lord also reminded me of the people we bought our house from. At least thirteen years had passed since they had promised to repay the seven hundred dollars, we paid for the closing cost on our house when we bought it from them. Joe felt hard toward them, too.

I was overwhelmed when I realized we did have debtors, who owed us fourteen hundred dollars! I said, "Wow, Lord!" I couldn't wait to tell Joe the good news! So that evening, on the way to his mom and dad's house, I told him what the Lord said to me about us forgiving our debtors. He got so angry with me. He stared at me in disbelief. His eyes were bulging. He started yelling and cursing at me, until the veins in his neck stuck out! He nearly drove our car off the road, looking like a wild man, when he screamed, "Carol, are you crazy, asking me a question like that? Blank, no, I won't forgive them! Don't you ever ask me a stupid question like that again. I don't want to hear any more about it! This subject is closed, forever! Is that understood?" I sat there in the car beside him stunned, and very puzzled. I humbly agreed not to mention it to him again. I just knew the Lord had told me that wonderful news. The realization of my inability to hear God correctly hurt me worse then Joe's hateful, abusive curse words.

I went to the Lord the next morning and asked Him, "Lord, I

was so sure that it was You who spoke to me about forgiving our debtors as a way of tithing. Did You see, and hear how upset Joe was with me last night when I asked him about it? I thought I knew Your voice, but I guess I didn't hear You this time. Please help me to understand? Are You mad at me or something, Lord?" I nearly spilled hot coffee all over myself when He calmly answered, "Daughter, you planted that seed. Now give Me the rest of the day to water it. Ask Joe again tonight." I said, "Oh Lord, You've got to be kidding? I'm afraid I'll make him angrier! Are You really sure about this, Papa?" I could sense Him smiling down at me. He was not amused at my frustration, but I knew He wanted me to trust Him. He didn't say anything else, and I never thought much more about it, until later that evening when Sandy and I were sitting at my kitchen table, talking. Joe was sitting in the living room watching a ball game on television. Suddenly, I blurted out, "Hey Joe, have you thought any more about what I asked you last night? Remember, how God told us to forgive our debtors, the people who owe us money for the house and the car?"

I was amazed that I'd asked Joe that question so easily. I was even more shocked when he answered my question the way he did. He said peacefully, "Yes Carol, I have. As a matter of fact, I haven't stopped thinking about it, last night and all day, today. The more I thought about it the better it sounded to me. So I've decided to go ahead and cancel their debts. Trying to get our money from them, all these years, has only caused me to have more hurt feelings. I've been angry with them long enough. I feel really good about just letting go of their debts and forgiving them. Once and for all. Go ahead and call or write them and tell them they don't owe us anything. Who knows, if we help them, maybe someone will give David a break." I kept glancing at Joe, and then across the kitchen table at Sandy, the whole time Joe was talking. She and I kept giving each other some quiet thumbs up signs. We sat there smiling in utter amazement. We witnessed, first hand, the awesome power of Almighty God! Joe's Nephew was so happy when I told him Jesus loved him, and He told us to erase his debt. The other couple who owed us money for the house were happy, too! "O' God, thank You for helping me not disobey You. I love You so dearly, Papa God!" (1 Corinthians 1:27) "God takes the foolish things of this world and confounds the wise."

I had another disturbing dream about Carrie. In the dream Carrie was off in another room where I couldn't see her; But I knew she was in a casket, because everyone was moaning and weeping as they went in and out of the room, "Carrie was too young to die. She always said she would be killed in a terrible car crash at the young age of nineteen!" When David called, I told him about the dream. He told me Carrie had always confessed those exact words over herself, since she was very young. Now that I knew the power of life and death is in our own tongue, I knew I'd better do something quick. Carrie's nineteenth birthday was in the month of April. I had the dream in March. She had prepared her own death, by speaking those words over herself, all those years. I started interceding for her. I pled the blood of Jesus over those negative words and broke there power off her life, in the name of Jesus! Thank God. Carrie's birthday came and went, without what she was speaking over herself coming true. The Lord spared her life. Jesus said, pray for those who persecute us. I did.

One afternoon, my friend Dixie stopped by. She asked me to go to church with her and stay afterward for prayer. I more than gladly accepted her offer. As soon as the service ended, I was the first one in line for prayer. Dixie and some of her friends anointed me with oil. When they started to pray for me, I couldn't seem to concentrate. I could barely hear them praying. Instead, I kept hearing a woman right next to me screaming to the top of her lungs, "JESUS! OH, DEAR, JESUS! PLEASE HELP ME DEAR JESUS?" The women screamed awfully loud in my ear. She really got on my nerves! Her screams were so loud. They were distracting me. It sounded like something horrible was being pulled up out of her? While the others were praying for me, it was as if I was watching a fast forwarded video on a television screen, and the movie was about me? All of the past years of my painful

103

memories, from birth to that present day, flashed quickly before me. I heard several loud, powerful voices, commanding spirits of pain, hurt, and shame to come out of me, in the name of Jesus! At the same time, I heard and saw myself having conversations with David, Carrie and Rebecca. I saw little Rebecca reaching for me, and I heard her loud cries! I saw the horrible scenario with Carrie, Rebecca, and the rubber worms again, too.

Suddenly, I realized it was me screaming! It wasn't someone else. I was the woman who couldn't stop screaming! I was the one. God healed me from the inside out. He pulled all of that old garbage up out of me. I was as relaxed as a rag doll. A woman named Mary Ann Huber scooped me up in her arms from the floor where I was still lying. She said boldly, "Carol, you have nothing to be ashamed of! God loves you. He has called you and your whole family! The enemy will be sorry he ever did this to you! The Greater One inside of you, is rising up within you! You will snatch many people out of darkness, and bring them into the light of God's kingdom, in Jesus name!" (Matthew 8:17) "Himself took my sickness and carried away my diseases and with His stripes I am healed." I told Sandy about my inner healing the next day, with tears of gratitude running down my cheeks. She agreed that God cares about us. He makes us whole, past, present and future. I was so grateful, I kept saying, "Thank You so much, my sweet precious Jesus! I love You so dearly, wonderful Jesus!"

I'd been praying almost constantly in the spirit for David, because I knew his court date was coming up really soon. I am so thankful for the dear precious Holy Spirit helping me pray until David's court date finally arrived. "Everything hidden MUST be revealed, everything covered MUST be uncovered." (Matthew 10:26) "Now dear Father, I'm asking You to reveal, expose, up root, and lay bare, any hidden truths that could help David, in Jesus name? You are his lawyer, dear, Lord Jesus, and I'm believing You will do a fine job of representing my son." I prayed, as I paced the floor. David finally called, and he was excited. He talked pretty fast! He said. He'd gone to bed scared the night before, just as he'd been doing for several months while he was awaiting his trial. He said he had tossed and turned most of the night, until around three o clock in the morning, when the Lord shook his shoulder and woke him up! God said, "Son. I want you to get up, get dressed, and go over to that Court House. Walk around it seven times, praying in tongues. And then, praise Me, and come on back and go to bed." Tears of thanksgiving streamed down my face, "Thank You for David hearing Your voice, Papa."

He said he sat straight up in his bed, rubbed his sleepy eyes, and turned his light on. When he looked at the clock, it said three a. m. He scratched his head, and looked all around the room, thinking he was only dreaming. He turned off the light and laid back down on his pillow. The Lord shook David's shoulder, a little harder, and He firmly repeated the message to David the second time. David laughed when he said, "Mom. God's voice was so loud and clear, I thought it was my commanding officer waking me up to go to court today." The second time the Lord spoke to him, it was really loud! The Lord shook his shoulder extra firm! David got up, got dressed, and obeyed God. He said it was really dark outside, and it was drizzling rain. He knew if he got caught they would put him in jail right then, for breaking curfew! David said he was so scared. His teeth were chattering really hard! Afterwards, he praised the Lord, and came back to his room, just like the Lord told him . He changed, out of his wet clothes, and went on back to bed. David said he slept sound the rest of the night. He hadn't slept that peacefully since he had left home. David asked, "Mom, are you sitting down?" I quickly grabbed a chair at the kitchen table, and said, "All right son, I'm sitting down!" He said. When he got up that morning, he looked outside his window at the Court House. The skies were still full of dark scattered rain clouds, but the sun was shining behind and between them. He looked up and saw a huge double rainbow stretched out, directly over the Court House! I yelled, "SWEET JESUS, I LOVE YOU!" I knew my neighbors heard me, but I didn't care. I was absolutely sure God was speaking to us through that rainbow. David confirmed my suspicions when he said, "Mom, I ran and grabbed my camera and took two pictures for you of the double rainbow! I will send them to you as soon as I get them developed. Ok. I told you about the double rainbows. Now, I'll tell you why I believe God put them there. When I got inside the court room, the judge pounded the gavel down, and then everything got quiet. The judge looked over at me. He said, 'Son, all I can say is, apparently someone has been praying for you. Evidence has been found, which we thought was lost six months ago, and it's in your favor.' "Mom, the judge brought my sentence down from ninety-one years, to ten!" I jumped up and yelled, "PRAISE GOD! OH, PRAISE GOD FOREVER!" David agreed, God is so awesome!

I was so happy! I kept praising God! I thanked Him, again and again for revealing and exposing all the hidden evidence. He promised it in His word. Hallelujah! I later told Sandy, "I don't know which one makes me happier, David hearing God's voice and obeying Him, or God bringing his sentence down from ninety-one years, to ten? I think I'm equally happy about them both. Glory to God!" Sandy was somewhat shaken, too, when I told her the only sad news, "David called me from inside the prison. As of today, he is incarcerated." The thought of my son being locked behind prison bars, made me feel very sad. I was really thankful he was on minimum security. He shared the whole prison with only twenty seven other inmates. He was allowed to leave the prison and go and play racket ball. He was also allowed to go and play other sports activities outside the prison grounds, but had to be back inside the prison before the eight o' clock curfew. I was thankful God gave David a lesser sentence. I thanked Sandy and all of our friends, and my family and Joe's too, for praying for us.

My youngest son, Joey, and his girlfriend Diane, broke up when he found out she had run off with her boss. He was a married man. Diane ended up getting pregnant. Joey moped around the house and sat in his room a lot. He was depressed and hurt. It wasn't long before he met a pretty red haired, brown eyed girl named Shelly. They started going steady. I was happy to see Joey laughing again. He was finally getting out of the house and having fun. A particular scripture kept coming across my mind, and I was puzzled, "Be ye wise as serpents, and gentle as doves." (Matthew 10:16) At first, everything was going along fine, until suddenly Joey's personality began to change drastically! His normal easy going, pleasant personality, switched. He became angry and he had developed abnormal mood swings, and terrible temper tantrums! I kept asking the Lord, to teach me how to pray for Joey! I needed Him to reveal to me whatever was wrong with him. This was so unlike Joey's good nature. He'd always treated me with love and respect, but he wouldn't even hug me, whenever he left or came home. Since he was a little boy, he'd always openly shown me affection. He wouldn't let me or Joe touch him now. He also stopped associating with all of his buddies that he grew up with. I prayed in the spirit constantly. I held up my shield of faith.

He walked in the house one day and rudely announced he was sick and tired of living with us! He wanted his own place! So, he moved into an old rundown, rat infested farmhouse with all his new friends, a bunch of strangers. Things got so bad. I couldn't even talk to him without getting into a terrible, shouting, and sometimes screaming argument! He worked hard every day. He got paid good wages, but his bill collectors were angrily calling me! They wanted their money. One morning, I'd had just about all I could take. So, I called Sandy and asked her to help me pray for Joey. She and I prayed nearly every morning together, but that day we prayed only for Joey. She and I placed ourselves in the hands of the dear, precious Holy Spirit. We asked Him to help us pray this thing through, until a breakthrough came for Joey. We also asked God to give us wisdom and understanding. As soon as we started to pray, the precious Holy Spirit showed me a vision of an ocean filled with dark, thick, muddy, looking water. It looked like black oil. The sky above it was really spooky, too. It was filled with heavy black clouds. Sitting on this dark scary ocean, was an old wooden boat with a green two- headed monster in it. The ugly green two- headed monster resembled something out of a horror movie. I thought, "This must be the outskirts of hell!"

I knew the two- headed, horridly ugly green monster was a

female, because she had all her green, ugly babies with her in the old boat. She'd roar, and then she'd let out another loud blood curdling, triumphant scream! She did this each time she threw back one of her ugly, green heads and long, green necks. Her long, red tongue kept slithering in and out of her mouth, between her jagged sharp teeth, like a snake. The vision shifted. Suddenly, I saw my son, Joey! He popped straight up out of the black, thick, murky waters. His scream sent chills up and down my spine, "JESUS! PLEASE, HELP, ME, JESUS!" The ugly green, two-headed monster threw back one of her long neck and heads. She let out another bone-chilling screeching scream! Using her second long neck like a whip, she threw her head forward and slammed it down, right on top of Joey! She did this several times!

She kept biting him! Her jagged, razor- sharp teeth kept tearing at his flesh! She kept knocking Joey back down under the black muddy waters, and every time he popped up screaming, "JESUS! PLEASE HELP ME, DEAR SWEET JESUS?" We kept on praying fervently in tongues. I watched her feed her ugly babies in the boat, all around her with my son, Joey's, flesh and blood. Every time Joey popped back up out of the dark murky waters with his arms raised towards heaven, he'd scream, "JESUS! PLEASE HELP ME, DEAR JESUS!" I couldn't bare to hear Joey scream like that! However, I hung onto the Holy Spirit and prayed.

Sandy and I continued to pray aggressively in the spirit, until I watched the old boat push backwards and overturn in the dark, muddy ocean. The two- headed ugly, green monster yanked her long necks and heads back and forth violently! She screamed and roared as she drowned in the dark waters! Her ugly, green babies all drowned with her when the old boat capsized! "Hallelujah!" Sandy and I stopped praying, and started praising God! We knew for certain we had prayed through to victory, because we both had peace. After I finished telling her about the vision the dear precious Holy Spirit showed me, she explained. She heard the Lord say "Drugs, and lies." Also the Lord showed Sandy a coke bottle, washed up on a beach. Since she wasn't familiar with what cocaine looked like, God gave her something she could relate to.

There wasn't a doubt in our minds what the two- headed monster, who was trying to kill Joey, represented. Lies and drugs. I was still sitting at my kitchen table talking to Sandy when I looked up and saw Joey's truck pulling into the driveway. When I told Sandy Joey was home she quickly said, "Oh Carol, I wouldn't miss this praise report for anything! I'm on my way! Bye!" Joey came running up our porch steps, and through the door, smiling. He grabbed me and hugged me! He even kissed me on the cheek the way he used to! He was so happy! He was laughing, when he said, "Hey mom! Do I ever have some good news to tell you? I had to come home from work and tell you I've just been set free from cocaine!" Sandy came rushing through the kitchen door just as Joey was tearfully explaining about God's supernatural intervention! We were all laughing and crying at the same time. Joey said he was standing on a scaffold about three stories high. He was putting new windows in one of the new homes they were building for his boss, even though Joey was afraid of heights. He said he couldn't take it anymore, so he let go of the ropes that secured him. He raised his arms towards heaven and cried out, "JESUS PLEASE HELP ME? PLEASE HELP ME, DEAR JESUS! HELP ME TO GET OFF THESE DRUGS, PLEASE JESUS! AND DEAR JESUS HELP ME TO QUIT LYING TO MY MOM AND DAD? OR ELSE, LET ME FALL OFF THIS SCAFFOLD AND DIE!" "God had mercy on you son."

Joey was so excited! He could hardly talk without crying. He said, "God set me completely free, that instant! I know, beyond a shadow of a doubt. I'll never touch drugs again!" I kept repeating, "Thank You so much dear Lord, Jesus!" I told Joey about the vision the Lord gave me. Sandy told him about the empty coke bottle washed up on a sandy beach. She told him God spoke to her, and said, "Lies and drugs." The only sad part was, Joey told us his two older Aunts got him on the drugs, along with his other young cousins. I knew our work in prayer and intercession was not over, until they were delivered, too. God helped them and gave them every opportunity to quit the drugs. Joe's older sister Jill was injecting liquid cocaine into her veins. Her heart nearly exploded.

One day the police caught up with her. God intervened. Reverend Frank lead her in the sinners prayer, right there in the jail! "Papa God, I praise You for Your unconditional love and tender mercy."

Finally, our day in court had arrived. We were actually on our way to the Court House to get grandparents' rights to see our little Rebecca. "Praise God!" Sandy and Ron went with us, to give us moral support. We were so grateful for their help. Our lawyer forewarned us, "Carrie might make up a lie against one, or both of you. She doesn't want you to get visitation rights to see Rebecca. So, be prepared, ok?" We were all shocked when Carrie boldly walked into the Court House. She was showing plainly to be about seven or eight-month's pregnant. We knew the baby couldn't be David's, even though she was still married to him. My heart was sad when I recognized Carrie and Janet's angry expressions were directed mainly toward me in that courtroom. They were staring daggers through me. My Lawyer was right. Carrie lied against me. But I still wasn't prepared for what happened. Carrie's lawyer stood up in front of the judge. He told the judge, and everyone else in that room, I was crazy. Her lawyer said I was supposedly taking all kinds of pills for a manic depressant disorder. He said I was suicidal, and very dangerous. He even told the judge I could possibly harm Rebecca! I couldn't believe my ears as I listened to Carrie's lawyer try and convince the judge with the lie that I was, more or less, crazy or insane!

My heart was breaking and I was so angry, I wanted to scream, "Judge, Carrie is lying! She's the one who put the rubber worms in Rebecca's pretty, red hair! She ripped the worms out of Rebecca's sore, tender little head, until her own baby cried and nearly passed out from all of the pain and terror! She and Janet are the ones who leave Rebecca alone with only a dog to babysit her!" I had to sit there instead, and listen to all the lies they were telling about me. We were warned beforehand, by our lawyer. We were not to say anything. We were told to allow him only to do our talking for us. Our lawyer glanced at Joe, then he looked back at me. He leaned forward and whispered, "Is any of this true?" Joe was angry, too, but we tried to remain calm. God gave me grace. Joe explained everything to our lawyer. I couldn't understand why Carrie tried to use some of what happened to me more than twenty years before, against me? She twisted the truth to suit her case.

I was never violent, nor was I a manic depressant. She knew I'd been abused as a child. All that other stuff had happened to me, way back in my early twenties. Thank God. I wasn't on any medication. Carrie and Janet both knew me. They knew I was never diagnosed as crazy, violent, or insane. I'd never try and hurt little Rebecca. So, why did she lie? After Joe explained everything to our lawyer, our lawyer explained it all to the judge. The judge granted us visitation rights every other weekend. "Hallelujah!" I came out of that courtroom relieved. Although, I was angry and hurt, because of the lies and injustice Carrie tried to bring against me. I was so agitated with Carrie and Janet, but I had to forgive.

I asked Sandy, "Can you believe the lies Carrie tried to make the judge believe about me? She tried to keep us from being allowed to see our own little granddaughter! Why Sandy? What have I ever done to her?" She hugged me and said, "Well, Carol, you just rejoice! Remember, 'Blessed are they that are persecuted for righteousness sake for theirs is the kingdom of heaven.' "So, rejoice, my friend! God knows the truth, therefore, you are blessed!" (Matthew 5:10) I looked at her and started laughing! We agreed that was all that really mattered. We finally had the chance to watch our little granddaughter grow up. More than anything else, David could talk to his little girl when he called! We all went out to lunch and celebrated! "Thank You for giving us the victory, Papa! Please forgive my anger Lord, I forgive them." Rebecca looked so happy riding her new bike we bought her. Joey loved Rebecca dearly, too. We were all so thankful we could see Rebecca often and know that she's all right. No more begging. "Thank You, wonderful Jesus!" "Blessed are the poor in spirit, for theirs is the kingdom of heaven." (Matthew 5:3)

Around three o' clock in the morning I had a really disturbing dream! Sandy was pounding on my back kitchen door! She was yelling, "Carol! Carol, are you in there? Oh, Carol, please hurry up and open this door! I need your help!" In the dream, Sandy's desperate cries for help were so real! I threw the covers off me, and ran into the kitchen as fast as I could! Hurriedly, I unlocked the door, and flung it open wide! I ran outside on the porch looking for Sandy, tipped-toeing in my bare feet, until I went all the way around to the other side of my porch, whispering, "Sandy? Sandy, where are you?" The night air was so chilly. It brought me fully awake. Suddenly, I realized it was just a dream. Here I was, standing outside in the darkness, in the middle of the night, in my night gown. "Sweet Jesus!" As my brother Gene used to say, "Feet don't fail me now!" I ran like a sprinter in a race around the side of the porch to get inside, and I slammed and locked the kitchen door behind me! I stood there shivering and breathing hard while I leaned my back against the kitchen door. My clock on the kitchen wall said it was three o-clock in the morning. I said, "All right, Lord. I know You woke me up with the dream for a purpose. What's wrong with Sandy, or her family?" He answered me with three simple words, "Come up hither." I knew He meant pray, and pray now! I said, "Oh, dear Lord, it must be urgent!"

I went into my living room, and lay on my face before God. I asked the dear, precious Holy Spirit to help me pray for Sandy and her family. I pled the blood of Jesus, in the name of Jesus, over Sandy's daughters and everything else around them, including the air they breathe. I laid there on the floor praying for them the rest of the night. I didn't stop until the alarm went off at six thirty the next morning to wake Joe up for work. I didn't feel the least bit tired, but felt refreshed, and happy. I fixed Joey and his dad's breakfast, and I packed their lunch without feeling the least bit sleepy. I kept remembering when Sandy told me she'd been sensing something evil hanging around her two daughters, Betsy and Jenny. She'd also told me the girls had been getting angry with each other for no reason at all. They were even calling each other terrible names. Sandy said in the past they sometimes had a slight argument like all close sisters or brothers do, but they always made up quickly. This unruly behavior, however, wasn't like Betsy and Jenny at all. Something was definitely wrong! I didn't get to talk to Sandy, until she called me, two days later. When I told her about my dream a couple of nights before, she said, "Carol, what you dreamed, really did happen! I came over to your house last night, the night after you had the dream. I frantically banged on your door, just exactly like I did in your dream! When you didn't answer, I turned your door knob and when I saw it wasn't locked I came on in. I walked all through the house, calling your name! I thought maybe you were downstairs doing laundry, so I went down there, too. I finally I realized you were gone. So, I left." Joe and I'd gone to his mom's that evening. We left the house unlocked for Joey. Sandy explained, she knew God gave me the dream, because Betsy and Jenny were in grave trouble when I woke up from the dream and prayed for them at three o-clock in the morning that same exact night. "Sweet Jesus!"

The girls confessed. For the past several months, they had been playing with a evil board game, with a few of their friends. They had opened themselves up to all kinds of demonic activity. The girls told Sandy. They thought it was fun at first. They also thought it was just an innocent game. They didn't realize how dangerous it was, until some of their friends were badly hurt in terrible car accidents! Some were even killed! While I was laying on my face praying at three o' clock that morning, the Lord woke up a spirit- filled prayer warrior, who was a bible believing, devil stomping, Christian woman! He directed her to the house where the girls were staying. The Lord told her to go and rescue them. She obeyed God. She got Betsy, Jenny and all of the girls out safely. Betsy and Jenny cried and told Sandy everything when the nice, Christian lady took them home. The girls immediately repented and denounced the works of Satan off their lives, in Jesus name, and by the blood of Jesus. They all repented of ever playing with the evil game board. "Praise God!" "Who the Son sets free is free indeed." (John 8:36) I was thankful to God when Sandy said, "Oh Carol, I'd hate to think of what might have happened to my girls, if God had not awakened you to pray for them, that awful night?" We agreed, God will never fail to keep

His promises, "The seed of the righteous shall be delivered." (Psalm 11:21) "O, Lord, how merciful You are to all of us!"

I was so grateful when my friend Dixie told me the Lord had commissioned her to wake up every morning a four o'clock, to pray for David. Dixie can not possibly know the heavy weight she lifted off of my shoulders that day. I couldn't thank God, or Dixie enough, for her obedience, and Him for asking her to pray for David. That was such an unselfish act of love. I told her. She's a precious gift from God, Himself. One morning, Dixie called and told me her husband Jim requested prayer for David. Jim attended the Full Gospel Business Men's Association meetings. A prophecy was given from one of the other men in the prayer group concerning David that day. Jim told Dixie this man prophesied David was going to be moved from the prison in England to a much larger, overcrowded military prison, here in the United States. David was being sent there right away, on a mission for the Lord. I cannot explain how I felt. I knew I had to trust God.

Even though the prison Jim mentioned was in the United States, and much closer to us. I was so afraid for David! This was the first time he'd ever been in real trouble with the law in his life. I'd heard horror stories about these larger, more over crowded prisons. So, I had good reason to be afraid for him. As soon as I hung up the phone, I fell on my face, and I cried out to God! I prayed for God's protection over David. I knew in my heart this was a very special mission, and it was between God and David. I felt in my heart I couldn't question the Lord about this special mission, or ask Him to alter it. I also knew I shouldn't ask the Lord how long this would take David, either. About a week later, David called to tell me. The commandant of the prison had just announced, the prison there in England needed desperate repairs. So, they were sending him and all the rest of the inmates, immediately, to the much larger, overcrowded prisons here in the United States. It was exactly what the man, who'd never met David, prophesied would happen to him. I settled it in my heart. David was going on a mission in the larger, over crowded prison for the Lord, so He would protect my son. I told David about the prophecy, to try and comfort him. I knew he was terrified, so I said, "Son, I know God would not send you on a mission for Him, and not take care of you."I needed to hear myself say that. I wrote David every day, to encourage him. He wrote me back everyday, too. Sometimes I felt overwhelmed. I'd just say, "Oh Lord, please, help me! What can I say to David to encourage him today?" The precious Holy Spirit always gave me the words and scriptures to help my son. I told him constantly to trust the Lord with his life. I kept saying, "Son, have faith in God. He will give you the grace to go through this." I pressed into Jesus harder than ever before.

I couldn't even imagine what it was like for him in that awful place. I prayed, and I asked God, "Lord, please send David the biggest, and the strongest friend You can find for him in that prison, in the name of Jesus?" No wonder we sing, "God, You are more than wonderful, You are more than marvelous, You are more than amazing." God sent him Jason. He was six foot three. Jason weighed more than two hundred and seventy pounds of solid, screaming, muscle. Jason is African American, and a black belt in karate. All the other inmates knew Jason as a cold- blooded murderer. The other inmates didn't know David told him about Jesus. He became David's born again, Christian friend, who no one wanted to mess with. "Hallelujah!" I agreed with the word of God for David. (Ephesians 6:10) "Be strong in the Lord and the power of His might." I kept saying, with all of my heart, "Thank You so much, my very own wonderful Papa, who cannot lie. I love You, dear Papa! I love You, dear Lord, Jesus! I love You, dear precious Holy Spirit! Thank You so much Lord for taking care of my son David, and all of us." I kept thanking God for His word in Psalm 91, "No evil shall come near me or my family, especially my son David, and neither shall any plague come near us. A thousand shall fall at our sides, and ten thousand at our right hand but it shall not come near us." "Precious Jesus, because You live, I can face tomorrow. Because You live, Jesus, I can confess at all times, it is well with my soul." Jesus is Lord over my life, and He is Lord over my family's lives, too. "Praise God forever!"

Chapter Four

The author and finisher

I was standing in front of my bathroom mirror one day, combing my hair, when all of a sudden I saw a vision of David, and Sandy's oldest daughter Betsy, getting married. They looked happy, and so much in love as they said their vows in front of the preacher. Betsy was wearing a beautiful white wedding gown. Her veil had tiny, white beads of pearl and baby's breath, which cascaded down the left side of her pretty cheek. The love between her and David was so strong. It nearly overwhelmed me! My eyes filled with tears. In the vision, they stood there staring lovingly into each others eyes. I thought, "This kind of love is ordained by God, Himself." The Lord was joining David and Betsy together, forever, with the strongest love there is, His Agape love. "What God has joined together, let no man put it asunder." (Matthew 19:6) I was so happy I could hardly stand it. I just kept laughing!

I practically sat by the phone all day, until David called. When I told him about the beautiful vision God gave me for him and Betsy, he received it gladly! He knew the word, and he also knew, I'd never tell him a lie. "Receive a prophet and receive a prophet's reward." (Matthew 10:41) In the natural, looking at it with our finite minds, we could never see how this could possibly happen. After all, David was still married to Carrie, and tormented by his love for her. David and Betsy hardly knew each other, but he believed and trusted God had spoken to me, through the vision. When I called Sandy and told her about the vision, she and I started laughing and discussing how beautiful, and anointed our grandchildren will be, and how great it will be to share them! "Hallelujah!" We knew, Carrie had already moved in with her boyfriend Bobby, in a big townhouse apartment, and was about to give birth to his child. David called back, bright and early the next morning, and said, "Mom, I prayed before I went to sleep last night. I asked God, 'If the vision my mother had of Betsy and myself, is really from You, then please take Carrie out of my heart, and all the painful memories with her, and put Betsy in?' After I finished praying, I rolled over and went to sleep. When I woke up this morning, I couldn't even remember what Carrie looked like. This is so wild! I can hardly believe it myself, but it's true, mom! He did it overnight while I slept! Now, all I can think of, is Betsy. I'm calling Carrie, today, and telling her I'm going to give her the divorce she wants." I kept saying, "Wow, David!"

The care of David learning about Carrie and Bobby, was gone. I said, over and over again all day, "Wow! Jesus, thank You for healing David's broken heart." Sandy came right over after I called her and said, "The Holy Ghost did surgery on David while he slept last night! He healed him so completely, he can't even think about Carrie. All he can think of now, is Betsy!" We danced and praised God for a long time, "What a Mighty God we serve! What a Mighty God we serve! Angels bow before Him, heaven and earth adore Him, what a Mighty God we serve!" "With God all things are possible." (Luke 1:37) "Lord, You are so awesome!"

I remember one night I'd stayed up late, long after Joe and Joey had gone to bed, so I could sit quietly and enjoy looking through a catalog in peace and quiet, without any interruptions. All of a sudden, the Lord gently shook my right shoulder, and said, "Carol, go to now, and comfort thine husband, for he has great need of thy comfort." I argued, "Lord, this can't be You, because You know how angry Joe gets, if I wake him up? Just recently, Joe was furious and cursed me out, before I could get into bed, only because the ice clanged against my glass when I sat it on the nightstand! No, Lord, I'm sure this isn't You." I no sooner went back to flipping casually through my catalog when the Lord shook my shoulder really hard, and said, LOUD and firm, "CAROL, GO TO NOW, AND COMFORT THINE HUSBAND, FOR HE HAS GREAT NEED OF THY COMFORT!" I thought, "Just do it!"

Suddenly, I knew it was the Lord, and I was sure He meant business! I leaped out of Joe's recliner, barely using the handle to pull it down into a sitting position, and ran into the bedroom, as fast as I could! As soon as I laid down and snuggled up against Joe's back, he started yelling, and cursing at me for waking him up! Even though I was so afraid of his anger, I took a chance, and told him what the Lord had just said to me! I was shocked, when I realized Joe was crying! His shoulders shook so hard. The entire bed was vibrating! I knew it was especially difficult for Joe to cry, and show his true emotions. He let go of his macho Italian image, and was just himself. For the first time ever, Joe laid in my arms and cried like a baby. For over an hour, he poured out his heart to me, asking, "Carol, why did all these terrible things have to happen to our sons, and little Rebecca?" He cried and talked, until he fell asleep, in my arms, exhausted. I think Joe would have exploded, if I had not obeyed the Lord. I'm so thankful, God loved Joe enough to keep trying until He finally got my attention, and I'm thankful He wanted Joe to let go of that hurt, instead of holding it all inside. I said, "I praise You, my very own wonderful Papa! I praise You, my blessed Lord Jesus! And I praise You, dear, precious, sweet Holy Spirit! I love You so much, Lord."

One afternoon, Sandy and I were standing in my living room, praying for David! We were pleading the blood of Jesus over him, and the prison, when all of a sudden, Sandy saw this horrible grotesque demon, controlling the main front prison gate! Seconds later, the Lord revealed Sandy's vision to me, also! Its long, greasy, dirty grey hair was all the same length. The demon tried to frighten us, he growled at us and beared his ugly, sharp jagged teeth! We saw the keys to the front gate of the prison, dangling from one of its long skinny fingers. The ugly demon had long, dirty fingernails which curled around and overlapped each other! That awful, evil spirit was so gruesome and nasty looking, wearing a long black hooded robe. Under the leading of the precious, Holy Spirit, Sandy and I started yelling, and in the name of Jesus we bound the enemy off the prison David was in, and commanded the evil spirit dominating that prison gate to give us those keys! We also commanded that thing to get off the premises, in the name of Jesus, and by the blood of Jesus! That ugly demon glared at us, growled at us again, and snarled its hairy upper lip! Its sharp jagged teeth resembled the fangs of a wild boar, or a mountain lion! It tried to make us afraid, but instead, when we yelled the all powerful name of Jesus, it turned into a whimpering, terrified, whiny, wimp, and flung those keys at us in submission! "Thank You, Jesus!" (Matthew 16:19) "And I will give you the keys to the kingdom of heaven, and whatever you bind on earth will be bound in heaven, and whatever you loose on earth will be loosed in heaven." Jesus is the Lion of the tribe of Judah. Sandy and I did what the word said, "Thank You Papa God that our names are written down in the Lamb's book of Life!" We know, all of heaven backs us up, when we speak the name of Jesus, and the blood of Jesus! Sandy praised God with me, because we knew that prison was a whole lot safer for David. I felt much safer, too, knowing Joe and I were going there to visit David in a few days.

Neither Joe, nor I, had ever been inside a prison or a jail before, so we were a little on edge. Thank God, the thirteen-hour trip, driving straight through, wasn't nearly as hard as we'd first thought, because we knew every mile was taking us closer to see our son. A couple of times when I got fearful, I'd hear God's word, "My grace is sufficient for you." (2 Corinthians 12:9) The Lord constantly reminded me, He was right there with us, watching over us, especially when I heard Joe yell just as we crossed the State Line, "Hey Carol, look at that big, colorful, double rainbow!" Immediately, I remembered the double rainbow which stretched across the Court House in England, right before God granted David that big miracle. My heart was encouraged. I kept thinking about David, and how much I loved him. I thought of all that we had gone through as a family, and I was so thankful we had our Papa God, Jesus, the precious Holy Spirit, the name and blood of Jesus, God's Word, and His holy angels on our side.

Finally, we checked into our motel room, tired, and exhausted from the long trip. Joe stretched out across the bed and fell asleep, immediately. I slept peacefully during the night, too. We could hardly wait to see David the next morning! After standing in a long line outside for over an hour, we finally inched our way inside the prison, only to wait another half hour before our names were called. We were than taken into another room, where we were given a locker for our things. We went through a metal detector. We were directed by the guards into another large room. After we stepped into each room, heavy metal doors with bars automatically slammed, really LOUD, and locked behind us! I felt myself starting to panic, and a strange, horrible fear gripped hold of me! I knew that kind of fear was demonic, and straight from the pits of hell! It was coming from inside the prison. I quickly spoke to the Lord from my heart, "Now Lord, I can't handle this fear! Papa, You knew this was going to happen to me a long time ago, so please, Papa, in the name of Your dear Son, Jesus, take this fear away from me, and hurry Lord! Please, please hurry, Jesus!"

Immediately, I felt something like a huge, soft powder puff of love, hit me from behind! I felt God's, agape love wash over me, and instantly, instead of the awful fear, God filled my heart with His perfect love for each and every one of those hardened criminals. I felt as if I was their mother, or something. It was all I could do to keep from embracing every last prisoner, including the guards, and telling them how very much Jesus loves them! I can't effectively describe the gratitude I felt in my heart toward God that day, for His miraculous transformation inside of me. All I know is, I was very thankful God took the fear out of me. Just as I turned to tell Joe what happened, I looked up and saw him hugging David. My mouth dropped open when David held out his huge muscular arms to hug me! In his life, he'd never been that big! I remembered him telling me, when he first found out he was in trouble, "Mom, if I'm going to prison, I'm going to work out every day before I get there. I'm going to get big and muscular, so no one will mess with me!" It was all I could do to hold back the tears, when I looked at the dark, sunken, yellowish, circles under David's big brown eyes. It was plain to see he'd suffered inwardly, much more than his dad or I could ever have imagined.

We were given four plastic chairs, as one of the guards led us out into the inner circle of at least three hundred prisoners, and their family's, before we found an opening. I sat down in the chair beside David. Joe sat directly across from us, in one of the two remaining chairs. We huddled together, trying to hear each other talk. At first, the noise made it impossible to hear each other talking! It was almost too overwhelmingly loud, with everyone talking to their families, and at the same time children were running around, playing, screaming and hollering, too! We were packed tightly in that overcrowded prison building, like a can of sardines! We were front to front, side to side, and back to back, but somehow, with God's help, I finally got used to it, and adjusted by drowning all the others out, and concentrating on just our conversations. I sat close to my son so I could be near him.

David cried a steady stream of silent tears, from the time we got there, until we left. I don't think he was even aware that he was crying. He hadn't seen any of us, his family, for such a long time, or felt a loving touch. I believe God was healing David through the release of those tears. I had sent David photographs of Betsy, and they were writing each other. He was impressed by her beauty, and I was so thankful he was falling more in love with her each day! Finally, we told him about Carrie's new boyfriend, Bobby, and everything that had happened to little Rebecca since he'd been away. We also told him why we kept it a secret, and he understood. I know it would have been much more difficult if the Lord had not healed David's broken heart and caused him to fall in love with Betsy. I kept thinking "My God is so merciful and kind to us. Because Jesus lives in us, all fear is gone."

I will never forget the look on Joe's face when David looked over at his dad and said, "Dad, I want to tell you something I read in the bible, in Luke 13:6-9. This is a story about a conversation between our heavenly Father, talking to His Son, Jesus. God, looks down on earth, and He sees a tree that's not bearing any fruit, so He tells Jesus, 'Let's cut it down.' But Jesus pleads with Him to give it one more year. Jesus said, 'I'll cultivate it and dig about it, put some fertilizer around it, and perhaps it will grow. Then if it doesn't grow, we'll cut it down, but please let me try, first?' Dad, I was like that tree. I wasn't bearing any fruit, so Jesus rescued me, and He gave me another chance. Listen dad. I said all that, to say this; You think you're a free man, just because you can walk out of this prison and I can't, but you aren't. If you don't have Jesus as your personal Lord and Savior, you're not free. I may be in this prison, and locked up with every kind of murderer, rapist, and thief, but I am still a free man, because Jesus has set me free from death, and hell." Joe blinked several times, and wiped the tears from his eyes. I never dreamed part of David's mission would involve being a perfect laborer for his own dad. Joe didn't say much to David, but I knew the Holy Spirit was convicting him.

Later that week, Sandy sat in my living room, and listened quietly while I cried and told her, "Sandy, I can honestly say, leaving David in that awful prison, was one of the single most difficult things I've ever done! I thought my heart would break saying goodby to him, and coming back home without him. I know the Lord will free him from that place when he completes His mission. Sandy, God is teaching me something through this, about Himself. For instance, there is absolutely nothing my sons could ever do that could make me stop loving them. I've learned more about God's unconditional love toward us, our children, and grandchildren, through His word, and my experiences with my own family. I realized when my own children got in trouble, I loved them more, not less, and God's love is billions of zillions times greater, than our love for our children!" (John 3:16) "For God so loved the world, He gave His only begotten Son, that whoever believes in Him should not perish but have everlasting life." When I told Sandy what David said to his dad about being a free man in that prison because of Jesus, she asked how Joe responded. I said, "He didn't say anything, but I'm believing he will one day soon say the sinners' prayer." She agreed.

Carrie's new boyfriend, Bobby, was an experienced meat cutter who worked at a well-known restaurant. Carrie worked there too, as a waitress. Sometimes when we'd pick Rebecca up or drop her off, I'd get this terrible uneasy feeling, if Bobby had his knives laying out on their kitchen table, sharpening them. From the very beginning, we'd had multiple problems with Bobby and Carrie. They convinced Rebecca her real daddy, David, was dead. Therefore, Rebecca was told, her last name was the same last name as Bobby's. They also told her Jesus was dead. God have mercy on them! I was furious when this happened, and contacted our lawyer who sent out letters to Carrie and Bobby, and put a stop to their lies, immediately. Thank God, with a little persuasion from the law, they had no choice, but to finally tell Rebecca the truth. Bobby had truly influenced and changed Carrie.

Several months had passed since we'd last seen David at the prison, and I missed my son. I knew he was on an important assignment for the Lord, so out of respect, I chose not to ask God, when he was coming home. However, the Lord knew my heart, and He honored my silence by giving me new hope. One evening while I was relaxing, I heard the Lord say, "0800 hours." I waited quietly for a while to see if the Lord was going to add anything else. He didn't, but I knew He was giving me a special word. I got so excited, I asked Joe what it meant. He told me to ask Sandy's husband, Ron, because it sounded like it was military. It just so happened we were going there for dinner that evening. I was given another piece to the puzzle, when Ron explained, "0800 hours means, 'eight o clock in the morning', military time." Sandy and I knew God was getting ready to do something good for David. We knew he'd be coming home soon. "Papa Your so wonderful!"

Rebecca wanted to go with us to the prison to see her daddy, but Carrie was being very stubborn. She was calling all the shots. Her answer was a defiant, "No!" Our lawyer agreed it would be good for David and Rebecca to see each other, but the final decision would be Carrie's. After spending a lot of time, doing spiritual warfare in prayer, I was convinced it was God's will for Rebecca to go with us to see her daddy. Finally, Carrie said she could go.

However, at the very last minute before we were to leave, Carrie changed her mind again, and said, no, firmly! Hot, angry tears streamed down my cheeks, as I made my way into the bathroom to pray again! I remember, I was aggravated, tired and anxious, and just as I knelt to pray beside the bathtub, the Lord spoke so LOUD, He shocked me, "STAND! YOU'VE DONE ALL, NOW STAND!" In one swift movement, I felt a gush of wind as He pulled me to my feet again! I knew, God was serious. I wasn't to pray about the situation again. With an excitement and new hope in my heart I began to praise and thank the Lord! "Sweet Jesus!"

I stood up, praising God, "Papa, I praise You! I believe Rebecca is going with us, in the name of Jesus, and I'm standing, according to Your word in, Ephesians 6:13! Also, When I am weak, then am I strong in Christ Jesus. Hallelujah!" (2 Corinthians 13:9) I could hear the phone ringing as I flung the bathroom door open! Carrie decided to let Rebecca go with us, and I praised the Lord for His supernatural intervention, once again! (Psalm 18:6-10) " . . . In my distress I called to the Lord; I cried to my God for help. From His temple He heard my voice my cry came before Him into His ears. The earth trembled and quaked, and the foundations of the mountains shook. They trembled because He was angry. Smoke rose from His nostrils; consuming fire came from His mouth, burning coals blazed out of it. He parted the heavens and came down. Dark clouds were under His feet. He mounted the cherubim and flew. He soared on the wings of the wind . . . "

David was as happy to see his little girl as she was to see him. Rebecca hadn't seen her daddy for at least a year and a half, and yet she picked him out of three hundred inmates coming through the doorway, and yelled, "There's my daddy!" She ran to him, and he scooped her up in his arms! It was glorious to see David and his little girl together again. After things settled down, I told David, God said, "0800 hours." After I told him what Ron said, I asked, "Son, what significance does 0800 hours have to you?" At first he looked puzzled and then, it dawned on him. 0800 hours is the only time they release their prisoners to go home! We all got so excited, because we knew David's mission for the Lord was almost over. God was telling us, David's coming home soon! David asked if God gave me a specific day or the month? I said,

"No son, but don't be discouraged. I believe the Lord wants you to be encouraged. Concentrate on your mission for the Lord, and before we know it, you'll be leaving here at 0800 hours."

We took Rebecca to a nice park, in between visits with David, and let her swing and slide all she wanted. We took her swimming in the pool at the motel, and we also took her shopping and bought her new clothes, and a few toys. She was such a good little girl, she never cried once the whole time we were there. We laughed so much that weekend, and had such a good time, it felt like we were on a vacation, instead of visiting in a prison. God's word taught me how to lean on, and trust in Jesus. "Perfect love casts out fear." (1 John 4:18) Rebecca was sound asleep in David's arms when he handed her to his dad. David leaned over to kiss her one last time before we left. It was as if God was speaking to all of us through David when he whispered, "Daddy loves you." I hugged David and said, "Who knows son, maybe today you will lead just the right person to Jesus, and he will carry the burning torch of God's love. Then His glory will shine over you and your work will be done here." He smiled, and patted me on the head when he said, "Mom, please keep praying I do His will, so it won't be much longer." I agreed. I was always happy to pray for him. We were sad to leave him there, but at least we had hope.

Early one Monday morning during our prayer meeting, I asked my friends to come into agreement with me. I needed a financial miracle, in the amount of fifteen hundred dollars to pay my bills, on a specific day. 'That day!' My friends prayed in agreement, that somehow the money would come, A.S.A.P. We sent out an S O S, to God, LOUD, and clear! He knew I was desperate, and we knew it is His will to prosper us. We prayed in agreement, according to God's word. When I waved goodbye to all my friends, as much as I believed God was going to help me, I never dreamed I'd be calling them back so quickly with such a wonderful praise report! Later that day I walked across the street to my mailbox. There were two letters inside the mailbox. On the envelopes upper left-hand corner of the first letter, the return address read, "Father in heaven, Streets of Glory, Heaven." When I opened it, tears burst from my eyes as I read the large, bold black letters, "Dear Carol, your Father says in, Isaiah 41:10, "FEAR THOU NOT FOR I AM WITH THEE, BE NOT AFRAID FOR I AM THY GOD, I WILL STRENGTHEN THEE, YEA, I WILL HELP THEE YEA, I WILL UPHOLD THEE WITH THE RIGHT HAND OF MY RIGHTEOUSNESS, saith the Lord." Typed underneath, "With love, Your Heavenly Father." I looked up to heaven and said in my heart, "Lord I don't know who You used to send me this letter, but I know it really came from You, Papa!" I cried tears of joy!

As I walked back across the street, I quickly tore open the other letter. There was a check inside for eleven hundred dolors! Wow! My faith was getting stronger by the minute! The phone was ringing, so I ran up the front steps and into the house! I cannot reveal who the person was on the phone, but they told me another check for seven hundred dolors was sent out to us the same day they mailed that one. I received it the next day! "Sweet Jesus, I thank You so much!" I paid every bill and had a couple hundred dolors extra to spend. God told the person who gave us the money, to give it freely. We both knew it was the Lord Himself who supplied the money anyway! God gave it to him to give to us. I was so grateful, I sang, "Oh ho, I've got a feeling everything's gonna be alright!" I couldn't talk without crying grateful tears when I called Sandy and the rest of our friends to give them the awesome praise report. They were overjoyed, to say the least! It shocked Joe when I told him about the money, too. He couldn't believe God answered my desperate prayers so quickly, and without ever having to pay the money back, no less. I also showed Joe the return address on the other envelope from my heavenly Father. He walked away mumbling, "Carol, this is TOO, far out! It's WAY over my head!" I smiled and said, "Can you believe it Joe? Jesus loves us!" I was finally seeing mega glimmers of hope. I laughed and sang and praised God light heartedly, "I love You, my very own Papa, my sweet Jesus, and my precious Holy Spirit!"

Even though David was on minimum security, he was forced to share the same building under one huge dome with all the other hardened criminals, who were called lifers. These inmates were very dangerous, and the terrible conditions with the overcrowding didn't make it any easier. David had never told me where his cell was located in the prison, but one day while I was praying in the spirit for him, the Lord took me there. In the vision, I saw several huge, bright white angels guiding me swiftly past the other inmates and guards, and up three flights of a winding black rot-iron staircase. I continued to watch as the angles lead me half way around an inner circle of cells, until we came to David's cell. He was sitting on the side of his bunk with his head in his hands, weeping. I sat down beside him on the bed, and put my arms around him to comfort him, and the angels did exactly the same. God's angels cuddled David and loved on him, too. I felt God's agape love strengthening David, and myself. The angels and I stayed there with David until he was refreshed and feeling better. I always checked the time as soon as the vision ended.

About an hour later, David called and told me he'd heard me call his name about an hour earlier, and he felt my presence there in his cell with him. He said it was so real. It was as if I were sitting right beside him on his bunk. He was shocked when I told him I was there, in spirit, and I knew where his cell was, because the angels took me there to comfort him. I told him the angels hugged him, and kissed his cheek when I did. He said that was precisely when he'd been feeling really depressed and hopeless, because the devil had him so full of guilt. He was tormenting him about the people he'd hurt, especially his little girl. The Holy Spirit set him completely free, instantly! This scripture took on a new meaning, "God is close to the broken hearted." (Psalm 34:18) Mine and David's faith was strengthened that day, when we realized God actually sends His angles to comfort us. David also said they finally gave him what he'd been asking for, a cell downstairs on the main floor. "I am my beloved's and my beloved is mine."Song of Solomon. 6:3 By faith, I receive God's mercy which is beyond comprehension, without the Holy Spirit's help.

Many times David told me it was a constant struggle just to keep his sanity. He explained how anyone in that prison was allowed freely to worship anything. Satan worshipers with 666 written on their foreheads, and all cult practices were welcomed. Jesus loves everyone of those prisoners and wants to break the chains of darkness off them. I couldn't even imagine how difficult it was for David in that awful place, but I believe he still told anyone who'd listen, about Jesus. He was given favor at the prison and they put him in charge of the night shift in the printing department. I liked stationary with wide lines, so he designed all different kinds of beautiful stationary with wide lines, and with scriptures at the top or bottom of each page. He even did some with the footprints of Jesus walking in the sand, which were so popular. Everyone I showed them to loved David's work. It had been eight months since my son had been incarcerated.

Finally, David was up for parole and the lifers knew it. They tormented him to try and make him angry so he'd fight with them, and knock himself out of his parole. David called one morning, angry and upset with a couple of the other inmates who had been steadily harassing him. He said he was under tremendous pressure from the lifers who resented him coming home so soon. So he allowed the enemy to steal his joy through them. I said, "Son, watch your confession of faith! Don't give into this trap of the devil, he's just using these men to try and keep you from getting your parole. David, please don't listen to his lies?" His frustration got the better of him, as he gave in to his anger. I tried to warn him again, not to let his temper go too far, but he was weary from the battle. He said, "Mom, I just can't take it in here anymore! I wish I could get into trouble, and they'd throw me in the hole! At least maybe I'd get some peace and quiet down there, so I can study my bible without all the noisy harassment!" Suddenly, he sounded really funny and said he had to get off the phone.

After I hung up the phone, and in the days that followed, I knew something was wrong. My wrists, waist, and ankles started to burn and hurt, like something was rubbing and pulling against them. I kept rubbing my wrists, waist and ankles constantly until they were red and irritated. I started feeling so depressed and awful, but somehow I knew it was David's depression not mine. I couldn't eat anything, either. I cried nearly all the time, and I didn't understand why. I felt an overwhelming need to intercede in prayer for David, constantly. I couldn't do anything but pray in tongues, and grown in my spirit. I began to suspect something was really wrong with David when several days passed and he didn't call. When the symptoms grew increasingly worse, Joe wanted to take me to the doctor. I told him, "Look Joe, I know this sounds crazy, but I know this suffering is not in my own physical body. I know this is spiritual, and I know it has everything to do with David and whatever it is he's going through. That's all I know, but I'm not sick, David is. I don't expect you to understand completely, just trust me, ok?" He shrugged his shoulders and walked away mumbling something underneath his breath again.

I confided in Sandy, and told her, I knew I was involved in one of the most intense spiritual battles I'd ever been in. Sandy comforted me by saying, "Carol, God will help you and David escape out of this trouble. The Lord will also reveal to you where David is, and why he hasn't called? God said in His word in, 1 Corinthians 10:13 "No temptation has overtaken you accept such as is common to man; but God is faithful, who will not allow you to be tempted beyond what you are able, but with the temptation will also make a way of escape, that you may be able to bear it."
I had red swollen eyes from a constant steady flow of tears. I couldn't stand anymore waiting so I called the prison and asked why David hadn't called me. The woman I spoke to at the prison assured me over the phone, David wasn't in any kind of trouble. She said he wasn't on their list, so that meant he wasn't in the hole, either. When I insisted something was wrong, because David hadn't called us for several days, and he especially called when his little daughter Rebecca was at our house for the weekend, she got really nasty with me and said, "Well honey, did you ever think that just maybe your little sonny-boy doesn't want to talk to you?"
Immediately, I went over her head and called the Washington

Parole Board office. I also called our Congressman and asked for his help again, too! They agreed to check up on David and find out what was going on, right away. I stood on God's promise, and quoted, "In the name of Jesus, and by the blood of Jesus Christ of Nazareth, it is written devil, "Everything covered MUST be uncovered, and everything hidden, MUST be revealed." I called Sandy at midnight, and asked her to pray with me. I apologized for calling her at such a late hour, but David weighed so heavily on my mind, I couldn't sleep. She told me to never apologize for needing prayer, no matter what time it was. She was always ready and willing to pray with me, at any hour, and she readily agreed with me, "In the name of Jesus my son, David, is coming out of trouble!" When we prayed in the spirit for David, I saw a vision of him sitting on the side of his bunk with his head buried in his hands, crying. As he lifted his hands in prayer, I saw that he had chains on his wrists, and as the vision shifted, I saw he was wearing connecting heavy chains around his waist and ankles, too.

I felt his deep sadness as if I were he, and I knew his thoughts as if they were my own. He was thinking of how much he missed talking to his little girl, and us. He wanted desperately to get out of that awful hole. He was so miserable! Horrible thoughts of hopelessness swept over his emotions continuously, like relentless waves in a stormy sea! His cry for help was the most gut wrenching, a helpless, hopeless cry I've ever heard! It was a cry that hurt way down deep inside. The torment inside David's heart and mind was almost unbearable. We prayed in agreement, and asked God to send His angles into David's cell to comfort him, and give him the peace that passes all understanding, in the name of Jesus. We also pled the blood of Jesus, in the name of Jesus, over David, his body, mind and spirit, and every crack and crevice of his cell, that hole, and everyone down in there with him. We never stopped praying until we finally felt God's peace.

When I told Sandy about David's chains, she could hardly believe it, either. However, we knew God wouldn't show us anything that wasn't true. She was as angry as I was when I said, "Sandy, how could this happen to David, in America?" Sandy

131

said, "We don't understand it Carol, but at least this explains why your wrists, waist and ankles were hurting." I told her, when I saw David in the vision he was wearing his favorite brown checked shirt, and jeans instead of his prison uniform. We believed God was telling us He's bringing David home soon, wearing his casual clothes. "Thank You, Jesus!" The following evening, when Sandy and I were standing in her kitchen discussing David wearing chains, our husbands overheard us, and they sharply disagreed. Ron said, it wasn't possible, because David wasn't sentenced for anything that harsh. Joe agreed with Ron. Things like that just don't happen in America. Sandy and I quietly agreed God will reveal everything that's hidden, and bring it to the light.

Sandy had forgotten to tell me, while we were praying for David the night before, I said the name Michael several times. She whispered, "Carol, I almost forgot to tell you what happened last night while we were praying for David! I interpreted, as you were praying in the spirit, and I heard you clearly say the name Michael, several times." We were excited because we knew God was giving me another hidden treasure. I thought about it a minute, and said, "Wait a minute Sandy! Isn't Michael, God's own archangel?" She ran and got her bible and looked it up in the concordance. Michael was indeed God's very own great archangel who protects the Jews. We both stared at each other, looking puzzled, and wondering why God brought that particular angel's name to my attention? We finally resolved, whatever the name 'Michael' meant, God would reveal it to me, in His timing.

David called right after we got home from Sandy and Ron's house that same night. He told us he'd been locked up in the hole for eleven days. The guards let him out of his cell, just long enough to make one phone call. When I asked him about the chains, I saw him wearing in the vision, he cried and told me, "Yes mom, it is exactly as God showed you. I am wearing chains on my wrists, and connecting chains around my waist and ankles. Pray that I'll get out of this hole soon, and go back upstairs! It's horrible down here!" Joe was shocked when David confirmed everything I'd been experiencing and feeling in the spirit realm was really happening to him, including the serious depression and loss of appetite. He told me when they slid his food tray under his cell door three times a day, he'd open his bible and read, 1 Corinthians 11:24 "Take eat, this is My body that was broken for you." David said. He'd only been taking a pinch of his bread, and some water, as he read the scriptures and took the sacrament, and he'd been doing it, three times a day, for eleven straight days. He said. He was too sick to eat or drink anything else. David also told me, the guards and the Commandant seemed somewhat concerned, that he wasn't eating. I reminded him, that there were many strong prayer warriors praying for him, night and day, including myself. "Wonderful Jesus, I know You will help us!"

When Joe came home from work the following evening, he was excited as usual about going on a weekend trip to our cabin. Most Friday nights, Joe was always in a hurry to pack the car and leave as soon as he got home from work. However, I was relieved when he told me he wanted to go in the back yard and set the sights in on his new bow correctly before we left. He said, "Carol, I know you haven't been getting much rest lately because of David, so put your feet up and relax a while." I quickly took his advice and leaned back in the recliner and closed my eyes. David was on my mind, but I felt so exhausted I couldn't keep my eyes open. All of a sudden, I automatically started praying in tongues, aggressively! While the Holy Spirit prayed through me, a strong, swift, powerful spirit of prayer engulfed me, propelling me to pray for David! I don't think I can ever remember praying in tongues so hard.

While I was praying, I saw a vision of David, his friend Jason, and a few other men climbing up some black rot iron stairs which resembled fire escape stairs. It was difficult for David and the others to climb the stairs because they were still shackled in chains, on their ankles, waist, and wrists. David and the other inmates with him were also balancing a stack of books, leaning against their chests. There was a huge, bright, white glowing angel leading David and the other men up the stairs. When the vision shifted upward to the next floor, I saw a guard kneeling down and turning a huge handle which opened up a round metal door. The

133

round door resembled a submarine door, or an old cellar door that opens up from the floor. The guard pulled up hard on the door and opened it, and David and the others walked straight up and out of the lower level, the hole. The guards moved David and the other men over beside an elevator. The elevator doors opened and two guards got off the elevator wheeling a big silver metal cart of food trays, exactly like the carts used for food trays in hospitals. I was so amazed as I watched the vision unfold before my eyes.

Suddenly, I heard David's thoughts when he prayed under his breath and asked God, not to let him pass out, because he felt so weak. The huge, bright, white glowing angel reappeared. He was so big and tall. He had to bend way over in order to stay inside the same room with them. He was much brighter than a florescent light and he vibrated with pure, intense energy. At first I thought he was Jesus, but I couldn't see any nail scares in his hands, so I realized he was an angel sent from God. When David began to weave back and forth like he was going to faint, the angel reached down and picked him up in his huge, glowing, right hand. The angel cupped his left hand behind his right hand, and began to massage David with his huge, glowing, gentle thumbs, starting at the top of David's head and working his way down to his feet, and from his feet to his head again. David's limp body fit perfectly in the palm of the angel's hand. The angel completed the whole process three times, until he had massaged life back into David. God's love for us is so much greater than what we can imagine.

The angel tenderly brought David up closer to him, and then he blew his breath over him, starting at the top of David's head, and on down to the soles of his feet, and he worked his way back up again, three times. It must have been fresh, clean air from heaven itself, because David wasn't nearly as frail looking as he was a few minutes earlier. The angel held David, as a mother comforts her child. He cuddled him up under his bright glowing neck, while rocking him back and forth and patting him. "As a mother comforts her child, so will I comfort you." (Isaiah 66:10) I watched as the huge, bright, glowing angel cuddled David against his cheek, whispered something in his ear, and sat David back down beside the other inmates standing next to the elevator doors. I couldn't hear what the angel whispered to David, but I was sure it was wonderful, because of the broad grin on David's face. My son glowed with new health and energy, and kept on smiling, so I knew he was thinking happy thoughts. The big angel started moving around some of the other guards with his bright, glowing, right hand. He'd pull them up to him, and whisper something in their ear and then, put them back in their places again. It was incredible to watch. While I watched the vision, in my heart I kept thinking, "Oh Lord, thank You for loving my son, David."

The elevator doors opened and the guards moved David and the other inmates onto the elevator. The angel's work must have been finished because I didn't see him again. When the elevator doors opened, David and the other inmates with him were guided by the guards into a large room, where they removed their chains. David and the others were so happy to get their chains off! They were all laughing. Then, they were escorted by the guards back into the center dome. I saw someone's hand signing a bunch of papers, and than I saw David and the others again. They were all glad to be back upstairs, even with all the noisy, overcrowded, horrible conditions. The vision shifted to a close up of David and his friend Jason as they shook hands. I heard Jason say, "Well David, what are you going to do first?" David breathed a sigh of relief and answered, "Man, I thank God, we are finally out of that depressing hole, it makes this place actually look good! Ok, first, I'm going to check into the doctors office like they told us to, and then I'm going to eat all of whatever they will give me for dinner in the chow hall. After that, I'm going to take a nap, and then call my mom." Jason laughed and agreed he was going to do pretty much the same thing. The scripture took on a new meaning where Jesus said, "I was in prison and you visited Me." He loves the prisoner.

Again, the vision shifted to a long hallway with a wide opening at one end leading to the outside, and into a beautiful resilient sunset, with bright colors of orange, yellow, pinks and purples. Row after row of convicts wearing dark chocolate brown uniforms were walking toward the outside and into the gorgeous sunset. I could see David plainly as he stepped out of the line and walked over to a black phone on the prison wall. Once again the vision changed, and I saw a man sitting at his desk with his legs crossed. He was wearing a light tan khaki shirt and matching pants. As the vision shifted again, I was looking over his shoulder, and on his lap were a bunch of letters, and a picture of Rebecca. I was sure it was the parole package we sent to the Washington, D.C. Parole Board office. As suddenly as I went into that prayer, I came out of it and the whirlwind of prayer stopped. I looked at my watch, to check the length of time I'd been praying. It had been exactly, one hour. A couple of seconds later, Joe walked in the door, ready to go. Amazingly, I felt more rested and refreshed than if I'd slept soundly for that hour. I felt especially hopeful, and relieved about David getting out of that horrible hole. My heart was so full of love and gratitude to the Lord, "Thank You, wonderful Jesus!"

Normally, I wanted our weekend to last longer, but this time I could hardly wait to get home and ask Joey if David called while we were gone? When Joey answered, "No mom, David hasn't called all weekend." I was really puzzled about the vision God gave me Friday night, and the name of His very own archangel, Michael. I couldn't call Sandy and talk to her, because she and Ron were staying with relatives in Michigan, and they wouldn't be home until Tuesday. Ivy was the only one who came Monday morning for prayer group, and she was in such a hurry I didn't have time to tell her about the vision, or the name, Michael, either. She had rushed through the door saying, "Carol, I am so sorry I don't have time to fellowship with you this morning. They changed my work schedule this week, but I do have time to pray with you, for David. He's been on my mind this week, so strong." I hadn't talked to Ivy in more than two weeks. So, she knew nothing about David being in the hole, or wearing chains. Since she didn't have much time, we immediately started praying.

As soon as she and I finished praying in the spirit for David, Ivy was so excited she couldn't talk fast enough. She said she kept interpreting, as I prayed in tongues. I said the name, Michael, clearly several times. In the meantime, she said she saw a vision of a huge, great angel standing on a pinnacle in the heavens with his arms folded across his chest, as if he were awaiting his orders for something. Instantly, my eyes of understanding were opened, and I knew exactly what I was supposed to do! I grabbed Ivy's hand and asked her if she'd lock her arms of faith with mine, and agree with me? I said, "I'll explain everything to you, later." I pointed my right hand and arm out in front of me, and in the name of Jesus, I ask God to send Michael, His very own archangel, to go and complete the vision He had given me three days before, on Friday. I asked Michael to go and get David out of that hole, in the name of Jesus! Afterward, when I quickly told Ivy about David wearing chains, she could hardly believe it, either. I had perfect peace in my heart that day, knowing I had obeyed God. When David called me from the prison, he confirmed everything God showed me in the vision was exact, including the beautiful sunset. My arms, waist and ankles stopped burning as of David's release.

Tears silently rolled down my cheeks as David explained what he felt when the angel picked him up in front of the elevator. He said he felt as if warm oil was being poured all over him, but he never dreamed it was an angel massaging him. I cried because of the tenderness of God toward us, His children. I finally understood why God sovereignly moved and sent His own archangel, Michael, to deliver David. David had been studying about God's arch angels, Michael and Gabriel, in the bible. He made a strange vow to God, "Lord, if You'll send me an angel like Michael to deliver me from this horrible hole, I promise You, I'll name my first son Michael, if I ever have one." David said. He'd asked the guard that morning if his name was on the list to leave, but the guard shook his head no, and said, "I'm sorry, David, your name isn't on here, and I was sure it would be today." He said as soon as the guard walked away, he turned his face to the cell wall, like Hezekiah did in the bible, in, 2 Kings 20:2-5. David said he repeated three times, "I'm leaving this hole today, in the name of Jesus! I confess it with my mouth. I'm getting out of this hole today, in the name of Jesus!" The angel heard the name of Jesus.

David said all of a sudden that same guard came running back, yelling, "Well son, I don't know how I missed your name, but here it is, right here on the list. You are leaving this hole today, after all." I was amazed at the revelation knowledge God gave us both, to get him out of that hole. I told David, "Son, the word says, the angel's were sent here to work for the heirs of salvation." (Hebrews 1:14) David said. The doctor who examined him was baffled because of how healthy he was, even after being in that horrible pit for thirteen days, and not eating or drinking much of anything. He said 'Big Brass' was checking out the prison. Some of the top workers there were undergoing an intense investigation. I kept saying, "Wow!" These officials uncovered many problems that had been terribly wrong with that prison system for years. "Hallelujah!" David and I agreed, the mission he was on for the Lord involved more miraculous repercussions than we could ever dream. I danced and sang, "Now tell me, who's report are you gonna believe? I will believe the report of the Lord! Praise God!"

I'd always wanted a bigger house, and after all; we could well afford it. We sold our house, and in the same day we signed the contract and bought a newer, big, red brick home. One minute Joe and I were sitting at the kitchen table eating supper, and discussing moving into our new house, when all of a sudden Joe started cursing me! He jumped straight up from the table, turned his chair over on the floor, and slammed his food down in his plate; splattering it all over the table, me, the walls, and the windows! I didn't say a word. I got up quietly and went into the bathroom and shut the door behind me to pray. I bound the spirit of anger off Joe, in the name of Jesus! I pled the blood of Jesus over us, and I quoted, "It is written, "The husband has not power over his own body but the wife." (1 Corinthians 7:4) I was shocked when Joe came looking for me a few minutes later, and apologized. I cried and said, "Joe, you have really changed for the good, and I know it's because David's been talking to you about the Lord, lately. Please don't get mad at me, but I've just got to know, are you saved, Joe? I want so much for you to know Jesus." I prayed silently, "Lord, please help Joe, not be angry with me?"

When I looked over at him, I realized he was crying, too. He said, "Yes Carol, I have been listening to David, and I've been talking to the Lord. A couple of weeks ago at work, while everyone was gone out to lunch, I got down on my knees, there beside my desk, and I asked the Lord to forgive me." I was so happy, I bawled like a baby, and said, "Oh, no wonder the enemy tried to make you so angry again, Joe? Sweetheart, this has got to be one of the happiest days of my life!" "Thank You Jesus!"

A few weeks earlier, Joe's mother had gone to bed one night and glanced over at their clock radio we'd bought them for Christmas. Instead of the bright red letters reading the time like it always did, the bright red letters on the clock said, J-E-S-U-S! Joe's mother yelled for her husband! When he came running into the bedroom, he found her hiding underneath the covers. Her muffled cries from underneath the covers begged him to look at the clock on the night stand and tell her what it said. Joe's dad slowly read the bright, red letters, "J-E-S-U-S!" Without taking her head out from under the covers, she ordered him to do something! He threw his shirt over it! The next morning the doctor's office called to confirm a test Joe's dad was supposed to have done on his colon the following week. Joe's dad and mother went to church. They were saved and baptized that same week. The following week after they did the test they found cancer. The doctors successfully removed all the cancer. "Praise You Jesus! Glory to Your Name Lord!" That was such an unusual miracle. God answers prayer! "Wow!"

Joe started taking me to church every Sunday. Joe's whole family was going to church, too. I cried with tears of joy when Joe began to stand up every Sunday morning and testify about the things God had brought us through, and the wonderful victories He'd given us. We started practicing singing gospel songs with Joe's brother, Ed, and his dad, to sing on stage in church. Finally, instead of them playing old bar drinking songs, Joe and his family were playing their guitars, and other instruments, for the Lord. While we sang on stage at the church, I was so happy! I thought, "Lord, I am so very grateful to You, I can't possibly say thank You enough!" I went around the house singing, "I sing because I'm happy! I sing because I'm free! Papa, You make my heart sing!"

When I told Sandy what had happened to Joe, she grabbed me! She started laughing and crying, "Oh, Carol, my friend, I am so happy for you and Joe! God is such a good and wonderful God, isn't He!" I smiled and said, "Sandy, look at God's amazing grace." "The fervent effectual prayer of a righteous man (or women) avails much." (James 5: 1) She and I rejoiced together!

We usually went back to Joe's mother and dad's house for a cup of coffee and to fellowship after church. I remember one special Sunday when our Pastor, Reverend Frank, preached a sermon about stepping out in faith. Joe paced the floor at his mother's house, while talking to his dad and brother Ed about stepping out in faith, and starting their own machine shop. I was especially concerned, because we'd just bought a bigger house, and with Joe's present job, we could easily afford the large payments. The past several years, Joe worked at one of the best jobs he'd ever had. He made an excellent hourly wage, and benefits, a company car, and a free gas card. I felt uneasy about it, and I told Sandy, "I wish Joe had prayed about going into business with his dad and brother first, because I don't feel like it is God's right timing, yet." None of them had any money saved to fall back on, in case they ran into trouble. I prayed many times, "God have mercy on us!"

Joe was too excited about owning their own machine shop to listen to any advise or heed the warning signs. Joe, his brother Ed, and his dad started their own machine shop, and quit their regular, steady, good paying jobs. Sometimes, if it was a good work week, Joe brought home maybe half of what he had normally made each week. We no longer had the luxury of a company car, or a free gas card to help us, and there were NO more benefits. I did what I'd heard Gloria Copeland say she did, to break the habit of worry in her life. I quoted the scripture she used, "I roll all my works (cares) upon the Lord, commit and trust them wholly to Him. He will cause my thoughts to become agreeable to His will and so shall my plans be established and succeed." (Proverbs 16:3) Like Gloria Copeland, I quoted scripture to stop worrying, like an acholic stops drinking, one minute at a time, and it worked. Month after month, Sandy and I agreed in prayer, asking God to send Joe and his family work. We stood together on God's word in, Philippians 4:19, and the Lord heard our desperate cries for help! He was kind to us and sent Joe and his family work every time. Sometimes paying our bills came real close to the deadline, but each time, my God supplied all our need, according to His riches in glory by Christ Jesus. "Thank You Papa God, for Your mercy!"

(Psalm 68:13) "Though you have lain among the pots, yet shall you be like a dove with wings of silver and of golden dross." I was sitting cross- legged on the bathroom floor with old newspapers under me, cleaning the commode when I heard the Lord speak His words of comfort to me. I memorized them instantly, not knowing at the time they were scriptures, or where they were located in the bible. We were cleaning for a poor man whose house had been condemned. The house was so dirty the authorities were going to board it up, if he didn't find someone to clean it and quickly. All the cleaning companies turned him down, flat. Finally, he saw our C & S cleaning add in the paper and called us. He was so desperate, we felt sorry for him and said yes. This poor man's wife had left him and all he had to keep him company were several cats. Animal control came and took his cats away, too. The man was pitiful, depressed, and lonely, so we had to help him. In all the years Sandy and I had cleaned houses together, we'd never seen one in such horrible shape. Daily, we pled the blood of Jesus over us, and his whole house, including the air we breathed.

Sandy and I were scrubbing everything in the man's house with S O S, throw away cleaning pads. We had to wear face masks for extra protection to keep us from breathing the germs. I ran into the kitchen to tell Sandy what the Lord said to me. She started laughing at me! Suddenly, I realized how funny I sounded trying to talk to her through my face mask. Right in the middle of all that horrible mess, God gave us such joy! He spoke directly to us with words of encouragement about our situation. Here Sandy was, cleaning molded greasy pots and pans and dishes in the kitchen, and I, myself cleaning an old dirty toilet, which is also considered a pot. Believe me! There was nothing funny about the dirt and grime in that house we were cleaning or the long exhausting hours of hard work. Jesus, The Son of righteousness arose with healing in His wings and gave us His joy which is our strength. He caused us to laugh at ourselves, with pink soapy bubbles from the S O S cleaning pads, all over our bright yellow rubber gloves, masks and old clothes. "Thank You, sweet wonderful Jesus!" Later, I found Psalm 68:31 in the bible. I also found, (Jeremiah 29:11) "For I know the thoughts that I think toward you, says the Lord, thoughts of peace and not of evil, to give you a future and a hope."

I remember feeling really uneasy early one morning in our new house in the country. Joey and his dad had left for work about an hour before sunrise, and it was storming outside! I jumped as constant LOUD crashes of thunder, and bright, white streaks of lightning lit up the dark, eerie looking sky! All around the house, strong winds whipped through the great, big, and unusually tall pine trees, right outside our windows! I kept pacing the floor and whispering, "Sweet Jesus!" As I hurried around the kitchen, and tried to fix myself some breakfast, I started communicating with the Lord, silently from my heart, "Papa, in the name of Jesus, I think I'd like a dog to keep me company. I'd like a little dog because if I had a BIG one, I'd be more afraid of the dog, Lord. I'd like the little dog to be about a year old, and I'd like it to be already house broken. I don't want to house break another dog." Suddenly, I realized what I was saying, and I said out loud, "Oh; Never mind, dear Lord, I'm being way too picky. That's just too much to ask of You, Papa."

Before I could finish apologizing to the Lord, the phone started ringing. As soon as I said, "Hello?" Joe said, "Hey Carol, how would you like a dog?" I said, "Oh, ho, ho! You've got to be kidding me, Joe?" He said quickly, "Now, just wait a minute Carol! Don't answer until I'm finished talking, ok? Before you say no, just listen to me for a minute. They have to put this little dog to sleep tomorrow, if we don't take him. He's about a year old and he's already housebroken. They will neuter him for us, for free, if we want them too, that is, if you want him? My friend's daughter works for a veterinarian, and she is a Christian. She told me, she's been praying for him to find a good home for the past six weeks, so they won't have to put him to sleep. Someone dropped him off at their clinic, after they broke his left front leg and cut his hair in every crazy length imaginable. He's been abused, and he's a really humble, little dog. He only weighs about a pound and a half, so he won't eat much either. Honey, before you answer, please listen? He's a very expensive purebred Yorkshire Terrier, and he's worth about four hundred dolors. You don't want the little dog to die tomorrow, do you Carol?" I knew I'd love that little, abused dog.

I finally squealed, "Joe, are you kidding? Of course I want him!" Joe could hardly believe it when I told him I'd prayed and asked God specifically for a dog with most of those same qualifications, just seconds before he called. And when I told him I'd prayed without saying a word out loud, he was extremely shocked and amazed! Isaiah 65:24. "It shall come to pass; That before they call I will answer; and while they are still speaking, I will hear." Joe's friend's daughter, Regina, brought my little dog, who I named 'Jacob,' to my house that same afternoon. I told her I believed her prayers for Jacob prompted me to pray and ask God for a dog! I thanked God again and again for His goodness. He not only saved Jacob's life, He gave me a constant companion who never left my side, and He answered a young Christian girl's prayer, too. I laughed when I told Sandy, "The Lord even gave me an expensive dog, because He knew all of my neighbors have expensive dogs, too. Wow!" She and I anointed Jacob with oil and prayed for the Lord to heal his broken leg, and his abusive memories. (Psalm 37:4) "Delight yourself also in the Lord, And He shall give you the desires of your heart." She and I sang praise songs, "Oh how I love Jesus." "Oh, victory in Jesus!" I said, "Lord Jesus, I love You so!"

The holidays were drawing near again, and neither Joe nor I could stand to go through another year, without spending at least part of it with David. We discussed it with Joey and he was happy we were going to see David. We decided to spend Thanksgiving with Joey, and Christmas Eve and Christmas day with David at the prison. Joey was engaged to be married to Diane, his girlfriend. He spent most of his time with her, and one year old son, Tyler, and their pretty little two-month-old daughter, Megan. We knew the trip would be expensive, but Joey didn't mind us spending a little less on gifts that year because he understood how important it was for us to see David. I was grateful our grandchildren were still pretty small, including five year old Rebecca.

I was so excited! I could hardly wait to tell David the good news, but when I did, his reaction completely surprised me. He was almost angry when he said, "No mom, definitely not! I will not let my mother and dad spend Christmas Eve in a lonely motel room, or prison, and especially not on Christmas day! No way!" We argued back and forth for a while, but I finally won when I said, "Son, our hearts have broken without you here to share our Christmas with us. In the past two years we haven't had you with us for the holidays. Now I insist we are coming, and that's our firm decision! No matter what you say, you're not going to change our minds because we love you too much." The argument ended when David realized it didn't mean anything to us to stay home for Christmas in a cozy warm house with gifts to open under a tree, if we didn't have him to share it with. One of David's concerns had been the weather. A thirteen-hour trip, driving on the expressway, over wintery, slippery roads could be very dangerous, especially in consistent, blowing snow from the open fields. But, God gave us blue skies and puffy white clouds which reminded me of great white, feathered wings stretched out over us, all the way there. The Lord confirmed, He hears my prayers every morning. Psalm 91 We who dwell in the secret place of the Most High, shall abide under the shadow of the Almighty. He shall cover us with His feathers and under His wings we take refuge.

I was so glad to see they had painted the walls of the visitation area inside the prison with a clean, refreshing, cream color, and trimmed it in burgundy. Instead of the old dingy yellowed walls, everything was bright and cheerful. "Thank You Jesus!" "What

144

concerns us concerns God!" (Psalm 138:8) The inmates were also allowed to decorate a Christmas tree in the visitation area with unbreakable bright colored bulbs, and trimmings. We laughed and talked and even sang Christmas carols in a soft, low, whispering voice with David. Out of the corner of my eye, I noticed one of the solemn-faced, motionless guards crack a slight smile when I jokingly whispered, "Twas the night before Christmas" to David and Joe. We all laughed quietly together. "Thank You Jesus."

Thank God for His grace. Later, Joe and I didn't tell David, but we had to admit he was partly right. Going back to that empty motel room, without family or friends, and no decorated tree on Christmas eve, was absolutely one of the strangest experiences imaginable. It felt so odd to be far away from home, alone, and in a distant big city, too. I can't properly describe the feelings of emptiness. Just knowing our son was in prison, on Christmas Eve, seamed to magnify the wilderness we were in. Joe and I knew we were not alone in our suffering. In the restaurants where we ate, and also at our motel, we saw many familiar, sad faces of the other parents, wives and children whose sons, husbands, and fathers were in prison with David. "God have mercy on us all."

As we drove to the prison before sunrise, at five thirty-Christmas morning, I whispered, "Oh Lord, please help me? I agree with Your word. Indeed, my spirit is willing, but my flesh is so weak." (Matthew 26:41) It was freezing cold, and we couldn't even get a hot cup of coffee or breakfast, because everything was closed for the holiday. Normally, I was thankful when others didn't have to work on Christmas day, so I repented of feeling sorry for myself. Thank God, Joe's mother had given us some of her delicious homemade cookies before we left, we were so hungry we ate every last crumb. I shivered as we walked to the back of the extremely long line of people already waiting to go into the prison. The air was so cold, everyone's breath looked like great white, billows of smoke. I smiled through my chattering teeth and spoke to each person in line, as Joe and I walked past them, "Good morning. Merry Christmas!" Most of them responded, with the same reply, others just nodded, some even grunted.

Joe struck up a conversation right away with an older man and his wife in the line in front of us, whose son had been in prison for several years. And they didn't see any signs of him getting out in the near future. Again, I repented in my heart for feeling sorry for myself. And I was really embarrassed for feeling such sympathy for just my own little family, when a tall, rough looking woman with two small children, playing with their toys in the snow behind me, told me her story. When her husband got in trouble several years before, she took her children out of their hometown, and away from their grandparents, friends and family, and moved them and what little belongings she had left, to this strange, big city so they could be close to her husband, their father. She said it was especially hard for her children on the holidays. She had to drag those little kids out of their warm beds early, make them open their gifts quickly, and leave the comfort of their cozy house to come to the prison and stand out in the freezing, cold weather.

I knew she must really love her husband to make such a sacrifice. As I stood there listening to her, I thought of how much God loves the prisoners and their families. My heart was overwhelmed with compassion for this poor woman and her little children. I know Jesus loves each and everyone of those prisoners. I prayed for them. David introduced us to a young friend of his, and his parents. They didn't have much happiness in their faces, because their son had murdered someone. I exchanged addresses with the young man's mother. We'd decided to write to each other. I told her about Jesus and how He helped us. I couldn't stop thinking about the prisoners and their families, and how they were suffering. I thanked God, He took me out of my comfort zone and showed me the needs of His broken, hurting people.

The Lord blessed us with beautiful weather all the way home, again. Sunshine, blue skies, and tiny puffy white clouds; I felt so safe dwelling underneath the shadow of His Great wings. We had to hurry home because Carrie and Bobby were going on a vacation, and they were dropping off Rebecca for a week. Rebecca and I sang and danced and made home made bread, and cookies. Her grandpa Joe even played dollies with her. I was so thankful, Jesus loves us. (Hebrews 11:1) "Faith is the substance of things hoped for and the evidence of things not seen."

I will never forget what happened one day when Sandy and I were preparing to clean for one of our regular customers. We had taken all of our cleaning supplies in and sat them down in the kitchen, but just as she and I were discussing which one of us had cleaned the kitchen or bedrooms last, we heard someone yell from the back part of the house! We looked at each other with eyes as big as saucers, and than we grabbed each other's hands! We stood there whispering, "What was that, Sandy?" "Someone besides us is in this house, Carol!" I said, "Sandy, I KNOW I cleaned the bedrooms and back part of the house last week. So, it's your turn to clean the bedrooms. It's my turn to clean the kitchen this week." She got right up in my face as she yelled in a loud whisper, "Carol, you're the one who needs to GO! Remember, it was you who took karate lessons with Janet a couple of years ago! So, you go and see who it is, or what it is, that made the noise." I said, "Oh no! I'm not going back there by myself, either! Come on Sandy, we'll both go!"

Their house had a walk-around-hallway. So, Sandy went in one direction and I went around the other side. I couldn't believe we were actually two, strong, Christian women, when we accidentally backed into each other in the hallway and screamed until we suddenly heard someone else screaming, "AL! IS THAT YOU, AL?" When Sandy and I heard our 'regular weekly customer' yelling for her husband, Al, 'the one who paid us our paychecks,' we were so shocked! I said, "Oh my goodness Sandy, it's Ella! She must have stayed home from work today!" Sandy said, "Oh Carol, what are we going to do now?" We prayed below a whisper, "Oh please help us, dear Jesus? Don't let us lose our job! We need the money, Lord?" We said, "Ella, it's ok, it's just us. It's your cleaning ladies, Carol and Sandy. Honestly, we didn't mean to scare you. You scared us! We didn't know you were home today? You are always at work when we come here, remember?" Although it wasn't very funny at the time, later,

Sandy and I couldn't help but laugh at ourselves, acting so ridiculous. We were thankful to God we didn't scare the poor old woman any worse then we did. We were also thankful she didn't fire us right there on the spot! (Proverbs 15:13) "A merry heart makes a cheerful countenance." Ella laughed at us, and with us, when she realized what happened. "Thank You, sweet Jesus!"

I remember one day, I was walking through my house, crying out to God in desperation, "Lord, I'm so thankful we live in this house, but I'm lonely! I'm way out here in the country, and my friends hardly ever come over to pray with me anymore, it's too far away! It's also long distance, so they can't even call me to pray with them, nor I them! Oh, dear Lord, I don't understand? I'm an intercessor, and yet, I don't have anyone to pray with, except Sandy, sometimes!" Suddenly, I felt the Lord's hand on my right shoulder. He said, "Daughter. It's time for you to write that book now." I remembered this book, 'Which way? What way? Your way Lord.' I was so excited, I squealed out with joy! I ran and got my typewriter out, and sat it on my desk in the dining room! My little dog, Jacob, was right on my heels, barking, as I hurriedly rummaged through my closets and found my typing paper and everything I needed to start writing my story. I began to write all day and on into the evenings. Many times I'd stop writing, and lay my head over on my desk, sobbing. I felt a process of healing taking place inside of me. God was healing my painful memories. Finally, I could write about what God had done for Sandy and I.

Every morning after Joe left for work, I always went into my large bathroom and shut the door behind me, so I could pray. (Matthew 6:6) The room was nice and long, so I paced back and forth as I said my prayers. I was deep into prayer, but just as I turned around, I gasped out loud, and stopped suddenly! Standing there, looking at me, with one foot propped upon the closed toilet seat lid, his elbow resting on his leg, and his peaceful face leaning against his hand, was a neat, clean looking young man with short brown hair. I sensed he was listening to me pray. He was wearing a clean, starched and ironed, light khaki shirt, and matching darker khaki tan pants. A dark khaki patch in the shape of a cross was on his top right shirt sleeve. I was so surprised when I saw him, I turned around, flung the bathroom door open, and ran into the dining room! I stopped suddenly once again, when I almost ran into two more of the young, brown haired men, who dressed and looked exactly like the one I saw in the bathroom. The one in the bathroom followed peacefully behind me, and came and stood quietly beside the other two men, next to my dining room table. I started to say, "I rebb," but the Lord stopped me in the middle of my sentence. He opened my spiritual eyes, to see the supernatural. They were angels on assignment. I repented and He forgave me.

I smiled at the angels and said, "I am grateful and so very happy to 'know' you are angels God sent here to listen to my prayers and help me, aren't you?" They just smiled peacefully, nodded their heads and turned around to walk away, and than they disappeared. It was just breaking daylight outside, and I knew in my heart everything was going to be all right. I went back into the bathroom to finish saying my prayers. I was so glad God allowed me to have another glimpse of His angels He sends to help us. (Hebrews 13:2) "Do not forget to entertain strangers, for by so doing, some have unwittingly entertained angels." "Papa, Your love is so sweet."

When I called Sandy and told her about the book, and my encounter with the angels, she came right over. We talked about how the dear, sweet, precious Holy Spirit led us to pray, Psalm 91, over our family's every day, and Psalm 103. We love to plead the blood of Jesus over ourselves, and our family's every day, including our cars, homes, and even the air we breathe. I pray Psalm 23 "The Lord is my Shepherd, I shall not want." I also pray the prayers in Ephesians 1:16-23, and Ephesians 3:14-20. God has taught us separately, individually and together many things about prayer. We knew we had to stay in the word to learn more. We pray in tongues especially. The Holy Spirit is our close friend.

One sunny afternoon, I was laying on my couch resting, and looking out my window. I'd painted my kitchen and living room walls, so I was extremely tired. I stared up into the beautiful blue heavens, communicating with God. He is my very own Papa, who I dearly love with all of my heart, and I was telling Him so. As I was enjoying my fellowship with Him, and praising His wonderful name, I was thinking of how many times in the past several years I'd seen visions of Him taking me upon His lap, and letting me rest my head upon His chest. I remembered all the times when I came to Him crying, I'd see myself as a small child standing at the foot of His throne, looking up at the rainbow of beautiful vibrant colors that surrounded Him. He was never too busy to reach down and pick me up and sit me on His lap. Sometimes I'd see Him stroke the back of my head while I cried. I told Him every little detail on my heart that was hurting me. It was there, on His lap as a little girl, I fell in love with Him. I was learning how to receive a Father's love. "Papa God, I love You so much."

Suddenly, it dawned on me, "Wait a minute, Papa, Your word says, You are a consuming fire, from Your loins up to Your loins down! Oh dear Papa, I've never known a father's love until now. You made me fall in love with You, and now, how can I ever truly hug Your neck someday? You'll burn me up!" My heart was so broken. I lay there hopelessly crying, and thinking about God's word. (Hebrews 12:29) "For our God is a consuming fire." (Revelation 1:14) "His head and His hair were white like wool, as white as snow, and His eyes like a flame of fire." (Revelation 4:5)

"And from the throne proceeded lightnings, thunderings, and voices. And there were seven lamps of fire burning before the throne, which are the seven Spirits of God." (Ezekiel 1:27) "Also from the appearance of His waist and upward I saw, as it were, the color of amber with the appearance of fire all around within it; and from the appearance of His waist downward I saw, as it were, the appearance of fire with brightness all around." It hit me so hard, I kept crying uncontrollably until it dawned on me, I will be in my glorified body then, where nothing can harm me. I heard Him say, "Carol, get up and read My word in Isaiah 54, than read Psalm 14 and let Me bless you." I quickly reached for my bible! When I read Isaiah 54, I didn't know until later, I was to pray that prayer every day, over myself and my family, "No weapon forged against us shall prosper." Later I received that very prayer in Isaiah 54 from Kenneth Copeland, confirming I was to pray Isaiah 54.8-17. The Lord also blessed me that day when I read Psalm 14:2, "The Lord looks down from heaven upon the children of men, to see if there are any who understand." My heavenly Father is so good to me; He took the time to let me know He was looking down from heaven at me, at the same time I was looking up at Him that day, and He comforted my soul once again. I'd finally found what I'd longed for, for so long, a Father's love, and it will never be taken away from me. "Thank You for Your love, Papa!"

One night I was laying in bed, drifting off to sleep, when all of a sudden I saw myself in a vision, rising upward through the Universe. The vision was so real, I thought maybe I was on my way to heaven, right then. As I saw myself in the vision moving steadily upward, I kept passing horrible looking demons with wild crazy hair, and bulging red eyes. Their fingernails were long, dirty and scraggly. They bared their ugly fangs at me, snarled their upper lip and growled at me, trying to make me afraid of them. I commanded them to get out of my face, in the name of Jesus! The moment I spoke the name of Jesus, those ugly demons were deflated, like a balloon when the air is let out of it suddenly, and they disappeared. In the vision, I looked very peaceful as I glided upward through the Universe. It was so beautiful at night with all its twinkling stars. The vision seemed so real, it felt like I was standing on a firm foundation when I finally came to a harmonious stop, in mid air. Peace engulfed me as I watched a thin, sheer curtain blowing softly in heavens breezes. I tried to peek in, to see what wonderful things could possibly be behind the curtain. Instantly, I saw myself step inside. I was sitting at the most beautiful, breath taking, and eloquent table I'd ever seen. God's wonderful love permeated the crisp clean air. I noticed there was no fear anywhere to be found up there, either.

I knew I was a welcomed guest, as I sat at the beautiful table. I kept whispering, "Wow!" It was so awesome, I felt comfortable,

151

and I knew I belonged there. I looked, but I couldn't see any end to the long, beautiful table. An elegant, hand woven, creamy-white ivory tablecloth, without seams, covered the lovely table. Interwoven in the tablecloth were very fine thin silver and gold threads. The elegant napkins perfectly matched the tablecloth. Each napkin was held together with one gold, and one silver napkin holder ring, resembling expensive wedding bands. The silverware were highly polished fine silver and gold, too. The royalty in this heavenly place cannot be properly described with my inadequate, simple words. Each place setting had royal, rich looking larger plates on the bottom, with a smaller plate, a large flat, round bowl, and a smaller bowl stacked carefully inside the other. Each place setting also had matching cups and saucers, and a leaded cut glass crystal goblet. Every dish, plate, cup, saucer and bowl was made of the finest creamy-white ivory bone china. Soft, pink, tiny rosebuds with tiny green stems were delicately hand-painted on every piece of the fine china, in exquisite beauty that blessed my eyes to just sit and look at it. Each piece of china, including the cut crystal goblets, and even the large graceful gravy dishes and coffee earns, were trimmed with one generous, fine ring of silver, and one ring of pure gold around the outer edges.

I sat straight up in bed and asked the Lord, "Is this really happening, Lord?" I looked over at Joe, who was snoring peacefully beside me, and got my answer. I laid my sleepy head back down on my pillow, thinking, "My Papa is undescribably rich, powerfully rich. What am I saying? He is the richest one there is! There is no one who could possibly top Him in anything, and I am His daughter, wow!" As soon as I closed my eyes I saw exactly the same vision of myself climbing steadily upwards through the Universe, and rebuking the demons, in the name of Jesus! I sat at the same beautiful table again, too. Apparently, God wanted me to remember it well. Jesus paid for my place at that table with His precious blood. The next morning, I thought about Ephesians 6:10-12, "Finally my brethren, be strong in the Lord and the power of His might. Put on the whole armor of God, that you may be able to stand against the wiles of the devil. For we do not wrestle against flesh and blood, but against principalities, against powers, against the rulers of the darkness of this age, against spiritual hosts of wickedness in heavenly places." And, Luke 22:30, "That you may eat and drink at My table in My kingdom."

1 Corinthians 2:9-10, "Eye hath not seen nor ear heard what God has in store for them that love Him. BUT God has revealed them to us through His Spirit. For the Spirit searches all things, yes, even the deep things of God." Psalm 23, "You prepare a table before me in the presence of my enemies." I said, "Praise You, loving, glorious Papa! Praise You, wonderful Lord Jesus! Praise You, sweet, precious Holy Spirit." Jesus said, "What do you want Me to do for you?" When I told Sandy about the vision, she and I prayed, "God, we believe we receive our inheritance from You! Oh dear Lord, we do believe. Help, Thou, our unbelief."

Finally, David was eligible for parole. We were all excited and busy writing letters to the parole board office in Washington, D.C. We prayed and waited several weeks with expectant hearts, only to hear David call and say, "Mom, they turned down my parole. I won't be coming home." I couldn't believe the awful news, and I started crying, too. I put David on hold and called Joe on three way calling. The three of us cried and talked for a few minutes, then suddenly I said, "Wait a minute David, Joe! I know God will help us, if we pray and ask Him to give us another plan that will outsmart the enemy, in Jesus name." Thank God, Cindy, Reverend Frank's daughter, was there with me that day. When she heard me crying, she came and sat in the living room and prayed for us in the spirit while I talked with David and Joe on the phone. I asked David, Joe, and Cindy to come into agreement with me while I prayed to the God who heals broken hearts and mends shattered dreams. We asked Him, in the name of Jesus, to give us an alternative plan, a plan that will not fail. Instantly, David said, "I know; Let's appeal it right away!" I knew deep down in my heart. This was God's plan for us to gain the victory for David's parole! "Thank You Jesus!" (Galatians 6:9) "Let us not be weary in well doing for in due season we shall reap if we faint not."

About three weeks later, my friend Cindy was visiting me again. We were sitting at my dining room table, talking, when all of a sudden, she yelled, "Carol! Something, or someone as tall as your house just walked past your big picture window, and they were dressed in all bright, white clothing!" I shrugged my shoulders and answered, "Not too long ago, I saw three angels here in this house. So, I'll bet it was another angel you saw. You're seeing into the spirit realm, Cindy." She got up and ran outside, walking all around my house, looking for the angel. As I shuffled along behind her, I kept hearing a song over and over in my head. "The King is passing by." I told Cindy about the song I kept hearing. I said, "When I teach the juniors' class in your dad's Sunday school, I tell them about one of my favorite scriptures in Luke 8:45 'And Jesus said, "Who touched Me?" She looked at me with a blank stare. I said, "Cindy, don't you understand? We touched Jesus with our faith, and the King of King's, Himself, passed by here to let us know, a miracle is on the way, yahoo!" She smiled, and willingly came back in the house with me. She had received the baptism of the dear, precious Holy Spirit, and I was teaching her some things I'd learned over the years about seeing into the spirit realm. Jesus baptizes us in the Holy Spirit, and He shows us things as we pray in tongues. I love the precious Holy Spirit.

A few minutes after Cindy left, David called to tell me his appeal was granted, and he was coming home! Tears of joy instead of tears of sorrow, rolled down my cheeks. "Sweet Jesus!" "Praise You Papa! Praise You Jesus! Praise You dear, precious Holy Spirit! Oh merciful God, I thank You so much for Your goodness and mercy that follows us all the days of our lives!" I told David about the supernatural visitation Cindy and I'd had about an hour earlier. "Jesus, Himself, passed by our house today David, to tell me, everything's going to be alright!" I knew David must have completed his mission for the Lord. I was so happy, I thanked God again and again for being so good to us! I called Joe, Joey and Sandy first, and then I called all of our family and friends to tell them the good news! I couldn't thank them enough for all their prayers and support on David's behalf. It felt so good to think happy thoughts, and make happy plans to go and get my precious son out of prison. (Numbers 23:19) "God is not a man that He should lie nor the son of man that He should repent." I knew the following three weeks, waiting to go pick up David to bring him home, were going to be three of the longest weeks of our lives. "Oh, Lord please help me to be able to wait on You!"

Late Sunday afternoon, Sandy and I were sitting on her living room couch talking while our husbands, Ron and Joe, were in the family room watching sports on their big screen television. The house was pretty crowded because of all Betsy and Jenny's friends that were there that day, too. There were girls sitting in the kitchen, eating. Some of them were standing, some were seated on the floor, laughing and talking in the living room with Sandy and me. A couple of the girls were watching baseball in the family room with their boyfriends. This was very normal in Sandy and Ron's big, comfortable home. Sandy and Ron always shared what food they had. Anyone was welcome to come and eat if they were hungry. Jenny's boyfriend, Brad, her best friend Gerald's half brother, knocked on the front door. A few times when I'd met Brad before, I heard the Lord whisper, "Drugs, drugs." Brad was standing in the doorway with the sun shining behind him. When I looked up at him the Lord began to speak to me about him, "Carol, if you don't lead this boy to Me before Midnight, he has set that time to kill himself. Every time you've been around him before, I've told you about his drug problem. I want you and Sandy to lead him to Me tonight." I also felt Him telling me not to worry about the others, He'd take care of them. I knew just to trust Him, and go on and do it. I felt the anointing strong in me.

I got Sandy off to the side and told her. She said I was the perfect laborer his mother had been crying out to God to send across her son's path. It looked impossible. The devil tried to tell me I was going to look pretty stupid when I told this handsome, young, man what God wanted me to do. But I didn't really care what the enemy thought about it. I intended to do God's will. Isaiah 45:2 "God has gone before us to make the crooked places straight, and broken in pieces the bars of iron, and cut in sunder the gates of brass." Joe stood up three times and called for me from the family room, "Carol, let's go home!" Each time, by the grace of God, he'd sit back down when I'd answer back, "O k, Joe, I'll be ready in just a few minutes." Ron worked nights and we usually left early, so he'd have plenty of time to get ready for work, but not this time. The Lord had other plans. As soon as Ron went into the bathroom to get ready for work, I went into the family room and quickly explained everything to Joe. He sat back down and agreed to wait. Ron no sooner left for work, when all of a sudden all the girl's friends left, too, except for Monica who was sitting on the floor in the living room talking to Brad.

Sandy went in the kitchen and asked Betsy and Jenny to call for Monica, and they did. I had no fear as I looked down at Jenny's blond, blue eyed, handsome twenty one-year-old boyfriend. I told him what the Lord said to me earlier when he came in. He stared up at me in disbelief. I finished my story by saying, "Son, I believe I am the perfect laborer your mother has been crying out to Him for." He kept on nodding his head while I talked, but before I finished, he buried his face in his hands and cried, "Oh dear God, I didn't think You were listening!" He told us through many tears. He had been shot at and hit, and he had been ordered to kill others on assignment. He said he had lost everything, and he never dreamed God would hear his desperate cries for help! Sandy and I led him like a little lamb to the Lord that very night. This tall, handsome, young man didn't care if Jenny heard him crying in the next room, or anyone else. He received Jesus into his heart that night, and he left there a happy man. "Praise You, Father, Son, and dear, precious Holy Ghost! Oh, dear Papa, Your word delivers us!" I am so glad the Lord trusted Sandy and me to be a part of His plan for Brad. Oddly enough, Brad and Jenny broke up right after that. Jenny went back to an old boyfriend she'd dated before, named Zak. I guess Brad had a lot of unfinished business to take care of. Both he and Jenny were happy with the separation.

Early one morning, Sandy and I were cleaning a house for a

customer. We also had another house close by to clean that day in the same area, but Betsy was on Sandy's mind. After we finished cleaning the first house, we decided we'd better go back to Sandy's house to check on Betsy, even though it was several miles out of our way, and in the apposite direction. When we arrived at Sandy's house, Betsy was crying and couldn't seem to stop. She was heavy with symptoms of severe depression, because no matter how hard we tried to cheer her up, she'd cry even harder. I kept following Betsy all through the house. As we walked, she kept crying, and pouring out her heart to us. My heart was overwhelmed with compassion for her, because I had lived through the torment of depression and hopelessness, until the Lord set me free! I was so grateful to Jesus. I wanted to help others to be healed from depression, too, in His name. The Lord kept telling me, Sandy and I needed to pray for her and anoint her with oil, and He'd set her free from demonic oppression. Betsy cried and told us she had struggled for so long with everything wrong in her life, she just wanted to die. I felt the Lord urging us to anoint her with oil, and to do it now! I asked Betsy if she wanted to be set free from that torment, and she said, "Yes! Please help me?"

We didn't waste any time. Betsy agreed to let her mother and I pray for God to deliver her from that awful agony. She went with us willingly back to her bedroom to let us pray for her. We laid hands on her and prayed for her in tongues, as she sat weeping on the edge of her waterbed. We no sooner started praying for her when all of a sudden I saw pinkish red 'Casper' looking ghosts inside Betsy. The strongest one was the most stubborn, hateful spirit of suicide standing wedged in the front wall behind her chest and rib cage area. Its hands were firmly pressed up against the inside of her with its feet stubbornly planted apart. I was standing directly over her with my hands on her shoulders when I did what Jesus told us to do in, Mark 16:17 "And these signs will follow those who believe; In My name they will cast out demons; they will speak with new tongues;...... they will lay hands on the sick and they will recover."

The strongest spirit of suicide, their leader, told the others what to do. It buttoned its lip tight, and shook its pink head back and forth. It yelled in a deep eerie voice, "NO!" That stubborn thing planted its feet firmer and said again, "NO! WE ARE NOT COMING OUT!" Its voice echoed with the other evil spirits in her. The Lion of the tribe of Judah roared up in me and Sandy, and under the anointing of the Holy Ghost, in a loud voice, Sandy and I commanded those evil spirits to come out of her, in the name of Jesus, and by the blood of Jesus! The Lord was working with us, showing signs and wonders! Jesus set Betsy completely free right at that moment. I saw several pinkish- red, evil spirits come up out of Betsy. They came out, one by one with their pink hand's clasp tightly together, in submission to the name of Jesus and the blood of Jesus. It looked like a mighty vacuum cleaner sucked them right up out of her and they were gone, forever! Betsy was never troubled with suicide or depression again. Sandy and I praised God, and we sang all the way back to work that day! We always sing God's praises, because there is none like Him.

"OH, We, are, in, the army of the Lord; We've been bought with the blood and we are going forth; There is nothing that can stop us; This mighty moving force; With a SHOUT, of PRAISE, and a two edged sword-----------. Every stronghold of bondage has to fall beneath our feet; Every prisoner held captive MUST be freed; Our deliverance has come through the power of the Son; Oh the blood bought; The church; The redeemed!" "Praise You, dear merciful, loving Papa! Praise You, wonderful Lord, Jesus! Praise You, sweet, precious Holy Spirit!" Sandy and I agreed, "God You are so good to us! Thank You, dear Lord, for loving us and helping us receive Your great love for us, always!" He is the Most High God. His mercy is new every morning. In Him there is peace, healing, love, joy and hope that makes us not be afraid. "Thank You, Jesus, for loving us, and shedding Your precious blood for us on the cross, so that we can be set forever free from darkness." I always know one of the reasons I recieve answers to prayer so quickly is because my sister Peggy is in complete agreement with me too. She's an awesome prayer warrior. She loves my family and I as much as I love her and her family. Her prayers get heard.

Chapter Five

We Are More Than Conquerors

I never told David, but Betsy had started dating a young man named Mark, who had two young sons. Betsy said she was falling in love with Mark. They became engaged several weeks before we heard about David's parole. The enemy was trying to tell me the vision I'd had of David and Betsy getting married wasn't real. Oh, but I knew what the Lord did in David's heart was real. God changed and healed his broken heart and mind, in one single night. I knew God's word. He cannot lie. He always keeps His promises. The vision of David and Betsy, and their strong love for one another, was still very vivid in my mind. However, I couldn't fault Betsy for trying to end her relationship with David and start another one with someone else, because she didn't have the vision, I did. I had to admit, if I were walking by sight and not by faith like Betsy was, I probably would have given up, too. After all, things really did look rather hopeless to her in the natural.

Jesus said, in Matthew 19:26 "With men this is impossible, but with God all things are possible." Daily, the accuser of the brotherhood reminded me of how impossible the circumstances looked, in order for the vision to come to pass. Everything especially worsened the day we went to the prison to pick David up, too. On and on the enemy kept talking to me, until he thought I couldn't hear him correctly, so he started hollering, and asking what I'd tell David when he ask about Betsy? Reminding me, I had a vision and my son believed me, and he's fallen in love with Betsy, only to get his heart broken all over again! Ha! I just drowned out the enemy's words, singing praise songs about the blood of Jesus! I had walked with the Lord for quite some time. He had never let me down. Jesus said, "Only believe." I believe God.

160

Joe and I were so excited! We knew we'd never have to visit David in that horrible prison again. "Thank God!" We were finally going to take our son out of that awful place and bring him home with us. The next morning after Joe left the motel to go and get us something to eat for breakfast, I switched on the weather channel. They were predicting terrible storms and severe weather from state to state, on our exact route home that day. I got so angry, I ran into the bathroom to pray again, but there was so much commotion going on in the room above us, I could hardly hear myself pray. I commanded the devil to stop causing the loud ruckus upstairs, in the name of Jesus! It immediately got quiet. I asked God to please remember, He is no respecter of persons. He promised me in, Joshua 1:5. What He did for Moses, He will do for me. I asked Him, in the name of Jesus, to split that storm system right down the middle, just like He did for Moses at the Red Sea, and let us bring our son home from the Egypt we had been in, on dry ground.

We picked David up from the prison at exactly 0800 hour, just like God had promised us. I humbly thanked God over and over. We never saw one single drop of rain that day, either. We had nothing to distract us but beautiful sunny blue skies. Doubts and fear tried to harass my mind about David and Betsy again during the long trip back home! I whispered, so Joe or David couldn't hear me, 2 Corinthians 10:5. "Casting down every evil imagination that tries to set itself up against the power of Christ, and bringing into captivity every thought unto the obedience of Christ." I also quoted, 2 Timothy 1:7, "For God has not given us a spirit of fear, but of power, and of love, and of a sound mind." I'd insisted David sit in the front seat of the car, so he could fully enjoy the scenery on the way home. We were all so happy! We laughed and talked about everything. David wanted to stop and have his favorite pizza for lunch, and so we did. We also went shopping and then had dinner wherever David wanted. While I sat in the back seat of the car the doubt tried to steal my joy again, until the thought crossed my mind which settled it in my heart, once and for all. "If this thing is of God, it will happen, and if it's not, it won't." I wouldn't want anything but God's will to be done in David and Betsy's lives

161

anyway. That was the end of my dilemma. From that moment on, I had total peace about David and Betsy. "Praise, You, Jesus!"

As for the duration of the trip home, once or twice, the enemy tried to bring up the subject of Betsy's engagement to Mark by calling to me, way far off in the distance. I refused to listen to him. Instead the word of God came to my rescue, immediately, "Lean not on your own understanding. In all your ways acknowledge Him and He will direct your paths." (Proverbs 3:6) Joe and David were baffled by the weather, because it was the exact opposite of what the predictions had been for that day on all the weather channels. I just laughed every time they said something about it, and I said to myself, "God has brought us out of Egypt, and we are crossing the red sea on dry ground! Hallelujah!" Some things I didn't share with Joe. He was too young in the Lord to understand. I figured they were better left unsaid, as opposed to casting my pearls before the swine, and being trampled by them. God gave me wisdom.

As we pulled up in the driveway, the headlights from our car reflected the huge, bright red letters painted on a sign hanging above our garage door, which read. "WELCOME HOME DAVID!" Joey, and some of their close friends surprised David with a party as soon as we stepped inside the house, with colorful balloons, streamers, and lots of handshakes and hugs! David never stopped smiling when I showed him his room, and the rest of the house. We stayed up late, and talked on into the night. We were really enjoying our time together as a family again. Early the next morning, Betsy knocked on the kitchen door. I asked her to wait in the living room until I told David. While he ran into the bathroom, to shower and freshen up, I told Betsy, I had not mentioned her engagement to Mark. She agreed. It was up to her to tell David. She and I had just walked into the kitchen to get a cup of hot coffee. We were standing there talking when David walked into the room. He said shyly, "Hello, Betsy." She smiled back at him, and reach out her arms toward him, as she walked across the room. She faintly said, "I just came to give you a welcome home hug, and kiss." David smiled, and opened his arms wide to receive her hug. Wow! I felt that same awesome agape love, exactly like I did in the vision when Betsy walked in front of me to get to David. Suddenly, I realized I needed to leave the room, because they were still kissing a few minutes later. As I walked into the living room, I thought, "Sweet Jesus! You are no doubt, standing there with Your arms around my son David and Betsy, because this was Your idea! I know You have put Your stamp of approval on them. Thank You Jesus!" I was so happy for them, I hugged myself!

Immediately, Betsy broke her engagement to Mark. Betsy and David saw each other every day, and they fell more in love with each other, with each passing day. They couldn't stand to be separated from each other for very long either. It blessed my soul when Joe had to admit he was wrong. He finally recognized the vision I'd had of David and Betsy's true love for one another was really from God. Joe had acted terrible! He'd made fun of me when I told him about the vision. Sandy and I were thankful Betsy and Rebecca already knew and liked each other. Betsy had known Carrie as a casual friend. She babysat Rebecca for her from time to time, too. Before David came home, at different times when Betsy came over with Sandy, and Rebecca was visiting me, they'd have so much fun together! "Praise the Lord!" Betsy and Rebecca loved to do handstands, and somersaults in our yard. They'd pet the neighbor's horses across the fence, and sometimes fed them a carrot or an apple. "I love You so much, wonderful, Lord Jesus!"

One afternoon when Sandy stopped by to visit me, her youngest daughter Jenny was on her mind. Every time we tried to talk about something else, the subject always came right back to Jenny. So, we decided we'd better ask the dear, precious Holy Spirit to help us pray for her. When we began to pray in the spirit, Sandy's voice got lower, and deeper! She sounded different. It was as if she were angry with someone, or something. She sounded almost like a man with a deep voice. She prayed violently, too! Afterwards, Sandy still felt uneasy, so we pled the blood of Jesus, in the name of Jesus, over Jenny again, and everything she touched, including the air she breathed and food she ate. We always depended on the dear, precious Holy Spirit. He's our comforter and our guide, especially when we didn't have the slightest idea why we had such a burden to pray for someone. We prayed for Jenny, and God's protection over her, until we felt somewhat peaceful.

Later that evening I went on to work with Joe, David and Joey. I often went with Joe when he had to work late. Many times I fixed everyone dinner and took it to them, so they could eat a good, hot meal. I also helped out, by cleaning their bathrooms and offices. That evening after we all ate, I was sitting in Joe's office, reading my bible, when the phone rang. I was startled when I heard Sandy's raspy voice, "Carol, it's Jenny! She's been in a terrible car accident and they don't expect her to live through the night! Pray Carol! Pray, as you never have before! The femur bone in her leg was shattered, the doctor said, it looked like the pages of an open book! My baby's pelvic bone hit the gear shift in the middle of her boyfriend Zak's truck where she was sitting! It did a lot of damage to her inwardly. Her other friend, Gerald, sat on her right side and Zak on her left. The two of them together crushed her when they hit a slick spot in the road and crashed against a tree! They said my child may not make it through the night! Please pray for her, Carol, and I will agree with you!"

Tears of compassion streamed down my face as I began to pray and intercede for Jenny, Sandy, Ron, and Gerald, her friend who was in a coma and not expected to live, either. In the middle of all the pain and confusion, I heard the Holy Spirit speak to me softly, and quiet my mind. (Psalm 118:17) "Jenny will live and not die, and she will proclaim the works of the Lord." I repeated God's wonderful words of comfort and hope to Sandy, again and again, reinforcing them into her spirit. Sandy explained how Jenny was riding in the middle of Zak's small truck, straddling the gear shift on the floorboard. Her boyfriend, Zak, was driving. Her nineteen-year-old long time friend, Gerald, was sitting on the passenger side. When Gerald saw they were going to hit the tree, he tried to shield Jenny with his upper body. The large tree crashed through the car window and crushed the right side of his head, causing him to have dangerous blood clots and brain damage. Jenny had lacerations and cuts on her face, arms, chest and legs. She, too, had a horrendous amount of internal damage, and bleeding. The jaws of life had to be used to cut them free from the truck. They were care flighted to the hospital by helicopter. Zak, Jenny's boyfriend, was the only one who was able to walk away from the wreck completely unharmed, without a scratch. He was drinking alcohol.

I went out into the shop, and quickly explained everything Sandy had just told me to Joe, David and Joey. David immediately went to get Betsy and we met them at the hospital. Our friends, Sandy and Ron, were a pale, chalk white. I'd prayed on the way to the hospital and asked the Lord to help me not to break down and cry. I asked God to help me be strong for them. Both sets of Jenny's grandparents were already at the hospital along with the rest of her family and friends. When I looked down at Jenny's frail, limp body, still covered in broken glass and her own dried blood, she whispered, "Carol, the first thing I did was make my peace with God. When I saw we were going to wreck, I asked Him to forgive me of all my sins. I wanted to make sure I was going to go to heaven, in case I didn't make it." Her dark, pretty eyes were full of pain and suffering. The Lord spoke to me right then and told me to go to the hospital every day with Sandy and stand in faith with her for Jenny. So, I did. We felt God's comfort, His mercy daily.

Sandy was weary, and she couldn't eat for several days while her child lay in intensive care. However, her weakness in body did not reflect on her strong faith in God's ability to heal her daughter. Sandy never moved from her stand of faith for Jenny's healing. Not even when she saw the doctors put Jenny's leg in heavy weights for traction with sandbags and bars hanging from her feet, and bars across her bed. Sandy still believed God's word, even when they hooked Jenny up to every kind of machine you can think of. Her confession remained the same, "Carol, I don't care what it looks like. As far as I'm concerned Jenny is healed, by Jesus stripes." Each day, I agreed in prayer with Sandy as she and I walked the halls of that hospital, speaking God's promises, and agreeing with His word in prayer. We kept reminding each other of all our past victories. We talked about them throughout the long hours of the days and evenings we spent together in the hospital.

Sandy's faith did not waver and neither did mine. We began to see Jenny's healing taking place, day by day. Our determination for victory against insurmountable odds paid off as we kept on speaking God's word. "Jenny will live and not die. She will proclaim the works of the Lord." We refused to let go of the hem of Jesus garment, and we saw new improvements in Jenny every day. "Praise God!" We prayed for the Lord to guide the doctors hands at all times. Sandy and I agreed. We thank God for the doctors who God so mercifully used to help Jenny survive that awful wreck. We are thankful for good doctors who really do care about people and want to help them. Sometime He uses doctors.

Sandy and I knew the power of agreement in prayer is where the rubber meets the road. She and I talked to Gerald's mother and told her, "Jesus miraculously healed your son two thousand years ago. If you'll only believe He took your sons sins and carried away his sickness, because He is so full of compassion and mercy for us all, your son will be healed." The doctors had given up many times on Gerald's ability to pull through, but his mother believed with us and he too, began to recover, although he was still in a coma. No matter how bad the doctor's report was, Sandy and I agreed on God's word in, Isaiah 53:5. "By His stripes, Jenny and everyone of us were healed." Sandy grabbed my arm and said, on the way to the chapel to pray, "Carol, agree with me? Jenny will not be in excruciating pain, like the doctor said, in the name of Jesus!" As soon as we got inside the Chapel and saw that it was empty, Sandy yelled, "Devil, take your hands off my child, this instant, in the name of Jesus, and by the blood of Jesus Christ of Nazareth!"

We prayed, " Father, in the name of Jesus, we plead the blood of Jesus over Jenny, us, our husbands, our children, and my precious grandchildren. You said in Your word; The fervent, effectual prayer of a righteous man, avails much." I followed quickly behind her, praying in the spirit. Sandy had such a rage in her against the enemy, even I shivered. I'd never seen such a strong anointing on her life. Woe be it to anyone or anything that tried to stand in the way of her child's miracle. (Zachariah 4:6) "Not by power, not by might, but by My Spirit, saith the Lord." "Praise God!" Instead of

166

Jenny spending months in the hospital, she was released in just a few short weeks. The doctors were all amazed. A metal rod was put in her leg. She had to have extensive therapy to help her walk again, but she's alive and well! She was never once in excruciating pain beyond what she could bear, with God's help and medication.

Not only was I a little tired from spending all those days and evenings at the hospital with Sandy, but every night David woke me up out of a sound sleep in the middle of the night, to get up and pray for him. He was having terrible chest pains, and panic attacks. One night when David woke me up to pray for him, I suddenly remembered a warning dream God had given me right before we went to pick him up at the prison. In the dream, Joe dropped me off near an old, wooden, park bench that sat out in the middle of nowhere. I remember thinking how strange it was that only one person was allowed to go into the prison to pick up our son? David had gotten parole and Joe had to leave me way out there in that barren, spooky place by myself, and at night, no less. I hesitated as I sat down on the old, half-rotted park bench, which had one lonely rusty, brown metal light hanging above it. Every kind of bug that had wings swirled around the dimly lit light. Joe said, "Believe me, Carol, it's much safer out here than it is inside the prison. As soon as I get our son out of that horrible place, I'll be back as quickly as I can to get you. You'll be all right." I slowly nodded my head yes. Even though I understood the rules, I was really scared to stay out there by myself, in the dream.

I sat there shivering and feeling awfully uneasy as I watched the headlights on our car winding its way up the long, dusty gravel road to the prison. My eyes squinted as I searched through the darkness, hoping to find another light from a friendly looking farm house, but there was nothing. Pitch blackness seemed to have darkened out the moon and stars. The ground beneath the old wooden park bench was dry and barren with only a few spindly blades of grass struggling to force its way up through the parched, cracked earth. All of a sudden, I felt an overwhelming sense of fear and danger lurking in the darkness beside me on the old wooden bench. The fear was demonic, and overpowering! It felt like it was trying to smother me. I forced myself to slowly turn my head to the left, to see where it was coming from. I caught my breath when I saw a huge, ugly, bald- headed demon. It resembled a heavy weight boxer. Even its bald slick head had large rolls of muscle and fat rippling down the back of its huge neck. Its arms and chest were hairy like an ape. When I looked up at it, it glared at me with hate in its mean looking eyes. It snarled its upper lip, then it growled at me like a wild untamed beast! Again, it roared really loud! And in one swift movement, it raised its huge hairy, right arm and hand up over my head, and then, with a terrible force, it brought it back down! It grabbed my left arm in a terrible painful grip! That thing reminded me of a sumo wrestler. It was impossible for me to break free from its grip in my own strength.

I tried to speak but I couldn't, and that's when the Holy Spirit rose up on the inside of me, and I screamed out fearlessly, "LET ME GO, IN THE NAME OF JESUS! I TELL YOU, LET GO OF ME RIGHT NOW, IN THE NAME OF JESUS!" I woke myself up screaming those same words out loud, and pounding the bed with my fists. Joe was really mad at me that time, because he was innocently standing in the bathroom at five thirty that morning, shaving before going to work. He said, "Carol, I nearly slit my own throat with the razor when I heard you scream like that!" I'd nearly forgotten about the dream since I'd been so involved with Sandy, and prayer for Jenny's survival at the hospital. Every night when I came home late from the hospital, I'd fall into bed exhausted. I guess I'd been too tired to realize how important the dream was. That is, until one night when I was praying for David and that same evil spirit I saw in the dream, revealed itself. That same ugly, bald- headed demon, which resembled a sumo wrestler stared boldly into my face with its hands gripped tightly on David's shoulders. It was the spirit of fear. I bound that hateful, tormenting spirit of fear off David, in the name of Jesus, and by His blood.

I told David to memorize and use the sword of the Spirit, which is the word of God, against that spirit of fear too. (2 Timothy 1:7) "God has not given us a spirit of fear, but of power, and of love, and of a sound mind." I understood, that spirit of fear was a stronghold in David's life from all that he'd gone through, before and during his prison experience. It was something that had to be dealt with forcefully, in the name of Jesus, more than once. We even had to rush David to the hospital several times because of the chest pains and panic attacks. Sandy and I kept binding that hateful spirit of fear off him, in the name of Jesus. The strangest thing happened while my mother was visiting us from California. One night, she told me she ran into a big, bald-headed man running down the hallway. I told her about the dream God had given me to warn me about David's condition. I said. "Mommy, that was the hateful, evil spirit of fear. I commanded that thing to leave David, in the name of Jesus, and you saw it, too?" She described the ugly spirit of fear exactly as I had seen it. I anointed every room in my house with oil, in the name of Jesus. She and I agreed. That evil spirit of fear that she saw leaving my house, cannot come back across the blood of Jesus! "I praise You, wonderful Lord Jesus."

A couple of months had passed since Jenny had been in physical therapy, and she was walking as good as new again. She was enjoying her life, although her monthly periods hadn't started back to normal yet. When Sandy took Jenny to the doctor, she found out Jenny was pregnant before the accident. Once again, Sandy's voice was low and raspy over the phone, and once again, the Lion of the tribe of Juda rose up inside her, stronger then ever. In righteous anger, she said boldly, "Carol, every doctor we've seen is insisting on Jenny having an abortion! Oh, but I say. The devil is a liar, and the father of lies! We've seen three different doctors, including our family doctor who brought Jenny into the world, and he even agreed with the other doctors. He told Jenny to get an abortion, too!" Sandy was very angry when she yelled out, "NO, DEVIL, YOUR NOT STEALING MY FIRST GRANDCHILD, OR ANY OF MY GRANDCHILDREN, IN THE NAME OF JESUS! NOT NOW, OR EVER, IN THE POWERFUL NAME OF JESUS, THEY ARE COVERED IN HIS BLOOD!"

I kept praying fast and fervent in tongues. I was in total

agreement with Sandy. Then she said very seriously, "Carol, the doctors are saying the wreck, the operation, the morphine and all the other medications, and the heavy sedation when they put Jenny to sleep to operate on her leg and put in the metal rod." Sandy broke down in tears again, "Carol, they are saying that all of this did a lot of damage to the baby. What they are saying is, it will be born without some of its limbs, and perhaps even have some serious brain damage. Oh, but I say, God created that baby in the first place, and He will recreate in my grandchild whatever it needs to be born perfect and whole, in the name of Jesus!" (Psalm 37:26) "Carol, I don't receive any of that negative hogwash spoken over my grandbaby, in the name of Jesus! The blood of Jesus covers my grandchild, and nothing evil can cross that bloodline!" I agreed with Sandy, one hundred percent, for her grandchild's healing, by Jesus stripes. From that day on, we spoke beautiful blessings over the baby. No abortion was going to intrude upon the life of her first, or any grandchild of hers, or mine, in the name of Jesus, ever, and by the blood of Jesus! We asked God to heal any imperfections in her grandchild, in the name of Jesus, and He did. "Praise God!" Sandy's beautiful grandson, William was born, on time, and in perfect health from the crown of his little head, to the souls of his tiny feet! "Thank You, wonderful Jesus!"

We were all still spending time in hospital emergency rooms with David. He kept having chest pains and panic attacks. He was still struggling, and we realized the symptoms David was experiencing were similar to a nervous breakdown. The Lord showed my sister, Peggy, it was because of what he'd gone through. She loved David dearly, too, and prayed for him almost constantly. Since David had never been in any kind of bad trouble, it nearly scared him silly when he entered one of the largest, meanest, and most horribly overcrowded prisons. It scared him so bad, it was as if he were driving on a freeway at ninety miles per hour, and putting on the brakes every few seconds! His divorce was painful enough, but the shame of prison life was even more difficult to go through with a broken heart. He had to face the shame of his court martial without his wife and daughter, too. All of it together had taken its toll on him. "Sweet Jesus."

Rebecca and her daddy were getting acquainted again. She loved Betsy, too. The three of them were planning their lives together, until we suddenly began to see an intense, strange change in Rebecca's behavior and personality. Rebecca had never been afraid of her daddy, Betsy, or any of us before. All of a sudden, however, when we picked her up every other weekend for visitation, she started pacing the floor, crying, and wanting to go home! She turned against all of us, including her grandpa and me. She'd pace back and forth, crying, and say she didn't want to come and visit us anymore. We couldn't bare to see her cry and be so unhappy. So, we'd take her right straight back home again. We were all puzzled, and confused at her sudden change of heart. David was so disheartened. He cried, too. He'd finally built up such a good relationship with his little girl, and now someone, or something, was tearing it all apart. The Lord kept reminding me of, Ephesians 6:12. "We wrestle not with flesh and blood, but against principalities, against powers, and against wickedness in high places." I kept praying, "Lord, please teach me how to pray?"

David hated arguing and fighting with Carrie, so Joe and I continued to pick Rebecca up and take her home. She was already comfortable with us making the exchange, anyway. Sometimes Joe went to pick Rebecca up by himself, if I was too busy. Rebecca usually loved it when her grandpa stopped by his tool shop on their way home. She loved to stop and see her daddy, uncle Joey, and her great aunts and uncles who worked there, too. One day while my mother was visiting us from California, Joe went and picked up Rebecca. Joe said when they stopped by the shop on their way home, Rebecca acted totally different. She usually marched in there like she owned the place. Everyone bought her candy and pop from the machines, because they loved her so much. Joe's brother, her uncle Norm, always saved her his brand new, shiny pennies in his office drawer, but when he tried to give them to her this time, she burst out crying uncontrollably! He and everyone else were shocked at the sudden change in Rebecca! Joe squatted down to her level and tried to talk to her. "What's wrong Rebecca, honey? Please stop crying, and tell grandpa what's wrong?" She burst into tears again, and cried, "Oh grandpa, pretty soon I won't ever see you, or grandma, or my daddy again as long as I live! Mommy and daddy Bobby keep telling me to get use to the idea of never coming over to see my daddy or any of you ever again! We are going far, far away, right after my daddy Bobby's birthday!" Rebecca's birthday was the day after his, in December.

David scooped his little girl up in his arms and told her, none of it was true. He tried several times to calm her down. He told her, "If Carrie and Bobby try to take you away from me, I'll call the police on them!" It was hard to try and undue the damage that was already done. After all she trusted and loved the two people who had lied to her. By the time they reached the house, David, Joe and Joey were so angry at Carrie and Bobby for tormenting little Rebecca's heart and mind, and scaring her with their devious plan. Chills went up and down my spine when Joe and David explained everything to Betsy and my mother and me. No matter how hard we tried to tell Rebecca the truth, her crying only worsened. It broke our hearts to see her cry. Rebecca and I were inseparable before this evil thing happened. Strangely enough, my own grandchild became so paranoid, she wouldn't even go shopping, the park, or anywhere else with us again. My mother couldn't believe the change in Rebecca, either. I knew I had to fix my eyes on Jesus, stop worrying, and wholly trust God. "I trust You Jesus."

Before we took Rebecca back home, I asked Sandy and my mother to help me anoint her with oil and pray for her. Sandy, and mommy and I gathered around her. They agreed while I prayed, "Papa God, Your word says, 'If anyone hurts a little child, it's better that a milestone were hanged about their neck and they were cast into the sea.' "I'm asking You, Papa to cause, whoever it is that's doing this to Rebecca, and causing her emotional turmoil, to feel the weight of that milestone, and pull them to their knees to repentance, in Jesus' name. Please dear Lord, heal little Rebecca's mind and heart and give her peace and joy, again." We didn't see

Rebecca for a long time after that. Carrie and Bobby wouldn't answer their phone, so we were not able to talk to our little red, curly headed girl. I prayed constantly God's protection over her. When I prayed in the spirit for little Rebecca, I kept interpreting, "Agape love." I knew the Lord was reassuring me. His agape love hovers over Rebecca. She abides under the shadow of His great wings. He has covered her with His love and protection. (Psalm 91) I'm so thankful the dear, precious Holy Spirit helps me pray.

David was in the process of taking Carrie and Bobby to court, because he was worried about Rebecca's welfare. I was so exhausted, I laid down in the middle of the afternoon and took a nap. While I slept, I had a strange dream of Joe, David, Carrie, Rebecca and myself, in a huge courtroom. In the dream, I saw Joe, myself and David sitting in a courtroom on wooden chairs. We were waiting for the judge to hear our case. David was sitting on my left and Joe on my right. We sat there and watched several times as the judge pounded his gavel and said, "GUILTY!" If the people lied to the judge, they were executed. When the judge pronounced the people guilty, guards in military uniforms carried them off to be executed in gas chambers or the electric chair. The people were weeping and crying out to the guards as they were being dragged away, begging not to be executed! The people kept saying they were sorry, but no sympathy or forgiveness was granted to them. However, we three continued to sit there very peacefully, while all the people cried and wept all around us.

Suddenly, I turned around and glanced over my shoulder and saw Carrie and Rebecca standing in a hallway. I was startled when I saw a large, mean looking women with her large hands gripping Rebecca's small shoulders. I yelled, "Rebecca, come to grandma?" She started to run to me, but the hateful woman jerked her backwards, and held her firmly by her shoulders! The strong, muscular woman with yellowed grey hair pulled back in a bun, glared at me as if defying me. Her jaws were clenched tightly as she held Rebecca's small shoulders in a death like grip. I started screaming, "YOU CONTROLLING SPIRIT, I COMMAND YOU, IN THE NAME OF JESUS, LET MY GRANDDAUGHTER,

REBECCA GO! I BIND YOU EVIL CONTROLLING SPIRIT, GET OFF MY GRANDCHILD, IN THE NAME OF JESUS! LET HER GO NOW! I SAID YOU LET GO OF HER, THIS INSTANT, IN THE NAME OF JESUS!" Joe and David locked their hands together and brought their arms down over my chest and shoulders on either side of me. They said, "Sh. Be quiet mom!" "Carol, stop it! You can't yell like that! Remember, we're in a courtroom, so be quiet!" I struggled hard to get out of their tight grip! I kicked my feet and legs, and tried to get up out of the chair to get to Rebecca, but they held me firm! They couldn't stop my mouth from using the wonderful name of Jesus, though.

I watched as that big, ugly, evil spirit let loose of Rebecca's shoulders! The name of Jesus deflated it like a big balloon with the air suddenly let out of it. The controlling evil spirit was sucked right out of the building with God's supernatural vacuum cleaner! In that same instant Rebecca bolted toward me, and grabbed me around the waist. Carrie looked at me as if she were terrified and motioned for me to come closer. I left Joe and David sitting there and walked over to her. Carrie moved closer and in desperation, she whispered, "Oh Carol, I'm so scared!" Her eyes kept darting all around the room, and over at the judge, and back at me several times. I patted her shoulder and said, "Why Carrie, there's nothing to be afraid of." She took another step forward, until she was right up in my face and whispered, "Carol, I'm scared, because I think we've lied to the judge, and we're going to die by execution!" As soon as Carrie said that same sentence the second time, I woke up. I didn't waste any time. I bound that evil, controlling spirit off Rebecca, in the name of Jesus, after I woke up. "I love You Jesus."

When Sandy came over, she interpreted my dream. She said, "The reason you, Joe, and David were so peaceful in the midst of all the turmoil was because you were telling the truth. Bobby and Carrie are lying to Rebecca and scaring her." I remembered Bobby was supposed to come into some kind of great wealth on his nineteenth birthday. That was a couple of weeks away. I realized that was how they intended to move far, far away, and take Rebecca. Sandy agreed with me, "They will never take Rebecca away from David, or any of us, in the name of Jesus." It had been several long months since we'd seen or heard from our little Rebecca. It was getting harder for all of us each day, wondering what was going on in her young life? The enemy was working overtime trying to put terrible thoughts in our minds concerning Rebecca's well being, but I kept reminding myself, "In the name of Jesus, this and every battle belongs to the Lord. The victory is ours, no matter what it looks like." (Job 42:1) "I know that You can do everything, And that no purpose of Yours can be withheld from You." (Proverbs 11:21) "The seed of the righteous will be delivered." I never stopped, day or night, in crying out to God for Rebecca's safety. Little did any of us realize why the urgency in me was so strong to pray for God's protection over her continuously. "Oh God, how I thank You for the blood of Jesus."

On Rebecca's sixth birthday, the day after Bobby turned nineteen, I was sitting in the living room talking to David and Betsy when Joe rushed in the door from work, saying, "Quick, Carol, turn on the six o clock news, hurry! You guys are not going to believe what happened today! I was listening to the radio on my way home from work, when all of a sudden the disk jockey said something that made me pull my car off the road so I could hear him correctly." Joe kept talking very fast! He kept pacing the floor, and making funny circles with the palm of his hand each time he hit himself in the forehead. He just kept repeating. "I can't believe what I just heard on the car radio!" We all kept saying, "What did you hear them say, Joe?" "What is it, dad?" Joe said, "I cannot believe my little granddaughter was living in the same house with that murderer." David's face went white, but Joe wouldn't answer any of us, accept to tell us to be quiet, and listen to the six o'clock news. Joe turned the television sound button up on loud. The man on the news showed Bobby's picture and said, Bobby robbed a man, shot him 'executioner' style, and stuffed him in the storeroom freezer of the restaurant where he and Carrie worked.

Carrie and Bobby worked at a well-known restaurant. When they showed Bobby and Carrie's pictures, and said his last name, we knew it was unmistakably Rebecca's step- father. The newscaster told the location of the restaurant and Carrie and Bobby's home address. I kept thinking, "Lord, where is Rebecca? Please, Lord, protect her little heart and mind from all of this." On the news they told about the large sum of money Bobby was supposedly coming into on his nineteenth birthday. Bobby had lied to everyone, and since he was under such extreme pressure to come up with some big money, he killed that poor man for a few thousand dolors. They put Bobby's picture back up on the screen and said if convicted, he'd die by execution, the same way he killed that man. Sandy called and said, "Carol, remember the warning dream God gave you a couple of weeks ago, about the courtroom?" I realized, God had already warned me, and He protected little Rebecca even when they said Bobby came back home and slept in the same house with Rebecca, afterwards. I said, "Sweet Jesus."

Several months had come and gone, since we last saw or talked with our little Rebecca. David's lawyer wanted to serve Carrie with a subpoena, but we couldn't find her. In March I still had our Christmas tree up and decorated with Rebecca's Christmas and birthday presents underneath it. In silent vigil, we waited for her to come and open her presents, by leaving our tree up. I prayed constantly, and fervently, "Lord, please change this situation? Help us find Carrie, and our little Rebecca? I can't take this waiting, any more Lord, please help us?" I had my ironing board set up in Rebecca's room, and I was praying in the spirit and ironing, as fast and furiously as I could! In my heart, I was begging God, again, to help us find Rebecca! God broke through my unbelief and said sternly, "Hush, daughter, and stop that crying! If you really believe I've heard your prayers, and indeed I have then praise Me for the answered prayer which you've already prayed. Now, stop crying and begging Me, and start praising Me. The answer to your prayers is on the way. Straighten up your thinking, remember what I've already taught you, and straighten up this room! Get this room ready for your granddaughter. From the way it looks right now, she'll never come here. Daughter, if you really believe in your heart that I am able to do this, clean up this room and get ready for your granddaughter. Believe it, and act like it's true. I've taught you to walk by faith, not by sight, now do it!'" Sandy laughed so hard when I told her, "I'll tell you, my friend, I needed that scolding from the Lord. And before He was finished speaking to me, I had Rebecca's room spotless. I had the ironing board taken down, and put in the closet where it belonged, the sweeper run and the furniture polished." Sandy and I laughed at how God's tough correction set me free! Oh, how I love my very own Papa. I never appreciated anything so much as I did that good ole fashion balling out from my heavenly Father. I never opened my mouth again on the subject of Rebecca, except to praise God and speak faith to anyone who would listen to me. "Sweet Jesus!"

David helped me buy a new comforter, sheets and pillow cases to match for Rebecca's bedroom. I bought extra matching sheets and I made her bright cheery Priscilla curtains, ruffled pillow shams and dust ruffle. I even had enough material left over to make her dolly cradle, a comforter, pillow sham, and sheets to match. By the time I'd finished redecorating Rebecca's room we'd discovered Carrie had moved in with Bobby's mother. Carrie told David she didn't have the money to go to Court, so she let us have Rebecca every other weekend, without a fight. (2 Corinthians 4:13) "For we walk by faith not by sight." I finally did, after I obeyed God. "Thank You for helping me to obey You, Papa God."

When Rebecca came over to our house, it was as if nothing had ever happened. She was happy and never once cried to go back home. "Praise You, dear Papa! Praise You, wonderful Jesus! Praise You, sweet precious Holy Spirit!" (Hebrews 11:1) "Now faith is the substance of things hoped for and the evidence of things not seen." I told Sandy when I was sewing the curtains for Rebecca's room, God blessed me when He gave me Psalm 126:6, "They that sow in tears will reap in joy. He who continually goes forth weeping, bearing seed for sowing, will (doubtless) come again with rejoicing, bringing his sheaves with him." I was sewing Rebecca's curtains and sowing precious seeds of faith and prayers. He is a rewarder of them that diligently seek Him. Although part of the dream I have yet to understand? Sandy, admitted she too was a little puzzled that Carrie was the one the Lord chose to warn

177

me, but it was Bobby who got convicted. I said, "Sandy, all I know is, God has given us back our healthy, happy, Rebecca, and I praise His holy name! Why did Carrie say, 'Carol, I think WE lied to the judge?' Whatever it meant, it's between her and God." She agreed.

Mine and Sandy's families sat in the church enjoying every minute of David and Betsy's wedding. My beautiful daughter-in-law stood there wearing her lovely white wedding dress and her veil with beads of pearl and tiny off-white baby's breath flowers cascading down one side of her sweet face, just like I remembered it in the vision. Betsy's cousin Debbie had made her veil. Standing close beside her was my handsome son David in his gray tuxedo. In my heart, I kept thinking, "Oh Lord, You are so wonderful!" David and Betsy stood there gazing lovingly into each others eyes, and the agape love between them was stronger than ever.

Rebecca was dressed in a beautiful white wedding gown and veil to match Betsy's. She was their flower girl. Pastor Frank's red headed grandson, George was the ring bearer. George's mother Cindy, and I commented on how much he and Rebecca resembled each other. Later at the reception, a very special thing happened between Rebecca and her daddy. They were playing David and Betsy's love song, "You Are The Wind Beneath My Wings." Betsy was in the back changing clothes, so David picked Rebecca up in his arms and danced with her throughout the entire song. Rebecca knew the song and melody by heart. She sang every word of it to her daddy, while they moved joyfully across the dance floor. What a celebration we had that day! "Thank You, dear Papa, wonderful Jesus, and sweet precious Holy Spirit!"

We were so happy when Betsy and David announced, she was pregnant. About a week later, I was laying across my bed watching the squirrels playing outside my bedroom window. I thought, "I wonder if my next little grandchild will be a boy or a girl?" I no sooner had that thought, when I heard the Lord say, "That's Michael, Carol. David will keep the vow he made Me, and name his first son, Michael, just like he promised Me." I could hardly wait to tell David and Betsy. The enemy tried to stand at distance and yell, "Hey, your going to look really silly when Betsy doesn't have a boy!" I ignored the enemy and told David and Betsy what the Lord said. Betsy agreed with David. If it was a boy they would call his name Michael, after God's own arch angel. A few months later Betsy's ultra sound reveled, it was a boy. "Sweet Jesus!" David and Betsy decided to call his name Michael Anthony. Just the sound of it brought joy to my heart, because I knew David was keeping a promise he'd made to God. I just had to say, "Is there anything to hard for You, God? No! No way! Oh Lord, how can I ever thank You enough. You are so wonderful!"

David was still seeing three different doctors for the anxiety attacks. He and Betsy were living part time in their own apartment and part time with us. Even though we were seeing signs of David's recovery, there were still some nights when David used his key to unlock our door and come in and wake me up to pray for him. Earlier, God gave Betsy a dream to see her through the troubled times. She dreamed an angel visited her, opened the bible and pointed his finger to Psalm 34. The angel gave her God's word for her and David. I got so excited when Betsy told me about the dream. She asked me to read Psalm 34 and tell her what I thought. I said, "God is personally telling you and David to trust Him, and He will deliver you!" Psalm 34:7 "The angel of the Lord encamps all around those who fear Him, and delivers them." God is so good, all the time! Between Carrie trying to withhold Rebecca's visitations from us again, and David's past prison experience causing the panic attacks, God knew Betsy needed His word to hold onto. Sandy and I were excited about God speaking to our children through dreams. We dearly love the precious Holy Spirit!

I told Sandy the Lord had given me confirmation of Betsy's dream in a vision. In the vision, David and Betsy were nearly drowning out in the middle of a dark ocean. The white foamy waves were huge and the raging stormy waters tried to overwhelm them! Several times' David and Betsy were almost swept under by the huge violent waves crashing down on top of them! They were fighting the terrible storm, and desperately trying to make contact with each other. They were screaming, "Jesus, please help us!" David and Betsy frantically struggled to reach each other, even though the violent undercurrent tried to pull them under, and the wind and the waves beat against their exhausted bodies. I prayed in tongues as I continued to watch David and Betsy struggling against the almost impossible storm that was trying to destroy them. Finally, David and Betsy's fingers touched, and in that same swift instant, two huge white hands came down from out of the sky, grabbed them by their soaking wet hair, pulled them straight up out of the raging dark waters, and sat them down gently inside a beautiful white battleship, trimmed in expensive gold. The battleship was well advanced in every kind of the most sophisticated equipment man's intelligent technology could possibly come up with, that is, maybe in the distant and far reaching future. Even though the storm didn't stop, David and Betsy were safe and warm inside the ship, with every kind of comfort anyone could imagine. "Thank You Papa for deliverance."

Sandy asked me, if I remembered Jenny's friend Brad? I said, "How could I forget him. The Lord used you and I to set him free from drugs and thoughts of suicide." Sandy said, "Carol, I know you also remember Gerald, Brad's half brother who was in the accident with Jenny." I said of course I remembered him. He tried to shield Jenny with his own body when he knew their truck was going to hit the tree. He'd been in a coma. She squealed, "Just wait until I tell you what happened! Carol, Brad was standing beside Gerald's bed with a soft drink in his hand, when all of a sudden, Gerald woke up from the coma, sat straight up in bed, took the drink from Brad's hand, and drank what was left in the bottle. Brad said he was shocked as he stood there watching his half brother, Gerald, gulp down the rest of his soft drink." I said, "Wow! Look at the power of God!" Sandy put the icing on the cake when she told me Gerald graduated with his class that year. He was in a wheelchair, but thanks be to God, he's alive and well, and able to graduate with his class! I shouted, "I love You Jesus!"

Joe came up to me one evening and started apologizing and crying. The past several months had been very difficult for us financially, because his shop wasn't doing well. He said, "Carol, you were right. I shouldn't have tried to start my own business at the same time we were buying this house. We are going to lose our new home, our ten thousand dolors we paid down on it, and my company. I am so sorry!" Joe said he also found out, our real-estate agent who we'd known for many years and trusted had lied to us about the house. It had several outstanding leans against it. I so liked that red brick house. I felt such darkness overshadowing us, and that house. It really shocked me when Joe cried and apologized to me because he usually never, ever, said he was sorry for anything, much less admit something was his fault. He'd stopped going to church with me and immediately fell back into his old ways of verbally abusing me. Joe had a terrible temper and he would curse and yell at me in front of family, friends, and even strangers, if I said or did anything wrong. It didn't matter if we were in a grocery store, shopping center, or a restaurant, he yelled and cursed at me. I felt as if I wasn't his wife, but a hated stranger.

Sometimes our friends or family were with us when Joe spoke to me like that in public. I'd try and fight back the tears and cover my shame while I stood there looking humiliated and embarrassed. Joe couldn't seem to control his sudden angry outbursts toward me. His cruel words broke my heart. I remember telling Sandy one day, "Some of things Joe has done to me are so bad I wouldn't even dare talk to God about them, let alone, you, my best friend." However, even though Joe was mean to me, I loved him so much I didn't know what to do. He was so sad about losing the house and his business. He was pitiful. All I felt for him was forgiveness and compassion. He was depressed and worried all the time. If I hadn't had Sandy to stand in faith with me, I think I would have given up sooner. No matter how much we prayed though, things just seemed to get worse concerning Joe's shop and the house on Ross Rd. I kept on believing God for a miracle, regardless of our circumstances. I didn't speak it, but somehow I knew it was God who was shutting the door to the house on Ross Rd. "Sweet Jesus."

Betsy went into labor, and several hours later our beautiful new grandson, Michael Anthony was born. There were no complications with mother or baby either. "Praise You, Papa!" Betsy didn't even ask for a pain shot, before, during or after the delivery. It happened just like Dr. Leon Stutzman had prophesied over her. Dr. Leon Stutzman called David and Betsy out of the audience. First he spoke words only the precious Holy Spirit could have given him for David. David was slain in the spirit. He told Betsy God was healing her of a blood decease and she would amaze the doctors and nurses because she wouldn't need anything for pain. I kept praising the Lord, "Dear Jesus, I praise You for healing my son, Betsy and Michael." I praised God for blessing us with Pastors Lee and Connie Stutzman. They are God's anointed.

David and Betsy brought the baby to our house, and stayed with us several weeks. Rebecca was happy and excited, because she loved her little baby brother. Our grandchildren, were precious and special to us, but our joy was overshadowed by losing the house on Ross Rd. Joe's business steadily going under didn't help either. We were trying to withstand the pressure to just give up, quit, and move out. The odds against us to do so, were unsurmountable. Joe said we were so broke, we couldn't even afford to rent another house. The lady who sold us the house on a two year Land contract contingency plan was calling me constantly, insisting we hurry up and move out! Finally the judge, court ordered us to move out of the house. I forgave, by the grace of God, our real-estate agent who had told us everything was legal and binding when we signed the papers. I also forgive the lady who sold us her house, and kept our ten thousand dolors. It was none refundable. I knew, even if there were no outstanding leans against the house, we still weren't able to keep on paying the large house payments. I said, "In the name of Jesus, I thank You, Papa God for restoring everything that was stolen, back to me, seven times over, according to Your word."

David and Betsy were kind enough to ask us to move into their tiny little apartment with them for a few months until we could get on our feet financially. We moved in with David, Betsy, and little

Michael a few days before Christmas, and all I did was cry. We felt terrible moving in with them because they were still considered newly weds. It felt like God was far, far away from me, even though I knew His word said, "He will never leave us nor forsake us." (Hebrews 13:5) We were so cramped for space in their small apartment, we were in each others way constantly. Joe was just relieved to have the burden of those large house payments off his shoulders. Living with people didn't affect him like it did me. I was miserable and felt like I was invading our son and daughter-in-laws' privacy. I kept crying, "Oh God please have mercy on us!" The highlight of my life was helping Betsy with little Michael.

After several months, Joe and I moved in with his mother and dad. I'd get up about four thirty in the morning before everyone else, just so I could pray and read my bible or I wouldn't have made it through that troubled time. Although I was very grateful for everyone helping us out, I wasn't used to several televisions going all day long, and constant company coming over. I was used to my house being peaceful and quiet throughout the day. One morning Joe's mother asked me if Joe was giving me any grocery money. I told her, "No, he always says he is broke when I ask him for money." She was angry because her husband, Joe's dad worked in the same shop and he knew Joe was making more money then he was telling me about. Joe's dad also told me Joe had bought himself a boat. He had failed to tell me about that also. We'd been living with his mother and dad for several months and Joe had not offered to help out once with their groceries or anything. I was ashamed and embarrassed. For thirty years I'd had my own home.

Finally, I got angry enough to tell Joe I couldn't take any more of his lies or living with other people. I also told him we were going to find us a house and move in it and I didn't want to hear, "Honey, we just don't have enough money to move into our own place yet." I told him I knew he'd bought himself a boat, and I knew he'd been keeping all the money back for himself for several months too. He was always gone, but I was stuck there. I also found out Joe's terrible, out of control habit of collecting baseball, hockey, football and basketball cards, had gotten a thousand-times worse. I'd heard from very reliable sources, Joe was paying huge ridicules prices to feed his crazy addiction for the ball cards. I finally found a house for rent within our price range, but Joe said we couldn't afford to pay the deposit and pay the rent too. I kept on praying and believing for a house. Thank God, my friend Jean happened to know a man who owned a house for rent. She said if he'd let us, she would help me paint, wallpaper, and fix it up in exchange for the deposit and part of the rent. He agreed to let us rent the house on those terms. "Oh Papa God, please bless my friend Jean bountifully!" Jean used her professional enterer design and wallpaper hanging skills, and I helped with the cleaning, painting and sanding the walls smooth. She furnished all of the wallpaper herself to help me get started on the house. She hung beautiful wall paper and mixed the paint to match perfectly for the walls in every room of the house. In eleven days, we completely refurbished that house, including ripping up the old green carpet in the kitchen and replacing it with clean tiles that was on sale for the perfect price. I said constantly, "Oh Papa, thank You for giving me the desires of my heart, and You have not withheld the request of my lips! OH YES! THANK YOU JESUS! I love You Lord!"

Jean was even kind enough to give me material to make curtains and a tablecloth in the kitchen, and chair pads. I sewed every stitch with such joy in my heart I thought I'd scream with excitement! I was so thankful to God for giving Joe and I our own home again. I played my praise tapes loud, and danced abandonedly like David danced before the Lord! I honestly cannot correctly describe my feelings with words. I prayed for God to bless Jean one hundred fold for all her beautiful hard work. "I love You, dear Papa God! I love You sweet Jesus! I love dear precious Holy Spirit! Yahoo!"

My friend Dixie was so excited one day when she called to tell me about a 'Women Aglow' retreat weekend in April of that year, 1990. She asked if I could come with her and her husband Ron. I said, "Dixie, if it's God's will for me to go He will have to make a way where there seems to be no way. I don't have the money for my hotel room, my meals, or the dress clothes I need to wear." She agreed, God would make a way if it was His will for me to go with her, and God supplied my every need. "Sweet Jesus, I love You!" I went to my first 'Womens Aglow' retreat. My very own Papa God even moved on Joe's heart and he provided me with several nice dresses and shoes to wear. I kept saying, "Wow! Thank You Papa God!" Dixie and Ron payed for my room and food the whole weekend, and I was more then happy to help them sell Pastor Clink's anointing oil. On the last day there, when we were ready to leave, I was sitting in the main lounge at the hotel waiting for Dixie and Ron to finish packing up Pastor Clink's anointing oils. They insisted I go out in the lounge, and relax and enjoy myself.

A nice friend I'd met at the retreat named Donna, came and sat down beside me on the couch and we started talking. It wasn't long before several other women were sitting there with us, because Donna kept stopping them, saying, "Come and listen to Carol's powerful testimonies about how God delivered her oldest son out of prison and her younger son from drugs! He healed her marriage too!" I never got tired of giving my testimony, because God has done so much for me. I knew Carol Pettit, Judy Hammons, Nellie Vega, and Donna Wolford and I would be good friends. Nellie laid hands on me and prayed for this book, "Which way? What way? Your way Lord." The other ladies stretched out their hands toward me, and prayed in agreement with her. Carol Pettit laughed at me when I told her I'd always had trouble in the past talking to other women in leadership positions, like herself. Carol told me, God had placed her in my life to show me the ropes. I told her about the prophecy over my life and how I'd always ran from it, because I couldn't even try to imagine myself getting up in front of others to tell my story. Carol had pretty blue eyes. She made me laugh at myself. A couple of months later, Carol Pettit told my mother, she had gone on before me, and she was going to help me get to where I was supposed to be in God's plan for my life, upon the stage speaking. I loved every one of my new friends, God gave me. He really blessed me at that meeting.

I continually apologized to Joe for everything! I asked the Lord to help me, "Papa God, please help me to do something that will please my husband." Most of my life I was made fun of, and told how stupid I was, but when I saw myself in the mirror of God's word, that stuff began to irritate me. I recognized, I am a new creation. I refused the devil's lies, in the name of Jesus! I believed the truth. I had always been so self conscious of everything I did, including the way I walked, talked and laughed. First my dad, and then Joe's ridiculing remarks against me made me feel unworthy. I finally realized it was just the enemy using them to try and stop God's plan for my life. As I read God's word, I allowed Him to renew my mind and everything in me started to cry out for change! In Joe's backslidden misery, his anger towards me worsened.

One day while Carol Pettit and I were talking on the phone, she mentioned that I needed more inner healing, in order to be more effective for God to use me, and to finish this book. I was skeptical as to why she felt I needed her and Nellie's help when all I had needed up to that point was Jesus working with me alone. Sandy, Dixie and Jean were concerned about me. All I did was cry, until Carol, and Nellie came and helped me allow the dear precious Holy Spirit to set me free. I'd just read, (God's Crippled Children, By Lana Bateman.) The book prepared me to understand, that I needed more inner healing. That wonderful book opened my eyes wide, and it helped me so much. "Thank You, wonderful Jesus!"

As Carol and Nellie sat beside me at my kitchen table praying for me in tongues, I saw what looked like a television screen of my whole life pass before me! It was terribly painful to watch. I couldn't believe, I even had to forgive my wonderful mother of some things. I instantly forgave her for leaving me alone with daddy. Mommy took my sister Peggy and went to California to see my older sisters. She didn't have enough money to take both Peggy and myself. Peggy was three years younger then I was, so I had to stay home with daddy. I hid in the closet underneath the dirty clothes for several hours, until daddy stopped searching the house for me. I didn't know which one I was more afraid of, the thought of the big black water bugs and roaches crawling all over me, or daddy. Finally, daddy stopped yelling my name. I listened hard while he fixed himself something to eat in the downstairs kitchen. After he was finished eating I heard the television playing really loud as usual, so I knew he'd lay there on the couch and watch it, until he feel asleep in a drunken stupor. I knew his pattern well.

I was so afraid as I snuck quietly down each step and peeked through the banisters, watching and holding my breath to see if daddy was asleep yet. I crawled on my hands and knees to the black phone which sat on a small table in the otherwise empty dinning room. When my older sister Louise answered the phone, she told me, "Carol, honey don't you worry. I'll call Curt home from work, as soon as we hang up. I'll get Linda and the girls ready, and we'll come and get you as quick as we can, ok sis? I love you sweetheart, by." I was so scared, I crept back up the stairs and resumed my place in the dark closet under the dirty clothes with the bugs, until almost three hours later when my sister got there to pick me up. They had to come all the way from Ypsilanti Michigan to Dayton Ohio to get me. This happened several times. I don't believe my precious mother ever meant to hurt me. I was more terrified of daddy then she realized. My sister Louise's oldest daughter Linda had grown up with Peggy and I. We were really close. They came and stayed with us for parts of the summers and we stayed with them too. We always loved it when they came. Daddy was respectful of Louise, so he treated us half way decent.

I was so thankful the Lord sent Carol and Nellie to help me. "Thank You, Papa for never giving up on me." I found myself laughing more often, and crying less. (Psalm 30:5) "Weeping may endure for a night, but joy comes in the morning." I had cried so hard when I had to say good-buy to my little dog Jacob. I gave Jacob to Joe's niece and her husband. I knew they would be good to him. They allowed him to sleep with them in their waterbed.

After Carrie's divorce was final with Bobby, she married a man named Rick. He seemed to be a nice person. He and Carrie were happy, but I prayed he would love and except Rebecca and be good to her. God knew I was concerned about Rebecca's happiness and her adjustment to another new step dad, so He gave me a lovely dream about her. In the dream Rebecca was doing a cheer. She jumped straight up in the air, turned around and landed with her feet spread apart, yelling loudly, "VICTORY! VICTORY! VICTORY!" She had a great big smile across her pretty freckled face. She was wearing a bright rainbow colored ball cap with an extra big bill, a pair of matching rainbow colored tennis shoes and socks, and blue sweats. Her curly red pony tail trailed out the back of her ball cap. Directly across the bill of the cap was written in bright yellow letters, "VICTORY!" I knew God was reassuring me, no matter what the situation looked like to us, everything was going to be all right. I've held onto that dream all through the many hard changes that little girl has gone through in her young life. (2 Corinthians 2:14) "Now thanks be to God who always leads us in triumph in Christ, and through us defuses the fragrance of His knowledge in every place." I said, "I praise Your wonderful and awesome name, Lord Jesus! I love You so much dear Lord!"

I received some really good news. "Hallelujah!" My sister Sally and her husband Don decided to move to Manchester Ohio. She was only two and a half hours away from me. Her and Don had come to mine and Peggy's rescue so many times when we were growing up. Sally refused to let the past beat her, so she always smiled her pretty smile. She chose to be happy. Peggy and I loved it when our phone rang and Sally and Don wanted to take us to the drive-inn movie with them and there two young sons. We loved to stay the night and sleep upstairs under one of Don's mother Grace's warm home aid quilts in the winter time. I remember once when they lived in a large house in the country, Don built Peggy and I a play house. Joe didn't want to take me to see my sister Sally very often. He mostly liked to be around his people. It was still nice though. I felt comforted just knowing she was nearer.

Sandy went to Kentucky to clean and paint her granny's house, as she usually did in the early spring. When She came back from her trip to Kentucky this time she told me, "Carol, right before we left I was taking some things down to the basement to put them away for granny when all of sudden her old-fashioned cellar door fell on my head and nearly knocked me unconscious!" Her granny had the old fashioned heavy cellar door which opened up from the floor, and when it fell on top of Sandy's head it knocked her down the stairs and onto the cold hard cement floor of the basement! Sandy said she immediately started praying in the spirit and she asked the Lord to not allow her to lose consciousness. She lay there in horrible pain, quoting scriptures and praying in the spirit, until help came. Everyone kept begging her to go to the hospital, but she argued, "No thank you, I really am fine. Jesus healed me with His stripes." Sandy looked up at me and laughed, gently rubbing the top of her head. She said on their way back home, later that same day as they were coming down around those mountains in the darkened car, the enemy started questioning her judgment, in not going to the hospital.

Sandy said the enemy also tried to convince her, she needed to admit she had a concussion. She said before she knew it, her head started throbbing again. It was so sore she could hardly stand to touch it. The enemy of her soul yelled LOUDER! The spirit of self pity was oozing from his voice, "Oh Sandy, I think you really do have a bad concussion and you'd better tell your husband to drive you straight to the nearest hospital!" She said the enemy kept on harassing her until finally she whispered underneath her breath, "Lord, do I really have a concussion?" Instantly, He asked her, "Sandy, do you want a concussion?" She answered Him quickly, "No Lord, I don't want a concussion!" He answered her sternly, "Then, you don't have a concussion, Sandy." She smiled and told me, the minute God told her she didn't have a concussion the pain left and the fear went with it. (Mark 9:24) "Immediately the father of the child cried out and said with tears, "Lord, I believe, help my unbelief!" God's words of correction got rid of Sandy's unbelief.

My dear brother Gene had been on my mind almost constantly. Several other family members and especially my mother told me Gene had been depressed, drinking and staying up in his room. I knew what that awful depression was like, so I prayed for him even more. I missed him so much. I had not seen him or his wife Nancy, in about nine years. Not since his oldest daughter Lydia was a baby. Since then they'd had three more beautiful little girls I was longing to see too. I didn't even know for sure where he lived? Every time I'd pray for him and his family, I kept hearing the Lord say to me, "Carol, go down to Lo Debar and bring your brother out." I knew what Lo Debar meant, not only because I'd been there myself but I had read about it in 2 Samuel 9:4. I read about King David wanting to bless Mephibosheth, the son of his friend Jonathan. David brought him out of Lo Debar to bless him.

God had called all of my brother's family to pray to the Lord for Gene, the same way they prayed me out of Lo Debar. Every one of my family members were in prayer and asking the Lord to help my brother get out of Lo Debar, 'depression.' I finally discovered where he lived and I got his phone number. So, I asked Joe if he'd take me to see him. Joe said Gene lived down near our cabin. He and David were going there the following weekend. So I called Gene, and he and his family welcomed my visit like the flowers in springtime, Gene said. I was so happy, I could hardly wait to see them all. Joe dropped me off there. He said he and David would pick me up several hours later on their way back home.

I sat at Gene's dining room table with him and his family talking about our lives growing up together. We laughed and talked, but in my heart I knew Gene wasn't happy. He had been suffering, I could feel it. (Isaiah 61:1-3) "The Spirit of the Lord God is upon me, Because the Lord has anointed Me to preach good tidings to the poor; He has sent Me to heal the brokenhearted, to proclaim liberty to the captives, and the opening of the prison to those who are bound; to proclaim the acceptable year of the Lord, and the day of vengeance of our God; to comfort all who mourn, to console those who mourn in Zion, to give them beauty for ashes, the oil of joy for mourning, the garment of praise for the spirit of heaviness; that they may be called trees of righteousness, the planting of the Lord, that He may be glorified." Through the power of the Holy Spirit, I rebuked the devil off Gene, in the name of Jesus! He will never use my brother for a mouthpiece again, in the name of Jesus! Gene was set free from that hour. My wonderful brother Gene that I loved so dearly was his old self again. We talked and laughed. I looked at my precious brother who I'd been so close to growing up. He was such a gentle sweet natured man. "Praise You, Papa God, for the anointing that removes burdens and destroys yokes!"

When Gene was young daddy would beat him unmercifully sometimes. Daddy pulled Gene's red curly hair until he'd pulled him straight up out of a chair! Daddy had his shoes on when he'd kick him hard too! I remember the last time daddy ever whipped Gene. For some reason we lived for the first and only time in an upstairs apartment 'way out in the country.' Gene and I were sitting on our tiny little porch right outside the kitchen door talking when daddy came home, drunk, angry and cursing us, as usual. We tried to stand back so daddy could get in the door. He kept on cursing us until he got to the top of the steps, but then he grabbed Gene by the hair and drug him into the kitchen! I wanted to scream for help, I was so scared of what daddy was going to do to him again. He knocked Gene onto the floor, and kept on relentlessly kicking him! My poor brother was curled up in a ball while daddy kicked him until he was bloody! Mommy tried to say something to make daddy stop, but it only made him angrier at Gene. Daddy looked crazy! I couldn't move for fear of daddy. I stood there on the porch, trying to look away, but afraid not to see if daddy was going to kill him this time? Inside my heart, I cried out to Jesus!

I know daddy broke or fractured some of Gene's ribs or his hip when he repeatedly kicked him like that. I immediately ran in the house and tried to help my poor brother to get up off the floor, but he wouldn't let me, mommy or Peggy help him. Gene laid there I'm sure in horrible pain until he was able to get up. However, this time when my brother Gene got up off the floor after another one of daddy's cruel beatings, he did something that shocked all of us. He staggered into the living room where daddy was about half asleep on the couch. Gene stood there glaring at daddy with a terrible mean fearless look in his eye. My brother got right down in daddy's face, pointed his finger and said, in a deep hurting voice, "Look old man, if you ever try to whip me or kick me like that again, I'll kill you the first chance I get! I'll get my hands on a gun or knife! I'll get something that I can kill you with! Do you hear me old man? And if you ever hit my mother or my sisters while I'm around, I'll kill you the first chance I get for that too! I'm just looking for a reason too kill you! Are you listening to me old man? You'd better be listening to me! You will never kick me or beat me like that ever again! You got that?" Daddy never attempted to beat up on my brother Gene again. He never tried to hurt him or us while my brother was there either. A few years later Gene, like all the rest of my brothers, joined the armed services. I missed my brother's broad smile, red curly hair and big blue eyes when he left. I missed daddy leaving us alone too. I thank God, we got through those hard times. "Papa God, Your grace is sufficient."

I had the privilege of making Gene and his family new curtains, table clothe, matching chair pads and I even made him new cushions for his favorite rocking chair and footstool. I made Gene and Nancy and their sweet pretty little daughters all bedspreads, and matching ruffled Priscilla curtains, pillow shams, dust ruffle, and throw pillows. I even made matching bedspreads and pillow shams for the girls' doll cradles too. God has given my precious brother back his life and made him whole. God's love is greater than any Lo Debar. "Lord Jesus, I am so thankful for Your love."

I was saying my prayers early one morning when all of a sudden I began to have an open-eyed vision of a brand new home being built. It sat up on a slight hill. I kept having this same open-eyed vision every morning while I was saying my prayers. As I watched this rather large home in the building process, I began to question the Lord about it. Proverbs 6:30-31 "People do not despise a thief if he steals to satisfy himself when he is starving. Yet when he is found, he must restore sevenfold; He may have to give up all the substance of his house." Suddenly, I knew the Lord was showing me this was my seven fold return on my stolen property, my house on Ross Rd.. I recognized this was my sevenfold return of the ten thousand dolors and my red brick house. I yelled, "Oh, thank You

Papa God, for restoring back to me seven times over, all that is rightfully mine according to Your word, with interest compounded daily, in the name of Jesus!" Every morning I continued to watch this same house on the hill being built. Finally one day, I asked the Lord to please show me where the house was located.

When Joe and I were taking my mother down to visit my sister, Sally, I kept seeing the vision of the house again. I asked the Lord quietly in the back seat of our car, "Lord, why am I seeing the house again? I usually only see it in the mornings when I pray." I heard the Lord answer, "Your seeing the house because you are very close to it." I said, "Where, Lord?" He said, "Look up to your left." Sure enough, there it was, exactly as I had seen it every morning in the vision. The silver paper with the large red stamped letters on the outer sides of the insulation was around the big two story house which sat up on a slight hill. I got so excited, I told Joe and mommy about the house! Of course my mother believed me, but Joe didn't. He made of fun of me. He said, even if he did believe that was our house he wouldn't live there because it was too far away from where he thought we should live. Later, I told Sandy, I didn't understand everything, but I knew that house would someday be mine. Jesus is the Master Carpenter, and He built that house for me, and I WILL live in it one day, but only in His timing. My friend Dixie took me to see my house when it was completed. It's a much larger red brick home then the one I lost on Ross Rd. I know God built that house for me, and I will see my vision fulfilled someday. I learned a Christian family lived there, but when God's timing is right, I will buy it from them.

I told the Lord, until it was time to move on into the bigger house I was very thankful for the current rented house and all the beautiful wallpaper and fresh clean paint on the walls. I'd had so much fun sewing pillows to match my window seat in our bay window in the living room. The Lord made it possible to purchase real expensive tapestry for a very low price. It had been water damaged and stained, but Jean told me I could wash it and iron it. "Hallelujah!" It turned out beautiful! More then anything else I love my quiet time with the Lord, playing my praise tapes and enjoying my Christian television again too. I so enjoyed having my sons, daughter-in-laws, and grandchildren over for breakfast, lunch or dinner. Joe even surprised me, when he bought us, all brand new appliances, wow! I'd never, ever owned a brand new stove, refrigerator, washer, and dryer before. My new, smudge proof refrigerator even had the fancy new gadget on the front of the door for crushed ice, or water. I just kept saying, "Praise You, Papa God! Your mercy endures forever! Praise You Jesus, and praise You sweet precious Holy Spirit! I love You dear Papa! I love You wonderful Jesus! I love You sweet precious Holy Spirit!"

Chapter Six

The battle is the Lord's

I was sitting quietly in my recliner, relaxing one morning when the Lord spoke to me clearly and said, "Come on Carol, let's go to the barn." That old barn where I was molested, was the last place on earth I wanted to go. I 'd put off letting God help me deal with that part of my life for many years, because it still terrified me. I had not wanted to remember who it was that molested me as a child until I read, (God's crippled children, By Lana Bateman.) In her book she shed new light on, John 20:23 "If you forgive the sins of any, they are forgiven them; if you retain the sins of any, they are retained." Even though I'd read that particular scripture in the bible many times, it wasn't until I read Lana Bateman's book that I fully comprehended the true meaning of it, for those of us who have need of inner healing. When she illuminated my spiritual eyes to that scripture, I knew I had to allow God to help me grow up and face whoever it was who had molested me. I had to forgive them by name, in the privacy of my home with God alone, and let Him set us both free. Lana Bateman also helped me to understand my unnatural fear of dogs and heights was born out of the childhood sexual abuse I'd suffered. I was so tired of all the unexplainable memories of my past haunting me and filtering through my heart and mind in parts and pieces. And until Jesus asked me to go with Him to the barn I thought I was ready to face the fear of knowing who it was head on, and get on with my life.

I'd already told God several times that I forgave whoever it was who had perpetrated these unkind acts against me. I was so afraid to remember, I curled up in my chair in a tight ball and said, "No Lord, not now. I'm here alone. Don't You think it would be better to wait until Carol or Nellie are here with me to help me?" All of a sudden I felt such a wonderful peace come over me as I watched myself with Jesus in a vision. I was a small child again, holding tightly to the Lord's hand. We climbed up a wooden ladder and into the loft of the old barn. Jesus was so big, He filled up the whole loft with His gleaming white garment which flowed out and over the sides of it. I couldn't see any other part of my small body except my big wide eyes blinking as I peeked through a tiny open space behind Jesus where I was standing. The old barn didn't look so spooky to me anymore. In that one swift flicker of time, Jesus took the fear and shame away from my heart and mind which had tormented me for most of my life. Jesus also reminded me, the place where He was born was similar to a barn. Jesus showed me that He was there with me all the time, and I praised Him for His gentle loving ways. I was still a little puzzled though. He didn't make me remember who it was who raped me yet. I realized the Lord was giving me a little rest in between healing's.

After Wanda Herman reviewed my manuscript, she said I needed to allow God to bring back my childhood memories. She said the enemy had stolen the good memories with the bad ones. Wanda prayed for me along with many others who God sent, and I was able to remember enough of my childhood to write almost half a chapter instead of the few pages I'd written previously. When Wanda asked me if I had any allergies, I told her all my life I'd been allergic to gasolene. The fumes made me nervous and triggered an unexplainable anger in me. Immediately, Wanda told me there must have been a gasoline can stored either in the barn or behind the barn to be used for the tractors. I said, "Wow! I never once thought of that." Wanda prayed for me, and God healed me miraculously from that allergy, and I've never had it again. "Praise You, Papa God for healing me! I love You, Lord!" The Lord graciously sent me, so many strong believers to pray for my inner healing. They prayed for me and encouraged me to finish this book. Nellie told me as many times as she has prayed for inner healing for other woman, she had never seen any other inner healing like mine, because it was so intense. She said she had never seen so much abuse in one persons life, as she had seen in mine. Nellie also encouraged me to tell it like it really was. In other words, she told me. "Carol, how can abused women relate to you, unless you tell the truth? Even though it may hurt a few people to hear the truth, it will help many others."

One afternoon I sat quietly watching a young dark haired man named David Ruxer give his testimony on T B N in Indiana. David Ruxer told how he was molested when he was a little boy. I listened closely while he told about his life of substance abuse and how he thought it was closely related to the repeated child molestation he'd experienced. He told about his past drinking, smoking and drug habits that plagued his life. He couldn't seem to break free from them even after he got saved and stood in many different prayer lines. David Ruxer told about his new powerful ministry. He teaches others how to break the chains of darkness. I wrote his number down, and called him. We talked for a while and then I told him about the repeated sexual abuse in my own childhood. I couldn't believe I was confiding in this stranger.

With great shame, I wept and told him I was so humiliated because I still smoked cigarettes, and yet I'd written a book about all the miracles God had done in mine and Sandy's lives. I told him, God had set me free from the addiction of taking twenty eight-prescription drugs a day, and the Lord had spoken to me and told me, the cigarettes will go out of my life forever, and they will, in the name of Jesus. I said, "God got me off the last ten pills, one day at a time, David, and the cigarettes are leaving too." "Thank You wonderful Lord, Jesus!" After we talked a little longer, he told me he'd come to my house on the following Monday, and council me for free. I was so relieved, he made house calls. "The Lord is my Shepherd and I shall not be in want." (Psalm 23:1)

Our conversation ended that Friday with a short, simple, but powerful prayer. David Ruxer prayed, "Father, please reveal and expose the roots of the cigarettes in Carol's life, in Jesus name we pray, amen." I was so shocked. I said, "Is that it?" He laughed and answered, "I'm sure that will do it for you." David Ruxer gave me a few instructions, and told me not to be afraid when different things started happening to me. He told me I'd start remembering things right away, and like the pieces of a puzzle, everything would come together quickly for me. He surprised me when he told me I'd remember who it was who raped me before he came to see me on the following Monday. He also told me before we ended our conversation, the reason I was afraid to remember who raped me was because I'd been hypnotized. He said, witchcraft was involved. He plead the blood of Jesus over me, and I denounced the witch craft off of myself and my family's lives forever, in the name of Jesus, and by the blood of Jesus. We knew it was accomplished. I felt jittery inside and I started to weep uncontrollably after I hung up the phone. I knew God was taking me from glory to glory, as I obeyed His voice. I was letting go of those weights that had so easily beset me. (Hebrews 12:1)

Later on that day I had a vision when I laid down to rest on the couch. I had just closed my eyes, but I wasn't asleep when I saw a vision of the man who had worked on the farm where we lived. Instantly, I remembered his face and I knew it was the man who had molested me so long ago. He was pitifully standing at the bottom of an old rusty looking well. The well was turned over on its side and he was standing near the bottom of it. The well was nearly empty, but I could see the rusty, murky water beside him at the bottom. He was so tiny, maybe a foot tall. He was looking up at me crying out to me, and begging me to forgive him! He kept saying, "Please forgive me Carol? I never meant to hurt you. I am so sorry! Please, Carol, can you ever forgive me? I've asked God to forgive me a thousand times!"

He kept raising his arms and hands toward me pleading, then letting them drop back down to his sides. Each time he'd drop his head and shoulders with his pitiful humble face starring toward the ground again. My heart was overwhelmed with forgiveness and compassion for this man! I burst into tears and cried out to God with great sobs as I forgave him with all of my heart. I prayed and asked God to forgive me for taking so long to allow Him to help me set this poor man free. I spoke his name in the privacy of my home. I asked God to heal him of those past hurts, "Oh Lord, please cause this man to know I've forgiven him completely. I know You forgave him the moment he asked You too, Lord."

By the time David Ruxer arrived early Monday morning, I'd had a weekend of memories flooding over me, until the pieces of the puzzle of that particular part of my missing past was completed. I told David Ruxer, I felt a joy, I'd never felt before. I kept saying, "Oh Lord, how I love You!" I also thanked Him for answering David Ruxer's short, simple prayer of deliverance! David Ruxer laughed when I told him how small the man was in the vision. "God is so kind and gentle, He even made the man who I'd been so afraid of in my past, totally none intimidating." From the moment I met David Ruxer, I felt like I'd known him all my life. He was so easy going and really down to earth. After we talked a while he asked if he could lead me again in a simple prayer of forgiveness for the man who had abused me so long ago. I'd never felt such peace and freedom in my life as I did when I repeated that pray after him. Unconscionable peace flowed over me in waves as I watched myself in a vision during that redeeming prayer of forgiveness. With all of my heart, I thanked God!

In the vision I was standing barefooted on a warm sandy beach. My five physical senses were so alive, it felt like I was actually standing there feeling the perfect temperature of the gentle ocean waves washing over my bare feet, and rinsing off the sand. A soft breeze was blowing, and the sky and ocean were an awesome vibrant color of blue. The sun was shinning so perfectly as I stood there talking to a lovely little dove sitting in my left hand. I felt such love for the little dove as it cooed softly. I pulled it up close to me and kissed it on its beak, then I lifted my left hand up high and set the little dove free. I watched as it soared gracefully into the beautiful blue heavens above me, and I knew this was a symbol of both myself and the man I'd just prayed for, flying free. We were both set forever free, because of the tender loving mercies from God's own heart. I told David Ruxer, I felt like that beautiful dove. My spirit was soaring through the heavens free at last. He surprised me when he suddenly asked me if I'd like to assist him in the prayers for inner healing for others? I gladly said, "Yes!" I felt so much peace and joy bubbling up on the inside me, I laughed more often, and heartier. The joy of the Lord is my strength. "Oh Lord, I love You so much! Thank You Papa God!"

The prophecy over my life began to manifest more as I received calls asking me to get up on stage and sing and tell my story. I was really scared at first, but my strong desire to help others and the hunger to do God's will over-road my fears. (Proverbs 4:11) "I have taught you in the ways of wisdom; I have led you in straight paths." I trusted Jesus to set me free from fear so I could work effectively for Him and give Him glory. He did the moment I obeyed Him and stepped upon that stage. "Thank You sweet, wonderful Jesus!" (John 8:36) "Therefore if the Son makes you free, you shall be free indeed." Joe wouldn't come and hear me speak or sing, but he didn't mind my having several of my friends over at our house for a weekly prayer and bible study. Joe didn't mind the ladies coming over at all, it only gave him another good excuse to leave me alone again anyway. I prayed, "God help us!"

My new friends asked me to teach them everything I knew about prayer. I taught them to pray the word of God. Psalm 91. Psalm 103. Psalm 23. I taught them especially to plead the blood of Jesus over themselves and their family's, and everything they owned. Before I knew it, God birthed in me a new prayer manual. A collection of prayers in compassed in the word of God.

My friend's Nancy Trimbach, Brenda Mays, and Carol Pettit helped me put the prayer manual together, and I sent it to my brother Myrlon and his wife Barbra who have a Christian printing shop out west in Arizona. They printed two hundred and fifty of my prayer manuals and sent them back to me, for free. "Thank You Jesus!" I prayed for God to bless each and every person involved in helping me publish my prayer books. Nancy did a beautiful job on the art work on the front cover, and her sister Susie's son did the art work on the back, again for free. Every Monday evening Nancy brought me something from my favorite Mexican restaurant. I never told her Joe wasn't allowing me to buy groceries, and I never told anyone in my prayer group Joe was leaving me alone nearly every night of the week until twelve, one, two and three o-clock in the morning either. Joe always said he was out looking for baseball cards in department stores, and I halfway believed him. My friend Judy and her sister Jan joined our prayer group too. They always brought home aid goodies to share with the other ladies and Joe. All of these special women in our prayer group carried my prayer manual to work if they had to, but they never missed faithfully saying the prayers every morning, they told me. When I pray the word of God, I know I am not praying vain repetitions. I've heard some of the comments from different people about repeating the same prayer's everyday being repetitious. The word of God will never return to Him void, but will accomplish what it says it will. (Isaiah 55:11) Praying the word always strengthens faith. I love the word of God. "I love You Papa, Jesus, and sweet Holy Spirit! You are so wonderful, Lord!"

Betsy and David blessed us with another precious grandson, Kyle Wesley. He's a special little boy with light blond brown hair and big brown eyes. His older brother Michael stayed with Joe and I a lot, and slept between us in our king sized bed. Even when David and Betsy were leaving from our house, and Joe and I were standing beside there car talking to them, before they could back out of our driveway, Michael would undo his seat belt from his car seat, roll down the window and climb out. The little fellow got into so much trouble when we'd all look up and see him waving to his mommy and daddy as he walked past the front of the car and into our house. He'd smile and wave, saying, "By mommy and daddy and little brother! I'm just gonna stay the night with grandma and grandpa again, ok?" Each time when David went after him, he'd cry to stay with grandma and grandpa! Sometimes David and Betsy just shook their heads and let him stay. I know Michael was attached to us, because Betsy and David lived with us until she had him. Afterwards she brought him home from the hospital and they stayed with us. We also stayed with them for about three months after we lost our home on Ross Rd. The more increasingly Joe's anger burned toward me, he rejected Michael too. I loved Joe unconditionally, and I forgave him consistently.

On a cold February afternoon I was sitting at my kitchen table gazing out the window, and admiring the beautiful blue sky while I ate my lunch. The wind was blowing briskly that day, and quickly whipping the puffy white clouds into thin vapor. However, I watched as a rather large sized white cloud slowly floated until it stood perfectly still against the deep blue sky outside my window. I remember thinking, "How strange it is, the big white cloud's not moving, and yet at the same time, the wind is whirling all the other clouds right past it, turning them into thin strings of white smoke, until they disappear?" The large white cloud began to take on the shape of a scull as it sat there in the blue sky starring down at me very peacefully. I said, "Lord, what are You trying to say to me?" He did not answer me, but I didn't feel afraid. Instead I felt rather calm, like the calm before a storm. I knew the Lord was warning me, because of the extended length of time the cloud remained stationary in the sky outside my window. I continued to watch mesmerized as all the other clouds swirled past the cloud in the shape of the scull. It was so odd to watch all the other white clouds whipping all around the large white cloud and disappear into thin vapor, while it remained.

After the large scull cloud finally disappeared, I called my friend Carol Pettit and told her about the strange phenomenon. She was quick to remind me, I'd told her a few days earlier something significant was going to happen on that particular day, February 29, 1992. Suddenly I remembered, I'd even written it in my bible, "Something very significant is going to happen on February 29, 1992." That evening Ron, and Sandy's family went with our family to celebrate Joe's birthday at his favorite restaurant. Our two families decided to celebrate Joe's birthday four days late, because it was the weekend and no one had to get up early for work the next day. Jenny, Betsy, David, and Joey left their children with a baby sitter so they could enjoy a quiet evening. Joey's wife Tina didn't go, nor did Jenny's bo, it was just the eight of us. After dinner, Ron and Sandy came back to our house for coffee, cake and ice cream. David, Betsy, Jenny, and Joey went to pick up all the children to bring them to Joe's party. It was still very cold and windy out, so we knew it would be a while before they came back. Coats and hats take time to button up and tie.

When we walked in the house I noticed the red light was flashing on the answering machine. It was a message from my nephew Donnie asking me to return his call as soon as possible. I turned around and looked at Sandy, and said, "It's my brother Jim, he's gone to be with Jesus." My sister Sally had told me several times, Jim was barely holding onto life and not expected to live much longer. After my nephew Donnie confirmed that my oldest brother Jim was dead, I sat down at my kitchen table and cried. I remembered the cloud in the shape of the scull I'd seen earlier that day and told Sandy about it. In the day's following, I cried for my precious mother when the Lord spoke to my heart and said, "Carol, do not take lightly the death of your mother's first born son." I prayed for God to heal mommy's broken heart. She wanted to go to heaven before any of us did. The Lord gave my brother Jim's second daughter, Melany a dream about her dad. She dreamed he was wearing a white suit, and looked happier, healthier, and younger then he had in years. Instead of seventy-three, she said he looked and acted about thirty years old. He still had his curly red hair instead of the streaks of mostly grey. He laughed and spoke to her, "Don't cry for me sweetheart, see daddy? I'm happy, and I'm well!" He beat on his chest, taking big deep breaths. Jim had three triple by pass heart surgeries within the past few years of his life. I sure loved my brother Jim.

I thought of the scull cloud again when Joey called and asked if he could move in with us. He and Tina hadn't been married a year, and they were getting a divorce. Ten minutes later Joey came in the door crying. I sat beside him at the kitchen table, listening as he poured out his troubles. Joey had been having panic attacks, so I anointed him with oil and prayed the prayer of faith, expecting the Lord to raise him quickly, but it only grew worse. I knew the divorce was really hurting him, however, I felt like something else was very wrong too. Joey, and his dad and I sat up late talking until around one thirty in the morning. I'd no sooner gone to bed and shut my eyes when suddenly, I saw what looked like a dark blanket stretched out across the sky above us. I felt it was something of evil intention, so I whispered, "Dear Jesus, what is that?" As soon as I spoke the name of Jesus, I saw these ugly black crow looking demons with big orange beaks turn around in unison and look over their shoulders at me. The blanket over our house consisted of thousands of these ugly black crow looking demons with bright orange beaks.

Again, I repeated, "Dear Jesus, what is that?" The micro second I finished the rest of that sentence, He answered, "Those demons have been assigned to destroy Joey." I threw back the covers and leaped out of the bed running, until I reached the room where Joey was. I fell to my knees beside Joey's bed and explained everything to him quickly. Joey said he was still so tormented. He agreed with me while I prayed and asked the Lord to show us clearly why this was happening to Joey, and what we needed to pray to stop it, in the name of Jesus? I'd no sooner finished praying when Joey started repeating what had happened to him one day while he was taking a shower. Joey said, being a fighter, he challenged Satan saying, Come on devil, I'll take you on and defeat you. Immediately, I plead the blood of Jesus over those words Joey had spoken, and commanded them to turn into powder and dissipate, in the name of Jesus! I bound the enemy off Joey's life in Jesus name, and commanded his assignment against Joey be destroyed, under the blood of Jesus. Instantly, Joey and I both felt peace. "Thank God." I explained, "Joey, you are no match for the devil without the name of Jesus." His eyes were opened. Joey told me he slept like a baby that night. Thank God, for the name of Jesus, and the blood of Jesus that covers and protects us, "Hallelujah!"

Joe kept saying we didn't have anything in common, and he kept staying out later and later. I knew the call on my life was to teach women to pray, but the more I prayed, Joe and I drifted farther and farther apart. None of my friends could believe I didn't take a yearly vacation with Joe. In thirty years of marriage I'd been allowed to accompany him on a couple of so-called vacations which consisted mostly of hunting, and fishing. We went to our first family reunion on my side of the family in Indiana once for three days. We had such fun. All of the rest of our family reunions had been held out west, in Arizona or California where the rest of my family lived. We never attended any of those reunions. I'd been mostly satisfied with taking weekend trips to our cabin.

I remember when my friend Judy Hammons took me shopping to find an undergarment which I desperately needed. She got so upset with me when I told her I wasn't allowed to spend eleven dolors on something no one would ever see. When I tried to pay a couple of dolors for the bra I usually bought, she took it out of my hand, put it back, and paid for the more expensive one for me. She along with all my other friends liked Joe. They simply couldn't believe he owned all those hundreds of dolors worth of ball cards, and all kinds of fishing poles, guns knives and etc., but wouldn't allow me to pay a normal price for a much needed bra. Joe always told me his ball cards, and equipment was an investment in our future.

When we got home Judy decided, she'd wait in the kitchen until I went back into the room where Joe was sorting through his many boxes of ball cards to see if he'd actually get angry with me about the price of my undergarment. I didn't lie or tell him I bought it, but he thought I did when I showed it to him and told him how much it cost. Joe didn't know Judy was waiting for me in the kitchen when he started cursing me! He yelled at me and said we couldn't afford to buy such expensive undergarments. Judy could hardly believe Joe's angry reaction over an eleven-dolor undergarment. Finally, after I'd proved my point I told him Judy bought it for me, and that she was waiting for me in the kitchen. She was so shocked! She hugged me good buy and left shaking her head in disbelief. One day my friend Carol Pettit, put her hands on my shoulders, looked at me with her big blue eyes and said, "Carol, my friend, as long as you want to be a door mat, your going to be a door mat. No one can change that but you." I told her I hated arguing with Joe, so I'd always apologize and drop the subject. He'd get very angry with me if I tried to ask him about the ball cards or hunting and fishing equipment coming before our rent, groceries, and other bills. Nothing I ever said to him changed the situation. I loved Joe so much and I wanted to save our marriage at almost any cost. He was nervously smoking more too.

Joe was scaring me. I'd never seen him so addicted to all his material things. He was also getting more hateful and abusive then ever. He didn't care if we didn't have any money for groceries or rent, or anything else. Our garage was so full of every kind of fishing pole and rods and reels. Inside our house were bowling balls, golf clubs, and hidden in every closet in the house were many different guns and knives. My room where I did the writing of this book was becoming fuller each day with large white boxes of expensive ball cards of every kind imaginable stacked up all the way to the ceiling almost. I prayed consistently for God to have mercy on Joe, and to free him from all of these addictions.

Joey went to see Reverend Frank and rededicated his life to Jesus, so he became a lot more peaceful. Tyler and Megan, Joey's two children were coming over every other weekend. Megan was four years old and Tyler was five. Tyler's cousin Jake was his same age, they were best friends. Tyler and Jake played together every day and road the bus to kindergarten together. Two weeks before Joey left their mother, Tina, Tyler's best cousin, Jake died suddenly one day. Joey was sitting apposite me on Saturday morning watching comics on television with the kids. Tyler become very angry with me after he'd said, "My daddy is my hero!" I pointed to a picture of Jesus hanging on my wall and said, "Jesus is my hero!" Tyler looked up at me with his angry big blue eyes and yelled, he was mad at Jesus, because He took his best cousin Jake away to heaven, and He'd also taken his daddy away from him too! I reached out my arms and tried to coax him to come and sit on my lap, but he stubbornly refused. Joey finally insisted, so he came and stood beside me. He was very hesitant, hostile and full of white hot anger toward me, and Jesus. My heart was breaking for him. I prayed silently, "Dear sweet Jesus, please heal my little grandson's broken heart!" I picked Tyler's stiff angry body up and sat him on my lap. As I held him close, I rocked him and talked to him about his cousin Jake's sudden death. I told him it wasn't God's will that his friend Jake die so young. Yes, Jesus took him to heaven so he could be well and happy there, but it wasn't God's will for Jake to be sick and die so young. I also told Tyler that it was his dad and mothers choice to get a divorce, because they had too many differences. That little fellow broke down and cried really hard for a long time. I continued to hold him close and rock him in my arms until he finished grieving. Once again I thought of the scull cloud. Tyler's trust in Jesus and his grandma has grown stronger since that day.

After Joey returned from taking the children back to their mother's on Sunday, I remembered the dreams my mother had concerning Tyler two years before. I told Joey, I was babysitting Megan one day while his grandma was visiting from California. When mommy woke up from her nap and came out of her room, she startled me when she said she had been burdened with strange dreams involving Tyler. In several of the dream's Tyler was walking around the edge of a big dark hole, lost and crying for his daddy! Mommy looked at me and said if Joey and Tina got married it wouldn't last very long. I knew my mother's walk with God, and she'd never say anything like that unless she knew it was from the Lord. She also told me some darkness and sadness were going to overshadow Tyler's life for a short time, but she said she knew the only reason Tyler didn't fall into that pit of total despair was because of my prayers over him, every day.

Mommy also said it was awfully dark in the dream where Tyler was, and except for a light shining above his head, which were my prayers over him, he would have fallen into the pit. "Psalm 119:105 "Your word, {Oh God,} is a lamp to my (grandson Tyler's) feet and a light to his path." Joey loved his grandmother, and highly respected her. Mommy said she may not live to see this happen, but it would happen, and it did. I praised God for the blood of Jesus saturating and protecting Tyler, and all of us.

Early one cold November morning, around six o clock, I woke myself up crying and sat straight up in bed! I'd had a disturbing dream, my mother died. The dream was so real it saddened my heart. I went out and sat in my darkened cold living room with a blanket over my lap and continued to weep for my precious mother. I knew the dream was a warning from the Lord, and it wasn't long before she became very ill. My blessed mother was eighty-seven years old. She had warned us many times, not to cry for her because she longed to be with Jesus whom she loved more then anyone or anything on this earth. All of us, her children, knew she loved us, but she had suffered long in her weary, frail little body. I knew I'd miss her so much, but the Lord gave me peace when He reminded me of the legacy of unconditional love and kindness she left all of us who loved her. Mommy always wanted to be a missionary. We told her she was one, because she prayed for each and every one of us until we all came into the kingdom of God's dear Son, Jesus. She also taught us about the precious blood of Jesus and what it stands for. I said, "Thank You, dear Holy Father for mommy teaching us about You and sweet Jesus, and the dear precious Holy Spirit!"

Joe didn't even try to comfort me concerning my mother's illness. As a matter of fact, he didn't want any part of my affection, except for intercourse. Joe wouldn't allow me to kiss him or hold him tenderly during these frequent acts of passion, either. He said he didn't love me anymore. He commented many times, "We only have one thing left in common, sex." Something strange was happening to my husband Joe of thirty-one years of marriage. I knew he was entertaining some kind of perversion, because he was acting so weird. Joe was gone a lot, both during the day to work and at night, and he was coming home later, and later. Our landlord was constantly calling and asking for the back, and current rent payments. I had very little money to spend on groceries so I was surviving on a backed potato and frozen green vegetables, lunch and supper. The strange thing was, Joe had just bought us all new appliances. I suddenly realized he bought them because he was feeling really guilty about something, (a woman.)

I'd always kissed and hugged Joe hello and good-by before he left for work and when he came home, but he stopped allowing me that pleasure too. When I'd try to hug or kiss him, he'd place his hand in the middle of my chest, and roughly shove me away! I'd lay on the floor on my face and pray in the spirit day, and night, begging God to save our marriage, just one more time! My heart was so broken over the impending lose of my mother, Joey's broken marriage, and now Joe's painful rejection, I couldn't stop weeping. I'd lay awake at night wondering where Joe could possibly be at that late hour? When he'd finally come home, if he made love to me, it was without any loving intimate emotions.

Afterwards, Joe always wanted to get up and talk about crazy things that didn't make any sense. He kept bringing up the past when I was sick, nearly twenty years before. He kept making me feel so guilty for something that was not only partly his fault, but that I had no control over back then. He told me almost constantly, if it hadn't been for me being so sick clear back in my early twenties, we could have had a bigger house, better clothes, nicer cars, etc., in our youth. I kept apologizing for something I couldn't have helped, but he would not forgive me! Joe said all the time, he wasn't happy, and he wanted to be free again. I was hurting so badly, I didn't know what to do. It seamed like the heavens were brass above me when I prayed for God to restore our marriage.

On January first, nineteen ninety three, I was sitting in the living room watching a football game on television with Joe. I was so happy he was home with me. I didn't even mind the roaring, and loudness of the games. Joe was watching a football game on our television set in the living room, and running back and forth watching another football game on a different channel, playing just as loudly on the television set in Joey's room. About nine thirty that evening I looked over at Joe sitting in his chair across the room from me. I was speechless when suddenly Jesus appeared to me in an open-eyed vision, directly above Joe's head. Jesus stared intimately into my eyes. With His beautiful heavenly blue eyes, He began to communicate some things to my heart and mind. I felt anointed waves of His agape love flowing over me.

Jesus squatted down and began to write something in the sand with His index finger. He kept lifting His head and looking up at me again, and again, as He communicated His thoughts to me about keeping my eyes on the glory just beyond the cross. He also reminded me of the time He took me to the cross with Him in the vision, and the miracles He preformed in mine and Sandy's live because of our agreement in prayer. He impressed on me, the title of a second book I'm to write for His glory called, "Seven Realms Of Glory." (Hebrews 12:2) "Looking unto Jesus, the author and finisher of our faith, who for the joy that was set before Him endured the cross, despising the shame, and has sat down at the right hand of the throne of God." He kept reminding me to look beyond the cross, and toward the glory. I fell in love with Jesus all over again as He searched deep into my heart and mind with those beautiful blue eyes of His. The love that flowed between us was so powerful, I felt like I was drunk with His agape love.

My heart was so broken and my mind tormented, I could hardly comprehend it, but Jesus said I would live the glory before I wrote the sequel to this book. I communicated with Him from my heart, and asked if I could see what He had written in the sand? Immediately, the vision shifted to the Lord's beautiful hand writing in the sand, which said, "I Love you, Carol." Jesus had put on the finishing touches by drawing a great big perfect heart shape around His written words. When I went to bed that night, I slept like a baby all night long. Not even Joe's cruel angry decision to divorce me interrupted my sleep that night. "Thank You Jesus!"

The next morning I was still happy after seeing Jesus in the vision. Romans 8:16 "And if children then heirs-heirs of God and joint heirs with Christ. If indeed we suffer with Him, that we may also be glorified together, for consider that the sufferings of this present time are not worthy to be compared with the glory which shall be revealed in us." I kept thinking, "The Lord must have really wanted my attention. He broke through two loud ball games playing on televisions, in a rare open-eyed vision, and on January first 1993, no less." "Oh Lord, You have taught me to be a prayer warrior. Please give me the grace to trust You even more, Jesus."

On the twenty-second day of the month of January, 1993, my sister Peggy called and told me, mommy went on home to be with Jesus. I yelled like someone hit me really hard! Peggy and I talked and cried together over the phone for a long time. Mommy had not only paid for her own funeral expenses, long before she died, but she also had already paid for the flowers from each of us, including all of her grandchildren, and great grandchildren. She was a very special lady who didn't want to burden her children for anything, not even the flowers on her grave. I know she is wearing a beautiful crown of pure gold on her precious head in heaven. I was constantly reminded of the odd scull cloud that hung suspended in the sky outside my kitchen window that strange day.

Joe refused to even comfort me after my mother's death. His anger toward me worsened, and he was coming home much later each night. My friend's Carol Pettit, and Nellie Veda prayed with me a lot during those long lonely nights and evenings while Joe was gone so much. They prayed for me so I could receive more of my necessary inner healing. I was scared and hurting so badly I knew I had to pray in the spirit almost constantly to survive another one of Joe's affairs with a younger woman, I dreaded it.

Joe's grandma died. She had been very special to me, but her last years on this earth were hard. She didn't recognize any of us, and I missed her long before she died. I was still grieving over my mother's death too. I had to ask the Lord to forgive me, because I knew she was healthy, well and much happier up there with Him. Joe hated my tears and wanted nothing to do with us comforting each other over the lose of our loved ones. Joe told me he'd already rented another house and was living with another woman named Jan. He kept telling me I needed to leave, but I didn't know where to go? Nellie tried to tell me about the law, and my rights to live in that house and make Joe pay for it, but I was hurting so bad I didn't want to be a burden on Joe or hurt him. I also kept on believing God was going to restore our marriage again. I'd lay there in bed at night, praying in the spirit and listening to my scripture tapes just to keep my sanity. Joe still continued to come home every night at twelve, one, two and a three-o clock in the morning, and most nights have sex with me, without any cuddling, kissing, or hugging. He said it made him feel too guilty if we kissed or hugged each other. Afterwards he'd insist I get up and go out in the living room and talk with him.

He talked about crazy things which made no sense. It always came back to when I was sick all those years ago and how it robbed something from him. I'd apologize, but it didn't help. Nothing helped this time, not even prayer and begging God to save my marriage to Joe again! Joe's mother and his sisters paid me, more and more frequent visits. I dreaded seeing them come to my house. How I wanted to run and hide myself somewhere away from their sight, so they'd leave me alone and stop badgering me. They'd tell me, they were so worried about Joe having a nervous breakdown, if I didn't leave that house. They said Joe couldn't stand the strain of paying for his rent and utilities, and mine too!

I hardly ever saw my friend's Sandy, Jean or Dixie anymore, and I missed them, but I especially missed Sandy. All my new friends called a lot to pray with me. Many times when Sandy called I'd be on the other line in prayer with someone else. I felt so badly about it, but it honestly seemed there was nothing I could do about it. I loved all of my new friends, as well as the others. Many of my days were filled with praying with different people over the phone. The last time I'd seen Sandy, she came over one special Monday evening. The ladies normally came for our prayer group on that night, but they weren't able to come for some reason or other. So, God worked it out for Sandy to come and visit me instead. She and I enjoyed our quiet time together, just her and I talked without any interruptions. She and I were sitting in the living room talking, just the two of us, like old times, when all of a sudden, I noticed Sandy kept staring at something on the wall above my head. When I asked her what she was looking at. She answered me as if she were in a daze, "Carol, the entire time you and I have been sitting here talking, I've been watching this big circle of stars on a rounded window, like the port hole in a ship. Inside the window I keep seeing you standing there laughing and talking to all kinds of different people. They are strangers, but you are talking to them as if you know them. As soon as I'd see you standing there laughing and talking to one person and their face left the inside of the window, another one took its place. Carol, you were talking to these people as if you had known them all your life, and I know you don't know any of these people. I wonder what it means?" We both looked puzzled at first.

She and I sat there questioning, if her open-eyed vision had something to do with the prophecy about my book, and the people I'd meet during the speaking engagements. However, she and I admitted, it all looked impossible, considering the way my life was headed right then. I looked at Sandy with tears filling up in my eyes and said, "Sandy, you've been my friend for a long, long time, and I've loved you just like a sister. You've stood on the word of God with me concerning my marriage before, but this time I don't know if the Lord is going to put it back together again?" Sandy wiped the tears from her eyes too. We passed the tissue box back and forth until we'd had ourselves a good hard cry. I said tearfully, "Sandy the bible says, if we leave homes, lands, sisters, brothers, and even husbands to follow Jesus, it will be given back to us, one hundred fold in this present time, with persecutions." She looked up at me with red swollen eyes and said, "Yes Carol, that's right my dear friend, and this sure is persecution, having to leave all your family and friends who love you so much!" We started bawling and fell into each others arms.

I wanted so much to share Sandy's vision of the port hole of stares with Joe, but he was worse then he'd ever been before. Hostile, bitter, and angry were mild words to describe the way Joe felt and acted toward me. And to top everything off, I felt as if I were dreaming one evening when a couple of ladies in my prayer group, who were supposed to be my friends, said, "But Carol, I don't understand this? As close as you walk with the Lord, how could this happen to you and Joe? If God won't heal your marriage, and after all, you're our teacher, then how can we possibly believe He will help us, and heal our marriages?" This was all I needed to hear. I was having a tough enough time dealing with my broken heart, and now I felt guilty too. Nothing had been the same for a long time. How I thank God for my friend Brenda Mays. She called often to check on me, and prayed for me and with me. I called Brenda one night and told her what the Lord had said to me while I was fixing myself a packed potato for supper. He said, "Carol, consider not the deadness of Sarah's womb." She looked it up in her bible, in Romans 4:19, and read it to me over the phone, "And not being weak in faith, he did not consider his own body, already dead (since he was about a hundred years old), and the deadness of Sarah's womb." "Lord, help me understand?"

Brenda and I also read Romans 4:20-22, "He did not waver at the promise of God through unbelief, but was strengthened in faith, giving glory to God. And being fully convinced that what He had promised He was also able to preform. And therefore it was accounted to Him for righteousness." One night Brenda told me, she was so crushed because of my brokenness, she cried out to God, over and over again in my behalf! She said she begged Him to please give her a dream about me, or something that I could hold onto. The Lord answered her desperate prayer and gave her an unusual dream about my future. In the dream, I had two handsome strong rescuers. One was named Mark, and the other was Joel. They both had dark hair and mustaches. Brenda said in the dream she and I were standing under an archway, and I was showing her pictures of my two new suitors. Mark and Joel were both handsome. In the dream, Joel walked in and put a ring on my finger and I married Joel. He picked me up and carried me to an upper room. Brenda said suddenly, I was naked and full blown pregnant. I was ready to give birth in this upper room where Joel had carried me. I soon gave birth to a lovely blue eyed, smiling baby girl with curly red hair. The baby girl looked a lot like my granddaughter Rebecca, who looks a lot like me. In the dream the little girl looked exactly like me, except for my dark hair and eyes.

Brenda said I was laughing and I looked happier then she had ever seen me. Brenda had known me since we were eleven years old, and she said she'd never known me to look so happy. Immediately, I compared the name's Mark, and Joel with the word of God. Brenda said she hadn't even thought of that. I reminded Brenda that Jesus teaches us in, 'Mark' Chapter 4:2-20 "But these are the ones sown on good ground, those who hear the word, accept it, and bear fruit: Some thirtyfold, some sixty, and some a hundred." I said, "Brenda Joel is a depiction of the former and the latter rain. God is going to give me back all the years the locusts have eaten away, and the one hundred fold return!" I yelled, "Oh thank You dear sweet Jesus!" Brenda laughed and said, "Carol, the way you love the word of God, I believe that God is speaking to you through His word, and I believe He will give you back all the years the locusts have eaten away, and the one hundred fold returns." Brenda had such a kind heart, she was always doing something good for me or someone else. I remember one day when I told the Lord what a good friend she is. The Lord spoke to me and said, "Brenda is my true Israelite in whom there is no guile." Jesus also said that about Nathanael, in John 1:47.

Several times Joe surprised me, and actually talked to me like I was a human being when he said, "Carol, I believe you are going to marry a Preacher or someone who is strong in faith like you are, after we are divorced." Every time he'd say that, I'd cry and tell him, I didn't want anyone but him. I even begged him to let me stay with him a little while longer, until I could get a job. I didn't even have a car, how was I going to find work and support myself? Each time he yelled a very loud, "NO!" I told Joe, "For thirty-one years I have been a good wife to you. One day you are going to tell anyone who will listen to you, that I was the best thing that ever happened to you. But maybe by then, it will be too late!" I had so much love to give my husband Joe, but all he did was shove me away, time and time again. I begged, "Oh God, please have mercy on us!" I constantly laid on the floor crying out to God, but nothing ever changed. Instead my marriage to Joe was crumbling before my very eyes. "Sweet precious Jesus, help me."

Two months earlier Joey kissed me on the cheek one morning and told me, he was moving out, because he knew his dad and I were having troubles. He said he didn't want to add any more strife to our already struggling marriage. I cried and asked him not to leave me alone, with his dad gone all the time, but he left anyway. I was so scared! I didn't know where I was going, or how I was going to make it on my own. I didn't even know if I wanted to go on without Joe. My mind and heart were so tormented, not knowing which way I should go? I had cried out constantly to the Lord, begging Him to not let them shut off my electricity, my phone, or water. For over a year I had barely any groceries, except for what I managed to pray in. Backed potatoes, and soup, and my friend Nancy bringing me Mexican food on Mondays was all I had. The landlord wanted me to get out, or pay the rent! I didn't know how much more I could possibly take, so finally I made my decision to leave. That night I begged Joe one last time to let me stay with him until I got a job! Again, he cursed, "Blank, NO! Carol, I told you, no!" I stood up and looked at him. With tears flowing down my cheeks, I said, "Joe, you would treat a dog better then you have treated me. In the morning I'll call my sister Sally, and ask if she and her husband Don can come and get me right away. They have been asking me to let them come and get me. As quickly as I can pack my things, I'll be gone." He begged me again to let him take my name off our cabin, but I refused. That cabin was the only thing we had, and I knew instinctively it should be sold and the money be divided down the middle between us. Joe didn't want me to mention our cabin in the disillusionment he wanted, but I knew I'd need part of that money to live on, he at least owed me that much, I thought.

My broken heart could hardly stand another night of Joe having sex with me, without any loving affection. I felt like I was being used, and I felt dirty, and cheep. Suddenly, I heard a choir of angels singing that night, and I saw a vision, right in the middle of Joe's abusive one-sided love making. "Up from the grave He arose, with a mighty triumph over His foes! He arose! He arose! Hallelujah, Christ arose!" While the angels sang so beautifully, I saw a vision of Jesus standing in front of a tomb commanding the person inside to come forth! I saw someone hobbling out of the tomb wearing old ragged grave cloves from head to foot. The only opening inside the grave clothes was a place for the eyes. Big wide eyes were blinking from within the grave clothes. I was sure it was Joe coming out of the tomb of spiritual death, and into God's glories light. After we made love, however, Joe was still firm about the divorce. I lay there trembling all over. I felt so cold, I pulled the covers up over my head, and cried myself to sleep again that night. I kept whispering under my breath, "Jesus."

Right before I woke up that next morning, I had a dream. In the dream, I was laying on my couch in the living room. My right elbow was propped up on the couch, and using my right hand as a pillow, I lay there crying, and looking very sad. Suddenly, Jesus walked right in my living room and stood there in front of me. He lifted His right hand and arm slowly until it was stretched out in front of me. His beautiful blue eyes gazed compassionately into my very soul when He said, "Daughter, always remember this; When you are the weakest, then are you the strongest, in Me. Not in your own strength, but in Mine." I woke up thinking, "I will always remember what Jesus told me." With one last futile attempt, I tried to hug my husband who I'd loved for thirty-one years good by before he left for work, but he shoved me away again. It hurt so badly, I slumped down in a chair, laid my weary head on the kitchen table and bawled like a baby. When I finally regained my composure, I called my friend Carol Pettit. She came over right away and just held me and let me cry in her arms again. Carol Pettit was one of the strongest friends I had to lean on while I was so weak and struggling. She helped me to keep on going even though Joe was being so cruel to me. She stayed by my side and helped me through one of the darkest trials I've ever been in. Carol Pettit held onto me, and she constantly showed me the light of God's love. I thank God for her mercy and strength.

Later that day when I was taking my clothes out of the dryer, I heard the Lord say, "Daughter, I will teach you to fly like the eagle, above the storms of life, and I will teach you to walk on the wings of the wind with Me." I wondered how I could hear God speaking such beautiful things to me at a time in my life when I felt like He was so far from me. He is close to the brokenhearted.

I remembered when I was packing to move from my large brick home on Ross Rd. in 1990, Sandy called and told me, "Carol, God said for me to tell you, to stay in the garden." I reach for my bible, and looked up all the scriptures about a garden. I'd already memorized some of the scriptures about the garden in Song of Solomon, 4:12-16 "Thou art like a garden locked up my sister my bride, a spring shut up, a sealed fountain.... Awake O North wind, And come O South! Blow upon my garden, that its spices may flow out..." I knew in my heart the Lord was relating to me about writing my book and singing and speaking on stage. I felt He wanted me to open up to Him, and allow Him to use me to tell others my testimony, about His great love. "God help me!"

Finally I'd started to see signs of the prophecy being fulfilled. I was singing and speaking on stage. I'd hoped my book might be drawing closer to being published. But once again my dreams were being put on hold, and my heart was so broken, I didn't have the strength to even care anymore. "Please Jesus, hold me."

Joe never came home that night. I found myself laying on the couch in my living room, sad and crying, just as I saw myself in the dream the night before. All of a sudden a strange car full of people started screeching their tires and blowing their horn while they pulled in, and out of my driveway! They were traveling at an extremely fast speed! Somehow, I had a feeling it had something to do with Joe and his new girlfriend wanting me to leave that house. Each time they did this, I could hear their car coming from clear down the street, blowing the horn and screeching the tires as they pulled into my driveway and stopped within seconds of hitting the garage door! I kept pleading the blood of Jesus!

Around three o clock in the morning, I couldn't take it anymore so I called my oldest son, David. I was afraid, if it was Joe, I'd get him in trouble if I called the police. My thinking was so weird at that time. Here I was worrying about getting Joe in trouble with the police, and him getting angry at me, and here he was, trying to kill me! David told me he wasn't coming in the house right away. Instead, he said he was going to pull up in front of my neighbor's house down the street and turn his lights off so he could see if it was his dad, or anyone he knew. David must have dressed quickly, because it wasn't long before I peeked out the window and saw him turn his car lights out, and pull up in front of the house down the street. I was so glad to see David, and know he was out side.

During the time this crazy car was pulling in and out my driveway at an incredible speed, I was getting very little sleep, so I began to write down instructions for David, and what I wanted him to do with my things. I knew I couldn't take our furniture because I had no where to put it. Joe said he wanted most of it for his house, because our king sized bed and some of our furniture belonged to his mother. When David finally came in, we talked the rest of the night with the lights out in case the strange intruders came back again. He stretched out in his dad's recliner while I lay across the couch. We talked until the sun came up the next morning. We must have fallen asleep out of sheer exhaustion. I woke up a couple of hours later, and then David went home to watch the boys, Michael and Kyle while Betsy came over, loaded down with empty boxes to help me pack. The Lord gave me a song like He had given my mother so many times when daddy ranted, and raved, cursed her, and gave her a hard time. No matter how bad mommy's life was, I never once failed to see her lift her weary arms, and sing praises to the Lord! Like mommy, the Lord gave me a song in my suffering also. My tears flowed unceasingly as I sang, "Peace, peace, wonderful peace, coming down from the Father above----Sweep over my spirit, and help me I pray, and fill me with Your wonderful love." I sang that over and over, day and night while my daughter-in-law Betsy and I packed my things.

Betsy and I worked hard. In two days, we hurriedly packed everything I had accumulated in thirty-one years. My sister Sally, and her husband Don were coming to pick me up that Sunday. Every once in a while Betsy would stop and look over at me, and start crying again. She and I had to keep comforting each other. Nearly as far back as she could remember, her family and mine enjoyed many happy times together. Betsy had loved Joe and I since she was a little girl. David brought the boys over and they all stayed the night with me, so I wouldn't be alone. David slept on the couch with Kyle, and Betsy and Michael slept with me in my bed. Little Michael was so upset when he came back with his daddy and saw me packing, he cried and kept asking, "Why are you leaving grandma? Where are you going?" We decided to tell him I was going on a long vacation, but his little two and a half year old mind just couldn't seem to grasp it. Betsy was getting aggravated because Michael kept on crying and wouldn't lay down and go to sleep, but I told her not to get upset with him. He knew something was wrong, and he was sensing my deep sorrow. As I held him in my arms, I kept repeating, "Sweetheart, everything will be all right, because the Lord Jesus will take care of us. Grandma will come and visit you very soon, I promise." I prayed softly, and asked Jesus to comfort him, and heal his little broken heart too. "Dear Lord, please give us more of Your grace."

Early the next morning, as soon as breakfast was finished, David took the boys back home with him so Betsy and I could finish quickly packing. Oh how I needed God's wisdom and strength when all of a sudden Joe's mother and sisters showed up to see me off. They were all laughing and asking if they could buy my curtains. They liked my hand made curtains, and they thought I wouldn't need them anymore. Joe's mother laughed and plopped down on my couch, grabbed my most recent hand made afghan and said, "I get first dubs on this afghan! I want this, how much do you want for this afghan, Carol?" They were all laughing and joking as if nothing was wrong. I burst into tears and yelled, "I fail to see what is so funny, ladies! This is one of the worst days of my whole life! Please don't ask me what price I want for my things! I can't even think straight right now because my heart is so broken, let alone tell you if I want to sell you my things! These are not just things, they are a part of my life, and my home that I've shared with Joe for thirty-one years! Please leave now! My sister Sally, and my brother-in-law, Don will be here to pick me up in a couple of hours, and I'm not finished packing yet! So, please, just leave us alone!" One by one, they cried, hugged me and apologized as they left quietly. It hurt so badly to think I'd been a loyal part of their family for all those years. I'd loved them, and prayed for all of them for years, yet they too treated me like a total stranger. "Father, I forgive them, bless them anyway dear Lord."

I'd saved packing my things in the bedroom for last, because it was the hardest. Just as I bent down to get my suitcases out from under my bed the Lord spoke to me softly, and said, "Come away with Me, My fair one. The winter is over and past, and the time of the singing of birds has come on the earth." I cried even harder, thinking, "Oh Lord, even though this is August twenty fourth, it is one of the coldest, most barren times of my life!" I heard Sandy talking to Betsy out in the kitchen, so I blew my nose, and wiped the never ending flow of tears from my eyes. Sandy took one look at all my things packed away in boxes and broke down in tears. It really finally hit her hard that I was actually leaving my home and everyone I loved behind. After Sandy left, I finished packing everything in my bedroom, then went and took my shower. I tried to put on some make up, since I hadn't been able to wear any for so long. I looked in the mirror at my red swollen eyes and puffy face, and the tears came gushing out like a never ending river. Again, I cried out to God, to please help me save my marriage! Immediately, He answered, "Remembers Lot's wife." I rolled His words over in my mind and heart and thought about it for a while and said, "Lord, are You saying I can never look back, or ask You to save my marriage to Joe, again?" I waited for His answer, but all I could think about were His last three words, "Remember Lot's wife." I had a feeling the Lord really meant business.

I was amazed that I actually felt a freedom after the Lord spoke those words into my spirit. I'd spent so many years living with Joe's constant rejection, thinking one day he will love me and except me for who I am, but I felt like God was saying, this abuse has got to stop. I knew if something did not change I was going to break under the consistent pressure, because I couldn't endure much more of him hurting me. I took a deep breath, looked up to Him and said, "All right then, Lord, if You are saying I can never look back to my marriage or my home being put together again, then I'm asking You to wipe away these tears from my eyes? Please help me Lord, to put on my make up, comb my hair, and leave this house with a smile on my face. Please Papa, help me to say goodby to Betsy, my sons and my little grandchildren without crying!" Instantly, my tears stopped. I had unexplainable joy. I was able to laugh and talk with everyone. God's grace is sufcient.

My little grandson Michael was so upset, he cried again before I left! He grabbed me by the hand and started pulling me into the bathroom! He pointed and told me to look and see, my towels were all gone off the towel holders on the walls! Again, Michael got really upset and cried because he thought someone took my flowers which always set on my coffee table. He kept crying and saying over, and over, "Grandma, who took your flowers, there gone!" I tried to calm him down when I pulled him up on my lap, and explained, I'd packed them away until I came back from my vacation. Kyle, was only a year and a half, so he didn't understand. My other grandchildren, Tyler and Megan believed I really was going on a long vacation, so they didn't cry or get upset. Michael spent a lot of time with me, so we were more attached. His little heart was so broken because I was leaving. My sister Sally and her husband Don, were so glad I was finally leaving Joe. I tenderly embraced Betsy, and my sons, then I kissed and hugged my beautiful grandchildren. David said, "Now mom, don't worry about your things, I'll take care of everything like I promised, ok?" As our car pulled away, all of them kept waving at us. God gave me peace in my heart to say goodby.

The last time I'd seen my granddaughter, Rebecca, she cried again to go back home. She told me she was afraid her step daddy was going to hurt her mother, and felt she had to be home to protect her from him. Rebecca even demonstrated with one of her dollies, how her step daddy fought with her mother, so we took her back home right away. I called Carrie and told her I was concerned about the fighting going on in front of Rebecca, and she got very angry with me. Angry enough to keep Rebecca away from us for well over a year. I had to lay the care of Rebecca at the feet of Jesus. I was trying to deal with so many hurts at one time, I had to trust the Lord for His protection over her, or else I knew I wouldn't make it. All of my family are protected by the blood of

Jesus, and we dwell in the secret place of the Most High God.

On the way back to their home in Manchester Ohio, my sister Sally told me each time she would start to kneel beside her bed to pray for mine and Joe's marriage, the Lord pulled her back up to her feet again. He told her, not to pray for mine and Joe's marriage to be healed, He had other plans for me. She said the Lord reassured her each and every time, I was going to be much better off without Joe. My sisters, Janie, Helen and Peggy, in Arizona said the Lord told them the exact same thing. Sally was such a wonderful cook, and I was so happy to finally have good food to eat. I ate every bite she put in front of me. On my second day there, I was laying across my bed upstairs when Don knocked on my open door. He said he wanted to show me how to use the stereo, tape player, so I could practice my singing. He encouraged me, by telling me God still had a beautiful plan for my life and I needed to keep on practicing singing gospel songs, for His glory. Sally started practicing singing with me. We sang and laughed, and cried together. My brother-in-law Don, had always been like a brother to me. I praised God, for allowing me to go to Sally and Don's big country home, to heal. They had bought nearly a hundred Akers. Their big two story white house sits down in a lovely valley, and is surrounded by big dark lush green mountains. Early every morning a white smoke like midst comes up off the river, and rises up through the great mountains.

We'd sit out on the front and side porches most of the day, and evening quietly talking. Sometimes, early in the morning and again right about dusk, we'd see deer walking and running through the open fields of Sally's front, back and side yards. Sally and Don had planted wonderful vibrant colorful flowers all around their house. Beautiful butterfly's in magnificent resilient colors came from everywhere to pollinate the bright yellow, red, purple, white, and pink flowers. Don had built Sally bird houses on every pole, and tree. I'd never in my whole life seen so many different kinds of brilliant colorful birds, and they too came from everywhere. Some came just to visit and drink from their pond, but the delicate little bright colored blue birds lived in their bird houses every spring and summer. I watched the pretty birds, deer and butterflies every day. I felt the calming effects of the peace and quiet, healing the strange circle around my broken heart.

Day after day, I sat for endless hours gazing up at the mountains which surrounded their property. I constantly communicated to the Lord from my heart, how very grateful I was to be able to look up at His beautiful blue skies and white puffy clouds. I loved hearing the hum of Don's tractor running, or the blue birds singing. Sally hugged and kissed me every time she walked past me, and told me that she loved me. It felt so good not to hear Joe's criticism, feel his painful rejection, or be a part of his confusion. It especially felt good to not be so afraid. So many times before I left Joe, I'd be afraid late at night, so I'd call my sister Peggy in Arizona. She'd cry with me. She had resented the way Joe pushed me around and degraded me far too long. She used to yell at Joe when he'd slap me. Sally got so angry at Joe when she'd see him purposely wrench one of my breasts if we were quarreling. She said, it's so cruel. Jesus healed me with His stripes 2000 years ago. He defeated the enemy, when He hung on the cross and was raised from the dead. "Thank You Jesus, I love You Lord."

I was constantly aware of my broken heart, and its subtle ache. Even when I laughed, the strange dull aching circle was still there. I remember one night before I left Joe my friend Carol Pettit took me to a prayer meeting at Marie Gosset's house. After we'd prayed for the different Chapters of Women's Aglow, Carol ask the ladies to pray for me. Marie sat me down in a comfortable chair in her living room, and not knowing very much about my life, she started to anoint me with oil. Just as she started to anoint my head, she acted like someone had hit her full force in the stomach. She cried out, "Oh dear Jesus! Please, heal this woman's broken heart!" She'd grabbed her stomach and bent over, praying fervently for me in the spirit. The other ladies gathered around me, and anointed my head with oil. They prayed for me too. When they had finished praying for me, I knew the sweet precious Holy Spirit had healed a great portion of my broken heart. "Dear Jesus, I praise You, and I thank You for healing my broken heart."

I kept thinking about the goodness of God, and how He brought me to a place of peace where I could rest quietly, and heal. I'd go upstairs to my big comfortable bedroom, play my accompaniment tapes, and practice singing. I'll never forget that first Wednesday night I went to church with my sister and her husband. The little white church had a red roof, and sat out in an open field in the country. It had old fashion wooden benches. The ceiling fans circulated the fresh night air coming in through the open windows. Sally and Don introduced me to their Pastor, Owen. I was impressed, because he let the dear precious Holy Spirit lead his service in that little country church. Instead of having his regular church service that evening, he told his small congregation he'd decided we could all just sit in our pews and talk. Owen also asked me if I'd sing something for them. I said, "Yes, I will sing if my sister Sally will sing with me." At first she said no, but I quickly talked her into it. We stood up and sang a couple of songs, without music. They all seamed to enjoy it, and afterwards they clapped their hands heartedly. Everyone in that little church hugged me, and ministered to me in a very special way that night.

Two of my older sisters, and their husbands, came from Arizona to visit Sally, and Don, and myself. Janie, and Clarence, Helen and her husband Ed. Janie had ministered to me over the phone, about two weeks before I left Joe. I'll never forget that day. The Lord gave Janie a wonderful prophecy, concerning my future. I was sitting at my kitchen table, crying, when she called from Arizona, and told me God's glory was going to hoover over my life, no matter where I went, or what happened. Joe couldn't stop it either, because no one can thwart the plan of God for my life. Janie understood how I felt, more then anyone else, because she'd had more then her share of heart aches with her husband Clarence, and younger woman. When we were talking up stairs at our sister, Sally's, she told me the Lord gave her a song for me. She has a beautiful voice, so I asked her to record it onto a tape. Since then, I've listened to that tape many, many times. "They that wait upon the Lord, shall renew their strength; They shall mount up with wings like eagles; They shall run and not be weary; They shall walk and not faint. Teach me Lord; Teach me Lord; To wait." I love that wonderful song and it's based, of course on, Isaiah 40:31. Janie didn't know Isaiah, 40:31, is one of my very favorite scriptures. I love Janie, Helen, and all my family so dearly.

I went to Sally's mail box every day hoping Joe had sent me at least twenty dolors, but he never once sent me anything. Sally and Don took me to the town nearby where I was born, so I could get my birth certificate and get some aid from the Government. Finally, after several weeks, I started getting one hundred dolors a month from them. My sisters and the rest of my family and friends were very upset with Joe, because he basically left me homeless. Thank God, they were there to help me. I'd never been on welfare in my entire life, and except for a very short time when daddy was really sick, way back when I was a little girl, I personally had never endured standing in those awful long lines, or felt that kind of terrible shame before. I wanted to get a job, but my sister and her husband lived so far away from civilization, it was hard to consider it. I'd had no formal education, no training, and except for cleaning houses, I didn't know what to do. After about six weeks, Joe started calling, and asking me again, to take my name off the cabin. He said he wanted us to get together and talk about it. Sally and Don both were furious! They, along with many others, advised me to never give into Joe and take my name off the cabin. At least half of it was rightfully mine.

I had another speaking engagement at the Huber Heights Chapter of Women's Aglow, so David came and got me. I was so happy to see David, Betsy and my little grandsons, Michael and Kyle. I'd missed them more then words could tell. The last time I'd given my testimony at the Huber Heights Chapter of Women's Aglow, was right before I left Joe. I remember, during the entire time I was speaking, the devil kept harassing me, saying, 'Why are you up here? Look at your life! How can you possibly tell anyone, anything? You're such a failure! BLA, BLA, BLA.' I felt like I couldn't teach anybody, anything, because my marriage had failed so miserably, but God had other plans. After I finished speaking,

I couldn't believe how long that prayer line was. Women lined up, one after the other, for me to pray for them. Audrey, a very pretty, redhead introduced herself and her friend, Cherri. They had come up in the prayer line, and I'd ministered to them. Audrey told me she had a Christian television program, and she asked if I'd like to be a guest on her show sometime in the near future? I was thrilled and said, yes, immediately! Cherri, a very anointed, and beautiful blond was also an ordained minister like her friend, Audrey. They asked if I'd like to come and visit their church in Fairborn Ohio sometime. "Thank You Jesus for Christian friends."

The first time I walked into Audrey and Cherri's church in Fairborn, Ohio, I felt the anointing, and it sounded like a song in my ears, the way they taught the word of God. A precious white haired lady came up and ministered to me after the service was over when I was standing in the prayer line. After she finished ministering to me, she gave me her phone number, and said, "Look honey, I don't even know you, but I felt lead to give you my phone number." Audrey and I had talked several times and become pretty good friends. I loved her friend Cherri too, because she was so humble and loving. She's a very powerful woman of prayer.

Joe called several times at David's house and before I knew it, I said I'd go away with him for the weekend. I still felt such strong love in my heart for Joe. I began to question if it really was God's will for me to divorce him. I was very confused and it was getting worse every time I allowed myself to see Joe. His confusion tormented me, undoing my ability to make the right decisions. I wanted Joe to tell me he still loved me, or talk to me about us getting back together, but he disappointed me every time. Only one thing was on Joe's mind, intercourse. I felt like a cheap used up whore, only he never paid me anything for my services. He'd talk crazy all night long. He didn't want a loving relationship. He wanted us to go ahead and get the divorce, live separate, but have more or less, an affair without any other attachments, or responsibilities. I'd always tried to be a submissive wife, but my mind and heart screamed, "Stop it Carol before Joe kills you! Remember Lot's wife?" I cried, "Sweet Jesus, please help me!"

My friend Judy bought me another book on how to save my marriage, so I thought maybe I should give in again and go out with Joe, once more. The book said I should be with my husband no matter what it costs me, in order to get our marriage back together. After all, it was a Christian book so I thought I could endure Joe's rejection. He was degrading me, and demolishing my self esteem, causing me to feel even more ashamed, and un-loved. I was so hurt, crushed and bruised inside, I didn't know what to do? I didn't know how to stop being a wife to Joe. Every time I gave in and saw him, I was worse off then before. It felt like I was incapable of making the decision to stop seeing Joe. Every time I saw him, his constant confusion and rejection of me was slowly killing me. His angry words felt like he was rubbing salt into my broken and wounded heart. I didn't want to go on living, because I felt like I was the most absolute worthless person on this earth.

Sally was dusting her living room furniture one morning, while I was vacuuming the carpet. Suddenly, she stopped, turned around and looked at me, and said something kind of strange. I turned the sweeper off, and asked her to repeat whatever it was she'd said to me. Sally said, "Carol, I really think you are to move to downtown Fairborn, and live in your own apartment, up above a Christian bookstore." I looked at her in shock, and started crying! I asked her why in the world she thought I should live in Fairborn. I didn't know hardly anyone who lived in Fairborn, except Audrey and Cherri, my two new friends. I cried even harder, and accused Sally of just wanting to get rid of me! What she said worried me. I panicked, and thought, "Oh dear Lord, I just can't do it! Please don't make me live alone, I'm too afraid!" I'd slept in the same room with my mother and in the same bed with my sister Peggy until I was seventeen. I'd been with Joe and my children for thirty-one years. I ran upstairs, and fell across my bed, desperately crying out to God! "Papa, You don't want me to move clear to Fairborn and live by myself, do You? I don't have a car, and where will I work? Oh Lord, help me to know Your will for me, and accept whatever it is?" Sally apologized for making me cry. She said she loved my being there with her, and once again I felt welcome to stay there with her and Don as long as I liked. It really puzzled me though, when she explained, "Carol, I honestly don't know why I spoke to you about moving to Fairborn, except that I suddenly felt it really strong. Before I knew it, the words came flying out of my mouth." We hugged each other and made up.

Nevertheless, I was beginning to feel more and more restless, whether I was at her house or staying with David, Betsy and the boys. I did love going to Audrey and Cherri's church in Fairborn. Every chance I got when I visited David and Betsy, I went to that church. About seven thirty one evening, I was sitting in the living room by the fire watching television with my sister, Sally and Don when Audrey called. She told me, she felt impressed to tell me, I should move away from my sister Sally's house and come and live in Fairborn, near her. She said I was like a baby eagle, and God was stirring up the nest, and bumping me out of it. I was really irritated when she laughed and said, "Carol, when God moves you out of that nest, you are going to land in Fairborn." I rejected her words just as I had my sister Sally's, but deep in my heart, I wondered if it was the Lord trying to tell me something. Why Fairborn, though? Finally, I decided it was just simply a coincidence that Sally and Audrey said the same thing about my moving to Fairborn, so I shrugged it off. I prayed in tongues much.

Audrey had been through some really rough times in her past. Her husband had beaten, and nearly killed her. She said she took her kids, and they lived in her car for a while, until she got a job and found them a place to live. She had given her heart to the Lord quit a number of years ago, and after that her needs were always met according to God's riches in glory, by Christ Jesus. "Praise God!" Audrey had a short stylish hair cut. Her dark red hair and big dark brown eyes lite up when she talked about the Lord. She was a sharp dresser, and she had a nice shape too, even though she'd told me parts of her were made up of silicone. She was a funny lady. She made me laugh at my circumstances. I knew if this woman could live through, with God's help, what she'd survived, then she was just the kind of friend I needed.

230

Memories of Joe and how things used to be in the early years of our marriage flooded over me one day. I remembered when Joe was almost kind to me at times. He even used to give me spending money and he allowed me to buy nice clothes and shoes, there for a while. A long time ago, Sandy and I reminisced about when she and I first met, I always seem to have money tucked away in my wallet. When Joe and I separated for the second time in 1985, once again, everything seemed to be alright for a little while after he came back, especially after he got saved, but he never was really happy with me. I constantly blamed myself for Joe resenting me. I couldn't be perfect like he wanted me to be. "In the name of Jesus, I choose to forgive Joe, today, seventy times seven, if that's what it takes Lord!" I'm so grateful to my Papa, God who loves me unconditionally. "I love You, and I trust You, my very own dear Papa, my sweet Jesus, and dear precious Holy Spirit. Thank You Lord, that you will never leave me nor forsake me."

Chapter Seven

My God shall supply

When I decided to try and ignore what my sister Sally and Audrey said to me about my moving to Fairborn, because it didn't make any sense to me, I had no idea I was fighting the Lord's perfect will for my life. Every time I said I wouldn't go to Fairborn, I might as well have put on boxing gloves. I was fighting my own fears, fleshly self will, and especially God, in a no win situation. I was so confused and broken hearted, I'd thought maybe God had changed His mind since He'd last spoken to me about mine and Joe's marriage, "Remember Lot's wife." I didn't even know the damage I was doing to myself when I kept on, knowingly and yet unknowingly disobeying God and seeing Joe, until it took its toll on me, physically, mentally, and emotionally.

I was pacing the floor in Joey's cold apartment on the nineteenth day of November, nineteen ninety three. I was praying fervently in the spirit, and weeping uncontrollably! Joe had dropped me off at Joey's apartment, after I'd spent another crazy, long horrible night with him making love to me, and yet breaking my heart with his rejection. I felt in my mind, I couldn't stand my life the way it was any more. It wasn't even safe or comfortable for me to go back to my sister Sally's house, because Joe had been seeing me down there too. I didn't have enough strength or courage to say no to the father of my children, the grandfather to my grandchildren, and the husband of my youth who I'd loved and cherished all those years. I was still wide awake when Joey left for work early that morning. I had not closed my eyes, but lay awake praying.

As I prayed in the spirit, I kept remembering Audrey and Cherri's Pastor, Jake, and how kind he seemed to be. I looked frantically through my purse, until I found the phone number

Audrey had given me to the church, in case I needed spiritual guidance or prayer. When I called, he was out so I left a message on his answering machine. Pastor Jake called me back within the hour. I couldn't talk to him without crying, as I tried to explain my situation. His voice was very compassionate, and kind. After I finished telling him my troubled story, he asked if he could pray for me. He asked the Lord Jesus, to reach down and touch me with the hem of His garment, since I was too weak to reach up to touch Him. He also asked God to open, only the right doors for me, new doors, in the name of Jesus, and slam shut in the devil's face, all the other doors, He didn't want me to go through. I felt that prayer strengthen me. After we hung up, I went on pacing the floor and praying in the spirit, until the dear precious Holy Spirit reminded me of the conversation I'd had with the sweet, white haired lady at Pastor Jake's church who gave me her phone number. Again, I frantically searched through my purse, until I found her number.

When I blinked back the tears, I saw that her name was Jenelle. Thank God, she answered the phone when I called. As soon as I introduced myself, she remembered who I was. We talked for a few minutes, and then she said something that totally shocked me! Jenelle told me she was an ex-police officer, and she recognized I was a perfect candidate for, 'The Domestic Women's Violence Shelter.' She told me I'd been abused, but I told her I didn't have a lot of bruises. She said, I may not have bruises on the outside, but I sure had some bad ones on the inside. She asked me if I'd go into a shelter if she could get me in, and I quickly said, "Yes." I had a feeling, this was one of those new doors, God was opening for me. Jenelle called back right away and told me they had room for only one more person, me. Jenelle made all the arrangements with the Domestic Women's Violence Shelter, came and helped me pack my things into her car, and took me there. By late that afternoon, I'd gone to the police station, and into the shelter with Jenelle, and no one knew where I was. I'd left Joey a note, saying I was with a friend, and I'd call him as soon as I could. God sent Jenelle, as the perfect laborer to help me to do His will.

The Domestic Women's Violence Shelter, was one of the

hardest doors I've ever walked through in my life. My mind was so confused, I didn't fully comprehend what Jenelle was talking about when she said she had to get me somewhere quickly, where I was safe. Somehow, in my tormented submissive state of mind, I still wanted to protect Joe, and his strange behavior toward me. I'd thought I was the one who was wrong, and I was the one who just couldn't ever seem to get anything right, until I read the papers in the folder they gave me at the shelter that night. I couldn't sleep, so I sat up most of the night reading pages, after pages of their information sheets about the abused, and the abuser.

Early the next morning I was sitting in a chair crying, holding their folder in my hand. A worker, leaving the night shift position bent down and patted my shoulder and said, "Oh now honey, it's going to get better soon, you'll see." I wiped the tears from my red swollen eyes, and looked up at her and said, "Lady, these are not tears of sorrow, these are tears of joy. After reading all this eye opening information, I finally see that I'm not the one who was always wrong or stupid. My husband was abusing me, and I didn't even know it. I'd always thought something was terribly wrong with me, not him. Lady, according to this information I've been reading, I've been abused, since the day that I was born."

I was so scared I was numb. I was allowed to contact my family members, by using a pay telephone in the shelter. I understood when the authorities told me this rule was for my safety as well as all the other women and children in the shelter. No one was allowed to ever know where this shelter was located. I didn't have the money to call long distance, so I asked Betsy and David if they could call Sally. Everyone was worried because of my sudden disappearance, they said. The authorities in the shelter frightened me when they told me, if I didn't obey their rules, I stood a good chance of being thrown out of the shelter. We were cautioned continually about their privacy rules, and how they were established to protect all the women and children in the shelter from their abuser. David and Betsy didn't understand why I couldn't come to their house for Thanksgiving. I explained to David, "Son, I was told by the authorities here in the shelter, if I came to your house, I'd run a risk of your dad showing up, and they said, I was not yet strong enough to see him. I know they are right David, because I still feel fearful and weak inside when I think of him. Please try and understand?" "Jesus, precious Jesus."

My nineteen-year-old room mate Gina, and I decided to fix Thanksgiving dinner for the twenty-three of us in the shelter. Even though the dinner went extremely well considering their's was a strange kitchen, and it tasted good, it still felt so odd not to look across the table and see one familiar, or happy face. I was thankful they were teaching me so much valuable information. They wanted me to become strong enough to leave the safety of the shelter, and get out on my own. I was terrified every time I thought about living in an apartment by myself, and especially to be alone at night. Night after night in the shelter, I'd wake up in a cold sweat, thinking about living alone and trying to support myself! I was so miserable standing in long degrading lines to try and receive my welfare checks at my new address instead of Sally and Don's for one hundred dolors a month. I got a part time job, working at a fast food place. Depression was so great, all I thought about was trying to make it through one day at a time, one second at a time. However, the only thing that came out of my mouth was, God's word, and laughter. I got up early every morning, said my prayers, took my shower, put on make up, fixed my hair, and went to work with a smile on my face, because I knew how God felt about grumbling in the wilderness. God's word gave me joy.

Consistently, I felt an unexplainable horrible emptiness inside the pit of my stomach and an utterly lost grey darkness clouded the window of my mind, but I never gave into the spirit of self pity, because I knew what it could do to me. I knew I had to stay focused on Jesus no matter what happened. When I obey God's word, in spite of how I'm feeling, He never fails to bless me. I also knew there were many unbelievers in that shelter, including the authorities who ran it. I knew they were watching my life, because I boldly told them, "I am a Christian." There was one precious Christian woman who was high up in authority in the shelter named Marie, and she was definitely on my side, "Praise

God!'" Most of the women in the shelter had children, so they were able to get help from the Government. They were assigned to a nice apartment with very low rent, and given food stamps. Since I was not over fifty, and I wasn't disabled, thank God, nor did I have small children in my care, I didn't fit into any of these categories in order to receive more Government assistance. I felt like I was living on the ragged edge, and I was extremely fearful of the unknown. I was forty-seven years old. Just trying to figure out where I was going to live and get a job paying enough to give me a substantial income to support myself without a car, made me very tired, and depressed. "Jesus, I'll rest against Your bosom."

I couldn't even afford a lawyer so I could get my divorce, and Joe would not help me with alimony payments, until I did. I was petrified because my short time given at the shelter was soon running out, and I still didn't have a plan. They only allowed us about sixty days to secure a job and an apartment. We ate whatever food was donated to the shelter. My room mate, Gina was a good cook even though she was so young. She fixed us T bone steaks a couple of nights. A company had donated them to the shelter, and we appreciated them very much. We each had our chores to do, and cooking for everyone in the shelter on our scheduled nights was one of them. We were each assigned different jobs to keep the shelter clean, besides our own rooms and outside work. We had a meeting every night somewhere else away from the shelter, and then again in the shelter on the same night sometimes. We watched a real life video of some women who was badly abused, and prayed to learn from her mistakes which ended up costing her, her life. Some of the other women's stories in the shelter were similar to mine, but some were much more horrible. We had a very strict curfew, and everyone obeyed the rules. When I called my friend Audrey from the shelter, she asked if I could start attending their church services. I was thrilled when the staff at the shelter said yes, and the Lord made a way for me to get there. "Papa God, You know I need to hear Your word."

A real kind, older gentleman who lived near the shelter volunteered to pick me up three blocks away, and never ask any questions about where the shelter was located. Carl picked me up, and brought me back to the shelter three times a week. It was quit a long drive to and from Fairborn, but I didn't mind it at all, because it gave me a break from the shelter. I thanked God that I could go and hear the teaching of His word. I sat in those pews every Wednesday night, Sunday morning and Sunday evening, drinking in God's words of eternal life. I loved hearing the word of God being taught. "I love You so much, wonderful Jesus."

I started in a school program the shelter offered, and I felt elated about finally getting my G E D! I couldn't believe it when the Teacher marked, 'excellent' on ALL my math papers. Joe and his family had always sort of laughed and made fun of my ability to keep the score at their silly card games, because of my lack of education. I was so proud of the fact that I actually got good grades on my papers. It was such an awesome feeling. "Sweet Jesus!" When I started using the school computers for the first time in my life, my Teacher gave me good grades in that area too. God was impressing on me to realize my potential, in Him. Instead of being so afraid I couldn't do it, I found myself finally trying to relax and enjoy the challenge, even though it was still very difficult for me. The enemy fought me hard every day, telling me I had no reason to go on learning anything, for what reason?

Although I felt like a salmon swimming up a stream, God never let the desire for learning the information I needed to make it on my own, without being abused, decrease in me. As I grew a little more knowledgeable each day, I began to feel, ever so slightly, stronger. Christmas Eve and Christmas day were hard for me to deal with. My sister Sally, and her husband Don came and got me Christmas Eve and took me over to their son Donnie's house for a while. I actually felt like a complete stranger with my own people. I was going through so many transitions all at one time, I didn't feel like I fit in anywhere accept with my new friends. Sally started crying when I had to tell her for the third or fourth time, they weren't allowed to drop me off in front of the shelter. She was afraid for me to walk all that way alone at night in the freezing cold weather. When I hugged them good by, I was hurting so badly I had to make myself want to keep on going. Any kind of sympathy opened a door, I knew I had to keep shut. A long time ago I promised God and myself I'd never pick up those old dirty rags of self pity again. I was fighting a raging battle within myself. I fought my flesh daily and kept on believing God's word day after day. "Oh Lord, I believe You! I thank You that the winter is over and passed in my life, just like You promised me, Lord." (Philippians 2:13) "For God is at work within me, helping me want to obey Him, and then helping me do what He wants."

I was so thankful the Red Cross donated Christmas presents for me to give to my grandchildren. I cried so hard on Christmas morning as I walked several blocks through the crackling ice and blowing snow to meet my son David and little Michael, at the fast food place where I worked. Betsy and little Kyle stayed home. It hurt so much to, not be allowed to be with them on Christmas day. Joe was the one who had pushed me out of my home, and yet he and his girlfriend were spending Christmas day with his family, and our sons and grandchildren. It didn't seem fair. I was only able to spend about a half an hour with David, and my precious little Michael. I kept repeating, "Please help us, dear Lord Jesus!"

I thought my heart would break, when I had to pull away from my little grandson, Michael. He cried as hard for me, as he had done so many times in the past! Always before, I took him with me, and he just didn't understand why I couldn't then. Everything in my life right then seemed as cold and grey as the weather outside that day. The tears flowed freely from my eyes as I walked back to the shelter. That was, without a doubt, one of the most difficult days of my life. Michael had grown so attached to me and me to him. The little fellow just simply couldn't understand why the grandmother who had always loved him and had been so close to him was pulling away from him now. "Sweet, precious, Jesus." Every time I thought of my family, I felt a deep sadness in my heart. I missed David, Betsy, Joey and my little grandchildren coming over for dinner. I also missed my friends stopping by or calling to pray. I missed my own home where I could quietly seek the Lord, and yet I still had a strange peace I can't explain.

In the shelter we were being given constant information, on how not to be abused. Loretta, and her three pretty little blond haired, blue eyed girls and I became friends in the shelter. Loretta, and her daughters came to church looking for me one night, and glory to God, they started coming regularly. Loretta got saved! "Thank You Jesus!" I'd been going with her when she dropped the girls off for their by weekly visitations with their dad, her abusive husband. Every other week the police met us when we dropped off her children in a public place, or picked them up. Loretta's husband was so angry one evening in the mall when he brought the girls back, he was throwing things, and someone called 911. It was after that incident the police had to be present with us. I remember when a woman' staff member on duty at the shelter told Loretta they finally got her and the girls a brand new, two story, low income apartment. It was so new they weren't finished laying the sod and shrubs in the yard. It was located in Fairborn.

I discovered my new friend Marie was the head authority in the shelter. I learned she had been a staff sergeant in the Army before she applied for the job at the shelter. She called me into the office two weeks before Christmas and told me, Pastor Jake's church, which was her church too, adopted me. A lady name Bev was assigned to the task of securing my apartment, and suppling me with food, clothes, and etc. I knew it was God supplying all my need, according to His riches in glory by Christ Jesus, but I was still scared to move in by myself. Constantly, I went from the fear of never being able to get out of that shelter, to being afraid of living alone and taking care of myself. Bev came and got me and took me to see my new apartment, which was in (down town Fairborn, up over a Christian bookstore.) I kept trying to imagine myself living there alone, and it literally terrified me! Loretta took me to the places I needed, so I could go through the process of getting my electric turned on for a really low monthly rate, until I could get my divorce and then receive alimony. Audrey called and told me she had talked to a friend of hers who owned a restaurant in, (down town Fairborn about three and some half blocks away from my apartment.) He said he'd hire me because

240

she recommended me. I could easily walk back and forth to work, and I had the job for sure, but I was still so scared. "Sweet Jesus!"

That night, I woke up having the usual panic attack and cold sweats! Again, I sat straight up in bed, thinking, "Oh Lord, how can I make it on my own?" Suddenly, I laid back down on my pillow, and for the first time in several months, I lay there quietly in the darkness. Finally it had dawned on me, "Oh my God, You really did speak through Sally, and Audrey about me living in Fairborn, above a Christian bookstore. I have a job downtown, so I can easily walk to and from work. You tried to tell me this from the very beginning, but I was too scared to listen to You! Oh my very own dear Papa, You had this planned from the beginning! Dear Lord, You even made sure my friend Loretta and her three little girls will be living right behind the place where I work. Oh, dear Lord God, You are truly a wonderful Papa! I love You Lord!"

I'd made my decision. I was ready to trust God and move into my apartment. I was ready to live alone. Marie had pointed her finger at me, more then once, and said boldly, "Carol, you are never alone!" I finally believed her too. I went in and filled out the application at the Italian pizza restaurant, and told them I was Audrey's friend. Mike hired me on the spot. I knew God had this planned, because I'd been going to that same restaurant for many years. It was my favorite pizza! "Oh, thank You wonderful Jesus!" Mike wanted me to start work at eight o clock the next morning, so I knew it was time to move on with my life. Dec, 28, 1993.

I called my sons, David and Joey and asked them to help me go and get my things from storage, I had to move into my apartment by that night. Several day earlier, Loretta found some nice ladies add in the paper who wanted to give her couch and chair away to anyone who would come and get it, free. A couple of helpful men from the church offered to take it up the stairs into my apartment for us. After she and I had went and got the couch and chair, we were not strong enough to take it up those stairs. Thank God, I was able to get it. It was all I'd have to sleep on until I could get a bed. By the time David and Joey picked me up at my apartment it was thirty-five degrees below zero, windchill factor. There were near white outs all along the freeway because of the blowing snow, but I was not afraid anymore. I was finally in the will of God, and I felt it. I unlocked my apartment door at the bottom of the stairs first, and then I half way ran on up the twenty-seven steps to unlock the top door, so David and Joey could help unload my things. After we finished, Joey and David stood there looking at me, as if to say, "Our mom will never make it by herself in this apartment." I reassured them, everything was going to be all right, especially now that I was sure I was where God wanted me to be. Audrey came just as they were leaving and brought me a small black and white television. I was so glad to see her.

She and I rummaged through the sacks of food left by the church, and put it all away. We worked for a while, and then sat on the couch and visited. I'd never met anyone quite like Audrey. She was a special lady. Audrey told me her husband abused her so badly, she ran from him! She took her two young sons and two small daughters with her and they lived in her car until she found a job and a place to live. She had been through some pretty rough times in her past too. She'd had cancer, and had to have part of her colon removed. She also developed cancer in her breasts and had to have them removed. She had been so badly abused, she was even sort of harsh speaking to me some times, but I loved her anyway. She was sometimes hilariously funny too. We sat up there in my apartment laughing until we cried from laughing so hard! She gave me the courage I needed to keep on going, telling me funny stories about her past. She gave me no pity, only tough, your gonna make it by faith talk. I thanked God for her.

All of downtown Fairborn was lite up like the beautiful huge Christmas tree which sat decorated in the middle of town and outside my window. The Lord knew I liked a night light. The next morning I bundled myself up really good, knowing it was still thirty-five below zero, with the wind chill factor. I kept thinking of Abraham. God told him to leave his family and go to a strange land too. I locked my top apartment door and made my way down the freezing cold stairway. I hesitated as I peeked out the partly frozen window glass on the downstairs door before I left, and I prayed, "Oh Lord, remember what You promised! The winter is over and past." I was fearful of crossing all the streets in the heavy snow, the hard days work that I knew lay ahead of me, and the new people I'd be working with, but I felt an umbrella of God's grace hovering over me. When I finally clocked out and sat down for my twenty minute lunch break, I was almost too exhausted to eat. Mike came over to my table, and complemented me on my hard work. He also gave me a forty-five-cent raise on the hour. In my heart I said, "Thank You dear Lord Jesus!" The young men that I worked with used that grotesque four letter 'F' word that I hated, fluently, and they took my precious Lord's name in vain, worse then Joe. They were vulgar, angry young men who were very rude to me most of the time, but I kept on smiling and treating them the way I wanted to be treated, decent.

I heard Mike yelling and cursing at some of the young men and the waitresses during the lunch, rush hour. I asked him to please not yell at me like that. I told him I'd heard enough abusive talk most of my life and I couldn't handle anymore. He smiled and told me not to worry, but he still crossed that boundary more then once, before that day was over. My second day there, I started my monthly period. I was so embarrassed because I hadn't thought to bring anything to put on. My manager seemed irritated when I told her my problem. She sent me back into the kitchen to ask some of the other ladies if they could help. By the time I clocked out to walk home, my body hurt so bad I felt like someone had beat me up badly. My sore feet and legs were numb, and they didn't want to walk across the busy streets when the lights turned. When I finally reached my apartment I was half frozen, and so tired I wanted to cry. After I unlocked and locked my bottom door behind me, I practically crawled up the twenty-seven steps, locked the top door behind me, and fell on the couch and went to sleep. Audrey woke me up by ringing my downstairs doorbell incessantly! She got me a twin bed. I was tired but grateful. We drug it up the stairs and into my apartment a little at a time, and set it up. Audrey made me laugh with her heavy Canadian accent. I loved the way she talked. I gave her back her T V, I liked quiet.

The first couple of weeks I didn't know if I'd make it through another day of work, I was so exhausted. Every muscle and joint in my body hurt, and even burned. God was so kind to me, and cared about the smallest detail of my life. It just so happened my friend Loretta was a masseuse. A couple of days a week I started walking to Loretta's house after work. She lived about a block and a half in walking distance behind the restaurant where I worked. Her three pretty little girls loved it when their mother worked on me. I had to lie on a mat in their floor. As she massaged my sore tired muscles, even in my feet, they laughed, rolled and tumbled on the floor all around me. Her smallest daughter, two year old Katie, loved to look back at me, upside down through her tiny legs and say, "Peek a boo." I hadn't stood on my feet or worked that hard since Sandy and I'd had our C & S Cleaning Company. I was at least ten years younger back then, and a whole lot stronger. Every day after work, or Loretta's I'd go home, start my warm bath water running, turn on the oven in the kitchen, clean a potato and put it in to bake, and some fresh frozen broccoli on low heat on the top of the stove. By the time I'd finish my bath, my dinner was ready to eat. I put plastic over my windows in the living room and bedroom, because there was ice frozen on the inside. I took down my thick heavy blue shower curtain in the bathroom, since I always took a bath anyway, I taped it over the bathroom window.

The brash young men I worked with lived only for their weekend pay. They went to the bars to drink, do drugs and party all weekend long. When a couple of the young men flirted with me, and actually asked me to go out with them, I was shocked! I was old enough to be their mother, and that was exactly how I thought of them, as kids. I laughed at them because I thought they were joking with me. I could hardly believe it when they got really angry with me for turning them down. They were especially mad at me for laughing at them! Those young men made my life even more miserable after that. I prayed for wisdom and the Lord showed me, it was like a student having a crush on his Teacher. I laughed and told the Lord, I felt kind of like Moses, after he'd gone through the wilderness. God gave him all those beautiful women to choose from. I was flattered, and I figured God allowed that situation to happen because my self esteem had been badly bruised. My first month working there I had three heavy periods. I was embarrassed, not having been prepared for any of them. Suddenly I realized I was going through the change of life. As soon as my body adjusted to the rigorous exercise, my periods actually became minuscule, lighter. I had to laugh at myself straining every mussel I had to keep on doing the deep knee bends at least fifty times a day at work. I said, "Oh well Lord, at least they're paying me to work out here. I don't have to go to a spa."

It wasn't long before I was finally able to afford a phone, but somehow Joe got my number. He started calling me late at night, and extremely early in the morning, harassing me. He kept asking if I'd go out with him? My answer was always the same, "No." Most of the things Joe said to me was too vulgar to repeat. Finally I said to him one day, "Look Joe, if all I wanted was sex. I work with several good looking young men who would be happy to accommodate me. I'm better then that, Joe. I deserve to be treated with respect. I am a lady and a decent human being." Suddenly, Joe's attitude changed and he said, "Your right Carol, you are better then that." My next pay check, I purchased an answering machine so I wouldn't have to speak with Joe. I knew I was getting stronger, because saying no to Joe came a little easier each time I said it. Less and less of me wanted my old way of life back with Joe. However, some of those old feelings were still slightly haunting me. The Lord told me to take it slow, one day at a time.

I felt so discouraged, I barely had enough money to get by on. I told the Lord one day, I couldn't take much more! I reminded Him, He was my husband. I'd stood looking out my kitchen window before I left Joe on my last day there, and said, "Lord, I take You as my lawful wedded husband. I know You will take much better care of me then any earthly husband." A lawyer name Dan who worked for the shelter called and told me, he was representing me in my divorce. Joe had to pay for it. When I told Dan I didn't have a car, he said he'd be happy to come to my apartment. He opened my eyes when he gave me information about my rights. I couldn't believe I'd been so ignorant of my rights. My lawyer was very angry with Joe. He told me I should have never left my home. I was shocked when he explained, by law Joe had to provide my groceries, rent, water, electric, and etc. When I told him Joe hadn't provided me with any financial help since I'd left him, and very little before that, he got upset with him again. Dan told me, there wasn't a judge in the County that wouldn't agree to make Joe pay me eight hundred a month alimony, and give me half, if not all the money for the sale of our cabin and land; And half the worth of Joe's ball card collection, fishing acquitment, guns, knives, and etc., and pay off all the bills. "Wow! Thank You Papa God, for taking good care of me!" Dan could not believe I was married to Joe for thirty-one years and he treated me like an unwanted animal, left at the side of the road.

My lawyer told me to inform Joe, the money he'd failed to give me since I'd left him, he'd have to make it up to me in back alimony payments, so he might as well start giving it to me every week. I knew Joe was afraid, not to respect the law, but he was furious when I told him what my lawyer said! He still insisted on only bringing me fifty dolors a week. I was very grateful for the money, but I wouldn't allow him to come up the steps, into my apartment. I'd lock my top door and meet him at the foot of the stairs when he came over. Joe always wanted to kiss, and hug me, but I'd pull away from him! After Joe tried to drag me down the street with him, I prayed and asked God for wisdom. Immediately, I started allowing Joe to only come there on Thursday nights. My prayer group was on Thursday nights, so I decided to have Joe come by then. My friend's Sharon, David Ay, Michael, Kathy, and Billy loved to pray too. It strengthened all of us each week to get together for prayer, and fellowship. I finally had something exciting to look forward to every week in between church days. It wasn't easy to pull away from Joe. I did, with wings like eagles.

My apartment had electric baseboard heat, and my electric bills had steadily climbed during those long bitter cold winter months. I knew whenever Joe and I got the divorce settled and I started getting my alimony checks, I'd have to pay the remainder of those bills off quickly. Everyone said it was the coldest winter we'd had in years. When the temperature went down to sixty-five below zero that year with the wind chill factor, my friend Marie took me home with her after Wednesday night church. Her kind husband Jim brought me all the way back to Fairborn in time for work the next morning. The next day at four thirty Audrey came by and picked me up at work and took me home with her. She made the most delicious home aid potato soup with cheese and broccoli I've ever tasted. She lived with and cared for an elderly lady in her home. May told Audrey, it was fine with her if I stayed the night. We laughed and had a great time. Audrey warmed the truck up before she took me to work the next morning.

The severe colder weather broke after that, so I was able to walk back and forth to work again. Although it was still terribly cold and I had to bundle up, it felt good to be in my apartment again. I remember that year we also had seven days of ice on the roads and sidewalks. I was terrified, but I never missed one day of walking and sliding to work that whole week. "Praise God!" Audrey had given me a wonderful pair of black leather boots. It was easier to walk through the snow and ice in boots. We had huge amounts of snow that year in 1994. The men in their snow plows shoveled it off the streets and onto the sidewalks into large piles. I fell into a big pile of dirty snow one day on my way to work. I couldn't walk around it, so I tried to climb over it, and I fell in it! "Thank You, sweet wonderful Jesus!" By the time I walked home that day someone had shoveled it off the sidewalk.

I couldn't afford to miss any work. I also started working on one of my days off. We were closed on Monday, so I went in and cleaned the restaurant. I started bringing in cookies every morning for the young men and the girl I worked with. God gave me favor with them. One young man who worked the ovens used to get very angry with me because I couldn't make his pizzas fast enough to suit him. I broke down and cried, and I explained my situation to him that nerve-racking day! After that, Scott and I became friends. The Lord was teaching me to speak up for myself. A young man named George kept harassing me because he knew I was a Christian, and he was a devil worshiper. I was glad I pled the blood of Jesus over myself every day. He combed his hair down the middle, and made little curls sticking up on the top of his head, he called horns. When I was making my preps he'd stand behind me cutting foil for the pizzas and chanting disgusting words, loud enough for me to hear him.

From the first day I started work there, I prayed softly or sang in tongues constantly to keep my sanity. One day George walked up to me and said, he was the devil. I said, "Well, if you are the devil then get out of my face and lay down on the floor so I can walk on you." His eyes got really big! He was offended at me and he said, "Aren't you afraid of me?" I said, "No, because Jesus Christ defeated the devil two thousand years ago and put him under my feet, in the name of Jesus." He walked away, and left me alone. I gave the Lord a high five on that one. "Sweet Jesus!"

I got up early every morning, so I could say my prayers and read my bible. Afterwards, I'd put on my praise tapes, LOUD, and I danced and praised the Lord for about twenty minutes. When I finished, I'd wash and dry my hair, put on my make up, eat breakfast, and walk to work. I had to force myself do all these things. Before I'd get up out of bed every morning, the deceiver rattled on, 'You are so useless, old and ugly. Why do you even bother to put on make up, and fix your hair? You don't have anyone who really cares about you anymore. After all, your kids don't even call you or come over and check on their mother. Your husband doesn't want you. Why don't you just jump out of that front window and kill yourself. You'd splatter all over the sidewalk, but all your misery would be over. Go ahead and do it, nobody cares if you live or die. At least then, you won't have to go to that horrible job, and listen to everyone yell at you. You wouldn't have to bus tables, scrub down the kitchen, catch up on your preps, or make pizzas anymore either.' I'd scream, "You liar! Casting DOWN, every evil imagination that tries to set itself up against the power of Christ, and bringing into captivity, every thought unto the obedience of Christ Jesus!" Even though I was surrounded by strong believers at the church I was attending, I still felt like I had very little reason to keep going. Day in, and day out, it was a constant struggle to stay focused. I kept on saying "Lord, I know that when I am weak, I am strong, in You, Christ Jesus!" Several people told me, they saw Joe's car parked outside my apartment at different hours of the night and day. I called the police and told them Joe was stalking me, so they drove by my apartment frequently. Loretta took me with her to the thrift stores and I bought myself some nice clothes that fit me. "Thank You sweet, wonderful Jesus. I love You."

James was one of the most eligible bachelors in the church. This handsome, dark haired, blue eyed, six foot two inch tall man came to my prayer group. He always drove his eighty one year old friend Abigail too and from church and out to eat afterwards. Abigail was no ordinary eighty one year old woman. She wore stylish clothes and beautiful rings on nearly every finger of both hands. Her fingernails were always filed to perfection and polished too. Her white hair was cut short, and her attitude was wonderful. Everyone in the church loved her and called her mother, including me. James and I loved to talk about the bible, but other then that, we were just friends. A couple of times he stood at the top of my stairs along with my other two friends, Michael, and David Ay, asking if I was having any trouble with Joe at the bottom of the stars. Joe didn't know it was my prayer group night, or that several of my girlfriends were sitting in my apartment too. Joe didn't know that I wasn't dating any of these handsome ordained minister friends of mine either. He'd just look up at them with a pale face, let go of me, and turn around and leave.

The men and women I made friends with were mostly ordained ministers. James told me, he wanted to learn to speak the word the way I did. I started enjoying myself when we all went out bowling on Friday nights. Audrey made me laugh at myself for being so self conscious, and she helped me try and relax. No one made fun of me, instead they told me we were actually bowling for fun, not blood. I started going into the jails and prisons with some of the

249

ministers at the church. I loved ministering to the prisoners, and telling them how much Jesus loves them. I told them how God brought David's sentence down from ninety-one years, to ten, and he spent only fourteen months incarcerated. I showed them the pictures David sent me from England of the double rainbow stretched out across the courthouse. I carried those pictures of the double rainbows in my bible at all times. My friend Sharon was the Chaplain of the Green County jail. She made copies of the Christian stationary David had printed when he worked in the prison. We used David's stationary to witness to the women prisoners. We gave them some of it to write their letters on. "Oh God, I'm so grateful for everything You've done for me Lord."

Sometimes on Sunday, Sharon took me home with her after church. She had a washer and dryer, and insisted I bring my laundry. We were always tired after a big lunch. Sharon said she enjoyed stretching out in her big comfortable recliner while I'd take a nap on her couch. She'd cover me up with a warm cozy blanket, and I'd fall into a deep sleep immediately. Most of the time, she wound up doing all my laundry by herself. She reasoned, she had an easy, and excellent paying job as a secretary. When I'd try to ask her, not to do my laundry, she'd just smile and say, "Carol, you were sleeping so peacefully, I didn't have the heart to wake you. I didn't mind, I don't have to work as hard as you do." God always took care of me, and gave me the best friends who loved Him, and me. Sharon was my age and she knew the work I did eight hours a day, standing on my feet was hard. I went with her to the Green County jail every Tuesday night and stood on my sore tired feet for several hours there too, but I loved every minute of it. We stood in line for hours, going into the prisons. I stood in the church choir and sang Sunday morning, evening, and Wednesday nights. I had one day off a week, Sunday. "Delight thyself in the Lord and He shall give thee the desires of thine heart." (Psalm 37:4) "I love You so dearly, Jesus!"

As I pray in tongues the Holy Spirit fills me with joy. Jesus said in, John 16:22. "Therefore you now have sorrow; but I will see you again and your heart will rejoice, and your joy no one will

250

take from you." Isaiah 53:5 "The chastisement for our peace was upon Him." Jesus bought and paid for my peace. (Nehemiah 8:10) Then he said to them, "Go your way, eat the fat, drink the sweet, and send portions to those for whom nothing is prepared; for this day is a holy day to our Lord. Do not sorrow, for the joy of the Lord is your strength." Matthew 12:34-37. "Brood of vipers! How can you, being evil, speak good things? For out of the abundance of the heart the mouth speaks. A good man out of the good treasure of his heart brings forth good things, and an evil man out of the evil treasure brings forth evil things. But I say unto you that for every idle word men may speak, they will give account of it in the day of judgment. For by your words you will be justified, and by your words you will be condemned." Every day, I pray, "Put a watch over my mouth, oh God, and over the door of my lips."

After a lot of coaxing from my friends, I signed up for the Student Minister classes at the church, against my better judgment. I didn't have enough confidence to believe I could pass the tests. I had been disappointed when I had to stop going to school, after I moved to Fairborn and went to work full time. I still had a hunger to learn, and especially anything about the bible. Every time I passed a test, I was shocked, and thrilled, all at the same time! I went to the classes at the church, three nights a week. I studied, and I passed every single test. "Thank You, Jesus!"

The head waitress Betty, another waitress, Linda, and Diana the office secretary were near my age. They stopped me in the hallway at work one day, and asked, "All right Carol, tell us your secret?" Starring at them a little puzzled, I said, "What secret is that, ladies?" They all talked at once, "We want to know what kind of vitamins your taking, because we want some too!" I started laughing and said, "Well, I take good vitamins, if that's what your asking me?" Betty, Linda, and Diana continued to bombard me with questions, "Look at you Carol! We know you are close to our age, and we want to know, where do you get all your energy? We know your going through some rough times, and yet we hear you laughing almost all the time! What is it that makes you look and act so happy? You almost never look tired, instead, you always look as fresh and pretty at four when you clock out to go home, as you did when you came in here at eight o clock that morning. We know you're in the middle of a divorce, and you were married to one man for thirty-one years. You've left your home, your children, grandchildren, friends, family, and still you are so happy. You never seem to have a bad day. How can you, NOT get angry with those mean, nasty young men you work with up front on the pizza line? We want to buy some of those vitamins, and we don't care how much they cost!"

I just smiled and said, "Yes, I told you I take good vitamins, but ladies that's not my secret for happiness. My happiness comes from knowing and loving Jesus. He gives me hope, and with His strength, He keeps me going on in the right direction. Look ladies, believe me, Jesus is the ONLY reason for my joy." I walked away thinking, "If they only knew how hard I've had to lean on Jesus. I can do all things, (ONLY), through Christ who strengthens me."

Joe refused to sign any divorce agreement that said he had to pay me eight hundred dolors a month alimony. He only wanted to give me two hundred and fifty a month, but I refused! We finally settled on five hundred a month, for five years, or until I remarried. My lawyer was so upset with me he told me if I wouldn't hold out for the eight hundred a month for the rest of my life, and half of everything, he'd quit my case! I cried and told Dan he wasn't walking in my shoes and barely getting by each week, financially. I didn't want to kill Joe, I just wanted to get my divorce. I knew Joe was so angry he'd never agree to sign those divorce papers, and I desperately needed my alimony checks so I could survive. I was so desperate to just be able to pay my rent and utilities every month, I agreed to sign the papers before a notary republic for a hundred dolor a month payment on my half of the cabin money. Joe begged me not to ask him to sell the cabin and split the money. He said if I'd sign, he'd give me one hundred dolors a month until my half was paid off, so I agreed. I knew I had to do it his way, in order to get anything from Joe. I also knew I'd told Joe from the very beginning, even though he was treating me horribly, I wanted to get the divorce peacefully. I refused to argue, because I knew I could only stay in the will of God, if I didn't get angry and quarrel with him. "Sweet Jesus, help me!"

One evening during our prayer group in my apartment, my friend David Ay gave me a prophecy from the Lord. On March fourth nineteen ninety four, these words spoke so clearly to my heart about my circumstances. "The winds of change are blowing through your life. They are like waves crashing on the rocks. When one ebb's, another wave seems to come right after it. God says, not to be overwhelmed by these changes. This season of change is there to bring you into the place that God has ordained for you to be since the foundation of the world." I knew the Lord was speaking to me through David, because His words gave me peace. David Ay is a wonderful friend who God sent into my life. I loved him like a son. He appreciated me like a mother. He was even kind enough to open my car doors for me, and treat me like a lady, I desperately needed that. He surprised me one day when he told me, the Lord told him to give me his little blue car. He was buying a new car. "Thank You sweet Jesus!" He paid my insurance for one year. He also paid for the tags on the car. I'd always been afraid of men. "Thank God!" He healed me of that fear before I left Joe. David and I had so much fun together. I trusted my dear friend David Ay, and I felt very safe with him.

One night I had a disturbing dream, and my friend Michael was in it. In the dream, I was sitting almost at the top of a huge black, granite rock mountain. I felt so tired and weary as I sat there listening to Michael talk to me. Looking up at him, I saw that he was still wearing his caramel colored rimmed glasses, but he was dressed like an angel, all in white. The only bright light up there illuminated from him. Michael kept motioning with his right hand and arm, beckoning me to climb up the rest of the way to the top of the mountain with him? As he was speaking, he kept pointing directly behind himself toward seven dimly lite steps. In order to climb the rest of the way up the mountain and get to the very top, I'd have to be very careful not to slip and fall off. Engraved in the side of the rock granite mountain were seven very treacherous steps. These steps resembled half rounded metal tire rims that fit inside the tires of a car. Each step was a half-rounded circle of thick metal and was embedded into the side of the rock granite mountain. Bubbling up from inside each metal rim was muddy water. I sat there on the cold hard barren ground as Michael tried very hard to convince me to go the rest of the way up to the top of the mountain with him. I stubbornly refused.

I shook my head, wearily, and said, "No, Michael, I'm not going with you. I'm so tired, I just don't care anymore. I don't want to go any further. I can't go on." He reached down and took my limp hand in his, saying, "Carol, come on! Get up and come with me! Let me show you how far you've already come." Michael lifted me to my feet and placed his right arm around me firmly, and he grasped my right hand in his. He held onto my left hand with his strong left hand, and walked me to the edge of the black granite rock mountain. I felt supernatural strength illuminating from him. He held onto me as I peered into the darkness. Adjusting my eyes, I looked down over the edge of the high mountain, and gasped for breath as I pulled backwards! I could hardly believe I'd actually come that far up the mountain. I could only barely see the bottom if I strained my eyes. The entire mountain was without any kind of vegetation, or signs of life. It did not even have a tiny little sprig of grass nor was there a tree to grab onto. There was only black nothingness everywhere my eyes could see.

Michael turned me around and started walking back to where we were before, and said, "Look Carol, 'YOU CAN DO ALL THINGS THROUGH CHRIST JESUS WHO STRENGTHENS YOU! GREATER IS HE THAT IS IN YOU THEN he THAT IS IN THE WORLD!" I looked up into his shining face, and said, "O k Michael, let's go!" The vision shifted and I saw my red fuzzy sock feet leaping and landing precisely on each metal rim, like the hind's feet of a deer, hallelujah! Again my dream changed, and

I was standing in a strange barren valley looking steadily at Joe standing a few feet from me, intimidating me. Joe stood there motionless, staring at me. His feet were spread apart, and his hands were behind his back, Army style. Suddenly, Pastor Jake came driving up in his white Cadillac. Pastor Jake got out of his car. He was wearing an expensive looking white suit. He stared sternly at Joe as he paced diligently back and forth between us. I could feel the anointing of the dear precious Holy Spirit removing burdens and destroying yokes off me.

Once again the vision shifted, and I was standing beside Michael. He was still dressed like an angel, but wearing his caramel colored rimmed glasses. We were standing there looking out over an icy road, which appeared to be very dark and slippery. Michael jerked his head, in a motioning manner, beaconing me to come with him on that awful slippery road. Abandoning all fear, I didn't even argue with him that time, I just nodded my head, yes, and went with him. We laughed as we skated smoothly across the ice. The dream shifted back again to Joe and me in the same barren valley. Joe was still standing there in the same position he was before, staring at me, except he was standing a little further back this time. I was sitting on a very tall stool, wearing a white gown. The only light in that terrible dark valley was coming from my gown. Once again Pastor Jake drove up in his classy white Cadillac. He stopped the car and when he stepped out of it, I could feel his strength, just like when he preached God's word with power on Sunday mornings. I woke up from the dream and sat straight up in my bed crying. I thought, "Oh Lord, that is exactly how my life has been for so long! I've felt for such a long time that I've been climbing straight up that steep cold, and barren, black granite rock mountain, with nothing to hold onto! I've been barely able to see my next foot-step of faith in front of me! I have held onto Your word though, Lord, and You have brought me such a long way in such a short time, and I am grateful." I cried for a long time until I fell asleep. When I told Michael about the dream at our Thursday evening prayer group, he and everyone else kept saying, "Oh Carol!" I also felt the Lord leading me to have that picture of Michael dressed like an angel, standing beside the seven dimly lite steps on the front cover of my sequel book, "Seven realms of Glory." The conversation I had with Michael, on the top of that mountain, will also be on the back cover of that same book. God had placed Michael in my life to help me climb that treacherous mountain of faith.

Michael is caring, kind, and gentle. He's happily married, and the Father of three beautiful little girls and a dog. He's an ordained Minister of the gospel and was led by the dear precious Holy Spirit to counsel me through one of the most difficult and dark times in my life. I thank God for him. Audrey's friend, Cherri also counseled me, and prayed me through some very hard times too. She and her husband Jim have become very dear friends. The Lord has sent me some of the most precious, encouraging strong and faithful Christian friends I could ask for. "Thank You Jesus!"

Michael, and Gabriel came in every day at four o clock to relieve me. Not long after those two young men started working there, my boss Shirley brought a pretty young blond haired women up to my unit and introduced us. She said, "Carol, meet Joy. We 've hired her to help you." I welcomed the sight of this five-feet nine inches tall women with a happy smile on her sweet face. I laid my pizza sauce ladle back into the pan and walked toward her slowly, quoting, "Weeping my endure for a night, oh but (Joy) comes in the morning!" "Sweet Jesus!" (Psalm 30:5) Joy laughed and said, "What did you say?" I said, "It's a scripture from the bible, and you are an answer to my prayers." She and I became friends right away, and I soon found out, she was just like her name. She's a joy to be with. "Thank You, dear Papa God!"

She quickly corrected the young men we worked with and told them off, if they said or did anything mean to me. She made them lift the heavy containers of shredded cheese and sauce for me, or else she lifted them herself. I was so thankful for my new healthy, and strong young friend. She didn't smart off when I told her about my love for Jesus either. Joy herself had, had dreams which came to pass too. One day, Joy and I, and a couple of the young men we worked with were standing at the end of our unit talking after the lunch rush was over. All of a sudden Joy said something that surprised me, "Carol, you're not like any of the other Christians I've met. You don't just say you are a Christian You live it. Carol, you make me want to be a Christian too!" Joy started coming to church with me and gave her heart to Jesus! "Thank You again, dear sweet wonderful Lord Jesus!" Joy and I began to pray together and talk to others at work about Jesus.

On a cold snowy day a pretty young waitress name Donna asked if she could drive me home from work. By the time we arrived at my apartment, she asked me how she could get saved. I lead her in the sinner's prayer, right there in her car! "Oh my Papa, Your wonderful!" Right after she got saved, Donna wrote songs about Jesus, and told others about Him according to, Romans 10:9-10

We also worked with a pretty young dark haired waitress who had the eye of every man there. Her name was Sherry. Sherry wanted a baby, but several doctors had told her she couldn't get pregnant. I prayed for her, and the Lord said she'd have a baby that year, but when I told her, she cursed me out! Her dark eyes shot darts of fire at me as she told me in not a few angry words, it was impossible for her to have a baby! I remained calm, and smiled when I looked her in the eye, and said, "Sherry, the Lord loves you and He is going to heal your womb, and cause you to be able to have a baby, this year." She and I had not been very good friends to say the least. However, when she discovered she was pregnant about six weeks later she stopped arguing with me, and treated me with respect. It dawned on her, God really loves her. She married her boyfriend. About seven and a half months later her beautiful little boy was born. His dark hair, and eyes were like his mothers. His high cheek bones, of Indian decent were especially like Sherry's. I said, "Oh dear sweet Lord Jesus, You are amazing!" Sherry also quit the pizza place to stay home and raise their precious little Zachary. "To You, God be all the glory!"

One night while I was standing in the Green County Jail ministering to the women inmates, I sang to one of several of the ladies who were holding my hands through the cold iron bars. My friend Karen was there, as well as several other ladies from our church, ministering to these precious women. Karen was in charge of all the music, and the choir at the church. When I finished singing, "Because He lives" to one of the lady inmates, Karen looked at me with those big beautiful dark eyes of hers and said, "Carol your going to sing on stage for us very soon in our Sunday morning church service." I was so shocked when she argued, "You have no reason to be afraid Carol. Why, you'd sing good if you were singing from the bottom of a garbage can!" I told her how I used to sing on the top of a garbage can lid when I was very young. She told several other people in the church, I could sing good. I laughed at her when she told them about the garbage can.

Karen wouldn't stop coaxing and encouraging me to sing, until I went to the Christian bookstore beneath my apartment, bought an accompaniment tape, learned the song and sang it on stage by myself. I was terrified, and I shook all over but I did it with the Lord's help. Jesus went up on the stage with me. My friend, David Ay was familiar with running the sound system at the church. He drove me down to the church several times during the week when it was empty and helped me practice singing with the microphone on stage. People came up to me after church and told me the song blessed them. Audrey always encouraged me to keep singing for the Lord. "Oh God, thank You for repairing my broken dreams."

The day finally came for Joe and I to appear in court before a judge to finalize our divorce. Joe offered to pick me up and drive me to the courthouse, but I told him I'd already asked my friend Brenda Mays to take me. She'd known Joe for many years. She was my maid of honer. Before we got in the car to leave, I hugged her and said, "Brenda, I know God told me to remember Lot's wife, and I'm not looking back at Joe, or our marriage, but I'm still a little uncertain. I know God hate's divorce?" She and I laughed outrageously hard and thanked the Lord for answering my question the minute we got on the ramp of the freeway! It was almost as if they were escorting us to the courthouse. All around us were BIG semi trucks with VICTORY written in Big red letters! Red, for the blood of Jesus. "Hallelujah!" These huge VICTORY trucks were in front of us, behind us, and beside us all the way there, and all the way back home again to my apartment. We believe the VICTORY trucks were a clear sign from God, telling me I was definitely still in His will. Joe had tears in his eyes, but I felt peaceful when I looked up at the judge and smiled after he announced, we were officially divorced. Upon leaving the courthouse Joe asked if we'd allow him to buy our breakfast. I saw no harm in it. Brenda agreed. After we ate, I excused myself and went to the ladies room. Later, on the way back to my apartment Brenda told me what Joe said to her while I was in the bathroom. Joe had tears in his eyes when he admitted to her, "Brenda I'm afraid I realized too late, Carol was the best thing that ever happened to me. She told me before she left me I'd one day see it, but it's to late." I thanked God for His healing mercy.

A nice looking man name Tony Allen started flirting with me each time he came into the pizza place where I worked. Everyone in the restaurant began to say, "Go out with him Carol, he really likes you! Tony Allen is a rich man. He's a part owner of a well known and prosperous meat Company." I was lonely for companionship because I'd been married to Joe, one day shy of thirty two years. However, I wasn't desperate enough to do anything without the Lord's leading. I knew I wasn't ready for a relationship. Jesus takes care of me. "The Lord is my Shepard, and I shall not be in want." (Psalm 23: 1) Tony Allen made the high stress level of my job at work a little easier though. I was always surprised and flattered. Every day he'd sneak up beside me, put his arm around my waist, and when I'd turn around to see who it was, he'd kiss me! If I was helping my friend Shirley Thatcher in the kitchen rolling out pizza dough, sometimes I'd have flour all over me, including my face when Tony Allen kissed me. Shirley Thatcher asked him boldly, "Tony Allen, did you know Carol is a woman of God? Are you a man of God?" He said, "Yes I am!"

Tony kept wanting to take me out on a date, but I kept telling him I was too busy. Although after several months of his steady advances, I was weakening. I told the Lord how lonely I was, and that I was going to go out with Tony Allen unless He showed me a reason I shouldn't. When I got to work that next morning, my boss told me Tony Allen was living with a woman, and he was not the Christian man he said he was. I thanked my boss and especially the Lord for that eye opening information. From that day forward I highly discouraged Tony Allen from making any more advances toward me. He finally stopped coming around. The Lord knew I needed to feel like a lady, and Tony Allen's flirting with me really didn't hurt anyone. The truth set me free.

I worked really hard every day. I became physically strong, making dozens of pizzas, and preps, busing tables, and cleaning my unite and the kitchen down twice a day, every day. I looked so forward to my little twenty minute breaks for lunch so I could sit down and rest. The Lord gave me the energy and strength to stand in the prisons and jails, stand on stage and sing in the choir and sometimes by myself after being on my feet eight hours. I worked in the nursery, and cooked and cleaned for our, get to gathers at the church too. Three nights a week, student ministers classes. I studied hard until late at night, only to get up early the next morning for work. On weekends, laundry, clean my apartment. Friday nights we bowled. Saturdays, fun nights. Loretta, Audrey and I played cards until late. Sundays, church twice. Sometimes on my day off I'd drive my little blue car over to David and Betsy's house. They invited me to come and do my laundry and have dinner with them and my little grandsons. Visiting with my family were always happy times. I didn't get to see Joey very often, because he lived with his dad. I missed him. Rebecca and I talked on the phone frequently, but I never got to see her.

One day my friend Loretta gave me a wonderful old French phone. It was black marble and brass, and I dearly loved it. I asked a beautiful young redheaded woman with green eyes, a minister name Tammy to honor us by teaching and singing at our prayer group. Tammy was as sweet, as she was beautiful. She had an awesome voice, and played her guitar as amazingly for us as she always did on stage in church, and in the prisons and jails we went to together. Everyone loved to hear her teach, sing and play her guitar. After she taught our bible study and sang, she commented on how much she loved the French phone Loretta had given me.

She said she'd had one when she was a little girl. Soon after everyone left, I was sitting in my living room chair admiring my marble and brass French phone on my desk. I said, "Well Lord, Tammy sure did like my pretty French phone, didn't she?" Immediately, He answered, "Well, give it to her." I was disappointed when He asked me to do a thing like that, so I argued, "No Lord, I like it too!" I fussed back and forth with the Lord over the French phone for several days, until I heard Him say, "Plant a seed into her ministry, and whatever you ask Me for in its place, I will give it to you." I said, "What could I ask You for, Lord?" I'd no sooner had that thought when the answer came to me. I blurted out, "Lord, I want a word processor in its place! Ok Lord?" I called to check and see if Tammy was home, and asked if I could come over. Standing inside her living room, I told her about mine and the Lords conversation over the past few days. She was so delighted with the gift, she thanked me several times. We laughed, and she agreed with me for my word processor.

Three days after I gave Tammy my French phone, I was given a brand new word processor from a friend who asked me not to disclose their name. It's truly a gift from the Lord. I said, "Wow, Lord, thank You! You are amazing!" The Lord told my friend to plant that particular seed into my ministry and expect an immediate return in their own ministry. I was shocked when I saw my request answered so fast. This gave me such hope, it made my faith soar! I suddenly realized the Lord loved me more then I could comprehend. He had not changed His mind concerning the call He'd placed on my life. I felt so happy, I thanked the Lord for my new word processor over and over again as I put the words from my manuscript inside of it. Suddenly I realized, I was to tell the truth about Joe and my life of abuse. Finally, I was able to take

Nellie's advice and write the whole entire truth in my book. I had been blinded to the truth, because I loved Joe. "Thank You, Papa, for helping me to never give up on my dreams. I love You Jesus!"

I was standing in my unit making preps when I heard one of my bosses, the day manager Shirley, say, "Carol, someone is here to see you." Tears stung my eyes when I looked up and saw it was my older brother Ben. I was so happy to see him! He looked sad, and I noticed tears in his eyes too. I asked him what was wrong. He told me his best friend Earl had passed away, and then he'd heard the terrible news about me living in Fairborn, and going through a divorce alone. I hugged him again. Ben told me he and his wife Pat were in the process of selling their beautiful large home in Indiana and moving back to live near me. I cried and thanked my precious brother for caring. I was so happy I cried and laughed every time I thought about Ben and Pat's kind gesture. Ben was upset with Joe and he told me, if he had of known about Joe throwing me out with the dish water, so to speak, he could have hired a good lawyer and I would have never left my home. I told Ben I'd finally realized God had secret plans. He wanted me to live in Fairborn for reasons I couldn't completely understand, but I had a quiet assurance in my heart that everything worked out the way God wanted it to. I was finally content to live in Fairborn, alone in my apartment above a Christian book store.

My sister Peggy and her husband Harry came back to visit me. They came all the way from Arizona to make sure I was doing all right. I was so happy to see them walk into my work place, I laughed and cried all at the same time. My two older sisters' Helen and Janie came back from California to visit me too, along with their husband's Clarence and Ed. Peggy bought a birthday cake to celebrate my forty ninth birthday. Seeing Peggy and my other two sisters made me realize how strange and different my life had been for the past year. They were still with their same husbands. I felt like a fish out of water. However, they were all very proud of me. I was the only sister in our family to go to student ministers class to become a minister. They made me feel good about going into the prisons and jails too. I loved all of them and hated to say good-by when their short visit ended. Although, it had been very difficult for me to stay indoors and work all day while they were visiting. After they left, I felt lonelier then ever.

It was fun going to my brother Ben and Pat's new house. They both welcomed me with open arms. They insisted I bring my laundry and do it there and stay for supper. My brother Ben always made me laugh when he teased me and said, "O-k Sis, you have to sing for your supper." I gladly sang, and sometimes Pat joined in. I enjoyed sitting out on their back patio and visiting with them on weekends when I could. My sister-in-law Pat had visited David, Carrie and Rebecca when they were in England. I was so thankful when Pat also went to see David at Christmas. It was the first year David was incarcerated in England. She'd gone through a lot of trouble to visit him. She not only brought David a fresh fruit basket and goodies, she brought enough for the other inmates there and even the guards. It comforted my broken heart.

One day while Pat was visiting me at my apartment, she looked around at the electric heaters along the baseboards with concern. She said, "Carol, you know this apartment is too expensive to heat in the winter time. You'd better seriously be thinking of where your going to move so you can keep warm, and pay lower heat bills." I agreed, I couldn't afford to go through another winter in my big spacious apartment, but move where? Here was another big decision I had to make. I needed to do something soon, it was approaching the end of September. I requested prayer in Sunday night church service. I asked God to show me where I was to move next? Another friend insisted on paying my first months rent and helping me with the deposit. They didn't want a refund on their money. I was grateful and accepted their kindness. The Lord always takes such good care of me. "I love You Jesus!"

I had called about an apartment in the paper that was affordable. It was exactly the same walking distance to my work. After talking to Tina, the nice landlady and seeing the apartment I accepted it. I gave her my deposit and first months rent. I got my utilities changed over too. It was another upstairs apartment but it was smaller, cozier, and warmer in the winter. Tina was a Christian. She prayed, and the Lord sent Christians to live in her apartments. I also loved the name of the apartments, "Loveington Arms Apartments" Tina made me feel comfortable knowing she lived three doors down in the next set of apartments. The only thing I dreaded was the move itself. After standing on my feet all day at work, packing and moving did not seem possible. My brother Ben, his wife Pat, and David Ay helped me move in. By the grace of God we did it. "Thank You wonderful Lord Jesus!"

The first evening in my apartment after everyone left I fell on the bed tired, but happy. Psalm 103:5 "Bless the Lord O my soul, and all that is within me, bless His holy name! Who satisfies my mouth with good things, so that my youth is renewed like the eagle's." As always, before I went to sleep, I said, "I love You Papa! I love You Jesus! I love You dear precious Holy Spirit!" "Thank You Jesus, that by Your stripes I am healed."

The next morning just after sunrise I saw and heard the wild bright yellow canaries singing right outside my window. I thought, "Oh dear Lord, it is so peaceful here. Thank You for leading me here." I could feel the stress draining out of me each day. I actually enjoyed walking to and from work, and I loved coming home to my cozy, quiet apartment. I was getting a whole lot more sleep at night too. There were no more noisy horns honking in the night on the busy main street below my apartment, or motorbikes revving there engines while waiting for the light to change. No loud shouts from the half liquored up people emptying out the bar across the street waking me up at one, two and three in the morning! Sometimes I'd hear a train whistle blowing way off in the distance during the night. I dearly love to hear the sound of a train whistle blowing in the distance. I felt I was wrapped in the loving arms of Jesus in my new Loveington Arms apartment. "I am my beloved's and my beloved is mine." (Song of Solomon 6:3) Although I was still working, and busy going into the prisons and jails, I felt I'd entered into a part of God's rest. Pat rewrote some older songs for us to sing in the jails and prisons, they loved them.

Joe came to my door late one night to drop off his one hundred dolor cabin payment. He said he'd forgot to send it through the mail. I hadn't seen him in six months, not since the divorce. His visit wasn't a complete surprise. I'd called him earlier in the week to remind him I needed the one hundred-dollar payment he'd promised. He knew I needed it to help pay my second months rent. I was sound asleep when I heard someone knocking! Without turning on any lights, I peeked through the small peep hole provided on the front door. I whispered loud, "Joe what are you doing hear this late? I thought we agreed you'd come over early. You were supposed to call before you came so I could meet with you outside, remember?" I saw him shrug his shoulders. He said, "I'm sorry Carol, but I had to work late all this week. I brought it right over just as soon as I remembered." I asked him to slide it under the door, but there wasn't enough room. I left the chain on at the top of the door. My hands shook a little as I unlocked the other lock, reached my hand through the small opening and accepted his check. I told Joe I had to go to sleep in order to get up early for work. After I thanked him quickly, I locked the door back and listened for his footsteps down the stairs. Relieved when I heard the bottom door shut behind him, I went back to bed, crawled under the covers and cried, "Lord, this isn't the way it was supposed to be! I loved Joe and expected him to love and cherish me for the rest of my life too! Lord, it's still hard for me to turn him away, I was married to him for such a long time. I'm not saying I'm not glad You intervened, I'm just saying it's still hard for me to see him, dear Jesus." I cried myself to sleep.

Tina told me there were albino robins and squirrels in abundance all around the apartments. It was incredible to see these white albino birds and animals. We had many large beautiful trees on the properties to attract them. I noticed outside my kitchen window every evening at sunset, several doves gathered on the telephone wires. I'd stand there quietly observing them, and listening to their peaceful cooing sounds. I thought, "Lord, they must be praising You. Your word says, 'Let everything that has breath, praise the Lord." (Psalm 150:6) I was amazed at how all the peaceful doves looked so romantic paired in two's. A feeling of loneliness swept over me. I realized, it had been a year and two months since I'd had the companionship of a man. I was still thankful to God, however. He had blessed me with so many good friends to fill that empty void. I was thankful for my alimony checks, and also my cabin payments. "Thank You Jesus!" I finally had Joe's support, whether he wanted to give it to me or not, he absolutely had to, by law. "Yes Jesus, You really are wonderful!"

Another friend from church name Mary, helped me buy material to make pretty new cream colored cape cod curtains for my windows! "Thank You Jesus!" When Mary came to my prayer group, she usually brought her huge black Lab dog, Luke. She often visited in her roller blades after skating on the streets and sidewalks of down town Fairborn, her dog Luke running beside her. She was in the process of a divorce herself, so she understood how I felt. Her hearty laugh, and pretty smile didn't hide her heartache. I had gone with my friend David Ay to Mary's prayer group several times too. One evening I was standing in the center of the circle in Mary's living room for prayer. Kathy stood there silently holding my hands, waiting for the dear precious Holy Spirit to minister to me, through her. I was so nervous, I kept thinking, "Kathy is such an awesome minister and our Sunday School Teacher, nothing misses her. Why isn't she prophesying over me yet?" The enemy kept trying to bombard my mind with thoughts of how insignificant and utterly useless my life must be. After all, Kathy is so sharp in spiritual matters, nothing escapes her. She must not have anything useful to say about me. I noticed the others who were standing beside me, softly praying in tongues. I thought, "They aren't going to have anything about me, either."

I'd never seen Kathy cry before, I didn't realize she was under the anointing. She stood there weeping, until she finally broke the silence and said, "Carol, even when your hair and make up are perfect and each of your fingernails is filed and polished, and even your toenails. Your clothes are clean and ironed, and you look wonderful . . . " She started to cry again, until finally she said, "Even then, you don't feel like you're good enough to be the scum underneath someone shoes! Carol, the Lord would have me to tell you; For every day of darkness you've seen in your life, you will see great light. For every day of sorrow, suffering, depression and terror you've experienced, in its place, you will have great joy!" One by one the others in the prayer group encouraged me too. Someone else said because I delighted myself in the Lord, He's giving me the desires of my heart. "I receive Your words, Lord."

I was laying on my small couch, night after night until one and two in the morning talking to Audrey. Her doctors had found cancer again, and this time it was in her liver. My friend was so terrified at night, I had to stay awake and comfort her and pray with her. I was standing on my feet at work all day, exhausted, I asked to be excused from the prisons and jails. This went on for over a month until finally the day came for her surgery. "Praise God!" The doctors were amazed, and the small amount of cancer was removed. She walked into my work and saw me a couple of weeks after her surgery. The doctors diagnoses at first had been very grim, but God gave us a miracle. "Thank You, sweet Jesus!"

I walked to work one morning feeling so heavy, I cried out to God, reminding Him, He said He wouldn't put any more on us then we can bear! I had to pay extra money every single month on my old electric bill from the last apartment, and pay my current monthly electric bill, my other bills, buy groceries, and pay my rent too. I always paid my tithes and offerings first, so I thanked God for His word in Malachi 3:10-11 "Praise You, Papa God!" That same day I checked my answering machine after work, and there was a message from Micelle at the eclectic company. I called her back, and she had some good news. She told me they had passed a new bill. If I'd pay my current electric bill (only) every month on time, (which I did anyway) one year later they would wipe the amount of the old bill off my record. Micelle was a thoughtful caring person, and I thanked her several times. Oh, but I knew it was my Papa who really had the electric company come up with that bill, and pass it just for me. I said, "Thank You Jesus!" A representative from the electric company brought me a pot of yellow mums and a thank you letter the following spring, of 1995. My old bill was forgiven and forgotten, and wiped away.

Tina started coming to church and joined the Student Ministers classes. She had me over to her apartment often for a good home cooked meal. She and I loved Chinese food, and we ate every Monday at her friend Irene's Chinese restaurant. One day Tina called my house excited, "Carol, Irene wants to talk to you about your music! She loved the tape you made her! Come on and get ready, let's go to her place for lunch, ok?" I'd made Irene a tape, singing with my accompaniment tapes as I'd done for some of my friends and family. I was so thrilled Irene liked my singing, and I loved her Chinese food. I agreed to meet Tina downstairs in half an hour. I kept saying, "Wow! Lord, what are You doing now?"

I sat there with my mouth wide open when I finally understood Irene's broken English, partly translated through Tina. Irene said, she didn't care how much it costs, she wanted to help me make an album and get recognized by the public as a gospel singer. She said she had plenty of money and she wanted to back me all the way, financially. I kept saying, "Wow!" Irene said, the Lord told her, she had the money and I had the voice. She was willing to pay whatever it costs to help me. I was amazed, happy, shocked, and fully persuaded, God was turning those days of darkness into light, and days of sorrow and suffering into great joy, just like He promised. I felt so humble I didn't know how to say anything, but, "Thank You Jesus!" "Thank you Irene, thank you!" She said she'd find a producer with a studio. About a week later Tina called and said, Irene found a producer in Cleveland Ohio. I was so disheartened. How could I go all the way to Cleveland Ohio to make my album? We were sitting in Irene's Chinese restaurant wandering what to do. Tina wanted to drive me there every week, but I felt uneasy. I was so confused as to what to do, until I remembered Roy Lovely's name, his daughter Kristie gave me.

All of a sudden I yelled, "Wait a minute, I just remembered there is a man with a recording studio who lives right here in Fairborn! His daughter, Kristie is a pretty young woman' who worked in the Christian bookstore beneath my old apartment, she gave me his phone number! She was always nice and helped me find my accompaniment tapes. One day, she told me her dad has a recording studio here in Fairborn, in case I wanted to record an album! She also told me, her dad, Roy, is a Christian, and a producer too!" While I was talking, I quickly rummaged through my purse, and found his phone number tucked inside my billfold. I yelled again, "Here it is, I found it! I found Roy Lovely's number!" "Oh thank You, dear wonderful Papa God, thank You!"

Mr. Roy Lovely answered the phone later that evening when I called. His voice remained calm, kind and gentle as I excitedly told him about Irene backing me financially. I asked him all kinds of questions about his studio? His daughter Kristie was getting married. She hadn't worked in the Christian bookstore in several months. The chances of my having ever seen her again were very slim. I quote my beautiful African American friend, Debbie Berbige, "Look at God, honey, look at God!" I always tell Debbie she looks like Sophia Loran with a dark tan.

Chapter Eight

As He is so are we

I only saw my friend Sandy twice briefly during the first year and a half, after I left Joe. She came over to David and Betsy's house and stayed for about twenty minutes while I was there visiting. The third time I saw her, about six months later. She actually sat down and ate dinner with us. She was so excited when I told her a restaurant owner named Irene was sponsoring me finically to make an album. David and Betsy were also happy for me when I told them I had an appointment with Mr. Roy Lovely, a Christian man who was producing my album. Sandy had always encouraged me to sing. Sometimes she and I sang at work while we cleaned houses together. The seasons in my life had changed everything so drastically. Mine and Sandy's schedules had been too busy to see each other often. It seemed so strange for us, not to even talk or pray over the phone together. I'd missed her.

Mr. Roy Lovely kept our introductory appointment the Saturday following his youngest daughter Kristie's wedding. I already felt like I knew Roy just by talking to him a few times on the phone. He had such a kind and gentle voice, I felt myself relax within seconds of our first conversation. He kindly offered to pick me up for our recording session, after I explained I'd sold my vehicle. I stood outside my apartment door anxiously watching for the small red car Roy described to appear. Finally, I saw the hot July sun glaring on his windshield as he rounded the corner. I wondered if this tall handsome brown eyed man was married when he smiled and shut my car door for me. Roy's tanned muscular looking arm rested on his blue metallic guitar as we sat comfortably talking in his studio. I thought, "Surly Roy's married, he's much too handsome not to be." His slightly receding, dark brown wavy hair and mustache had light touches of grey. My salt and pepper grey hair still had decent amounts of black. I felt my cheeks blush red when Roy finally told me he was divorced. I was so impressed when he told me he'd finished raising his two daughters alone. During our conversation I discovered, Aimee was a strong Christian girl like Kristie. Suddenly, I recognized Roy and remembered I'd met him and his oldest daughter Aimee once before when he brought her to the church. She played the keyboard and sung several of her own well-written gospel songs, beautifully. Roy accompanied her on the guitar. He was so awesome, he played the guitar like no one I'd ever heard before. Kristie and Aimee are pretty. They have dark brown hair and brown eyes like their dad. I really enjoyed talking to them, especially when we talked about the Lord. Their bubbly personalities made it easy for me to like them.

Week after week it felt so strange, and wonderful to be standing in a recording booth singing with real head phones on. My heart was so thankful, God used Irene and Roy to make a lifelong dream come true for me. Roy made me laugh more then anyone ever could, except for my sister Peggy, and yet he was sensitive and not ashamed of tears in his eyes when something was said to touch his tender heart. I soon realized Roy Lovely was an extraordinary person. I knew he was filled with the love of the dear precious Holy Spirit because he was so special. "Hallelujah, too the Lamb!"

One evening Roy called, and after a few casual words of conversation he said, "Carol, when I was praying for you today at work, I clearly heard the Lord tell me to ask you something." I said, "Ok, Roy, I'm listening. What did the Lord tell you to ask me?" He said, "Carol, I'm supposed to ask you, if your going to the jails and prisons, student minister classes, working in the nursery, and doing all this stuff in church for the Lord, because you think 'He' wants you to do it for 'Him'?" Roy waited quietly for my response. I stammered, "W-e-ll, Roy, I, I think the Lord wants me to do all these things for Him, or at least I thought He did. Why, did the Lord tell you to ask me that question?" Roy answered softly, "Carol, I know you don't know me very well, but I know the Lord told me, specifically to ask you that question, and then He told me to tell you, He wants you to slow down. I think you need to ask yourself, if your pushing yourself beyond your own physical capacities for strength to do everything for Him, and if not for Him, then who?" I thought, "Oh, sweet Jesus, help me!"

Roy Lovely didn't know me well enough to figure all of that out on his own. I knew in my heart he was speaking straight from the mouth of the Lord. I'd known for a long time I needed to slow down, but I thought I couldn't possibly stop, if the Lord expected it of me. After I searched my own heart like God said, through Roy, I realized I was still doing a lot of these things because other people expected it from me. I broke down and cried, I was so relieved it wasn't God who wanted me to continue on at the rigid pace I'd allowed others to set for me. Immediately, I started distancing myself from the people who kept pushing me beyond my own capabilities. I refused to allow myself to be manipulated or controlled. I wanted too only be influenced and directed by the dear precious Holy Spirit. Before I knew what was happening another friend at church hurt my feelings, because I didn't do something the way they thought I should. Again, I was crushed.

I left the church in tears after the service was over. I walked several blocks in the direction of my old apartment until I realized I'd moved and I was extremely lost! When I urgently asked the Lord to please help me find my way home, He said, "Duck through the ally." I did, and instantly I found myself on a familiar street. I kept saying, "Oh, thank You so much, dear Lord, Jesus!"

My friend Tina, had also been saying negative things to Irene about my album. I was so upset I walked to her apartment first and gave her Irene's check back. She cried and refused to take it! She begged me to reconsider, but I left the check on her table and walked the rest of the way home, bawling like a baby! My pretty red silk dress was smudged with tear stains and black mascara. I was still crying when Roy called. I told him I had given Irene's money back, so I wouldn't be finishing the album! He asked if he could take me to a park or quiet place somewhere and talk. I told him I didn't want him to see me without my make up. My eyes were red, and swollen. My friend David Ay came looking for me since he couldn't find me after church. We usually went to lunch together along with several others. I cried and told him everything, so he took me to the park to try and cheer me up. We wondered aimlessly around the park for a while. I was so miserable, all I could think about was Roy's soft gentle voice. He sounded so discouraged when I said, no. I felt so bad for the way I'd treated Roy. It wasn't his fault, he was only trying to be kind and thoughtful. "God, please help me to do the right thing?"

After David dropped me off at my apartment, I called Roy back and apologized. Again he offered to take me to some quiet places to talk, and I turned him down a second time. Just as I hung up the phone the Lord spoke to me and said, "Stop crying now Carol, dry your tears. Go and wash your face, comb your hair, and put on your make up. Call Roy back and go with him, he'll show you a good time, you'll see." Immediately, a peace settled over me and I stopped crying. I got cleaned up and called Roy back. When I told him what the Lord said to me, he was happy God changed my mind. Roy took me to some of the most beautiful parks and places with waterfalls I'd ever seen. It was strange how I felt a slight tingling similarly to electricity when Roy took my hand and walked me over a bridge. A couple of young men were fishing near by. I struggled to get upon the rock, Roy so easily sat down on. When he reached out his hand to help me up on the rock, again, I felt slight tingling bolts of electricity go through me. I'd never in my life felt anything like it. We just sat there for a while quietly listening to the waterfall's trickle softly across the rocks.

I felt so safe and comfortable sitting beside Roy, I couldn't believe it. As we talked, we realized we had so much in common. His mother and dad had thirteen children, and they were poor too. Roy's people were from Kentucky like most of mine were. His mother had been a strong Christian too. His heart was so full of compassion, he promised he'd finish recording my album, free of charge. I'd never in my life met anyone like Roy. We never stopped communicating all day. He'd talk awhile, and I'd talk awhile. It was amazing how we never seemed to run out of things to say as we walked through lush green parks, observed waterfalls, swung, or sat at a picnic table underneath a shady tree.

I went out to dinner with Roy a couple of times. We enjoyed each others company and friendship. Roy was always a perfect gentleman. He'd walk me up the stairs to my apartment, then he'd smile and wave good-by after I unlocked my door. One Saturday when Roy and I had lunch together, I mentioned I was going over to my friend Mary's house. He kindly offered to drive me there. The three of us were sitting out back on her spacious wooden deck talking as she watered several large pots of her beautiful flowers with a garden hose. About a half an hour later Roy glanced at his watch and said he had some things to do at home. Mary reaffirmed she'd see me safely to my apartment after we were finished visiting, so Roy smiled, patted my head and said good by. Instead of Roy climbing down the deck stairs and out the back yard gate, Mary insisted he leave from the front door where we came in. It was a beautiful sunny day, so I stayed outside.

After they went inside, I leaned back in one of Mary's soft comfortable lawn chairs, and watched puffy white clouds lazily roll across the enormous blue sky. Off in the distance I could still hear Roy and Mary laughing and talking. I was fascinated watching two large puffy white, people looking clouds floating toward each other. Each cloud remarkably resembled a person with their lips positioned out, ready to kiss. The two clouds came together and honestly looked like they had lips that were kissing. Suddenly a gust of wind separated the two clouds, and as they separated, the cloud on the right looked exactly like Roy Lovely with his head thrown back laughing hilariously, as he so often did. I sat straight up in my chair and said, "Roy Lovely, Lord? Is he the man I'm supposed to marry, dear Lord?" I felt God smiling at me.

Nineteen ninety two, 93, and 94 were some of the darkest days of my life and Roy's too. Roy's mother went on to be with Jesus, as well as my own precious mother who died January 22, 1993. My oldest brother Jim went to be with Jesus, and Roy's older sister Patty died also. My ex husband threw me out, and Roy's second wife of only one year left him. Roy had fought depression especially in his younger years, just as I had. He'd suffered with ulcers in the past too. He laughed when he admitted he'd often been eating pop corn, sweets and junk food for dinner for more than ten years. With that incredible news I invited him over for a home cooked meal. I'd seldom cooked a decent meal for myself since I'd left Joe, so I was looking forward to it. The very first words Roy spoke when he came to dinner was, "Carol, I believe God will restore back to us, all the years the locusts have eaten, don't you?" The minute I agreed with him and God's word, I remembered my friend Brenda Mays dream. Before I'd left Joe. Brenda dreamed I married Joel, and after he'd carried me to the upper room, I had a little baby girl who looked just like me, except she had red curly hair and blue eyes. I knew in my heart the baby girl was Rebecca. Even though I had called Rebecca frequently, I had not seen her in more than three years.

Right before Roy left, I broke down and cried when I tried to tell him about Rebecca. He closed my apartment door back, walked me to the couch, sat down beside me and said, "Well Carol, if you'll tell me where your little granddaughter Rebecca lives, I'll take you to see her." Roy made me laugh. He looked up toward heaven and said, "Lord, if your not using me, You sure are confusing me!" After I told him what had happened to Rebecca since she'd been born, he looked sad. His words were so comforting. He'd sat beside me stroking the back of my hair with his big kind gentle hand. I told him, the only person who'd stroked the back of my hair when I cried was my mother and the Lord, Himself. I promised him I'd call Rebecca and schedule a time for us to see her. I was so grateful, I looked up at him and said, "Roy Lovely, you are precious to God and to me. Joe hated my tears, and made fun of me, but you didn't push me away. You've done the sweetest, kindest thing today." He just laughed, and bragged on my dinner again. "Thank You, sweet wonderful Jesus!"

After Roy left, I thought to myself, "Roy Lovely is tall and handsome. He also has dark brown eyes, hair and mustache." I knew I was falling deeply in love with Roy, and I was convinced he was the Joel in Brenda's dream. Later that week when I told Roy about Brenda's dream, he just sat there nervously smiling. He agreed, he was perhaps the Joel in Brenda's dream, manifested, but he looked fearful when he said so. He'd gone through two very difficult marriages that ended in divorce. I could see pain and suffering when I looked into Roy's brown eyes. I'd been praying for him. Roy mentioned Joel again when he told me, he and his first ex wife used to sing and play guitar like Joe and I had. His ex wife didn't want to sing or play the guitar for the Lord any more then Joe did. I said, "It's God's will to restore everything back to us according to His word in Joel 3:23-25." "Be glad then, you children of Zion, And rejoice in the Lord your God; For He has given you the former rain faithfully, And He will cause the rain to come down for you----The former rain, And the latter rain in the first month. The threshing floors shall be full of wheat, And the vats shall overflow with new wine and oil. So I will restore to you the years that the swarming locust has eaten, The crawling locust, the consuming locust, And the chewing locust, My great army which I sent among you." "Papa, Your will be done in Roy and I."

I knew my meeting Roy was not a coincidence. Every day, God clearly confirmed Roy was indeed the Joel in Brenda's dream. When I told him about my book, he offered to edit it for me, free. I discovered he could type more than seventy-five words a minute. Roy made the highest grades in school in spelling. So this dear man corrected both my spelling and grammar. Roy edited my book sometimes while I fixed us dinner or quietly crocheted. I didn't own a television. Three different people gave me one, but I gave it back to them. I'd had enough of the televisions roaring for too many years. I enjoyed my peace and quit. I didn't use an alarm clock either. Joe's alarm clock blared every morning for thirty-one and half years. I'd just ask Jesus to wake me early. He never failed to wake me on time. "Thank You, sweet Jesus!"

When Roy took me to see Rebecca, Carrie invited us to come in. After we sat and visited awhile, we took Rebecca out to eat. We laughed and talked about everything. Although my granddaughter looked and seamed happy, I felt uneasy and sensed something was wrong, especially when we dropped her off. She gingerly thanked Roy for bringing her grandmother to see her! I was surprised when she hugged him too. It was as if she and I'd never been separated for any length of time. I was so enthusiastic, thanking Roy for taking me to see Rebecca that night, before I knew it I stood on my tip toes, threw my arms around his neck and kissed him right on the lips. It was a short, swift kiss, but I could barely sleep that night just remembering the power of it. I'd never experienced anything like it before. "Wonderful Jesus, I love You, and Roy!"

Roy told me. He'd been depressed and lonely for several years. He prayed, "Lord, haven't I been good? I am so lonely, I want someone to share my life with. I'm going to be very specific this time when I pray, Lord. I want a woman who lives in Fairborn. I want her to live close by, so I won't have to drive very far to see her. And Lord, I want to date another musician. If we have our music in common, we will understand each other better. Oh, and last but most important, Lord, I want a woman who is more spiritual then I am. Thanks for listening Lord, amen." Roy looked at me seriously and said, "Carol, you called about the recording studio a week after I prayed that prayer." Roy's voice was still hesitant even after he admitted I was the answer to his prayer. He also said he knew he was falling in love with me too. He'd been so hurt and abused, and I'd been abused too. Oh but, I knew Jesus specializes in setting the captives free, spirit, soul and body. (Luke 4:18) "The Spirit of the Lord is upon me, because He has anointed me to preach the gospel to the poor.....To set at liberty those who are oppressed." "Thank You Jesus for Roy's freedom!"

Roy encouraged me to talk about my divorce and cry, if I needed to. I had not allowed myself to cry or talk about Joe or the divorce, except on rare occasions. I thought it was wrong to bring up the painful past. My unmarried friends who'd married once but never remarried told me, if I talked about my ex husband it would run another man off. I was finding out more and more about Roy each time I saw him. Roy said he really hadn't talked to anyone about his painful past much either, until he met me. We comforted each other. I learned that Roy was no ordinary man. He told me how hard his daughters cried after their mother left them in 1985. I could hardly believe how similar our lives had been. Nineteen eighty five was the same year Joe left me. When Roy told me, how hard it was to finish raising two teenage daughters without their mother, I felt compassion for him. I loved his humility and honesty, and his ability to be real. I especially enjoyed our oneness in talking about our Lord, Jesus together, and our love for Him.

Roy jokingly said he'd been sad for so long, he couldn't stand it anymore. He said, "I got up one mornin, and put my feet on the floor. I said, "Lord, I ain't gonna be depressed no more! I'm tired of feeling sad and I'm tired of feelen blue, today I'm going to start my life brand new. I believe I'm gonna make somebody laugh today!" He said his life has never been the same since. I told him, "That sounds like a song!" We wrote a song together to the tune of rock-n-roll. Roy had the most contagious laughter, but I knew he still needed inner healing, especially if we'd start to talk about marriage. Suddenly, he'd stop talking and change the subject. Sometimes I'd get really irritated, but I loved him too much to remain angry. I knew I had to keep my eyes on Jesus, and not allow myself to sink into a depression too. Instead, I rebuked the spirits of fear, self pity and depression off Roy, in the name of Jesus, and covered daily his, spirit, mind and body in the precious blood of Jesus! I had no doubt Roy was worth all the intercession and prayer I was making for him. I trusted the dear precious Holy Spirit to help me pray for Roy and see him set free. "Hallelujah!"

One day while I was cleaning the flour off everything in our kitchen at work from making our fresh pizza dough, the Lord spoke to me and said, "Carol, I have placed Roy Lovely in your life to bring you to the high places of the earth where I have called you to go for My glory, And I have placed you in Roy Lovely's life to bring him to the high places, spiritually, where I have called him to go for My glory." I ran as fast as I could and whispered everything God told me in Joy's ear. She raised her eye brows and said, "Wow! Wow!" All that day, Joy and I kept laughing and smiling at each other. She knew I'd asked God for sure confirmation that I was to marry Roy, and we knew this was His answer. When Joy and I went on our lunch break, I said to her, "If this isn't another clear confirmation from God that I'm to marry Roy Lovely, I don't know what it is, do you, Joy!" She smiled and agreed with me. Roy admitted many times, he'd been tough on me, because he was so afraid of another failed marriage.

I couldn't think of anything else the Lord could possibly say or do to make it any clearer to Roy that I was to marry him, but that night when I told him what the Lord said to me about taking each other to the high places, he thought of something. He said he wanted God to confirm it by putting it on a flashing light upon a billboard for everyone to see. THUS, SAYS THE LORD, "ROY LOVELY IS SUPPOSED TO MARRY CAROL!" If I'd been walking in the flesh, I would have thrown in the towel and called it quits right then. My pride would have gotten the better of me and I would have said, "See you later! Don't call me, I'll call you, sweetheart." However, I knew God wanted me to fight, and kill those giants out of my promised land, in the name of Jesus! I knew He wanted Roy free from the spirit of fear of marriage failure which He didn't give him. I couldn't afford to allow myself to get into pride or to be unforgiving. I knew the battle was the Lord's, and the promised victory was mine. I didn't intend to give up, give in, slow down, or quit! I knew Roy was such a caring tender-hearted person he was just trying to protect himself from getting hurt again. Roy laughed and told me, my anger did not intimidate him like the other women in his past. When he gazed into my eyes with so much love, everything else just melted away. "Bless the Lord, oh my soul and all that is within me! Bless His Holy name! I love You so much, Papa, Jesus, sweet Holy Spirit!"

Roy and I talked every evening on the phone. We couldn't bear to be away from each other very long. We had to see each other every day. Roy always opened my car door first. He'd stand there in the heat, cold, pouring rain, or blowing snow waiting until I was seated before he'd shut my car door and get in himself on the other side. He sent beautiful vases of flowers at work to brighten my day, and he sent romantic cards that showed me truly what was in his heart. Some of Roy's cards were hilariously funny too.

One evening my friend David Ay called and told me, he had a dream about me. He said, in the dream I was struggling to ride a slippery pale grey horse. David said every time I tried to ride on the horse's back it wouldn't budge, and I kept falling off. David was baffled. He couldn't imagine what the dream meant, but he felt he should call and tell me about it. The dear precious Holy Spirit revealed the dreams meaning to me immediately. I knew, God was telling me, I was not to mention marriage to Roy again. If I did, I was dealing with flesh and blood, and this was a spiritual battle. I decided I would not ride that old grey horse again, and mention marriage. God gave me a battle plan! I laughed at the Lord comparing stubbornness to an old grey, slippery horse who wouldn't budge. "Papa, You are so wonderful!"

1 Corinthians 1:27-29 says, "But God has chosen the foolish things of the world to put to shame the wise, and God has chosen the weak things of the world to put to shame the things which are mighty. The base things of the world and the things which are despised God has chosen, and the things which are not, to bring to nothing the things that are, that no flesh should glory in His presence." "Dear Papa God, I thank You for giving me a plan."

That evening when Roy dropped me off at my apartment I looked up into his pretty brown eyes, and said, "Roy, you will never have to worry about me mentioning marriage to you, ever again. But you, however will mention it to me, because you will ask me to marry you. I ask the Lord to saturate you in the blood of Jesus Christ our Savior every day. I will marry you Roy Lovely, because you are going to ask me too, you'll see. God is healing you of every heart ache and damaged memory of your past, because, I've been praying for you." He laughed at me and hugged me when he said, "Carol, please keep on praying for me. Don't ever give up on me, because I love you too, I really, really do?"

Roy decided he was ready to meet my oldest son David, Betsy, and my grandsons, Michael and Kyle. We laughed and had a great time, but when we started to leave I stayed behind hugging my grandsons while Roy went on to the car. Michael and Kyle started waving and yelling, "By grandpa! By grandpa!" I said, "Michael, Kyle, what did you just call that man?" Michael put his hands on his hips and looked up at me and said, "I calls him my grandpa, grandma, because I likes him!" My two grandsons were too little to understand. They turned around again and kept on waving and hollering, "By grandpa! By grandma!" My cheeks were blushing. I said, "Roy, I honestly didn't tell them to say that." He just laughed and said, "It makes me feel sort of special. Carol, don't worry about it. It's all right if they call me grandpa, really I like it." Roy tried to talk to me about marriage often, but I'd simply smile, nod my head, and remain completely silent on that particular subject. As I prayed for Roy, I noticed he looked more, and more peaceful. "I praise You and thank You, Papa, God."

The evening of September 11, 1995, I was walking through my apartment and feeling a little uneasy about Roy when I heard the Lord say, "Fear not little lamb, for I truly am the Great I Am. Let not your heart be troubled about these trivial things; For I truly am doing a work. I truly have placed the flower of your love deep within Roy Lovely's heart to stay." Tears of gratitude ran down my face as I praised God for His goodness and tender mercies, "Sweet Jesus! Oh how I love You, my dear sweet Jesus!"

Several months had passed since I'd put my own album aside, and instead encouraged Roy to finish his. He said he'd always wanted to make an instrumental album. Roy had written and produced some beautiful songs. Everyone who heard his music said, "Roy is truly anointed! He is an awesome guitarist, and recording artist." I loved to listen to his instrumental tapes. Roy's heavenly Father, who gave him the talent, taught him how to play several instruments, and record them. "Papa, You are amazing!"

Roy told me funny, but true stories he'd encountered on his job. He said when he first started working for a certain well known water softener company twenty three years before, he was shy and awkward. He said one day he'd gone to some lady customer's house to deliver a water softener. When he got there, she started yelling and cursing obscenities at him and the company he worked for! She was raging madly and waving her arms, screaming, "I've had nothing but trouble with you blank, blank people! And as far as I'm concerned your water softening company can just go to h-e-l-l!" Roy said he looked at her and said quietly, "Well, Lady, I'm taking this water softener to the basement, but that's as far as I'm going." Roy laughed and said she glared at him for a couple of long seconds and then she burst into hilarious laughter! Since then she's become one of their best costumers. Roy's soft gentle voice threw her off guard. When it finally dawned on her, what he'd said, she broke out in wild abandoned laughter! (Proverbs 15:1) "A soft answer turns away wrath, But a harsh word stirs up anger." Roy's soft spoken manner was like a stun gun toward that woman's anger. God turned it around for him because he used wisdom. "Thank You Lord, for turning Roy's sorrow into joy!"

On Saturdays Roy drove me to work, so I didn't have to walk. Roy was sitting on the couch while I gathered up my apron, jacket and purse. I said, "Roy Lovely, you are so precious to God and to me. The Lord loves you so dearly, and I do too." He looked at me and said, "Carol, please don't ever stop saying, 'Roy, you're precious to God and to me. Roy, I love you and God loves you so dearly too.' Carol, when you say that, I see you with a chisel in your hand, breaking down the stone wall I've built up around my heart to protect myself from being hurt again." I said, "I really do love you Roy, and you truly are precious to God, and to me."

For no apparent reason, Roy stopped calling or coming over to see me for two whole days. I was worried. When I called his house, his daughter Aimee told me he was busy working in his studio. I asked her if he'd indicated he was angry with me about something, if so, I wanted to apologize. She assured me he constantly talked about how much he loved and missed me. Roy had never gone that long without calling me or coming over. I was so sad I went onto bed early, thinking he wouldn't call again that night. Suddenly, the phone rang! When I heard Roy's tender caring voice telling me how much he'd missed me, I breathed a huge sigh of relief. I asked him, "Roy, have I said or done something wrong?" He laughed and said, "No Carol, I'm not mad at you, I've been busy making something for you for sweetest day. Listen to this song I wrote you, and tell me if you like it, ok?"

I cried like a baby, all the way through the song. It was the most beautiful love song I'd ever heard! For the very first time in my life I felt like I was important and special to someone. No one had ever done anything like this for me before. I listened to the words of, "Dear Carol I love you." I was overwhelmed with his wonderful mellow voice. I listened especially to the words of love that he sang to me from his heart. After the song was over Roy put the phone back up to his ear, and asked what I thought of it? He was surprised! I was crying and laughing all at the same time. My response made him cry too. When I played my song for my friends and family they said, "Oh Carol, Roy sings so dreamily!"

I plead the blood of Jesus, in the name of Jesus, over, any, and all, unnatural, ungodly soul ties between Roy Lovely, and his ex wives, ex girlfriends, other musicians he played music with in the bars, or friends, and even family who had caused Roy to feel defeated. I commanded those unnatural, ungodly soul ties to be destroyed, annihilated, disintegrated, burned up into ashes and cast into the sea of forgetfulness forever, in the name of Jesus, and by the blood of Jesus! I'd already prayed those same prayers between myself, my ex husband and others since I heard Marilyn Hickey teach on it. The results are seen and felt immediately.

"Thank You, dear Papa, for the blood of Jesus, and the name of Jesus! Thank You blessed Jesus, for Your sacrifice on the cross. Thank You dear sweet precious Holy Spirit!" Roy has never drank a single drop of liquor of any kind in his entire life, and he's never smoked either. He told me, he had played guitar as the lead guitarist in many different bands since he was a young man. He said he played in the bars on the weekends, because he desperately needed the money to raise his girls. One day, he prayed and asked God to help him stop going in that direction. The Lord helped him to make extra money elsewhere. "Thank You, wonderful Jesus!"

When Aimee and Kristie invited me to a surprise birthday party for their dad, I gladly accepted. Roy's brother Ed and his wife Hazel were there, and Aimee and Kristie's best friend, Ester. Kristie and her husband Rich, and Aimee and her faience Wayne was there among a few other friends, including my friend David Ay. Roy looked so handsome. I was a little concerned when I realized it was Roy's forty fifth birthday, and I'd just turned fifty. When I was able to speak to him alone, I whispered, "Roy, you're only forty-five years old and I'm fifty. I thought you were my age? I even thought maybe you colored your hair. I have lots of black in my grey hair, but you have dark brown hair with a few specks of grey, doesn't that bother you?" He threw his head back laughing and said, "Hey, it's better to have grey hair, then no hair." He bent over forward to show off his slightly receding hair and patted the top of his head. I laughed and said, "Now isn't that a switch! Joe always left me for a younger woman, and here the Lord surprises me by giving me a younger man!" "Papa God, You are so awesome, You thought of everything!" Roy also reminded me he was color blind anyway. He honestly didn't care what color my hair was. I thought, "Dear, sweet Jesus, I love You and Roy!"

On the kitchen table among Roy's other gifts, I noticed a small pretty box expensively wrapped in dark red foil with a beautiful shinny gold bow on it that sparkled. I wondered what it could be, or who bought it for him. After we sang happy birthday Roy blew out the candles and started opening his gifts. Finally, he picked up the small pretty box last and opened it. I was standing across the room, and on the other side of the table. I couldn't see what it was. He showed it to his daughters Aimee, Kristie and the others. He kept saying, "This present can't be for me, can it?" They agreed, "No way! It can't possibly fit you!" Then Roy said, "I believe this present belongs to someone else. This must be Carol's present." "Yes, I believe this present belongs to you, Carol." I thought he was playing a prank on me in front of everyone.

Suddenly, Roy started walking toward me, looking very serious. He stopped and stood in front of me. Roy took my left hand and lifted my wedding ring finger while holding a beautiful gold and diamond ring in his right hand. He lowered his voice to a soft whisper, and said, "Carol, will you marry me?" He was talking so low I couldn't hear him. I said, "Excuse me, what did you say, Roy?" He moved a little closer and spoke in a loud husky whisper, "Carol, sweetheart, will you marry me?" I was stunned, and I shouted so loud it shocked me, "YES! YES! I WILL GLADLY MARRY YOU, ROY LOVELY!" Everyone was clapping and cheering when Roy kissed me. Wow! I never dreamed, when I obeyed the Lord and shut my mouth, how fast God was going to work in Roy's heart. I was extremely shocked at how Roy proposed to me on his birthday, October 21, 1995. I thought he was such a private individual. "Oh, how I love You, sweet Jesus!" Hebrews 10:35-36 "Therefore do not cast away your confidence, which has great reward. For you have need of endurance, so that after you have done the will of God, you may receive the promise." I went to bed with a big smile on my face that night.

We planned our wedding for February 24, 1996. I'll never forget what my granddaughter, Rebecca said when I told her I was going to marry Roy. I asked her, how she felt about him and she said, "Grandma, if I'd just met you and you were not my grandmother, I'd love you the minute I met you and I'd want to be your friend. That's also how I feel about Roy!" Wow! What double compliments for both of us! All of my sisters and brothers who'd met Roy liked him very much. My sons, Betsy, and my grandchildren all liked and respected Roy. I thought Roy's people were all nice. His brothers were all funny and they made me laugh. Roy's dad was funny too. He made me laugh ridiculously hard when he told us stories about the past. It was hard to believe Roy's dad was sick, because he seemed so happy.

I guess, one day a squirrel got in the house, and Roy's sister Alice and the others were trying to catch it. Nelson, Roy's dad was in bed resting that day when all of a sudden he opened up his eyes from a long nap and found the squirrel sitting on top of his covers on his stomach, starring him in the eye. Nelson quietly grasped two double handfuls of the top of his covers and with one quick yank, flung the covers upwards, and snapped them back again, knocking the terrified squirrel clear across the room! Someone screamed, "There it is, let's get it!" They threw a heavy rug or something over the poor frightened squirrel and put it outside where it belonged. I thought Roy's dad was a very special man.

A few days before our wedding, I was suddenly having second thoughts about getting married. I knew I was very much in love with Roy, and I knew I wanted to marry him, but I was concerned. When I cried out to God, He answered sternly, "Mount up with wings as eagles." I said, "Papa, thank You for exposing that lie. I love You so much Lord, and I trust You completely."

One day while I was walking through my apartment, I stopped suddenly and said, "Lord, I see no reason for me to continue to have monthly periods, do You?" He showed me a vision of an hour glass with the sand running through it when I heard Him say, "Just as the sand runs through the hour glass, so will your periods cease." My monthly periods ceased almost immediately. "Oh Lord, thank You! You have given me the desires of my heart and You have not withheld the requests of my lips. I love You, Lord!"

Roy's dad kept getting worse. He was in the hospital, and not expected to live much longer. I asked Roy tenderly, if he wanted me to start calling everyone, and tell them we were canceling our wedding plans until a better time, but he said he knew his dad was

287

going to heaven to be with Jesus and his mother. Nelson, had suffered a long time. Roy's precious dad went home to be with the Lord three days before our wedding. It wasn't easy, but we buried Nelson on Friday and we were married Saturday afternoon at two o-clock, February 24, 1996. It was at Roy's insistence that we go ahead with our wedding plans, as scheduled.

Roy looked so handsome in his black and grey pin-stripped suit when he came to pick me up for our wedding. Our friend's Joe and Brenda Mays insisted on us getting married in their beautiful spacious home. I asked my friend Michael to marry us, and he gladly said, "Yes!"Aimee and her fiancee Wayne, sang beautifully at our wedding, and our reception. David and Betsy were there with my grandsons. Joey and his children came too. I was disappointed Rebecca wasn't allowed to come. Roy's daughter Kristie came by herself, her husband Rich had to work that day. David Ay and some of my other friends and family members were there. Those who couldn't attend the wedding, came to our reception. Brenda and Joe's house was full, even with the extra added dining room chairs brought out, so my two sons and grandsons were seated on the floor opposite where Roy and I were standing. I heard low levels of laughter throughout the house starting with my niece, Linda from Michigan when I smiled and slipped out of my black pumps. I said my wedding vows in my black nylon stocking feet. Roy, just looked at me and smiled.

I could not restrain myself any longer! I broke out into nervous giggles when I tried to get my snug engagement ring off! Roy was ready to place my wedding ring on my finger! I'd tried to keep my composure and not laugh, but the entire time I was trying to remain calm and repeat my part of our wedding vows, my four and five-year-old grandson's, Michael and Kyle were sitting there taking their lime green bubble gum and spreading it across their mouths and noses. Thank God, David saw what they were doing and made them behave. Roy thought it was hilariously funny too!

I loved our wedding ceremony! It was so beautiful. It began, and ended with faith filled prayers for us. It consisted of God's blessings being spoken over mine and Roy's marriage. I had written to Kenneth Copeland ministries and requested his book on wedding ceremonies, based on the word of God. God showed Kenneth Copeland that a marriage covenant made between a Christian man and woman is like the covenant between us, and Him. It was wonderful. Roy and I took the sacrament together toward the end of the ceremony, in remembrance of what Jesus has done for us. Michael quoted from the book, God's intention is for a woman to stand by her husband's side, not under his feet. He said, God intended for a man's wedding ring to be a semble of faith and love, not a shekel of dominance. I loved it when Michael addressed the audience and said, "This marriage is a miraculous thing, and it is of God. Woe be it to anyone who tampers with this marriage union, or its prosperity." God gave me a Christian man who will honor the covenant between us. "I love You Jesus!"

Our reception was so nice. Roy loves blue. That is the only color he sees perfectly, and it's easy for him to distinguish. So, I was wearing a royal blue suit, with a matching royal blue silk blouse. I believe Roy is healed from the color blindness by Jesus stripes. Jesus healed the blind, and He also carried away Roy's color blindness. My friend Brenda was smiling constantly, not only because I was finally happier then she'd ever known me to be, but especially because her dream was manifesting before our eyes. Our God is an awesome God! My friends, Carol Pettit, Nellie Vega, and Nancy Trimbach decorated our reception hall earlier that day. I prayed, "God bless them, everyone." So many of our friends and family bought us really nice gifts. Others gave us money. We were so thankful for their kindness. I communicated from my heart that was so full of gratitude, "Lord, You are so wonderful! Look how far You've brought me, and so quickly, Lord! I love You!" Roy made me feel like a queen. All my friends and family, marveled at God's blessings on mine and Roy's lives.

Roy and I went to Virginia Beach on our honeymoon. I didn't know the highest places of true unselfish love existed, until I married Roy. A man who spends time with God, his Creator, knows how to love his wife. "Praise You Papa! I must be highly favored by You, dear Lord, because You gave me Roy Lovely! He is exceedingly, abundantly, above all that I could ask or think!" Roy enjoys doing the things I like to do. We went to see Pat Robertson and sat in the audience for a live show on the 700 club. The Lord even gave us unseasonably warm weather for that time of year. We had so much fun, sight seeing, and shopping in some of the stores in town. I kept saying, "Thank You, dear sweet wonderful Jesus!" I'm no longer anybodies worm, I'm a butterfly!

Before I met Roy, my sister Janie said, "Carol, God is going to send you a man who will love, you, and you alone. This big handsome man will take you in his strong loving arms, look into your eyes and tell you he loves you, and you alone." Roy does exactly that. When my sister Janie prophesied over me, she truly spoke it from the Lord, because it came true. From the day Roy and I met each other until the day we married, it was exactly eight months. New beginnings. "My dear wonderful Papa, I love You so dearly! Thank You for Roy's relaxed, easy going, joyful personality, and his quiet soft gentle voice. But most of all Lord, I'm thankful he loves You! " Instead of listening to cursing and yelling, I'd rather sometimes say, "Huh, what did you say, Roy?"

After we returned home from our honeymoon, Roy woke up that next morning to the sound of hammering. I started remodeling his house, so it could become ours. Roy laughed and said, "You weren't kidding when you said, you wanted to get started remodeling the house right away, were you Mrs. Lovely?" Before we were married, I asked Roy if he'd mind if I made some changes in the house later. He had wooden stripes in each corner of the living room walls, in what is called English tooling. It looked nice, but I wanted the walls to be all one light color. Roy said, "Well then, its coming down, isn't it." I taped and mudded the drywall in the corners, Roy was impressed. For several weeks we did all of that hard strenuous work, and still continued to work our full time jobs. God helped us get through it, somehow. "Praise

You, Papa God!" The newly painted living room, hallway and two of the bedrooms turned out really nice. Aimee kept telling me, how much she loved the new improvements we made. I made all new cape cod curtains for the whole house too. Roy had just put in all new windows. The big bay window in our living room was my favorite. Roy liked the way I decorated, and so did the girls. I'd kept all of my "Home Interiors" shelves, sconces, and pictures.

I chose Kristie's bedroom as my office, or quiet room. Roy put my sewing machine and my recliner from my apartment in there for me too. I'd told Roy, I needed a quiet place to sit and read my bible and pray. I wanted to be able to work on my book without any interruptions. It takes a lot of quiet concentration to be a writer, and to study the word or pray. I am zealous when it comes to my secret place with God, my prayer closet. The early mornings are mine and the Lord's time together. Even when Roy and I were on our honeymoon, I got up early and went into the bathroom to pray. Since 1983, I've done this. I am so thankful to God for the privilege of prayer, by the virtue of the precious blood of Jesus. Each morning, I hear my sweet Shepherd's voice calling to me. Song of Solomon 2:10 "Rise up My love, My fair one, and come away. For lo, the winter is past. The rain is over..."

Aimee had written a scripture in the card she gave us for our wedding. Among the wonderful blessings she spoke over her dad and I, she wrote, Psalm 85:10 "Mercy and truth have met together; Righteousness and peace have kissed each other." Immediately, I thought of the two clouds I saw kissing that day at Mary's house when I said, "Roy Lovely, Lord? Is he the man I am to marry, dear Lord?" "Thank, You dear wonderful sweet Jesus! I love You Lord!" All of my grandchildren love Roy, and call him grandpa. My friends and family always say, "Carol, who could not love Roy? He is such a kind and gentle man."

I got so excited when Roy started teaching me how to write my own songs, from the heart. I was so happy! I could hardly believe it when Roy taught me how to write songs about my own life's experiences, especially when we wrote my song, "Little lamb." He showed me how to fit the very words that God had spoken to me before I left Joe, into my song. While I was at work one day, I began to hear a song playing over and over in my heart and mind. I heard the Indian drums beating too, "I can hear the winds of God's Spirit, blowing throughout this land; Get ready God's people; Jesus is coming again. Can't you hear the winds of God's Spirit blowing throughout the land? Get ready God's people, Jesus is coming again." The vision the Lord gave me when I prayed the prayer of forgiveness with David Ruxer, and I forgave the farmhand who'd hurt me when I was a small child, I knew belonged on the front of my album cover. I kept seeing myself letting go of the pretty gentle dove in my left hand and setting it free. I decided to name the album, "The Winds Of God's Spirit."

I was singing a couple of my new songs for a group of women at a Women's Aglow meeting in Huber Heights. Roy and I were scheduled to speak after I finished singing that day. As soon as I finished singing two songs, some tall, pretty, blond haired women stood to her feet quickly and spoke to me with such boldness, "Carol, if those songs aren't copy written, then you'd better get them copy written; And if those songs aren't on a finished album yet, then you'd better get it finished and get the album published; Because your songs are to minister to the broken body of Christ!" I kept saying, "Wow! Oh, thank You, Jesus!" I found out later her name was Phillis. She's an ordained minister. When she sat back down, I said, "Wow! Thank you for obeying God, and encouraging us to finish the album." I recognized the anointing on her. I've been told many times my album has an anointing on it to minister to the broken hearted. The desire of my heart is to minister to hurting women, and men. "God's will be done in us."

God bless my wonderful brother Myrlon and his wife Barb for designing and printing, one hundred and fifty of my albums cover. They did not charge me a penny. They also made Roy's album covers earlier, for free too. I prayed, "God bless Myrlon and Barb one hundred fold, for all their hard work." Roy is my producer, the engineer, back ground singer. He played every instrument on each and every song on my album. Everyone said Roy and I harmonize really well together. I love the way Roy brings out my God given talent along with his. "Praise You, Papa God!" My friend Brenda said, "Carol, You and Roy make sweet music together." I agreed.

I'd been experiencing some difficulty with my right hand. At work, I constantly lifted heavy wooden prep boards with pizzas on them. All day I lifted them in and out of the refrigerators in my unite. I also lifted them high upon the shelf so the pizza pie bakers could put them in the ovens. Sometimes when we were short handed, I also put them in and took them out of the ovens, opening and closing the heavy metal oven doors. I scrubbed down the kitchen and my unite twice daily. I used a heavy metal roller sliding it back and forth over the dough to make preps all day long too. I'd been standing on God's word for my healing, but I kept abusing my hand, until the pain was almost unbearable. Since I'd married Roy, Joy or Paul was picking me up for work, because it was too far for me to walk. Getting a ride back home was another story. I prayed for the Lord's guidance. I kept saying, "Thank You Jesus for healing my right hand and arm. You took my pain Lord."

One day while I was making preps, I looked out the window and saw someone's license plate on the back of their parked car in front of our restaurant. There weren't any numbers on it, just letters, "Escape." I ran and got Joy's attention. When she looked at it she said, "What do you think it means, Carol?" I quoted her the scripture in, 1 Corinthian's 10:13. "No temptation has overtaken you, accept such as is common to man; but God is faithful, who will not allow you to be tempted beyond what you are able, but with the temptation will also make a way of (escape), that you may be able to bear it." "God, Your speaking to me."

God spoke to me again through a dream. In the dream, I was leaving mine and Roy's house to go to work, only, instead of someone picking me up that morning, I was walking to work. When I shut the front door behind me, I noticed three extremely tall muscular angelic looking individuals, and except for their great height and muscular build, they almost looked human. Two of them dressed like women, and the third one was dressed like a man. The angels were standing at the edge of the street in front of our house. I kept starring at one of the really tall, strong looking angels with long blond hair wearing a royal blue suit. It was the exact same color and style of my royal blue wedding suit. As I hesitantly walked toward them, I came to the end of our front walkway, and started to turn to the right in the direction of my work. The tall muscular blond haired angel in the royal blue suit, looked at me and said boldly, "I THOUGHT YOU WERE GOING TO BE ABOUT FAITH?" The angel's voice sounded like many loud rushing waters! The angel turned his eyes toward heaven, clasped his hands together, loudly, and started to float in mid air on his back. His two companions followed his example. As I tried to walk past them, the furious winds which they were stirring up against me, made it impossible to continue walking in that direction! After I woke up, I told Roy about the dream. He didn't understand it. I knew they were angels. And I knew God was strongly warning me through the angels in the dream to read His word and strengthen my faith. I knew He wanted me out of the pizza restaurant I'd been working in for the past three years. "Please help me, dear wonderful Lord Jesus!"

The days and weeks following the dream were strange. When I'd try to get a ride home from work, it was almost impossible. Joy kept wanting to quit Mike's place. She was offered more money to work for Pizza Hut. Joy always left earlier then I did to pick up her three daughters from school. I was staying longer and longer. After work, I had to sit and wait for someone to take me home. Finally, Roy contacted a cab company and paid them in advance to pick me up from work and bring me home. Even that was awful. Unexpectedly, several of their regular drivers quit. They were frantically trying to find new workers to drive their cabs! So here I was, clocked out, smelling like pizza, hungry, exhausted, and sitting there waiting for the overworked cab drivers to pick me up from work. I waited an hour, hour and a half or two hours.

Roy wanted me to go to a doctor and have carpal-tunnel surgery, but I refused surgery, in Jesus name. God had a better plan. One day, Roy told me about a Christian Chiropractic doctor he'd been listening to on the radio, named, Dr. Michael C. Ewald. At Doctor Ewald's suggestion, I started immediate therapy for the carpal-tunnel in my right hand. He filled out the necessary papers so I could start receiving workmen's comp. I quit work that day. "Thank You Jesus!" Although I was obeying God, it was hard at first. Roy gave me his change every week for my spending money. Thank God, he always had a ridiculously large amount of change. Dr. Ewald loves our Lord, Jesus Christ too. I was thankful for a Christian Dr. God wanted me off that job, so the healing process in my hand could begin. Roy was so kind to me, he took really good care of me. I love my husband more with each passing day.

My boss Mike, argued against me for workmen comp. He said I hurt my hand while writing on my book or making curtains. After they turned me down for workmen comp., I forgave Mike. Proverbs 6: 30-31 "Men do not despise a thief if he steals to satisfy himself when he is hungry; But if he is found out, he must restore seven times (what he stole); he must give the whole substance of his house [if necessary; to meet his fine.]" {The amplified bible.} According to God's word, the enemy must restore back to me everything he stole, sevenfold, in the name of Jesus! "I thank You Papa, God, for restoring everything back to me sevenfold, in the name of Jesus." After several months of steady treatments three times a week, I didn't have any surgery, and my hand is perfectly healed. Nahum 1:9 says, "What do you imagine against the Lord? He will make an utter end: affliction shall not rise up the second time." Dr. Ewald let us make affordable payments. "Thank You so much, precious Lord Jesus!"

I was so happy when Rebecca asked, if she could come and stay with Roy and I for a few days during summer vacation. We had so much fun that weekend. Rebecca feels comfortable around Roy. Since I'd met Roy, he'd taken me to see her often. She wanted to stay with us another night, so she called her mother and asked to stay with us one more night. When Carrie said, "no" she cried really hard for a long time! I tried everything to cheer her up, but nothing worked. I loved Rebecca so much, I couldn't bear to see her cry. After Rebecca left with her mother, I was so concerned about my granddaughter. I knew she wasn't very happy. That little girl, had been sad for far too long. She told me she didn't agree with her step dad sometimes. I was furious when she cried and told me, he yelled at her and even kicked her in the stomach! She cried and begged me not to tell her mother. I ask God to surround all of my grandchildren with great warring angels, every day. I ask God to not allow anyone, or anything to hurt them, in the name of Jesus. I always plead the blood of Jesus, in the name of Jesus, over Roy, myself and our sons, daughters, son-in-law's, daughter-in-law's and grandchildren every day. I place all of us under the shadow of the Almighty each day, according to Psalm 91) I know God protects all of us, and keeps us safe. He hears and answers all of our prayers.

Joy surprised me when she called and asked, if I'd make some curtains for the Pizza Hut restaurant in Zenia Ohio where she worked as manager. I was so thrilled! I bought the red and white checked material and solid green. The Lord helped me come up with an excellent design for the curtains which hung between the booths in the restaurant. "Thank You, sweet wonderful Jesus!"

Sandy and I started seeing each other again as often as we could. We were talking and praying over the phone again too. Since I wasn't working outside my home, we had more time to catch up on everything. We reminisced about the vision she'd had of the porthole window with the circle of stars around it, and how it manifested. I'd met so many new friends since then. Sandy could tell I was happier then I'd ever been. I told her what happened to me just a few days after I married Roy, while I was standing in the bathroom fixing my hair and make up. As I looked at myself in the mirror, I realized I finally felt like a whole person. I even liked myself. I'd always felt like I was with a stranger while I was married to Joe. I looked at him sometimes and thought, "Who is he?" I said, "Sandy, from the day I met Roy, I've felt like I've always known him. Roy talks to me and he's interested in what I have to say too. Roy laughs with me, not at me and he never, ever makes fun of me." Sandy smiled and said, "Carol, I am so happy for you!" Sandy's name means, 'Helper of mankind.' She very lovingly cares for her family and many others.

One day, while Joy and I were still working together, she told me she dreamed she and her husband Mark bought mine and Roy's house. Joy and I were sure God gave her that dream. Four months after Joy's dream, Aimee was happily married to Wayne. Roy and I decided to look for a new home. Every time we started to put our house up for sale, I heard the Lord say, "Wait on Joy." Roy and I both wanted a bigger house. I didn't want to live in a house that was so full of Roy's past memories of his ex wives and neither did he. We finally found the house we both wanted, but we had to sell our house first. Joy kept trying to get a loan, but her financial situation looked pretty bleak. I was sitting at my sewing machine making curtains for the Pizza Hut where Joy worked. I was thinking about how much I wanted to buy the bigger house on Oakhill, when suddenly the Lord sang me a little song, "Tweetily Dee, Tweetily Da. Da., there's peace and good will, when you wake up every morning in your house on Oakhill." I had my answer, the house on Oakhill was ours! By a series of miracles, Joy's dream came true against seemingly impossible odds. "Thank You, dear Papa God, for giving us dreams and visions, and the faith to see all of our dreams and visions come true!"

Roy found out, I'd never had a doll house, so he bought me a huge one for Christmas. It's so beautiful. I painted my new three story doll house while Roy put it together in the upstairs of our new house. We had so much fun picking out furniture for both our new house and my doll house. My granddaughters love to play with my doll house. I like my two little white rocking chairs sitting on the front porch with a basket of red apples in the middle. Roy buys me gifts all year, not just for Christmas or my birthday.

"Oh Lord, how I love You, and I love Roy Lovely too." God also fulfilled a childhood dream for Roy. His dad and mom left them a sizable inheritance. Roy bought himself trains, and everything that goes along with them. He even made mountains, and tunnels. Our grandchildren love to come over to our house and play. The Lord is giving us back all the years the locusts ate away.

When Sandy visited me, she couldn't get over the abundance of all of the different kinds of food I had. My refrigerator, and my cabinets are always full. I said, "Sandy, God promised me, for every day of darkness I had in the past, I now have great light, and for every day of sorrow and suffering I experienced in the past, I have great joy instead!" "Thank You, Jesus!" She said tearfully, "Carol, I remember all the years when you hardly had anything in your cabinets or refrigerator, but look at you now! This is your one hundred fold returns, friend! Isn't God good?" I agreed! "Yes!"

Sandy just happened to be at my house when Roy walked in with a beautifully wrapped small package. On Valentines day Roy gave me an exquisite sapphire and diamond gold necklace. For Christmas he bought me matching sapphire and diamond earrings. He knows how much I love sapphires and diamonds. Sandy kept saying, "Wow!" I remember one Saturday when I was talking to my friend Brenda on the phone. Roy came home and handed me another beautifully wrapped small box. And lo-and-behold it was a sapphire and diamond, gold ring. I never dreamed a marriage could be this wonderful! "Sweet Jesus, how I thank You Lord!" (Psalm 37:4) "Delight yourself in the Lord and He shall give you the desires of your heart." "I do delight myself in You, dear Lord!"

I was so excited when one of the publishing companies I sent my query letter too, asked to see my manuscript. I thought I'd finally got excepted. After I sent them my entire manuscript I waited one whole year and they had not communicated with me any further, so I called them. They sent my manuscript back. My friend's Nancy Trimback and Debbie Berbige were here with me. "Thank God!" I cried really hard! I was so discouraged, I couldn't believe they kept my manuscript for one whole year and then decided not to keep it. I was so upset I wasn't going to work on the book anymore. I wanted to quit and give up on it. After having my hopes up so high for such a long time then being turned down, it was more then I could bear. I had not seen my actual manuscript since all the editing was finished. When I looked it over, I couldn't believe the mistakes I'd missed on it. I repented, and the Lord gave me new strength and courage to start again. Roy bought me a new computer, and my work on the book became so much easier. The Lord gave me the strong impression, I am to publish this book myself, but first, bring it up to date. The Lord showed me I'm to work on this book, one day at a time, one step at a time. I'll work closely with the sweet Holy Spirit, until we get it done.

My youngest son Joey met and married a pretty girl named Jennifer. We loved her immediately. She and Joey were sitting in our living room visiting one day when all of a sudden, Joey said he wished Jennifer would study the bible with him. Roy looked over at her and asked her, if she was saved. When she said she didn't know for sure, even though she'd gone to church when she was a child, Roy said, "Jennifer, if you don't know if you are saved, than you'd better get saved, right now, today, because the Holy Spirit has led us into this conversation!" I looked at Roy and said, "Wow!" I knew the Lord was working when I asked her if she wanted to say the sinners prayer, and she quickly said, "Yes!" Roy read a small book to her cute curly headed little two year-old daughter, Brandy, while Jennifer repeated the sinner's prayer after me. She gave her heart to the Lord that wonderful day! "Jesus, thank You for Your precious blood! You, bore our sins for us!"

On January 22, 1999, Joy stopped by with her three pretty daughters. Joy said, "We stopped by, because the girls want to say the sinner's prayer with you." Sarah, Joy's seven-year-old, pointed her finger at me and boldly said, "Carol, we came here tonight to get saved, and YOUR going to save us!" I hugged her and laughed when I said, "No Sarah. I can't save you, only Jesus can save you, and He will!" Joy's oldest daughter Reagan got saved the night before, so Sarah and Christy wanted to get saved too. They knelt in front of my chair. I opened my bible and asked them to read Romans 10:9-10. After I asked them a few questions about their understanding of it, they repeated the sinner's prayer and gloriously gave their hearts to Jesus! I said, "Thank You Jesus, for these precious souls entering Your Kingdom!" Nine-year-old Christy had on a yellow shirt with a big smile face on it. I thought, "How appropriate, dear Lord."

My youngest son Joey called and sadly told me, he'd just discovered his seven-year-old daughter Megan had been molested by her step dad, repeatedly. I was so angry and hurt for her! I ask God to saturate my grandchildren every day in the blood of Jesus, along with all the rest of us. I destroyed that curse off Megan and all of my grandchildren forever, in the name of Jesus, and by the blood of Jesus Christ of Nazareth! I thank God for stationing, great warring angels around all of us every day! I cried, "Dear God, please heal my little Megan, and keep her safe, Lord!"

Joey and I went to court with Megan. She testified against the man who hurt her. Joey stayed right by her side. He told her not to be afraid to tell the truth. My beautiful precious granddaughter came skipping out of the courtroom and told Joey, "Daddy I did exactly what you told me. I wasn't afraid. I told the judge the truth, and nothing but the truth, so help me God!" Joey hugged her and said, "That's daddy's good little girl. I'm very proud of you." After a year of waiting, they finally put the man who hurt her in jail for only one year. I forgave him, but I prayed and asked the Lord to never let her have to look at that man again, and she hasn't, "Thank You, Lord!" My friends and I prayed, Megan's step dad would never hurt another little child, in Jesus name!

Megan's big blue eyes and her thick long dark eye lashes are an expressive part of her beautiful little face. She has long dark hair and a small frame. She's sweet and quiet. She has a happy, bubbly personality, and she will stay that way, in the name of Jesus! My granddaughter loves Jesus, and she loves to sing with my album. She told me happily, she plays my album all the time and sings my songs with me. What more could a grandmother ask for. I believe the anointing on those songs on my album have helped to heal her broken heart. That yoke has been destroyed off Megan because of the anointed One in her, Jesus Christ, our Lord. My grandson, Tyler loved their step dad, but he loves his sister Megan more. Tyler, once again was confused and cried for his step daddy, just like my mother's dreams revealed. "God bless Tyler's heart too."

Rebecca started acting strange again when she came to stay the night with us. She'd acted this way several years before. She would be all right until it started getting dark. At bedtime she'd go frequently into the bathroom, saying she was sick. She'd even kneel in front of the toilet. She'd say she thought she should call her step dad and have him come and get her. I tried to talk to her and comfort her, but she was adamant about going back home. Rebecca would not calm down, until I'd let her call her step dad. I knew she really wanted to stay with us, but she was afraid her step dad might hurt her mother, if she wasn't there to protect her. She usually cried to go back home after Roy went to bed. My beautiful blue eyed granddaughter was acting the same way she did in 1988-89. I'd lived in the house on Ross Rd. It wasn't until Bobby was put in prison after he'd killed a man that she became normal again. Later, when she was eight-years-old, back in 1992, she told me she was afraid her new step dad was going to kill her mother. She felt, if she was home with her mother she could at least try and protect her. I prayed constantly for God's protection over all of us, and I especially cover my grandchildren in prayer. I felt so sorry for Rebecca, when she kept apologizing to me for leaving, "Grandma, I love you and Roy! I don't want to go home, but I need to be there to help my mom." I always hugged her and comforted her. I never made her feel guilty for leaving.

My friend Audrey called me, she was crying so hard I could hardly understand what she was saying. Finally, I was able to comprehend why she was crying. The doctors who'd finished all her tests at the hospital found cancer again, only this time it had traveled throughout her entire body. The doctor told her it was too late to treat her with any kind of medicine. He sent her home to die. I wasn't much help to my friend that day. I burst into tears and cried with her! As soon as I was able to regain my composure I prayed for her until she felt better. Those of us who loved Audrey were praying and believing God for a miraculous healing manifested in her body. As the weeks and months passed, her fears grew worse because of the pain! She was in the last stages of cancer. She called me several times a day and at night for prayer. She asked me one day if I'd sing her favorite song at her funeral, "Bulla Land." I cried and told her, I'd try. "Help us, dear Jesus!"

Audrey said, "Carol, my friend, all I know is, whether I live or whether I die, I'll be standing right there beside Jesus when He puts a crown on your head, because of all the prayers you've prayed over me. Thank you for being my friend and always praying for me night, or day." I cried so hard! I didn't know what to say, accept to reassure her, I loved her too. Audrey and I had remained good friends for several years, but until then I never saw her give up like that. Unfortunately, that was one of the last conversations I had with my friend Audrey. She was put on morphine and couldn't talk to me over the phone any longer. I called and checked up on her. Her children and grandchildren stayed with her around the clock, until she went on home to be with Jesus. Audrey lived much longer then the doctors expected her to. She even continued to work full time in a large hospital as Chaplain. She ministered to the spiritual needs of critical dying patients and led them toward the Lord. Audrey led her doctor who was from India to the Lord too. I will never forget my dear friend Audrey, she was a unique lady. I'm sure she is dancing through fields of flowers with Jesus. That was a long and very difficult year, because my sister Sally had been fighting a battle with sickness too. "Sally will live and not die, in Jesus name!"

Roy and I were traveling to Manchester, Ohio to see my sister Sally as often as we could. Sally had to have several serious operations. The doctors didn't give her much hope either. "God bless Sally's sweet heart." She is alive and well. While my sister

Sally was recovering from one of her surgeries, my brother-in-law Don had to undergo a very extensive surgery himself. God brought her and Don out of several years of sickness and suffering and restored everything back to them, according to His word! "Praise You, dear Papa! Praise You, blessed Jesus! Praise You, sweet precious Holy Spirit!" She and Don sold their home and property for a good price, bought a brand new house and moved closer to her oldest son and my brother Ben, and me. Sally and Don love Jesus. All of us, their family hung onto the hem of Jesus garment for them, and they are well now. "Thank You, wonderful Jesus!"

I really love Sharon, Roy's sister. She loves the Lord with all her heart the way I do. We have a lot in common. Sharon started coming over and bringing her crochet yarn, so we could visit while we made baby blankets. She and I were sitting in my living room talking with my other friend Nancy around ten-thirty one morning when the phone rang. I was shocked! I barely recognized Rebecca's voice, she was crying hysterically! I said, "Rebecca, honey, please try and calm down and tell grandma what's wrong?" I couldn't believe my ears when I heard her tell me an unbelievably grueling story! My fifteen-year-old granddaughter told me she watched her mother Carrie being murdered by her step dad, just the night before! I kept whispering, "Oh, dear sweet Jesus, please help my granddaughter." My heart was breaking for this sweet child that I loved so dear. I thought I was a dreaming.

Rebecca and her younger half sister Jaimee and her younger half brother Dale were in the house when this terrible thing happened! Rebecca was the only one who heard her mother screaming and woke up! She went down stairs, and saw her mother being stabbed to death by her step dad! I kept whispering, "Oh, dear Jesus!" Rebecca kept telling me every gory detail of this horrible story! As soon as Nancy and Sharon heard parts of my conversation with Rebecca, they cried too. They sat there praying quietly. Nancy prayed in tongues. I thank God they were with me, praying for us. Suddenly, I remembered all through the day, and up until the time Carrie was murdered the evening before, I kept vividly remembering a dream I'd had of her three years earlier. Right after I married Roy, I dreamed of Carrie hanging by rope from a tree. All through the dream, I tried desperately to help her! I took a ladder over by the tree and climbed up to help free her, but no matter how hard I tried I couldn't reach her. I climbed up the tree myself and out onto the limb to get to where she was, but she was just too far away, I couldn't reach her! She just hung there almost peaceful looking. In the name of Jesus, I asked God to forgive me for not praying for Carrie, and I know He did.

Carrie asked Rebecca to call 911, but she wasn't able to help her mother. She said her step dad had taken the phones off their hooks. I kept thinking, "Oh God Please help her! No child should ever endure such horror!" As Rebecca went on to describe every horrible detail to me, a steady stream of tears flowed from my eyes. Rebecca said, after her step dad finished killing her mother he came upstairs and told her to stop crying! She said when she asked him if he was going to hurt her or her sister and brother, he told her he would never hurt them. Thank God, for the angels watching over my little granddaughter and her sister and brother. The step dad took Rebecca, and her younger sister and brother over to his parents house and made the children wait in the car while he went in and confessed to his mother and dad what he'd done. They called the police and he gave himself up. Day and night, I cried out to God for this precious child, my granddaughter! Rebecca told me both of her step dads always fought violently with her mother. "Thank You Papa, God for Your protection over my grandchildren, night and day, Lord." Especially at night, I wrestled with visions of what my little granddaughter witnessed! I cast down every evil imagination constantly off my grandbaby who saw her own mothers murder! She loved her mother so much.

Roy remembered, I had told him at the beginning of the year, 2000, I felt the Lord was telling me, Rebecca was going to live with her dad, Betsy and her brothers in, 2000. Sandy remembered I'd told Betsy and David, Rebecca was somehow going to go and live with them, that year. I never thought Carrie was going to die. Nearly all of the years of Rebecca's young life, she discerned the spirit of murder in her step dads. She spent most of her young life trying to save her mother, but she couldn't save her. Only the Lord knows what she saw, heard and felt in her little heart and mind all those years, and only God can, and certainly He has healed my granddaughter of those terrible memories. "Thank You Jesus!"

Carrie's sister, Rebecca's aunt Wendy and her uncle Jack, wanted to keep Rebecca and her half brother and sister together with them. Rebecca was hurt and confused. She wanted to stay with what was left of her family, her brother and sister, and no amount of talking or reasoning could change her mind, either. Rebecca was a very angry little girl. She said she loved her daddy, but she didn't know him. God gave us His grace, sufficiently.

They had to cover Carrie's once pretty face with a veil because her stab wounds were so bad. They said Carrie's face was almost unrecognizable. The last day of the funeral Carrie's dad took David aside and told him, Rebecca's aunt Wendy and uncle Jack wanted to adopt the three children. David was hurt and angry! He wanted Rebecca to know the truth about him. David offered to take all three children and raise them. Rebecca was so angry when I told her she was in her dad's custody, because her mother was dead. I just wanted her to give David a chance. She was furious, and she told me off quickly about it too! I cried when I hung up the phone. I realized Rebecca knew I'd never lie to her, but her heart was just too broken to deal with much of anything right then. I consistently plead the blood of Jesus, in the name of Jesus, over my families brains, our minds, our memories, our imaginations, our thoughts, and dreams and visions. I prayed extra for Rebecca. It was so hard to watch my grandchild suffer. "God help her!"

I was riding in the car beside Roy when I heard the Lord say, "Carol, this is round two with Rebecca." I told Roy what the Lord said. I was more convinced then ever, that God was going to bring His promise to fruition. He'd said Rebecca was going to live with her dad, Betsy and her brother's Michael and Kyle in the year, 2000, and I believed God. Rebecca was full of uncontrollable anger. When she lashed out at us, it felt like we were in a boxing match with her. I prayed for God to heal her from the inside out.

I kept calling my sisters and brothers, and asking them to pray for her. My family asked their church congregations to pray for her too. My friend Carol Pettit put Rebecca on the Internet for prayer in our Women's Aglow prayer circle. "I love You, Papa God!"

Roy and I went to the trial against Rebecca's step dad. Rebecca was the only witness, the other two children were asleep in bed. I cried all the way through Rebecca's testimony while she was on the witness stand. No human being should ever have to die like that, nor should a child have to see her own mother die such a horrible death. Roy and I were sitting beside the jury. We didn't realize we would be able to plainly see all the horrifying pictures of Carrie's murder. The stab wounds on Carrie's face and frail looking body taken at the murder scene were horrifying to look at! I kept thinking, "My dear Papa, God, please have mercy on my little granddaughter who saw all of this happening to her own mother!" I could barely stand to look at those horrible grotesque pictures, but I made myself. I had to see what my little granddaughter saw with her own eyes that terrible night. I constantly prayed, "Oh, dear God, please, somehow wipe these terrible memories away from Rebecca's mind, and heart forever, in the name of Jesus!" Rebecca's step dad was charged with two counts of murder. He not only beat Carrie nearly unconscious with his fists, he stabbed her unmercifully too! "God, forgive him."

I bought Rebecca a stuffed bunny rabbit with a pretty red checked dress and matching bow above its ear. I glued an anointed prayer cloth from Marilyn Hickey ministries underneath the bunny's red apron on its dress. I also prayed over the bunny rabbit myself and anointed it with oil. After I sent it to her, I called and asked her if she would please sleep with it. She promised me she would sleep with the anointed bunny rabbit, and she did. I told her when I went in the Domestic Women's Violence Shelter, the lady who worked for the Red Cross gave me a bunny rabbit. It had a bow in its hair and a frilly dress with a white apron on it. I slept with that bunny rabbit every night, until I married Roy. I started to see some signs of improvement in her after she started sleeping with the anointed bunny rabbit. "Thank You Jesus, for healing my granddaughter." Roy and I had bought Rebecca and her sister, and brother a ceramic angel to remind them, they each had an angel watching over them. I prayed, "God help all the dear children."

Rebecca looked at me with tears running down her precious face and said, "But, grandma, why didn't my mom have angels watching over her too?" I admitted, I hadn't prayed for her mother for a long time, and I apologized. I reminded her, Carrie was in heaven now where no one can ever harm her again. She seemed satisfied with that answer. "Comfort my granddaughter, Jesus."

Rebecca's aunt Wendy and uncle Jack had obtained a lawyer and they took David and Betsy to court. They wanted to get full rights to Rebecca if the judge would allow it. One night I was wrestling with doubt of Rebecca going to live with her dad, until I heard the Lord singing, "Don't worry; Be happy; Everything's going to be all right." As I listened to the joyful singing, the Lord showed me a beautiful, peaceful vision of Himself sitting on a great white horse with a golden bridle. The white horse was prancing through a meadow of beautiful yellow flowers. David told me he prayed, "God, if it is Your will for me to have my daughter, then please give her to me! In Jesus name I pray, amen."

My friend Carol Pettit had a vision of me standing in my living room in the year 2000 with money stacked in my arms, and all the way up to the ceiling. Carol said she saw the money staking up in my arms so high, it kept falling into big bundles all around me on the floor. She also prophesied over me and said, the large amounts of money I knew I was coming into, Rebecca moving in with her dad and my book being published, was a triple braided cord. They were intertwined together. A triple braided cord cannot be broken. I said, "Papa, God, I praise You, and thank You for bringing my friend, Carol Pettit's vision You gave her of the money in my arms stacking all the way up to the ceiling and laying in big bundles all around me on the floor, to pass, in the name of Jesus! I thank You Lord for Your word, in Luke 1:45. "Blessed is she, {Carol S. Lovely}, who believed, for there will be a fulfillment of those things which were told her from the Lord." I said, "Money cometh to me and Roy Lovely, now, today, in the name of Jesus! My granddaughter is happy, and my book, "Which Way? What Way? Your Way Lord., is published too, in the name of Jesus, and by the blood of Jesus?"

My grandson's Michael and Kyle stayed the night with us. After we had taken them to the drive-in-kiddie-movies, we came back home and were sitting out back on our deck. As we swung in our large porch swing, the boys heard a noise and became fearful. I said, "Now listen boys, you must be hearing the wind from one of my great warring angels wings rustling the trees." Kyle looked at me with wide eyes after we came in the house and I was tucking them into bed. He said, "Grandma, do you have ghosts in this house?" I said, "Baby boy, the only ghost in this house, is the Holy Ghost, and He won't hurt you, He loves you! Now go to sleep." They did, after I promised them their usual pancakes for breakfast. The next morning, they were telling Roy and I about their dreams. Kyle dreamed of angels inside and outside our house. After listening to the way Kyle described the angels he saw, I knew he actually did see them. There is no way that little boy could describe angels like that, unless he really saw them.

Michael also told us boldly, he'd missed sleep because he was awake part of the night talking to Jesus. Michael had overheard his grandpa Roy talking about his job, he was concerned about it. There was an anointing on both my grandsons when they described their heavenly visitations. Michael said, "Grandpa, while I was up there talking to Jesus, I asked Him about your job, and He said to tell you, you are not to worry about it. Everything is going to be all right, grandpa." I'd had three of my bottom teeth pulled a couple of weeks earlier and, thanks too Jesus, I took no pain medication. Michael knew I needed to have four more back teeth pulled. So while Michael was up there talking to Jesus, he asked Him, "Lord Jesus, my grandma loves You, please help her get her other teeth pulled without pain too." Jesus told Michael, not to worry about his grandmother. He said, I would suffer no pain, and later when I had those four teeth pulled, I had no pain.

"Praise You dear wonderful Jesus!" Michael was so bold! He told us Jesus said the reason I had so many red birds on Oakhill, was because He knew I loved red birds, and the Lord just wanted to bless me. God poured out His Spirit on my grandsons! Michael told us truths from God, because everything came to pass.

When Michael was a baby, and he was still in diapers he'd be roaming around the house in his walker. The only thing he'd touch on my coffee table was my bible. He'd pull my bible down from off the coffee table onto his tray in his walker, reach his little hands and arms up toward heaven and say, "Halalula!" He said halalula, so much that my friends and family called him the little preacher boy. When he was a few years older, and he was helping his grandma Sandy clean, he'd say, "Please help me, sweet Jesus!" Everyone always said, "Michael is called of God." I believe God's hand is on Roy and I, and my sons and daughter-in-law's, Roy's daughters, and son-in-law's and our grandchildren, according to His word, in Isaiah 59:21 "As for Me," says the Lord, "this is My covenant with them: My Spirit who is upon you, and My words which I have put in your mouth, shall not depart from your mouth, nor from the mouth of your descendants, nor from the mouth of your descendants, descendants," says the Lord, "from this time and forevermore." "I love You, Papa God, Jesus, and Holy Spirit."

Michael and Kyle received Jesus into their hearts one day while they were watching Christian comics on television. They asked grandpa Roy and I a lot of questions, and before I knew it they were kneeling beside my chair and reading, Romans 10:9-10, from my bible. We were relieved knowing they are saved, before the age of accountability. "Hallelujah!" Or should I say, "Halalula!"

My youngest son Joey and his wife Jennifer gave us another little granddaughter. Danielle Nicole was born with dark hair and hazel eyes, and thick, dark eyelashes like her dad and mother. We all fell in love with her immediately. She's so precious, and beautiful. I started calling her, "Little lamb." My sister Sally says, she's quiet like I was when I was a baby. Danielle's big smile lights up a room. Her sisters and brother love her, and she loves them too. My son Joey and Jennifer asked if I would anoint Danielle with oil when they brought her home from the hospital, and dedicate her to the Lord. I was thrilled to do it. "Praise God!" In Jesus name, I believe my sons, daughter-in-laws, and my grandchildren, including Danielle are under the Samuel anointing all the days of their lives. They will serve the Lord all the days of their lives, like Samuel did in the bible. (1 Samuel, 2 Samuel)

The Lord spoke to me again and said this was the third, and final round of 'victory' for my granddaughter. The boxing match continued on between us and Rebecca, until she became really unhappy at her aunt and uncles house. About three weeks after that wonderful sure word from God, Rebecca, through a series of sudden changes in circumstances went to live with her dad, Betsy and her brothers. "Thank You, dear, sweet wonderful Jesus!" David and Betsy had almost given up the hope of her coming to live with them. Finally, Rebecca was getting to know and love her daddy. However, Rebecca still needed a lot of repeated serious counseling to help her. She still needed to get healed from all the misery she'd gone through. She got depressed sometimes and even suicidal, which I rebuked off her, in the name of Jesus. I prayed for her constantly. It was not easy for Rebecca to adjust to her new family with all the life threatening, sudden changes she had dealt with in her young life. It wasn't easy for my son David and his family to adjust to Rebecca either. They were dealing with a child who had grown up around murders. They had to deal with each others sudden bursts of anger, and frustrations. I knew this was a spiritual battle so I had to consistently keep my fleshly will out of it, and stand on God's word for David and all of his family. "Oh, God, I thank You for Your mercy and Your unconditional love."

One night God instructed Roy that when he got to work the next morning, he was to walk around his work building seven times. He didn't even tell me about it, until after he had obeyed God. Roy got to work early that morning, before anyone else was there. He laughed and told me he pretended he was picking up trash, in case anyone was watching him. Several weeks after that, Roy became the manager. A year later, he lost the job as manager, because a larger company bought them out. A new manager was brought in who treated Roy unfairly, and enjoyed every minute of it. One day while I was praying in tongues for Roy, I saw his boss, Al sitting at his desk in his office. Suddenly, the Lord started writing in black ink letters on the outside of his boss, Al's wall beside his office door. "MENE." I looked up the meaning of the words, MENE, in Daniel 5:25-26 "This is the interpretation of the matter: MENE, God has numbered the days of your kingship and brought them to an end."   A few months later, they closed Roy's work building down in Springfield, and merged with one of their sister companies in Dayton. His ex boss, Al was transferred along with Roy and the others to Dayton. Their new boss gave his ex boss, Al a lesser paying job. It wasn't to long after that, Al quit. Al sells cars now. Seven is the number of spiritual completion.

I had three wonderful similar dreams in 1998-99. "Hallelujah!" I dreamed, I lost the weight I'd gained after I quit working. I had two of the dreams in 1998. In the first delightful dream, I was looking for the lady's bathroom in an extremely large church. Everywhere I walked throughout the huge building there was wall-to-wall, full length mirrors. I was wearing a light and dark blue Chinese style dress. Every time I saw myself in the wall-to-wall full length mirrors, I thought, "I must have lost a lot of weight." I kept hearing someone say over a loud speaker, "THIS CHURCH IS ONE OF, THE, LARGEST CHURCHES IN THE WORLD!" In the second dream, I was talking to Sandy while I tried on my summer clothes from the year before. I kept saying, "I can't wear any of my summer clothes from last year! Sandy, look at me, they are all way too big for me now!" She kept commenting, "Oh Carol, you've lost so much weight! Now, we need to go shopping to buy you some smaller size clothes that will fit you!" On New Years Eve, January 1999, I had a third dream. The Lord told me I am to write a third book. In the dream, I was having a conversation with the Lord. We were discussing how I was going to write the third book, "How To Lose Weight And Keep It Off Without Dieting And Having Fun Doing It God's Way:" {By Carol S. Lovely.} God showed me the front cover of my third book. It is a nice pearl white color. The title words surround a five by seven, a slender looking picture of me on the front cover. The title letters stack downward, one on top of the other. They start at the top left side and follow all the way down, and across the bottom of my picture, in the shape of an 'L'. I woke up, having a discussion with the Lord about the book. I prayed, "Oh dear Lord, please teach me how to lose weight and keep it off, without dieting, and having fun doing it, Your way Lord, in the name of Jesus!" When I told Roy about the dreams and the book I'm going write on losing weight, he hugged me, and said he loves me no matter what size I am. He's so precious. Roy always compliments me, and tells me how pretty I look, even if I'm not wearing make up. Roy Lovely is indeed, exceedingly, abundantly, above anything I could have possibly asked God for in a husband. "Thank You, dear Jesus!"

Joy offered to pick me up, so I started working one or two days a week with her at Pizza Hut. I also made curtains for two of the Pizza Hut restaurants, and two of their carry out stores. I made the curtains that hang between the booths in one of their restaurants in Middeltown Ohio, and one of their restaurants in Zenia Ohio. I made the curtains that hang in the large front windows in one of their carry out stores in Springborro Ohio, and one in Centerville Ohio, too. Joy said the afternoon sun glared through the large front windows in their carry out stores, and made it difficult for them to read their computers properly. Everyone seemed happy with my cape cod curtains that looked very Italian. "Thank You sweet Jesus!" I knew God designed the first curtains, so I asked Him to teach me how to make the curtains for Pizza Hut. He did!

My precious husband Roy had been experiencing problems with his stomach since he was a teenager. Roy had to have the ulcer surgically removed, and the doctors also had to remove part of his stomach. He had to have major stomach surgery. Roy's surgery was on a Tuesday, the day before Valentines day, in the year, 2000. Exactly one week before Roy's major surgery, my oldest son David had to have major surgery on the Tuesday before. Three days before Christmas David had to have an emergency appendectomy. While he was in emergency, they did an M. R. I. The doctors found a tumor hanging from my son's right kidney. God brought David through the six and a half hour surgery, and then He brought my husband Roy through a tedious six-hour surgery the following Tuesday. Roy's stomach is wonderful now. He can eat anything and it doesn't hurt him at all. Roy says he's never been healthier. I constantly praise God for sparing my husband, and my son's lives. God is so merciful. Roy was in the hospital nine days and he kept the nurses laughing constantly by telling them jokes. David is doing well too, but only because of the healing power of Jesus. I am so thankful the Lord brought us through it all. "Praise Your wonderful name forever, Papa, God, dear Lord Jesus, and sweet precious Holy Spirit! I love You!"

Roy and I were so surprised when we found out his youngest daughter Kristie was pregnant. We were thrilled when little Jakob was born. Jakob has a sweet contagious laugh. He is so precious to us. He has blond, brown hair and pretty big brown eyes that seem to dance with pure energy. About a year and a half later, Kristie and Rich gave us another beautiful grandson, Joshua. Roy and I know, without a doubt that Rich and Kristie well raise little Jakob and Joshua in the knowledge, and the admonition of the Lord, because they are such strong Christians. Rich was able to get a wonderful job in Colorado Springs, Colorado. He's working for the well-known Dr. James Dobson. "Hallelujah!" Roy and I now have nine grandchildren. Each and every one of our grandchildren are special to us. They are precious gifts from God.

I was so shocked when I had a dream about my dad. I had never in my life, to my knowledge, ever once dreamed of my dad. In the dream, I was sitting in the front seat of a car on the passenger's side. My sister Sally sat in the middle and daddy was driving. My brother Gene was riding in the backseat directly behind daddy. Daddy was never fat, but in the dream he was kind of chunky. After I woke up from the dream, I understood why I dreamed of Gene, but I couldn't even imagine why I dreamed of my dad. Gene was recovering quickly from an illness. We were all praying and believing for his healing. "Thank You Papa God, that my brother Gene will live and not die and he will proclaim the works of the Lord!" "Thank You Jesus, by Your stripe's Gene's healed!"

A few days before I had the dream, I was praying for this book, and I heard myself ask God to give me honesty and integrity. It came right out of my mouth without knowing I was going to say it. I'd always prayed for wisdom. I ask God constantly to help me write this book correctly. I prayed "Papa, if honesty and integrity were not used all through this book, then please show me, and I'll change it, in Jesus' name." I knew there was a major reason I spoke that out of my mouth. While I was waiting on God's answer, I had the dream about my dad. My sister Sally called one evening to let me know how our brother Gene was doing. Sally and I prayed for him again. Before our conversation ended, I told Sally about the dream I had of daddy, her, myself and our brother Gene. I told her the dream was a good, peaceful and happy dream. Suddenly, I asked her if daddy had ever once said he loved me or did he ever hug me or show me any kind of affection when I was a baby. I told her what the Lord said to me about honesty and integrity. To my great surprise she said, all those years ago when I was in and out of the hospitals battling depression and even suicide, partly, because of how he'd treated me, daddy called her and my other sisters and brothers and asked them to pray for me, every day. I was shocked! I couldn't believe daddy loved me.

Sally lived in California near mommy and daddy. I lived here in Ohio. She said he also asked everyone to send me pretty cards and letters to cheer me up. He told them to make sure they reassured me, they loved me too. He told her, he and mommy were always sending me cherry cards and letters, and they always put money in them. He asked my sisters and brothers who lived out there to do the same, because he knew Joe and I were paying Dr. bills. I

314

never, ever knew he even cared. Tears, stung my eyes, especially when Sally said daddy actually called all of my family members, every day to remind them to pray for me. I have no recollection of this, including the cards or letters. The Lord knows my heart. He especially knows I didn't have any of this knowledge about my dad when I wrote this book, until now. During daddy's illness before he died, he told my sister he loved all of his children but the strong drink had stolen his ability to show anything but anger. She said he always bragged on my singing and my other talents to everyone. I didn't know any of this about my dad. "Sweet Jesus."

I cried for several days and thanked God for opening my eyes of understanding. I recognized why Sally was seated between me and daddy. She was our mediator. Later, my sister Louise called me. She also told me some things about daddy that was incredible news. Daddy bought me and my sister Peggy new shoes and dresses when we were little, before we left the farm. She said daddy played with me sometimes, and he held me in his arms. WOW! I was shocked, and blessed! I never knew there was a happy time with my dad. I guess the years of abuse erased my good memories as I tried to block out the bad ones. I kept saying, "Thank You, Jesus for reveling the truth to me. Thank You for healing my broken heart, completely." I kept thinking, "My dad really loved me." The dear precious Holy Spirit constantly leads and guides us into all truth, and the knowledge of the truth set me free! I decided not to try and rewrite this book, but to tell about this truth exactly as I learned about it. The Lord saved the best wine for last when He caused me to know the truth about my dad. Of all people, it was my dad rallying my family to pray for me, and God honored those prayers, and loosed me from that prison.

I remember when my brother Jim died in February of 1992. After the funeral my sisters, Helen, Louise, Janie, Sally, Peggy and I were all sitting in Sally's big comfortable living room talking when somehow the subject came around to our dad. I was completely amazed and totally shocked when they told me, daddy had asked for everyone's forgiveness before he died. When they finally asked daddy, if he was going to call me or my sister Peggy back in Ohio and ask for our forgiveness, he said. "No, I cannot ask Peggy or Carol for their forgiveness, because what I've done to them cannot be forgiven." I felt so terrible knowing my dad wanted my forgiveness and I didn't know it. Of course by the time I found this information out, God had given me an abundance of His wonderful precious grace to forgive daddy. Just knowing my dad died with that terrible guilt, made me feel so sad. Sally reminded me also that when daddy came back to visit, he always hugged us hello and good-by. I had no remembrance of dads' affection. God's restoring memories the shock treatments erased.

I never treated my dad with disrespect. Even when his poor old hands shook from withdrawals from the alcohol, I took him to the state store and bought him a bottle of whisky. I never allowed him to get drunk, especially in front of my sons. Daddy agreed to let me hide it from him. He and I both knew he couldn't stop drinking, until he was drunk and horrible acting. Whenever he asked, I fixed him a drink. I remember jokingly asking, "Daddy, do you want your whisky over the rocks, or without ice?" I knew he'd been addicted to alcohol much too long. To try and stop him from drinking as old as he was, seemed impossible. He was really pitiful sometimes. Suddenly, I realized how much daddy really did love us. He was terrified of heights and flying, and yet he flew here to Ohio to see us every year. When he'd fly back to California, mommy came and stayed with us for several months too. Mommy and daddy never owned their own home. When they moved to California, they finally had a nice clean rented house. I guess daddy had quite a green thumb. Beautiful flowers grew all around their house. They never flew back together and left their nice little house unattended. I saw a picture of their house.

As I continued to pray and seek God, I heard myself pray, "Dear Papa God, I ask You to please forgive me, in the name of Jesus, if there is any self-righteousness in me, or in this book. I repent of it. I ask You to show me were it is, and help me to remove it. I know You will not share Your glory with another." I was constantly checking myself to make sure I didn't offend my Papa.

Once again I started from the very beginning of the first chapter. With God's help I read carefully over every sentence. I prayed in tongues. If I found anything that even remotely hinted that I was trying to pat myself on the back, I repented of it, and corrected it immediately. I heard Jesus tell me to read John chapter 10. "Most assuredly, I say to you, he who does not enter the sheepfold by the door, but climbs up some other way, the same is a thief and a robber. "But he who enters by the door is the shepherd of the sheep. "To him the doorkeeper opens, and the sheep hear his voice; and he calls his own sheep by name and leads them out. "And when he brings out his own sheep, he goes before them; and the sheep follow him, for they know his voice. "Yet they will by no means follow a stranger, but will flee from him, for they do not know the voice of strangers..." "I love You so much dear Lord Jesus!" Daily, I ask God for discernment, and He gives it to me.

My sister Sally told me she kept feeling a heaviness to pray for someone in our family, before my oldest son David ever had to have any surgeries. Sally told me she kept kneeling at the foot of her bed, and asking God, "Dear Lord, I know I need to pray for someone in our family, because I can feel they need prayer, but who is it Lord?" Twice Sally dreamed the same dream of my son David and Jesus. She dreamed David was sitting under a shade tree talking to Jesus, on a sunny afternoon. David leaned back comfortably in a lawn chair. Jesus sat beside him in another lawn chair. Sally said David looked so peaceful sitting there talking to Jesus. She said Jesus, gently rubbed David's face and hair. David's hair and face glowed with the glory of God on him. Sally said it was a beautiful dream. She felt the strong healing love, and joy that Jesus was administering to David. She said, "Carol, Jesus loves your sons. David has the call of God upon his life."

Early one morning while I was watching the news with Roy before he went to work, I had an open-eyed-vision of my son David when he was a little boy. The vision was so bright and clear of David, even though the television was on. David's curly hair was white as cotton, just like it was when he was about five or six

317

years' old. He was wearing his favorite brown and yellow horizontal stripped short sleeved shirt, and his baggy yellow shorts. He was happily swinging on a swing, when suddenly the swing broke and he fell. He was crying! Large tear drops were popping out of his big brown eyes and spilling down his little ruddy cheeks. He got up rubbing the right side of his back. It was the same side he'd had the surgery on. He stopped crying and smiled. The vision lasted quit a long time. God always confirms the visions and dreams He gives me with His word. Later, I was watching Benny Hinn on Trinity Broadcasting Network, when he quoted a scripture from Job 33:25-26 "His flesh shall be young like a child's, He shall return to the days of his youth. He shall pray to God, and He will delight in him, he shall see His face with joy, For He restores to man His righteousness." This happened six months after David's surgeries. I could see such similarities between Sally's dream, my vision, and the word God gave me.

I went to bed the night of September, 10, 2001, praying for the peace of Jerusalem. I'd been praying extra for them, for peace. Sometime during the night, I sat straight up in bed and started praying in tongues. Suddenly, I started pleading the blood of Jesus, in the name of Jesus, over everything, and everyone in the State of Ohio. "I pled the blood of Jesus, in the name of Jesus, over all the electrical wiring systems, and water pipes, the electric poles, and water, the telephone poles, and wires, the telephones; The rivers, streams and lakes, the bridges and overpasses, underneath the bridges and overpasses, down in the sewers, and the sewage systems, and the tunnels; The post offices, and postal workers, the incoming, and the outgoing mail, and the machines they use to sort it, the mail trucks, mail boxes, and mail bags; The nuclear power plants, the gas and electric power plants; The water plants, and the chemical plants; The farmers and their farmland and animals, the grain and hay they use to feed the animals, the milk and the butter and cheese, the eggs and chickens, the small air planes, and chemicals they use to spray their produce; The gas stations and the hospitals, the churches, banks, schools and theaters, shopping malls and grocery stores, museums, homes, lands, and people, animals, birds and trees, parks, and all buildings of any size and any kind; Cars, trucks, vans, and busses, eighteen wheeler Simi trucks, police cars, ambulances, fire trucks, the ships, boats, yachts, and canoes, trains, air planes, helicopters, jets; All over the Cities of Fairborn, New Carlise, Oakwood, Medway, Park Lane, Crystal Lakes, Springfield, Cincinnati, Columbus, Dayton, Centerville, and the entire Miami Valley, the Write Patterson Air Force Base, and the entire State of Ohio. I thank You Lord for Your holy angels that watch over all of us and keep us safe, in the name of Jesus." I trusted the dear Holy Spirit as I prayed. I knew the weather was nice, but I pled the blood of Jesus in the name of Jesus over all of Ohio anyway.

While I was praying, I thought, "Lord, You've only led me to plead the blood of Jesus, in the name of Jesus, over the entire State of Ohio on rare occasions?" I laid back down and went to sleep. The next day was September 11. I've prayed this prayer over all our Cities and the State of Ohio, nearly every day since.

Twice, a small but powerful book was dropped into my hands. "Pray For Our Nation" 'Scriptural prayers to revive our Country. Published by Harrison House.' I've prayed those prayers almost every day since September 11, 2001. I have become more vigilant in praying for our nation. I thank God, for putting that little book of prayers into my hand. I also began pleading the blood of Jesus, in the name of Jesus, over all of our military men and women fighting over in Afghanistan or any where else in the world, every day too. I plead the blood of Jesus, in the name of Jesus, over all of their inner and their outer organs, and the food they eat, the liquids they drink, the air they breath, the clothes they wear, and their shoes, the shots and medications they take, their homes, family's, animals, their work places, schools and churches, the cars, trucks, and vans, military busses, trains, boats, ships, and submarines, air planes, jets, helicopters, and tanks they drive and ride or fly in. I thank the Lord for His holy angel who watch over them all, and keep them safe, in Jesus name. "And they overcame

319

they loved not their own lives unto death." {Revelation 12:11}
I pray many other prayers for God's protection over our military
men and woman too. I am so grateful for all of them and their
sacrifice they are making for our Country. It is a privilege to pray
for them. I pray, "God bless all of our military men and women."

Rebecca's heart was so broken. Thank God, Jesus healed my
granddaughter's broken heart 2000 years ago. I asked my
granddaughter if I could put two of her poems in my book.
Rebecca hopes, by sharing her poems others may receive comfort.

I Miss' You!

*"Oh mom; Is there ever not a day that I don't think about you?
You were my mom; My best friend; The reason I lived. You took
care of me when times were rough; I need you right now, because
it is so tough. My heart is broken; And it is sore; I can barely live
without you anymore. I miss the times we spent together; Going
shopping: And talking about whatever? You were so pretty; And
very young; You loved me with all of your heart; Now I have to be
living with us apart. Now we can't speak or even touch; How can
I tell you that I love and miss you so much?"*

Every day

*"Every day that goes by; I always wonder why? I miss your
smile; I miss your touch; Oh mom; I miss you so much! This is too,
much pain; I think about you night and day; All of this is such a
shame; The sun will never shine the same. You were so pretty; You
were so kind; It makes me cry all the time; Life is just not the
same without you; You were my best friend; You were like a sister
to me; You were so cool; But how could you die so cruel? Now
I'm left with nothing; Except pictures and memories; I love you
mom with all of my heart; I can't believe we have to be apart?
Now I know that you are in peace; No one can hurt you anymore;
Now I'll let you rest; Mom, you were the best."*

Chapter Nine

We're Crossing Over Jordan

The Lord encouraged me to stay focused on finishing this book as the year 2001 began drawing to a close. He knew I still needed to believe I was capable of writing a book. I'd never had much confidence in myself or anyone on this earth until I came back to Him in 1983 and started to read my bible. My merciful heavenly Papa gave me visions and dreams to hold onto, and He confirmed them with His word. (Proverbs 4:20-24). My son, give attention to My words; Incline your ear to My sayings. Do not let them depart from your eyes; Keep them in the midst of your heart; For they are life to those who find them, And health to all their flesh. Keep your heart with all diligence, For out of it spring the issues of life. Put away from you a deceitful mouth, And put perverse lips far from you." John 1:1-2 1:14 "In the beginning was the Word, and the Word was with God and the Word was God. He was in the beginning with God." "And the Word became flesh and dwelt among us, and we beheld His glory, the glory of the only begotten of the Father, full of grace and truth." "I love You so much Papa! I love You wonderful Jesus! I love You dear sweet Holy Spirit."

God keeps reassuring me like all those who have gone on before me in the bible that He loves me and He created me for His purpose. Consistently my dear heavenly Papa God has worked with me closely to help me receive His wondrous love. As I sit at Jesus' feet and renew my mind according to His word He gives me beauty for ashes and joy instead of sorrow. God even changed my last name, and gave me a wonderful Christian husband, and yet I still had a ways to go before I really, really believed I could write this book, publish it, and be worthy to be called its author. "Wonderful Jesus, You are the author and finisher of my faith."

Several years ago one of my good strong Christian friends who loves God and loves me, looked directly into my eyes and told me boldly, I was not a writer nor could I be the author of this book. She told me I needed a 'ghost writer' to write the book for me. Over the years I gave my manuscript to several different women with higher educations and brilliant minds, thinking perhaps they were supposed to help me write my book but God said, no, every time. When I gave my manuscript to each one of these women, they said they loved it when they read it, but they became so busy fighting so many battles on the front lines, they didn't have time to edit it for me. After several months, I'd feel the Lord strongly impressing on me to go and get my manuscript, but none of these wonderful Christian women wanted to give it back to me. Some of the women even cried, and some felt insulted. One lady was so angry she stomped off and when she came storming back into the room with my manuscript she threw it down at my feet! She told me the only way she'd give, (MY) book back to me was under the condition I'd have my manuscript placed on a word perfect disk and send it back to her. But again God said, no, no, no.

My wonderful Papa God wanted to take a woman like me who'd had an equivalent of a sixth grade education, and make me into a 'writer' and an 'author' so I could tell the world, "If God can teach someone like me to be a writer, He can help anyone do anything!" Hallelujah! God gets all the glory. "Wonderful Jesus, I love You." Certain family members said things to me about this book that hurt my feelings, but I kept believing God had called me to do this. Others thought I was using this book to bring dishonor to our family, until I cried and told them I didn't write the book to hurt anyone, but only to help others and bring glory to God! My sister Sally read my query letter and cried. She said, "Sis, you have written this book for all of us. This is a beautiful book!" The Lord has comforted me and dried my tears so many times. He has kept every promise He made me. He calls me His little lamb, as He teaches me to walk on the wings of the wind with Him, and sore like the eagles above the storms of life. The winter truly is over and past in my life, just like He promised me. "Praise God!"

God had mercy on me, because He knew I was still so afraid of criticism. When my precious husband Roy helped with the second editing of this book, a few years ago he kept telling me the book was good, but I was still hesitant of my family and friends reading it. I couldn't bear the thought of anyone else criticizing me. When I let my sister Peggy read the first chapter, she loved it. Peggy always encouraged me to write this book. She had such faith in my ability to do anything, especially if God called me to do it. I love Peggy dearly. I became a little braver, and I finally had the courage to let my brother Ben's daughter Sherry read my manuscript. She loved it so much, she went wild! "Praise God!" I felt encouraged when she kept saying, "Aunt Carol, I'm praying you get this book published and into the hands of women and even some men who desperately need to read it!" I love all my nieces and nephews. Sherry's spiritual walk is so much like mine. I love her and I value her opinion too. God's perfect love casts out fear.

One day I was telling my friend Cheri McKee, I felt so much pressure to get the book done. I'd been distancing myself from some of my friends and family so I could get alone with God, and work on this book. But every time my phone rang, which was several times a day, I'd answer it. By the end of the day, I was working late hours on my book. My sister Peggy told me many times, I should treat this like a nine to five job and not answer my phone during my working hours, BUT IF I DID OTHERS WERE OFFENDED! Cheri, prayed for me and saw it was God who was applying the pressure on me to finish this book! Wow! She also prayed God would give me the courage to work on the book without feeling guilty. I said, "But Cheri, I am a prayer warrior, shouldn't I answer the phone and pray with them?" Roy, Peggy, Nancy, and Cheri told me the same thing, "God will help them understand, He wants this book finished, now." "Please help me, Jesus!" My boss is my very own Papa and I want to please Him. I thank God for all of my friends and family who have understood my deep need to be tucked away with God so I could concentrate on completing this book. More then anything, someday I want to hear the Lord say, "Well done, My good and faithful child."

One night in December 2001, the Lord gave me the chorus to a new song. I couldn't go to sleep until I got up and wrote it down on paper. "Oh, don't give up; Don't give in; Just reach out and touch the hem of Jesus-garment until you hear Him say, "Who touched Me, I felt-virtue-go-out-from-Me-today." Wow! God gave me another anointed song of hope according to His word in, Luke 6:19 "And the whole multitude sought to touch Him: for there went virtue out of Him; and He healed them all." "I love You Jesus! Thank You for healing me according to Your word." I lay there in the darkness drifting off to sleep with a knowing in my heart, God was telling Roy and I to get ready to make another album together. It felt great to think about making another album. "I love You Papa. I love You Jesus. I love You dear Holy Spirit."

On the thirtieth day of December 2001, my friend Nancy was praying for me in tongues. When she gave the interpretation, it was about my sequel book, "Seven Realms Of Glory." She said God has been taking me from one realm of glory to another, as I draw closer to Him. Again, I knew God was encouraging me to finish this book. I got so excited! Nancy saw a vision of me sitting at my computer working on this book. But, she said I was writing on my book with an old fashioned quill feather ink pen, and the ink in the pen was writing out gold letters on the paper. " Sweet Jesus, I love You so dearly Lord!" Line upon line, Jesus helps me.

The Lord spoke to me clearly on the very last day of 2001. On December thirty first, New Years Eve, He told me to read Job 19. He said when I read Job 19, I'd find some nuggets. I found the nuggets immediately! "Praise You, my very own dear loving Papa!" I put the scripture from, Job 19:23-25 in my computer and printed out the delightful words God gave me. I taped them onto my printer, so that I could read, and reread them as I worked on my book. "Oh, that my words were written! Oh, that they were inscribed in a book! That they were engraved on a rock with an iron pen forever! For I know that my Redeemer lives and He shall stand at last on the earth." I prayed, "Please, dear Papa, help me to finish this book and get it published-I know Your precious Son, Jesus is coming soon." Precept upon precept, we'll get it done.

When Roy came home from work I told him what the Lord said to me earlier that day. I showed him the scripture, Job 19:23-25 on my printer in my office and he got excited too. Roy truly respects the anointing on my life. I always look so forward to the evenings when he and I talk about our day. Since Roy doesn't enjoy sports, our weekends together are also quite lovely. Life is so much easier now that I can talk openly about the Lord. He and I are not only still very much in love with each other, we are also best friends. I was still excited when we went to bed that night. Job 19:23-25 kept exploding in my spirit. My faith was already soaring, but God really wanted this to be an unforgettable December thirty first New Years Eve 2001. That night He gave me awesome visions to start off the new year of 2002. I love it when God gets my attention anytime, but especially at the beginning of the new year!

I was almost asleep when all of a sudden I saw a brilliant vision of my little two-year-old granddaughter, Danielle. She walked right up to the foot of my bed, pointed her tiny index finger at me and boldly said, "Ok ga-ma, it's time for you to move on up to the big house now!" She smiled her pretty smile at me as she made motions with her head and hands, nodding and pointing in the direction of the large red brick house I watched the Lord build me back in 1992. I was so excited I could hardly stand it! I said, "Oh Lord, You used my own pretty little granddaughter to prophecy to me! Yes Lord, I believe it is Your timing for Roy and I to move on up into our big red brick house You built for us in 1992! Papa God, I ask You in Jesus' name to bring it to pass, please."

I no sooner got myself calmed down and laid my head back down on my pillow when I saw another bright clear vision. In the vision I was walking up the sidewalk to my red brick house the Lord built for us. That vision was so real! The sun was going down--it was dusk and the lights were on in our house. I could see my mauve colored curtains hanging in the front window. I knew they were my curtains. Just as I approached the front porch of my house the door opened and I went inside. A beautiful wreath hung on the door. My house is lovely inside. "Oh Papa, I thank You that no good thing will be withheld from us who love You!"

Finally, I calmed down enough to try and go back to sleep again, but just as I closed my eyes I had another awesome vision of the red brick house the Lord built for us. In the vision I saw the front of our house. Roy was hard at work hammering nails in our big front porch that he was building. The studio was already built. It was also red brick to match our house. A beautiful lighthouse stood out in front of our "Lovely Lighthouse Studio" exactly the way we'd been planing to build it. Once again it was around dusk, the sun was going down. To my right I could clearly see the beautiful face of Jesus looking toward our house, studio, and seven acres of our property. I could only see the left side of His precious face. I didn't understand why He was crying. A tear was suspended on His left cheek. "I love You dear wonderful Jesus."

Before I went to sleep that night I had another vision. In this unusual vision I knew I was inside the vault of a bank. Large stacks of money was being moved out of the bank towards me. I knew it was my money the Lord had promised me. When I told Sandy the next morning about the visions, she said, "Don't you get it Carol? Weeping may endure for a night but joy comes in the morning." (Psalm 30:5) She and I agreed, He is faithful that promised. God never fails to keep His promises. "Yahoo!"

On January the fifth 2002, I heard the lord speak to me early that morning, before I got out of bed. He told me to read Joshua 3:10. After Roy left for work, I could hardly wait to read it. 'And Joshua said, "By this you shall know that the living God is among you, and that He will without fail drive out from before you the Canaanites and the Hittites and the Hivites and the Perizzites and the Girgashites and the Amorites and the Jebusites:" I was so happy! Wow! What a sure word from God! "Thank You Papa!" I shouted and I praised God, until, suddenly the chorus of another new song came to me, "Oh, we are crossing over Jordan--into the promised land; God's delivered us from our enemies--with His Great and Mighty Hand! We've left the wilderness behind us-- we'll never look back again you see; God's delivered us from our enemies-- cause He loves you--and me!" I sang that chorus nearly all day, and evening. Every time I sang it I felt such deliverance!

327

Early the next morning before I got out of bed the Lord spoke to me again. As soon as I opened my eyes He asked me if I knew how many enemies He's driving out of my life. I thought about Joshua 3:10, and all of a sudden, I said, "Oh Lord, I didn't count them yesterday when I read Your word in Joshua 3:10, but I just know there are seven of them Lord! After all, You've been speaking to me about my sequel book, "Seven Realms Of Glory." Once again, when I read Joshua 3:10 I laughed and I shouted, "Oh Lord, there are exactly seven! Thank You Papa God, that You are without fail driving out all our enemies! Hallelujah!" Suddenly I remembered learning what the number seven means when I took the student ministries classes at the church here in Fairborn. The number seven represents spiritual completion. "Praise the Lord!" When Roy came home from work, I told him everything that happened, and he was happy too! I love being able to share the things the Lord tells me with Roy. "Thank You wonderful Jesus!"

On January 24, 2002, the Lord told me to read Zechariah 10: I got so excited when I read Zachariah 10:6-7-8, "I will strengthen the house of Judah, and I will save the house of Joseph. I will bring them back, because I have mercy on them. They shall be as though I had not cast them aside; For I am the Lord their God, and I will hear them. Those of Ephraim shall be like a mighty man, and their heart shall rejoice as if with wine. Yes their children shall see it and be glad; Their heart shall rejoice in the Lord. I will whistle for them and gather them, for I will redeem them." I said, "Oh dear Papa, I thank You that according to Your word You HAVE already whistled for my sons and they follow You! Thank You Lord for Your mercy hovering over my sons." In the Amplified bible, Zachariah 10:8 says, "I will hiss for them (as the keeper does his bees) and gather them in..." I will never forget December 6, 1983 when the Lord hissed for me. Since that wonderful day I always said, "God will hiss for my sons like He hissed for me, and they will fall in love with Jesus all over again like I did." Now God has given me His word, He has heard my prayer of confession for my sons who obey Him. (Isaiah 54:17) "No weapon formed against me or my family shall prosper."

My friend Sandy has finally interred into a place of God's rest. Sandy has worked hard ever since I've known her. She is a certified nurses aid, she did in home care for the elderly. Sandy took care of several different elderly women after God closed the doors on our C&S cleaning company. I remember when her mother-in-law, Elaine was dying of cancer. Sandy and her husband Ron took care of Ron's mother and dad, Elaine and Watt before they went home to be with Jesus. Elaine and her husband Watt had lived near me for thirteen years when I was still married to Joe. They were the best neighbors I'd ever had. I have no doubt, those two precious Christian people are in heaven right now enjoying eternity with Jesus. The remarkable blessing that Sandy knows, as a Christian she will see them again at the rapture.

I also have no doubt Sandy did the very best she could all the years she put her own desires aside and took care of Elaine and Watt. Sometimes I'd get so concerned about my dear friend. Sandy was working full time taking care of two different elderly woman, in two different locations, besides taking care of Elaine and Watt. Finally she had to stop trying to take care of the other two elderly ladies and just take care of Watt and Elaine. I was so grateful when she quit her other two jobs. After Watt died, Ron and Sandy moved in with Elaine and cared for her full time. Sandy loved her mother-in-law and father-in-law.

Sandy also loves her own sweet mother Dolly and she helps her too. She takes her shopping and out to eat. She takes her to the doctor, or to get her hair done. Sandy also cleans her mothers house quite often. She always helped her little elderly neighbor lady too. Sometimes she'd cook her a hot meal or just rub her shoulders if she was hurting before she died. My friend also loves her family. She has had a busy life, but finally she has slowed down enough to enjoy herself. My friend deserves a quiet rest. Sandy's youngest daughter, Jenny wrote a poem about her grandmother and grandfather after they passed away. I knew she still had the loving poem she wrote about her grandpa, so I asked Jenny if I could put it in the book. With her permission I'll share Jenny's poem she wrote about her grandpa, Watt Howard.

329

"OUR LITTLE PAPAW"

Little papaw was the monarch of the Howard family, raising us with love; that's how he taught us to be. "Have faith in God" he would always say "Can't get through life any other way." There's lots of stories we could tell of him, especially mamaw, daddy, Carl and Tim. My sister and I have memories of our own, ones that we'll cherish now that we're grown. "Good-night-sleep-tight-don't let the bed-bugs-bite" he'd kiss and tell us every night. Six a.m., the clock would be dinging, here he'd come, crawling, barking, and singing. I remember driving to church at one hundred and ten. "Can't be late, that would be a sin."
Hanging garage doors at work all day, we couldn't wait for him to come home and play. Anxiously waiting for a great big hug, me and Betsy with our hands out for his lunch box and jug. "Whoopi" is something he always said, then he'd flick your ear and pat your head. He'd take off his lid, (hat) as he sat in his chair, we'd dress him up and put bows in his hair. The angels were singing on February 11, they knew the special man they were getting in heaven. 'Go ahead little papaw, it's time to rest, we'll take care of mamaw, we'll do our best.' (Poem, by Jennifer Howard).
One day after Sandy and I'd stood in Elaine's bedroom and anointed her with oil, the prayer of faith saved the sick and the Lord raised Elaine up off of that sickbed. He gave her two more good years before she died. Everything the Lord showed us came to pass. Elaine stood completely healed in the pulpit of her church and spoke to women's groups, with every beautiful silver hair on her head grown back, even curly, and her fingernails long and pretty. She always wanted long fingernails so the Lord gave them to her. Watt Howard was seventy nine years old when he died. He still had a head full of black hair. People used to tease him about coloring his hair, but he really didn't have one single grey hair. Elaine was seventy two when she went home to be with the Lord. Most of their fifty years of marriage were good. They raised four sons, and Betsy and Jenny spent much of their happy growing up years with their grandma and grandpa Howard.

I remember one day when I was sitting at my dressing table putting on my makeup. The Lord sang me a slightly different version of the song He'd sung to me a few years earlier, "Twiddly de--twiddly da--da; There's peace and good will, when you wake up every morning in your house on, the hill." It wasn't your house on Oakhill. This time He said, your house on 'THE HILL.' I knew immediately which house on "the hill" He was talking about! "Yes Jesus! After all, You are the Master carpenter! By faith I receive the house You built for me and Roy back in 1992. Thank You sweet Jesus for building it for us!" (Psalm 127:1) "Unless the Lord builds the house, they labor in vain who build it;" "I confess in Jesus' name, Roy and I are living in the perfect will of God."

February the fifth 2002 Sandy, Nancy and I were sitting in my living room visiting when suddenly Nancy heard the Lord say, "Divine appointment." We three agreed to start our prayer group going again, only this time on Fridays. The three of us pour out to others all week long in prayer and we minister to our families. We felt the Lord telling us we needed to pray for each other, so we began to pray and minister to each other every week under the anointing of the dear precious Holy Spirit. We've seen so many wonderful breakthroughs! "Hallelujah! Glory too You, dear Papa, dear Jesus, sweet Lamb of God, and dear precious Holy Spirit!"

Early one morning on February the twentieth I was sitting in my chair praying when I saw a clear vision of Jesus hanging on the cross with a crown of thorns pressed into His sweet precious, head. He glowed with a golden color. It was as if He was suspended in space. He turned His blessed head in agony and looked up at me and said, "It is finished." "Blessed Jesus, I love You so much! Thank You Lord for Your great love for us." That same night before I went to bed, I heard the Lord whisper, "Frankincense and myrrh." The very next morning when I woke up, I heard Him softly say, "Gold, frankincense and myrrh." I searched diligently through The New Testament where rich kings brought Jesus gold, frankincense and myrrh when He was born. Suddenly I remembered the Lord had already told me to read Song of Solomon weeks earlier. He prompted me to read it again.

I pray, Psalm 25: 4-5 "Show me Your ways O Lord; Teach me Your paths Lead me in Your truth and teach me, For You are the God of my salvation;" In The Amplified Bible on February the twenty fifth 2002 I found Song of Solomon 1:13 "My beloved (Shepherd) is to me like a (scent) bag of myrrh that lies in my bosom." On February twenty sixth the Lord gave me Song of Solomon 4:6. "Until the day breaks and the shadows flee away, (in my thoughts) I will get to the mountain of myrrh and the hill of frankincense (to Him whom my soul adores.") "Praise You Papa God!" Song of Solomon 4:14 "Spikenard and saffron, calamus and cinnamon, with all the trees of frankincense, myrrh, and aloes, with all the chief spices." I knew the vision of Jesus hanging on the cross was so significant for me personally. Jesus paid everything so that I could live life abundantly. "I love You sweet wonderful Jesus! Thank You Lord for giving Your precious life for me. I truly am Your little lamb." John 10:11 "I am the good shepherd. The good shepherd gives his life for the sheep."

One night after I'd been searching the scriptures to try and comprehend even more about His unconditional love, I had another dream. I dreamed a wedding ceremony took place at my house. It was an unusual dream, because first a young man came in the door wearing a white wedding gown over top his navy blue suit. An older blond haired woman also came through my front door wearing a white wedding gown, saying she just wanted to try it on. Right before I woke up, I dreamed I was standing in my kitchen washing dishes, thinking, "This wedding celebration is going take place here in my house and I only have until Tuesday! O my goodness, there is so much to do and so little time to do it!"

The Lord also lead me to reread Hannah Hurnard's sequel book to "Hinds Feet In High Places"---"Mountains Of Spices". In the very last few pages of Hannah Hunnard's book "Mountains Of Spices" she examines what the spices of myrrh and frankincense truly mean to us as Christians as we strive harder to be more like Jesus. I dearly love Hannah Hurnard's books. I've bought her books for others, but I've never given away my own very treasured and worn copies. Each time I've read them they've blessed me so.

Song of Solomon 5:1 "I have come into my garden, my sister, my (promised) bride: I have gathered my myrrh with my balsam and spice (from your sweet words I have gathered the richest perfumes and spices). I have eaten my honey-comb with my honey. I have drunk my wine with my milk. Eat, O friends (feast on, O revelers of the palace: you can never make my lover disloyal to me)! Drink, yes drink abundantly of love, O precious one (for now I know you are mine, irrevocably mine! With his confident words still thrilling her heart, through the lattice she saw her shepherd turn away and disappear into the night)." When I told Nancy about my dream of the wedding, she said a wedding means, salvation. She was also excited because she had a vision of Jesus looking through the lattice at her earlier in the week. Wow! God is speaking to all of us, all the time about His great love for us. "The Lord is my Shepherd and I shall not be in want." Song Of Solomon 5:5 "I arose to open for my beloved, and my hands dripped with myrrh, My fingers with liquid myrrh, On the handles of the lock." Song Of Solomon 5:11 "His head is like the finest gold." When I saw Jesus hanging on the cross He was a golden color. "Praise You Jesus!" Song Of Solomon 5:13-16. "His cheeks are like a bed of spices, Like banks of scented herbs. His lips are like lilies, Dripping with liquid myrrh. His hands are like rods of gold, Set with beryl. His body is carved ivory Inlaid with sapphires. His legs are pillars of marble, Set on basses of gold. His countenance is like Lebanon, Excellent as the ceders. His mouth is most sweet, Yes He is altogether lovely. This is my beloved, This is my friend, O daughters of Jerusalem." My beloved Jesus.

On February 27, 2002 Nancy prayed for me in tongues and the Holy Spirit showed her a vision of a train and the conductor looked at his pocket watch and said, "We're right on time." Sandy saw a vision of me sitting at my computer working on my book wearing a gold crown. God keeps reassuring all of us, everything is going to be alright. The Lord has shown Nancy, Sandy, Cheri, and Carol Pettit that Roy and I are financially richer then we could ask or think and we are seeing these prophecies fulfilled right before our very eyes. "Praise You, my very own dear Papa God!"

My dear friend Nancy had offered several times to critique this book for me, but as usual I was afraid of being criticized. Suddenly, one day after prayer group God helped me leap over the wall of being insecure concerning this book, and I heard myself ask Nancy to edit it for me. Wow! God's delivering me from my enemies with His Great and mighty Hand! I'm finally entering into my promised land. Nancy has made me feel really good about this book. She keeps telling me how much she likes my sentence structure. Nancy has had several years of collage, majoring in English. She is an anointed editor. I thank God for my precious friend Nancy, who kept saying, "Oh Carol, your book is so wonderful! This book is so anointed with the word of God in it, it cannot fail because God cannot fail! Girl, you've got to get this book published, and NOW!" Nancy was the perfect laborer, "mid wife" to help me bear down and give birth to this baby, my book! She has encouraged me, prayed for me, and gave of herself in time and prayer unselfishly again and again. "THANK YOU JESUS!"

Sandy finally had enough quiet time in her life just a few months ago to sit down and read the book, but of course she has always encouraged me every step of the way too. I laughed at Nancy when I offered to let her take the manuscript home. She immediately said, "Oh, no thank you Carol! I don't want to do that, because I KNOW what happened to the other ladies when you gave them your manuscript!" Instead she came here and I sat beside her so I could learn from her as she edited this book. I laughed again because she kept saying there wasn't much to do to it except change a quotation mark sometimes. Nancy wouldn't touch or change anything without asking me first. If I was out of the room she called for me. I so appreciated the respect Nancy gave me concerning this book. Nancy has always respected me and the anointing on my life as much as I do her and the anointing on her life. "Dear Papa God, I love You so much! Thank You Lord for giving me so many excellent friends who walk in Your love and Your sweet anointing." (Romans 5:5) "Now hope does not disappoint us, because the love of God has been poured out in our hearts by the Holy Spirit who was given to us."

On March the 15, 2002 God spoke to me and told me to read Joshua 1:9 "Have I not commanded you? Be strong and of good courage; do not be afraid, nor be dismayed, for the Lord your God is with you wherever you go." I kept listening to Dr. Leroy Thompson on Kenneth Copeland's daily broadcast. I also read his books on financial prosperity. I kept saying, "I will never be broke another day in my life! Money cometh to me now, today, in the name of Jesus!" Money came. March 27, 2002 the Lord told me to read Joshua 10:10 "So the Lord routed them before Israel, killed them with a great slaughter at Gibeon, chased them along the road that goes to Beth Horon, and struck them down as far as Azekah and Makkedah." God spoke to me and said, "This is your day of financial freedom." "Papa, I receive Your word for me and Roy. Thank You Lord!" Wow! I'd been standing on the word Benny Hinn gave us about financial freedom and Rod Parsley, Paul and Jan Crouch, Kenneth and Gloria Copeland, Dr. Leroy Thompson, Jerry and Carolyn Savelle, Pat Robertson and the 700 Club. I love pastor Lee Stutzman's teachings on finical prosperity. On March 29 the Lord also gave me Psalm 102:13, "You will arise and have mercy on Zion; For the time to favor her, Yes the set time, has come." "I receive Your financial blessings dear Lord."

Through the years God has encouraged Sandy and I by giving us dreams and visions concerning our financial blessings. He said in His word in 3 John 2, "Beloved I pray that you prosper in all things and be in health, just as your soul prospers." I will never forget the great words of encouragement the Lord gave us on March 22, 2002 when we were praying together with the dear sweet precious Holy Spirit over the phone. The Lord spoke to me again very specifically about our financial situation. I heard Him say LOUD and clear, "NO LONGER WILL MY PEOPLE BE MADE TO MAKE MORTAR WITHOUT STRAW, THEY ARE LEAVING EGYPT TODAY!" We shouted and praised God, because we knew God cannot lie. Numbers 23:19, "God is not a man that He should lie, nor a son of man that He should repent." "Thank You dear Papa God, I love You so much! I love You so much Lord Jesus! I love You dear precious Holy Spirit!"

One day as I was praying in tongues for Sandy I saw a clear vision of her and I standing in our bare feet wearing shorts and tee-shirts! A gusher of oil spewed up from the ground splattering all over our smiling faces! In the vision we were laughing and dancing while our hair and clothes were being saturated by the rich black oil. I continued to pray in tongues as I watched two huge metal rimes that had been fastened securely at the bottom of the oil gusher with nuts and bolts, jarring loose! Soon nuts, bolts, and rings all came flying up in the air, from off the bottom of the oil gusher! In the vision David and Betsy, Michael Kyle and Rebecca, Joey, Jennifer, Tyler, Megan, Danielle, and Brandy, Jenny and her children were all standing behind us laughing and rejoicing too! Sandy and I kept saying, "Wow! God is telling us, we are wealthy, hallelujah!" "Praise You Papa God-Your word will never return to You void!" Proverbs 13:22, "A good man leaves an inheritance to his children's children, But the wealth of the sinner is stored up for the righteous." Sandy and I have always stood on the word of God and believed Him for miracles, and we've always watched God honor His word. By faith I'd been packing ever since God showed me the vision of my large red brick house He built for us years ago in 1992. "Thank You Jesus!"

I woke Roy up one Saturday morning-he doesn't like to sleep past nine thirty. I laughed when he said, "I'm so glad you woke me up, Carol! I've been dreaming such clear dreams all night long about helping people we know, move into their new houses and I'm tired!" Roy told me, first he dreamed Sandy called us because her and her husband Ron were moving into their big new home and they wanted us to come over and see it. Roy said their house was spacious and really nice with tall white pillars on their huge front porch. When Roy told me Ron kept showing him all the cabinet space in all the rooms, especially the kitchen, I got really excited! There is no way Roy knew the desire of Sandy's heart is to have an abundance of cabinet space. Roy said he even knows where this house is located because in the dream there were real recognizable landmarks! God is increasing our awareness of His intended blessings! "Oh dear Papa God, I love You so much!"

Roy said he had another dream right after that one. He dreamed he and I were helping David and Betsy and Joey and Jennifer move into their new houses out in the country! They also had a red barn and one unusual thing he noticed was the fact that they had black Arabian horses and a huge race track behind the barn! Sandy was so happy when I told her later that day, she came right over so Roy could tell her in person precisely everything he dreamed. I kept thinking, "It's just like the people in the bible, Abraham, Mosses, and David. God didn't just make them wealthy, He made them, 'VERY WEALTHY'!" When I told my sons about Roy's anointed dreams they were impressed. I told them, God will bring those dreams to pass in His timing, in Jesus' name! We all agreed ONE black Arabian horse would be expensive, but a whole race track full of them, not counting the HUGE amount of land they would have to purchase to build a race track. When my sons were little we owned a Shetland pony. I thought, "Lord is this their sevenfold return on the Shetland pony they lost?" I don't think it matters that neither David or Joey were ever interested in horse racing. Sandy and I agreed with Roy, God is revealing the "BIGGER PICTURE" of how He will bless us, abundantly.

On the evening of July 5, 2002, I was watching TBN when all of a sudden Rod Parsley came on. I got so excited when I saw he was teaching about the Canaanites, Hivites, Hittites, Jebusites, Perizzites, Amorites, and the Girgashites and why God is driving them out of our lives. "Praise God!" I quickly grabbed a pen and paper so I could take notes from his important teaching. "Oh Glory to You Papa God!" God used Rod Parsley to open my eyes of understanding a little wider when He taught what each name represents, and in Jesus' name what they can't have in Joshua 3:10. The Canaanites, {family}, the Hittites, {faith}, the Hivites, {finances}, the Perizzites, {fidelity}, the Girgashites {freedom}, the Amorites {the future}, and the Jebusites, {final glory}. I kept saying, "Thank You so much Lord for Rod Parsley! He is a wonderful gift to the body of Christ." I knew God was speaking to me through him! The living God among us will (without fail) drive out from before us all our enemies in the name of Jesus!

337

I thank God for His word that has literally renewed my mind and caused me to believe it is God's perfect will to bless me and my family abundantly, in every area of our lives. The only rememberable experience I had in my childhood of my dad giving Peggy and I money was right after we came back home from another evil ride in his car with our friends. I ques mommy was upstairs sleeping that day. For some strange reason Peggy threatened to tell on daddy! She became jealous because he kept giving the girls money, after whatever it was they were doing with him. He gave them money to appease them and Peggy was furious! Especially since he never once gave us, not even a penny. She screamed and stomped her feet, while threatening to expose his diabolical plan if he didn't give us (hush money) too!

I was quivering while hiding behind the door in the next room! I remember I was so angry with my sister for causing him to yell for me to come in there with them. This thing wasn't my idea, I was terrified of him! When he reached in his pockets and handed her and I a hand full of pennies, she hurled them to the floor and stomped off crying! She yelled she didn't want pennies, she wanted silver coins like he gave those other girls. I wanted nothing to do with the whole ugly scenario! I resented my sister who left me standing there with daddy watching those pennies dance across the old linoleum floor. I cannot remember how I escaped from that room, or if I did without a whipping or getting my hair pulled or cursed out. We were just two young little girls, not thinking rationally. I know it had not crossed Peggy's mind that she should threaten to tell on him because what he was doing to those girls was so morally wrong. I believe the stress of it all was just to much for my little sister, and she temporally lost it. We lived our lives surviving each day and night, but we know now that Jesus was there with us all the time. When Peggy and I babysat we gladly gave mommy a percentage of our meager days wages without regret. All four of my brothers sent mommy an allotment from part of their pay after they left home and joined the military. "Thank You dear Papa God for renewing our minds with Your love for us in Your word. You are such a good Papa!"

Early one morning on August the eleventh 2002, I was standing in my kitchen running the garbage disposal when I heard the Lord speak to me over all the LOUD noise, "DEUTERONOMY! DEUTERONOMY! DEUTERONOMY!" It was as if the Lord was standing behind me, leaning over my right shoulder. I immediately turned the garbage disposal and water off and asked, "Lord where do You want me to read in Deuteronomy?" He said, "1,2,3,4,5,6,7. The first seven chapters of Deuteronomy." The Lord instantly gave me confirmation from His word. In my spirit He spoke this scripture, "You will hear a word behind you saying, 'this is the way, walk ye in it.'" Isaiah 30:21. I laughed when I grabbed my bible and opened it to Deuteronomy. That scripture was so perfect, because I actually heard Him speak a word behind me. "Wow! I love You Papa, Jesus, and sweet Holy Spirit!"

As usual my very own dear Papa had some extra hidden treasure for me in the last few verses of Numbers on the apposite page of the first chapter of Deuteronomy. I'd been interceding for someone special for God to help her get her rightful inheritance. The Lord made sure she found out that she and her two sweet daughters are next in line for a 'bigger then life' inheritance. My friend's mother married her real dad after she was divorced from her first abusive husband. Her mother already had three other children from her first marriage before she was born. For some reason her mother did not give her, her real dad's last name, but instead gave her the same last name as her other children from her ex-husband. I ques she didn't want them to feel like half siblings. It was after her real dad went home to be with Jesus recently that she found out about her rightful inheritance. She is getting her last name changed back to her rightful royal bloodline name so she and her daughters can receive what belongs to them. God assured me, the devil's not stealing her money in the name of Jesus, she will get her inheritance money! He gave me His word. Numbers 36:8 "And every daughter who possesses an inheritance in any tribe of the children of Israel shall be the wife of one family of her fathers tribe, so that the children of Israel each may posses the inheritance of his fathers." "Praise You Papa for confirmation!"

Deuteronomy 1:5-8 On this side of the Jordan in the land of Moab, Mosses began to explain this law, saying, "The Lord our God spoke to us in Horeb, saying: 'You have dwelt long enough at this mountain. 'Turn and take your journey, and go to the neighboring places in the plain, in the mountains and in the lowland, in the South and on the seacoast, to the land of the Canaanites and to Lebanon, as far as the great river, the River Euphrates. 'See, I have set the land before you; go in and posses the land which the Lord swore to your fathers--to Abraham, Isaac, and Jacob--to give them and their descendants after them.'" I said, "I confess in the name of Jesus Roy Lovely and I and our families are living in the perfect will of God! Thank You Lord for driving out all our of enemies from our promised land! I love You, Lord!" I could hardly contain my joy! "Thank You Jesus!" I'd been packing and cleaning everything in the upstairs excluding Roy's desk. Most everything downstairs in the basement is packed and ready to go too except our recording equipment. Part of our family room furniture stays here, some of it we sold in our garage sale.

Deuteronomy 1:21 'Look, the Lord your God has set the land before you; go in and posses it, as the Lord God of your fathers has spoken to you; do not fear or be discouraged.'" Sandy and I have always referred to Joshua and Caleb of the bible. Every time we go to the word of God for our situation, we believe the good report of the Lord. Many, many times we've looked at each other after agreeing in prayer then spontaneously started to sing, "Now tell me who's report are you gonna believe? I will believe the report of the Lord! His report says I am healed-- His report says I am filled-- His report says I am free-- His report says VICTORY! Now tell me who's report are you gonna believe? I WILL believe the report of the Lord!" Sandy and I have danced and sung that song so many times and the victory always came, the battle belongs to the Lord! "Praise You Papa God!" I love Deuteronomy 1:29-30 "Then I said to you, 'Do not be terrified, or afraid of them. 'The Lord your God, who goes before you, He will fight for you, according to all He did for you in Egypt before your eyes." "O, we are crossing over Jordan into the promised land!"

Deuteronomy 6:4-11 "Hear, O Israel: The Lord our God, the Lord is one! "You shall love the Lord your God with all your heart, with all your soul, and with all your might. "And these words which I command you today shall be in your heart; you shall teach them diligently to your children, and shall talk of them when you sit in your house, when you walk by the way, when you lie down, and when you rise up. "You shall bind them as a sign on your hand, and they shall be as frontlets between your eyes. "You shall write them on the doorposts of your house and on your gates. "And it shall be, when the Lord your God brings you into the land of which He swore to your fathers, to Abraham, Isaac, and Jacob, to give you large and beautiful cities which you did not build, "houses full of all good things which you did not fill, hewn out wells which you did not dig, vineyards and olive trees which you did not plant----when you have eaten and are full---- "then beware, least you forget the Lord who brought you out of the land of Egypt, from the house of bondage." "Papa, I pray in the name of Jesus, You will help me never, ever forget what You have done for us. I know You did it because of Your great love for us Lord." "Oh Lord thank You, You give us (houses) full of all good things."

Deuteronomy 7:1-2,9 7:14 "When the Lord your God brings you into the land which you go to posses, and has cast out many nations before you, the Hittites and the Girgashites and the Amorites and the Canaanites, and the Perizzites and the Hivites and the Jebusites, seven nations greater and mightier then you, and when the Lord your God delivers them over to you, you shall conquer them and utterly destroy them. You shall make no covenant with them nor show mercy to them." "Therefore know that the Lord your God, He is God, the faithful God who keeps covenant and mercy for a thousand generations with those who love Him and keep His commandments." "You shall be blessed above all people; there shall not be male or female barren among you or among your livestock. And the Lord will take away from you all sickness, and will afflict you with none of the terrible diseases of Egypt which you have known, but will lay them upon all those who hate you." "I am strong in Christ Jesus my Lord!"

A few weeks after I had the vision of Jesus hanging on the cross, when He said "It is finished" I had another sharp disagreement with one of my friends. I was a little bit agitated to say the least. I kept saying, "Lord what happened?" He answered immediately, telling me there are millions of prisoners in prisons all over the world who one day wake up behind bars asking that same question. Jim and Tammy Bakker also asked that question, and so did Jimmy Swaggart and other undiscerning Christians. Angry children hurting or killing others in their classroom ask that same question along with their parents. He told me to call my friend right away and tell her that this thing was of the flesh. He wanted both of us to nail that fleshly self will to the cross and never allow that subject to come up between us again. He said where He's taking us, we cannot go with this thing going on between us. He said He wanted to do a work in us through our prayers of agreement for the individuals we were disagreeing about. This 'HAD BEEN' THE ONE and ONLY discussion we could not ever have in our friendship, but God said He wanted that old garbage thrown out of our relationship forever! I heard a minister on television say Jesus weeps for us to lay aside childish things so we can go on with Him. To hate your brother is considered murder.

Jesus said these offences would come in the last days, but we have to get over them quickly if we want to go on with Him. I sat down in my chair and picked up the phone to call my friend when I saw a bird fly into the large bush outside one of my large living room windows. I said in my heart, "Lord if this is You telling me to call my friend and tell her all these things You told me, then let that red cardinal climb up out of that bush and sit on an outer branch where I can see it?" The beautiful red cardinal hopped up and out onto the outer branch immediately. I dialed my friends number and obeyed God. She was just as happy to obey the Lord's instruction as I was. "Praise You Lord!" He had also told me He wanted us to pray this thing off of these certain people so it could not go onto another generation. We humbly repented and that Jezebel spirit of control was bound off us in Jesus' name, forever! "Thank You Papa God for Your correction. I love You so Lord!"

In the name of Jesus and by the blood of Jesus, everything is being restored back to me sevenfold, including all that the enemy stole from my mother and dad! "In the name of Jesus, I thank You Papa God for restoring back to me seven times over all that is rightfully mine including my parents inheritance that was my rightful inheritance." Since I was a small child I heard my mother and some of my brothers and sisters talk about the farm where we lived when I was born. Mommy told me that the farm would have belonged to all of us after the owner died one day if daddy would have stayed on and continued to run it. When Mr. Howard the owner of the farm took pity on mommy who was washing clothes for all fifteen of us by hand, and bought her a brand new ringer washing machine daddy became furiously jealous and angry at Mr. Howard! For years I thought that was the only reason we left the farm until I talked with my brother Ben. Ben told me what also happened besides my dad getting jealous towards Mr. Howard. I believe it was God looking after mommy as He dropped the idea of buying her a ringer washer into Mr. Howard's kind heart.

Ben told me daddy left more and more of the heavy farm chores on him and our brother Myrlon until he caught my brother Ben reading a book in the barn between the cows who'd had the milking machines attached to them too long. Once again daddy threatened Ben and started to curse him and beat on him but this time my brother had about all of daddy's abuse he could take! So he in turn threatened daddy and told him not to even think about beating him again! My sister Janie and her husband Clarence were visiting from Dayton so my brother Ben went back with them and left the farm. Daddy quit the farm because he couldn't run it without Ben's help. Mr. Howard's only son wanted nothing to do with the farm. Mr. Howard's intentions was to give the entire farm, and all the livestock to my dad and mother. Daddy also threw one of the best curve balls anyone had ever seen. Some official people from the farm leagues wanted him. After he succeeded with them he could have easily gone on to one of the big leagues but he got scared and backed out, so that was stolen from him too. God will restore it to us who claim it, sevenfold.

343

I kept increasingly hearing myself pray, "Papa God, if it is Your will for me to babysit my granddaughter Danielle then I'll do it Lord." Before I knew it Danielle's regular babysitter quit and I started watching her full time. She is such a good little girl. She has long naturally wavy dark brown hair and big dark brown eyes that sparkle when she laughs, which is most of the time. She looks up at me with those beautiful eyes and thick long dark eye lashes of hers and she gets just about anything she wants. She is three years old and she is so attached to her grandpa Roy who loves her dearly too. She loves my album. Every time we are riding in the car or at home she wants to hear gand-ma's tape. She is my biggest fan. Each new day she is such a joy to be with. God created Danielle to be a blessing. Jesus loves her so much. I told my daughter-in-law Jennifer Danielle should have been given my mothers name, Lydia, because she loves all of her doll babies. If you ask her what she wants for her birthday or Christmas or any occasion, she wants another baby. We love all of our grand babies.

My prayer group has been temporarily interrupted, but my friends understand it is God's will for my little granddaughter to be here with me until God makes a way financially for her mother to stay home and take care of her. Sandy said she completely understands the importance of what I am doing. Sandy has really been busy helping out with her grandchildren, and our grandsons Michael and Kyle. Nancy has been a good friend for along time too and she is very busy with her family. I miss talking with them but I am having a special time with Danielle. I told Roy, my entire childhood years, I only had one old doll and half its hair was missing. I couldn't imagine having all the dolls Danielle has. He said, "Well Carol, now you have another old doll to love with half its hair missing, me." He is one funny man, and he's got lots of nice hair. Danielle raises her little hands while we are watching a Carman video and she praises the Lord with them while their dancing and singing. She reminds me of my grandson Michael when he was about her age. Michael was so precious like her when she says hallula! I praise God for all of our grandchildren who love and trust in the Lord Jesus. God bless our grandchildren.

Rebecca is very much in love with her boyfriend Christopher. He has another year of collage left. She is finishing her senior year of high school. Rebecca is smart like her daddy, she is making straight A's in all her subjects. I am so proud of her. My granddaughter is still in the healing process. Jesus is healing the memories of her mothers untimely death. Rebecca left her dads house and moved in with her aunt Linda a few months ago. After two years it just didn't work out at her dad's. God is restoring that relationship. I saw a vision one day of Jesus standing in my sons living room with His arms around David and Betsy. Michael and Kyle were standing there and Jesus opened His arms and brought the boys into the circle of love. Rebecca stood shyly beside the dining room table when Jesus beckoned for her with His precious nail scarred hands. She gladly came into the circle of love with them. Jesus has His loving arms around my granddaughter and her dad, knitting them together with His agape love. "God, I believe You are bringing that vision to pass quickly, in Jesus' name."

How often I have thought of Joseph and the story about his life in the bible. Persecuted for his dreams, his own brothers pushed him away, but God fulfilled his destiny. I praise God that Joe rejected me now that I know the 'lovely' life God had planned for me. I could never have finished this book and published it the way things were with Joe. I'm not angry or hurt at my ex-husband. I pray the Lord blesses him and his new wife especially with the knowledge of how much He loves them. Jesus died for them too. God had my destiny preordained to be fulfilled with Roy Lovely. God has given Roy an assignment concerning our singing and making albums in our studio and my books being published. I pray in the name of Jesus God keeps Roy Lovely and I in His perfect will. Through His guidance Roy is taking me to the high places of the earth where He has called me to go for His glory-- and I in turn am taking Roy to the high places, spiritually where God has called him to go for His glory. I remember when God told me the highest places are love and forgiveness. Joel, who is Roy carried me to the upper room so that I could give birth to this baby, the new me and this book. I shout, "God bless my precious husband Roy Lovely!"

For as long as I can remember back, I never liked my name. I didn't like to write my name nor did I like to hear someone call my name, not even my mother. I always wanted to be called by another name, although I did enjoy hearing grandpa and grandma Passqualucci say my name in Italian. From the time I was eleven years old and could afford to buy makeup, I've worn makeup. Now, however Roy thinks I am beautiful without makeup so I rarely ware it. When Roy says my name in that soft intriguing voice of his, I like my given name. I especially enjoy writing out my name with my new last name. Now, I wouldn't want to be called anything else. I even like myself because I finally know who I am in Christ Jesus without being persecuted for it. What I learn and read about God's love for me in the bible is no longer challenged with angry words. I am cherished and loved by my Christian husband who highly respects God and me. "I thank You dear Papa God for giving me my sweet precious husband Roy who encourages me to be all that You have created me to be."

There in my darkened kitchen before I left Joe I heard God say, "Consider not the deadness of Sarah's womb." Now, here I am nine years later seeing my book birthed because I obeyed God. Through it all I didn't let go of the vision God gave me. (Romans 4:16-21) Therefore it is of faith that it might be according to grace, so that the promise might be sure to all the seed, not only to those who are of the law, but also to those who are of the faith of Abraham, who is the father of us all (as it is written, "I have made you a father of many nations") in the presence of Him whom he believed, even God, who gives life to the dead and calls those things which do not exist as though they did; who contrary to hope, in hope believed, so that he became the father of many nations, according to what was spoken "So shall your descendants be."And not being weak in faith, he did not consider his own body, already dead (since he was about a hundred years old), and the deadness of Sarah's womb. He did not waver at the promise of God through unbelief, but was strengthened in faith, giving glory to God, and being fully convinced that what He had promised He was also able to preform." He said, "It is finished!"

I selected one of our wedding pictures with most of our family in it. From left to right, starting at the bottom row, are my grandchildren, Michael, Kyle, Tyler and Megan. Roy and I of course are the middle row. Top row, my good friend David Ay, and my youngest son Joey who's given name is Sammy. Roy's youngest daughter Aimee, and his oldest Kristie, my daughter-in-law Betsy, and my son David. Aimee's husband Wayne is barely seen, but he is standing behind his wife. "Glory to You dear Papa God, sweet Jesus, and dear precious Holy Spirit. Thank You for loving me, and teaching me, Your way dear Lord."